CLASSICAL PRESENCES

General Editors

LORNA HARDWICK
JAMES I. PORTER

CLASSICAL PRESENCES

Attempts to receive the texts, images, and material culture of ancient Greece and Rome inevitably run the risk of appropriating the past in order to authenticate the present. Exploring the ways in which the classical past has been mapped over the centuries allows us to trace the avowal and disavowal of values and identities, old and new. Classical Presences brings the latest scholarship to bear on the contexts, theory, and practice of such use, and abuse, of the classical past.

Ovid in French

Reception by Women from the Renaissance to the Present

Edited by
HELENA TAYLOR
and
FIONA COX

OXFORD
UNIVERSITY PRESS

Great Clarendon Street, Oxford, OX2 6DP,
United Kingdom

Oxford University Press is a department of the University of Oxford.
It furthers the University's objective of excellence in research, scholarship,
and education by publishing worldwide. Oxford is a registered trade mark of
Oxford University Press in the UK and in certain other countries

© Oxford University Press 2023

The moral rights of the authors have been asserted

All rights reserved. No part of this publication may be reproduced, stored in
a retrieval system, or transmitted, in any form or by any means, without the
prior permission in writing of Oxford University Press, or as expressly permitted
by law, by licence or under terms agreed with the appropriate reprographics
rights organization. Enquiries concerning reproduction outside the scope of the
above should be sent to the Rights Department, Oxford University Press, at the
address above

You must not circulate this work in any other form
and you must impose this same condition on any acquirer

Published in the United States of America by Oxford University Press
198 Madison Avenue, New York, NY 10016, United States of America

British Library Cataloguing in Publication Data
Data available

Library of Congress Control Number: 2023935837

ISBN 978-0-19-289538-7

DOI: 10.1093/oso/9780192895387.001.0001

Printed and bound in the UK by
Clays Ltd, Elcograf S.p.A.

Links to third party websites are provided by Oxford in good faith and
for information only. Oxford disclaims any responsibility for the materials
contained in any third party website referenced in this work.

Acknowledgements

The editors wish to thank all the authors for their contributions and their patient commitment to this volume. We would also like to thank the Leverhulme Trust, whose support has underpinned this project; Eleanor Hodgson, for her translations; and everyone involved in the publication process: the Classical Presences series editors, Lorna Hardwick and James I. Porter, our editor, Henry Clarke, our copy-editor, Ingalo Thomson, our anonymous readers, and the OUP production team.

Contents

List of Contributors	ix
1. Introduction *Helena Taylor and Fiona Cox*	1
2. Women's Wit: Skirting Ovid in Renaissance France *Emma Herdman*	21
3. Madeleine de L'Aubespine's Translation of *Heroides* 2 *Jessica DeVos*	44
4. *Belle* and *Fidèle*? Women Translating Ovid in Early Modern France *Helena Taylor*	67
5. Defending Phaedra's Glory: The Corrective Translation of *Heroides* 4 by Marie-Jeanne L'Héritier in *Les Epîtres* *héroïques* (1732) *Océane Puche, translated by Helena Taylor*	88
6. The *Letters from Julia to Ovid*, by Charlotte Antoinette de Bressey, Marquise of Lezay-Marnésia *Séverine Clément-Tarantino, translated by Eleanor Hodgson*	104
7. Metempsychosis, Sappho, and Adultery Laws: Ovidian Moments in the Career of Constance de Salm (1767–1845) *Thea S. Thorsen*	121
8. Corinne at the Capitol *Fiona Cox*	140
9. Playful *Metamorphoses*: George Sand's Ovidian Affinities *James Illingworth*	151
10. Cahun: An Ovidian Tiresias for Modern Times *Catherine Burke*	169
11. Marguerite Yourcenar's 'Feminism' and the Ambivalence of Ovidian Models in *Feux* *Florence Klein, translated by Eleanor Hodgson*	188

viii CONTENTS

12. Kristeva's Ovidian World: 'Un monde en mutation'   220
    Kathleen Hamel

13. 'Il faut raconter mon long parcours': Migration and Ovidian
    Presences   242
    Fiona Cox

14. Epilogue: The Soul That Is Chewed Up   263
    Marie Cosnay, translated by Fiona Cox

Bibliography   275
Index   297

List of Contributors

Catherine Burke, University College Cork

Séverine Clément-Tarantino, University of Lille

Marie Cosnay, author and translator

Fiona Cox, University of Exeter

Jessica DeVos, Yale University

Kathleen Hamel, University College Cork

Emma Herdman, University of St Andrews

James Illingworth, Cardiff University

Florence Klein, University of Lille

Océane Puche, University of Lille

Helena Taylor, University of Exeter

Thea S. Thorsen, Norwegian University of Science and Technology

1

Introduction

Helena Taylor and Fiona Cox

The early fourteenth century saw the first translation into a Romance language of Ovid's *Metamorphoses*, the French *Ovide moralisé* (c.1317–28). This moment represents the opening chapter of Ovid's distinctive and influential afterlife in France, an afterlife that has yet to be studied in detail. Though there have been important studies examining instances of Ovidian reception at specific moments in French cultural history, there has not to date been an in-depth study examining the trajectory of his afterlife over the course of centuries within a specific demographic. It is possible to track his influence in individual studies, examining the presence of myth in particular—and usually male—authors such as Ronsard, Hugo, Balzac, or Proust, or in particular time periods,[1] but the books that will show us what it means to think of a 'French' Ovid, across the centuries, remain, as yet, unwritten.[2]

Any figure whom we might name a 'French' Ovid is necessarily a composite of a host of different Ovids, who are born of different time periods, of different regions, different languages and political contexts; the Ovids of the dispossessed, of the elite. Our study also recognizes the impossibility of understanding the varieties of 'French' culture without understanding the ways in which that culture operates and has operated on the world stage. This is most strikingly demonstrated in the ways in which Ovid acquires new and different resonances in work by writers such as the French writer of Vietnamese descent, Linda Lê, and the French Marie NDiaye, both of whom use

---

This volume was supported by funding from the Leverhulme Trust, which the editors gratefully acknowledge.

[1] Paul White, *Renaissance Postscripts: Responding to Ovid's 'Heroides' in Sixteenth-Century France* (Columbus: Ohio State University Press, 2009); Helena Taylor, *The Lives of Ovid in Seventeenth-Century French Culture* (Oxford: Oxford University Press, 2017); Fiona Cox, *Ovid's Presence in Contemporary Women's Writing: Strange Monsters* (Oxford: Oxford University Press, 2018); Theodore Ziolkowski, *Ovid and the Moderns* (Ithaca: Cornell University Press, 2005); Marta Balzi and Gemma Prades, eds, *Ovid in the Vernacular: Translations of the Metamorphoses in the Middle Ages & Renaissance* (Oxford: The Society for the Study of Medieval Languages and Literature, 2021).

[2] A recent book represents a significant step in changing this: Stefania Cerrito and Marie Possamaï-Pérez, eds, *Ovide en France du Moyen Âge à nos jours* (Paris: Classiques Garnier, 2021).

Helena Taylor and Fiona Cox, *Introduction* In: *Ovid in French: Reception by Women from the Renaissance to the Present.*
Edited by: Helena Taylor and Fiona Cox, Oxford University Press. © Oxford University Press 2023.
DOI: 10.1093/oso/9780192895387.003.0001

2 INTRODUCTION

metamorphoses to think through questions of migration and dislocation in the context of France and its former colonies.

This volume will trace Ovids constructed by French-speaking women, and one writer we might describe as gender non-conforming (Cahun), from the Renaissance to the present day, Ovids bequeathed from generation to generation, and Ovids who emerge with particular significance at the moments in literary history when women have felt sufficiently emboldened to assert their writing identities. Such moments include the quarrels about female authorship in the medieval period, Renaissance humanism and the *querelle des femmes*, the salons of the seventeenth and eighteenth centuries, the surge of second-wave feminism marked by Cixous's seminal essay 'Le Rire de la Méduse' (1975) and the emergence of third-wave feminism which shaped the concerns of Marie Darrieussecq's Ovidian tale of metamorphosis, *Truismes* (1996). Such Ovidian moments continue. In the Anglo-Saxon tradition in particular they are evident in responses to the sexual violence and predatory seduction which pervade the *Metamorphoses* and the *Ars amatoria*, as present in Fiona Benson's prize-winning poetry collection, *Vertigo and Ghost*, which retells the mythological rapes from the perspectives of the victims, casting Zeus as serial abuser, and Donna Zuckerberg's analysis of Ovid's role as the original 'Pick Up Artist' in the online seduction community.[3] Ovid's interest in gender fluidity has also made him a focal point for inclusive and intersectional feminist movements, as discussed by Helen Morales and evident in works such as Ali Smith's *Girl Meets Boy* (2007).[4] Some of these Ovidian moments represent social and cultural shifts, and so correspond to the moments of transition that Marina Warner argues are especially conducive to resurgences of Ovidian reception.[5]

This recent turn builds on a longer history of scholarship, from the 1980s in particular, in which feminist classicists have sought to question dominant ways of reading Ovid (see, for instance, the 1986 and 1990 editions of the journal *Helios* with articles addressing feminism and Classics) which initiated scholarly interest in a poet often dismissed as lacking in seriousness for

---

[3] Fiona Benson, *Vertigo and Ghost* (London: Cape, 2019); Donna Zuckerberg, 'The Ovid Method', *Not all Dead White Men: Classics and Misogyny in the Digital Age* (Cambridge, MA: Harvard University Press, 2018), 89–142. See also Madeleine Kahn, *Why Are We Reading Ovid's Handbook on Rape?* (London: Routledge, 2005).

[4] Ali Smith, *Girl Meets Boy* (Edinburgh: Canongate, 2007). Helen Morales, *Antigone Rising: The Subversive Power of the Ancient Myths* (London: Wildfire, 2020). See also Tessa Roynon and Daniel Orrells, eds, 'Ovid and Identity in the Twenty-First Century', *International Journal of the Classical Tradition*, 26/4 (2019) [special issue].

[5] Marina Warner, *Fantastic Metamorphoses, Other Worlds: Ways of Telling the Self* (Oxford: Oxford University Press, 2002), 17.

such attention.[6] That year, the Women's Classical Caucus of the American Philological Association had, as a topic for its annual panel, 'Reappropriating the Text: the Case of Ovid'. This had an influential effect on the revival of scholarly interest shown in Ovid through the 1980s and 90s. Building on this, two important essays from 2006 and 2008 studied the relationship between feminism and Classics: Genevieve Liveley traced first- and second-wave feminist responses to Classics, and analysed in particular the third-wave, post-feminist movement as it offers a hermeneutics of reception in its plurality, self-reflection, and situatedness.[7] Vanda Zajko explored different models (and waves) of feminist reception in relation to Classics, underscoring the need for feminist praxis to challenge, innovate, and bring new voices to classrooms and readers.[8] Most recently, attention has turned once again to the complex problem of Ovid's representations of women and gender in an edited volume by Alison Sharrock, Daniel Möller, and Mats Malm, highlighting its topicality.[9]

Beyond the university, Mary Innes's 1955 Penguin translation of the *Metamorphoses* ensured a more mainstream female presence in Ovidian reception. This work and Mary Innes herself, who worked as a Classics teacher in a girls' school for most of her life, is emblematic of the wider access girls and women enjoyed to education, and specifically, to the study of Latin and Greek.[10] As a direct consequence of this emerged generations of alumnae whose classical knowledge was equal to that of men (before Classics became a subject principally taught by fee-paying schools): this is evident from the considerable presence of women writers in Philip Terry's edited collection of short stories *Ovid Metamorphosed* (2000) which features works by A. S. Byatt, Joyce Carol Oates, Margaret Atwood, Catherine Axelrad, and Marina Warner.[11]

---

[6] Marilyn Skinner, ed., 'Rescuing Creusa: New Methodological Approaches to Women in Antiquity' *Helios*, 13 (1986) [special issue]; see also *Helios*, 17 (1990).

[7] Genevieve Liveley, 'Surfing the Third Wave? Postfeminism and the Hermeneutics of Reception', in Charles Martindale and Richard F. Thomas, eds, *Classics and the Uses of Reception* (London: Wiley, 2006), 55–66. On the history of feminist Classics, see also Amy Richlin, *Arguments with Silence: Writing the History of Roman Women* (Ann Arbor: University of Michigan Press, 2014), 1–35.

[8] Vanda Zajko, 'What Difference Was Made?: Feminist Models of Reception', in Lorna Hardwick and Christopher Stray, eds, *A Companion to Classical Receptions* (London: Wiley, 2008), 195–206.

[9] Alison Sharrock, Daniel Möller, and Mats Malm, eds, *Metamorphic Readings: Transformation, Language, and Gender in the Interpretation of Ovid's Metamorphoses* (Oxford: Oxford University Press, 2020).

[10] Ovid, *Metamorphoses*, trans. Mary Innes (Harmondsworth, Middlesex: Penguin, 1955). See Fiona Cox, 'Women's Education and the Classics', in William Brockliss, J. Gnoza, and E. Archibald, eds, *Learning Greek and Latin from Antiquity to the Present* (Cambridge: Cambridge University Press: 2015), 156–65.

[11] Philip Terry, ed., *Ovid Metamorphosed* (London: Chatto and Windus, 2000).

4 INTRODUCTION

In the French-speaking world we are also witnessing a noteworthy land-mark in literary history—making this volume particularly timely—reflected in the striking response to Ovid on the part of francophone writers working in a variety of genres. In 2008 Marie Darrieussecq followed up on her fictional metamorphosis with a translation of Ovid's exile poetry, *Tristes Pontiques*, while Marie Cosnay's recent translation of the *Metamorphoses* was awarded the prix Bernard Hoepffner in 2017. Cosnay, who is a classicist, a teacher, a novelist and a political activist, had already written a novel entitled *Des Métamorphoses*, which is highly influenced by her understanding of the experiences of the refugees whom she tries indefatigably to help.[12] Ovid has also been used politically by writers seeking to articulate the horrors of occupied France (and subsequently the French-Algerian war), as Eurydice enters the hell of the camps in Michèle Sarde's *Histoire d'Eurydice pendant la remontée* (1991), where Eurydice's assumption of her own voice is darkened.[13] Sarde, Cosnay, and Darrieussecq respond to Ovid politically: their interest lies in democratizing the Classics, making classical works access-ible to people who will not necessarily have studied Latin and Greek in school, and using them to comment upon the political situation in France. Marie Cosnay's epilogue to this volume extends this political response to Ovid by examining his work in the light of green politics and, more particularly, the Covid-19 pandemic. As an example of creative-criticism, Cosnay's contribu-tion breaks down distinctions between creative and critical practice, breaking down boundaries and opening up the discipline.[14]

It goes without saying that Ovid's own writing about women and gender has provoked extensive debate: he has been seen variously as misogynous; as a champion of women; and as resistant to fixed notions of gender. These varying interpretations are evident both in critical readings of his own work and in its creative receptions. Ovid's writing about gender could in part be said to have provoked such a range of responses not only because of elements of ambiguity, but also because of its own variety: as Charles Martindale emphasizes in his now-classic *Ovid Renewed*, 'the variousness

---

[12] Marie Cosnay, *Des Métamorphoses* (Chambon-sur-Lignon: Cheyne, 2012); and *Les Métamorphoses* (Paris: Éditions de l'Ogre, 2017).

[13] Michèle Sarde, *Histoire d'Eurydice pendant la remontée* (Paris: Seuil, 1991).

[14] See Emily Hauser, 'When Classics Gets Creative: From Research to Practice', *Transactions of the American Philological Association*, 149/2 (2019), 163–77. Perhaps indicative of a new creative and multi-media trend in Ovidian reception is Clare Pollard's translation of Ovid's *Heroides*: *Ovid's Heroines* (Hexham, Northumberland: Bloodaxe, 2013), accompanied by a touring performance. In December 2020 Jermyn Street Theatre performed *15 Heroines*, inspired by Ovid's *Heroides*, by fifteen different playwrights, including Natalie Haynes.

of the responses to Ovid...mirrors the variety of Ovid's own writings.'[15] Ovid's *Heroides* in particular have been seen to champion women's voices, or an *écriture feminine*;[16] although this is ambiguous since the women are characterized solely by their passivity and emotive suffering, as he imagines the laments of mythological women abandoned by their suitors. The (eroticized) violence against women on display in the *Metamorphoses* in particular, and the gender politics at play in his love poetry, the *Amores* and *Ars amatoria*, as Valerie Traub suggests, are largely 'patriarchal, normalizing, regulatory',[17] and, as Amy Richlin has shown, valorize male domination and reveal Ovid's misogyny.[18] Others, however, emphasize his sympathy with female suffering (often citing, for instance, the Philomela story), such that Ovid's presentation of sexual violence was a way of criticizing gendered hierarchies of power in relationships and society.[19] In her systematic review of the representations of gender and transformation in the *Metamorphoses*, Sharrock highlights that for all Ovid's sensitivity to female subjectivity, this is only demonstrated in negative contexts, underscoring male-dominated power relations.[20] That being said, Ovid's attention to gender fluidity has made him a champion of non-binary and trans identities in reception, as explored by Morales; and a recent study of the medieval and early modern reception of the Iphis and Ianthe story in France and England traces how this tale and its afterlives are ethically and politically engaged with non-normative gender identities.[21]

This study proposes not to consider Ovid's representation of women and gender, which has been productively revisited in two volumes since 2020;[22]

---

[15] Charles Martindale, ed., *Ovid Renewed: Ovidian Influences on Literature and Art from the Middle Ages to the Twentieth Century* (Cambridge: Cambridge University Press, 1990), 5.

[16] Efrossini Spentzou, *Readers and Writers in Ovid's Heroides* (Oxford: Oxford University Press, 2003).

[17] Valerie Traub, 'Afterword', in Goran V. Stanivukovic, ed., *Ovid and the Renaissance Body* (Toronto: University of Toronto Press, 2001), 260–8 (p. 264).

[18] See Amy Richlin, 'Reading Ovid's Rapes', in Amy Richlin, ed., *Pornography and Representation in Greece and Rome* (New York: Oxford University Press, 1992), 158–79; Joan DeJean, *Fictions of Sappho: 1546–1937* (Chicago: University of Chicago Press, 1987), 60–78.

[19] Leo Curran, 'Rape and Rape Victims in Ovid's Metamorphoses', *Arethusa*, 11 (1978), 213–41; Ellen Greene, 'Sexual Politics in Ovid's *Amores* 3.4, 3.8 and 3.12', *Classical Philology*, 4 (1994), 344–50.

[20] Alison Sharrock, 'Gender and Transformation: Reading, Women, and Gender in Ovid's *Metamorphoses*', in Alison Sharrock, Daniel Möller, and Mats Malm, eds, *Metamorphic Readings: Transformation, Language, and Gender in the Interpretation of Ovid's Metamorphoses* (Oxford: Oxford University Press, 2020), 33–53.

[21] Valerie Traub, Patricia Badir, and Peggy McCracken, eds, *Ovidian Transversions: 'Iphis and Ianthe', 1300–1650* (Edinburgh: Edinburgh University Press, 2019).

[22] Sharrock, Möller, and Malm, eds, *Metamorphic Readings*; Melanie Möller, ed., *Gegen/Gewalt/Schreiben: De-Konstruktionen von Geschlechts- und Rollenbildern in der Ovid-Rezeption* (Berlin: De Gruyter, 2020).

6 INTRODUCTION

instead, we shall think about how women and gender non-conforming writers have used Ovid and how those responses reveal changing norms regarding identity, publication, and access to Classics from the Renaissance to today. Our historical range allows us to explore and challenge notions of collectivity or a female tradition, since the authors studied here do not all write from the same positions of marginalization or of being outside structures of patriarchal authority—some are explicitly interested in feminism, some are less so. And while we look at some examples of feminism in French via Ovid, we are not engaged explicitly with 'French Feminism', the post-68 movement, prioritizing instead, a longer historical view.[23] The inclusion of Claude Cahun in a study with 'women' in the title is not intended to flatten the complexities of her/their gender identity; however, in line with recent scholarship on Cahun, which uses a female pronoun, we also felt that excluding her/them might be a presumptive act and, without being able to ask permission, we include Cahun here, but do so with caution.[24] As Catherine Burke demonstrates in her chapter on Cahun, Cahun makes us think about the limitations of categorization according to a gender binary.

We are primarily interested in bringing to light a series of voices less known to Ovidian scholarship that productively help us think about how the traditional reception canon has tended to be male-dominated. While there have been some studies on Ovid's reception in France, the dominant focus in classical reception studies has been on Anglophone sources and often, particularly in relation to questions of gender, on more recent writing with only brief attention paid to earlier contexts.[25] From salon poetry to Revolutionary theatre, from realism to surrealism to autofiction, we trace Ovid's influence and uses across French literary culture.

Although many more women now receive an education equal to men's (the main barrier to a classical education now being class rather than gender, in the UK at least), for much of Western history women have been sidelined from,

---

[23] For other discussions of women's recent responses to Ovid, see Fiona Cox, *Ovid's Presence in Contemporary Women's Writing*; Fiona Cox and Elena Theodorakopoulos, eds, 'Translation, Transgression and Transformation: Contemporary Women Authors and Classical Reception', *Classical Receptions Journal*, 4/2 (2012) [special issue]; and Fiona Cox and Elena Theodorakopoulos, 'Female Voices: the Democratic Turn in Ali Smith's Classical Reception', in Stephen J. Harrison and Lorna Hardwick, eds, *A Democratic Turn? Classics in the Modern World* (Oxford: Oxford University Press, 2014), 263–75.

[24] For example, Jennifer Shaw, *Exist Otherwise: The Life and Works of Claude Cahun* (London: Reakton, 2017). See also the recent 2022 exhibition of Cahun's work in Rotterdam which, referring to Cahun's own practice, uses a female pronoun, although with caution. https://www.kunsthal.nl/en/plan-your-visit/exhibitions/claudecahun/

[25] Lively focuses primarily on the modern context, with some attention to the medieval Christine de Pizan. Cox also looks at some French writing (primarily Darrieussecq), but again the focus here is on contemporary works (*Ovid's Presence*, 155–74).

and have a complex relationship with, the two related activities that govern their reception of Ovid and the classical canon: education and authorship. They therefore, also, share an oblique relationship to Ovid. This story is made more interesting because, as noted, Ovid's own representation of women does not constitute an easy relationship: his representations of rape and violence against women are disturbing for all readers; his eroticism 'too extreme, too tormented, too sensationalist, and hence, too disturbing or dangerous for women writers' concerned, until recent times, with the propriety of author-ship:[26] women have, in the past, faced 'social opposition' to writing about Ovid.[27] Our study highlights such questions as: how has this story changed over time? What does this grouping suggest about the history and pluralities of feminism and the possibilities and limitations of the idea of a female tradition? How far were writers writing in a tradition of reception? How is this tradition shaped or challenged through Ovid's reception in the works of authors whose family histories connect them to cultures from outside mainland France?

This volume seeks to address these questions by offering the first coherent account of Ovid's presence from the Renaissance to the present day, with a particular focus on French and francophone literary culture, and on women and gender non-conforming writers. Our chapters address different forms of reception—from rewriting, influence, intertext, and translation—examining how each mode intersects with questions of gender, authority and access to classical learning. The intentions of the volume are twofold: to reveal lesser-known voices in Ovidian reception studies, particularly by shifting the focus onto French and francophone writing and culture, and to contribute a wider historical perspective on the complex question of Ovid and gender.

* * *

This study is also about the history of Ovid's reception in French, so the receptions studied here need to be placed in context. The year 1100—and indeed the medieval period more broadly—has been dubbed the 'aetas Ovidiana'. As James Clark has shown, Ovid had an important place on the curriculum, particularly because his *Metamorphoses* offered an insightful compendium on mythology: this interest expanded to the extra mural public from the late twelfth century:[28] for instance, Ovidian influences, including

---

[26] Traub, 'Afterword', 266.

[27] Heather James, 'Ovid in Renaissance English Literature', in Peter E. Knox, ed., *A Companion to Ovid* (Oxford: Wiley-Blackwell, 2009), 423–41 (p. 437).

[28] James Clark, Frank Coulson, and Kathryn McKinley, eds, *Ovid in the Middle Ages* (Cambridge: Cambridge University Press, 2011), 6.

8   INTRODUCTION

from his *Remedia amoris* and *Metamorphoses*, have been traced in the poetry of Marie de France.[29] But it was not until Christine de Pizan's engagement with Ovid through his presence in Guillaume de Norris and Jean de Meun's *Roman de la rose* (1230; 1275), as well as the *Ovide Moralisé* (*c*.1317), and Pierre Bersuire's Latin *Ovidius Moralizatus* (1340)—the latter two dominated the late medieval criticism on Ovid—that we see an extended critical response to Ovid mediated through a woman's reflections on her own authorship. It is largely thanks to vernacular versions that Pizan, although versed in Latin, had access to Ovid's work. In the three letters Pizan wrote against Jean de Meun's additions to the *Roman de la rose*, she tasks Ovid with misogyny in his embrace of erotic violence, championing her female cause and her place as an author.[30] Marilynn Desmond suggests that Pizan's 'understanding of Ovid conditions her to develop a similarly critical approach to the *Roman de la rose*' and that she 'reject[s] the Ovidian version of female identity and desire articulated by the "Vieille" in the *Roman de la rose*'.[31] As Desmond explores elsewhere, in Pizan's *Othea*, she 'queers the Ovidian obsession with metamorphosis and explores trans-species sexuality as a way of revising received notions of female sexuality and envisioning female desire'.[32] Pizan also makes Ovid new; as Jeremy Dimmick argues: 'Christine's detestation of Ovid does not make her unwilling to borrow from him; on the contrary, she does so repeatedly, and in a consciously revisionist spirit, appropriating mythological protagonists and narratives from the *Metamorphoses* for her own arguments.'[33] It is significant that Pizan makes it into Dimmick's survey of Ovid in the Middle Ages, confirming the importance of her reception of the ancient poet.

The 'Renaissance Ovid' was primarily author of the *Metamorphoses*. Humanist scholarship produced detailed commentaries of this poem in Latin, summarizing the myths and their allegorical meanings;[34] French translations of

---

[29] See Kristine Brightenback, 'The Metamorphoses and Narrative Conjointure in "Deus amanz", "Yonec" and "Le laustic"', *Romanic Review*, 72/1 (1981), 1–12; and SunHee Kim Gertz, *Echoes and Reflections: Memory and Memorials in Ovid and Marie de France* (Leiden: Brill, 2003).

[30] See David Hult, 'The Roman de la rose, Christine de Pizan and the querelle des femmes', in Carolyn Dinshaw and David Wallace, eds, *The Cambridge Companion to Women Writers: Medieval Women* (Cambridge: Cambridge University Press, 2003), 184–94.

[31] Marilynn Desmond, *Ovid's Art and the Wife of Bath: The Ethics of Erotic Violence* (Ithaca: Cornelle University Press, 2006), 155 and 164.

[32] Marilynn Desmond and Pamela Sheingorn, 'Queering Ovidian Myth: Bestiality and Desire in Christine de Pizan's Epistre Othea', in Glenn Burger and Steven Kruger, eds, *Queering the Middle Ages* (Minneapolis: University of Minnesota Press: 2001), 3–27 (p. 6).

[33] Jeremy Dimmick, 'Ovid in the Middle Ages', in Philip Hardie, ed., *The Cambridge Companion to Ovid* (Cambridge: Cambridge University Press, 2002), 264–86 (p. 267).

[34] Aldus Manutius, *Quae in hoc volumine continentur: Ad Marinum Lanudum epistola... Orthographia dictionum graecarum per ordinem literarum; Vita Ovidii ex ipsius operibus; Index fabularum et caeterorum... Ovidii Metamorphoseon libri quindecim* (Venice: A. Manutius, 1502).

the *Metamorphoses* were published in Paris in the first half of the sixteenth century by Clément Marot and François Habert, who produced close translations of Ovid's original, paying attention to stylistic features.[35] At the beginning of the seventeenth century, in 1601, another verse translation of Ovid's *Metamorphoses* by Raimond and Charles Massac was published.[36] These translations did not entirely abandon the trend of commentary writing, as moralizing allegorical interpretations of the myth were inserted alongside or after each story, or in the introduction. Condensed versions of the myths, in the form similar to the earlier commentaries, were still in demand, and a successful series of summaries of the fables from the *Metamorphoses* were printed in the vernacular, *Le Grand Olympe des Histoires Poétiques du prince de poésie Ovide Naso en sa Métamorphose* (1532).[37] Versions of the *Fasti*, *Amores*, and *Ars amatoria* were not as frequently produced in the sixteenth century. The *Tristia* and *Epistulae ex Ponto* fared little better despite their place on the school syllabus: and yet, the experience of exile recounted here chimed with the concerns of a period increasingly open to travel and its narration, and is echoed in Joachim Du Bellay's *Les Regrets* (1558).[38]

Despite the moralized and excised editions in circulation, Ovid still had a reputation for licentiousness. The Ovidian misogyny so criticized by Pizan continued to prove complex in the Renaissance. Women might have been avid readers of Ovid's verse, but as Traub and Heather James note, they were more reluctant to use him as a model in their writing, given the importance placed on decorum and propriety. On the face of it, it was Virgil who had a more prominent role for Renaissance female authors, attested by Hélisenne de Crenne's and Marie de Gournay's translations.[39] At the same time, however,

---

[35] Clément Marot, *Le Premier Livre de la Métamorphose d'Ovide, traduit de Latin en français* (Paris: E. Roffet, 1534); Clément Marot, *Le Second Livre de la Métamorphose d'Ovide*, in *Les Œuvres de Clément Marot* (Lyons: E. Dolet, 1543); François Habert, *Six Livres de la Métamorphose d'Ovide, traduits selon la phrase Latine en rime française* (Paris: M. Fezandat, 1549); François Habert, *Les Trois Premiers Livres de la Métamorphose d'Ovide, traduits en vers français; le premier et second par C. L. Marot, le tiers par B. Aneau* (Lyons: G. Rouile, 1556); and François Habert, *Les Quinze Livres de la Métamorphose d'Ovide interprétés en rime française, selon la phrase latine* (Paris: M. Fezandat and E. Groulleau, 1557).

[36] *Métamorphoses d'Ovide mises en vers français par Raimond et Charles de Massac, père et fils* (Paris: A. l'Angelier, 1603).

[37] *Le Grand Olympe des Histoires Poétiques du prince de poésie Ovide Naso en sa Métamorphose* (Lyons: D. de Harsy, 1532). This saw several reprints in Paris and Lyon.

[38] Joachim Du Bellay, *Les Antiquitéz de Rome et Les Regrets* (Geneva: Droz, 1960). See Stephen Hinds, 'Black-Sea Latin, Du Bellay and the Barbarian Turn', in Jennifer Ingleheart, ed., *Two Thousand Years of Solitude: Exile after Ovid* (Oxford: Oxford University Press, 2011), 59–83.

[39] Hélisenne de Crenne, *Les Quatre Premiers Livres des Eneydes* (Paris: Janot, 1541). See Fiona Cox, 'An Amazon in the Renaissance: Mlle de Gournay's Translation of Virgil, *Aeneid* 2', in Susanna Braund and Zara Martirosova Torlone, eds, *Virgil and his Translators* (Oxford: Oxford University Press, 2018), 97–106. See also Sharon Marshall, 'The *Aeneid* and the Illusory Authoress: Truth, Fiction and Feminism in Hélisenne de Crenne's *Eneyde*', PhD thesis, University of Exeter, 2011.

10   INTRODUCTION

more than ever, Ovid's work was both being directed at female readers and seen as offering moral exempla for women, namely through the Christianized versions of his *Heroides*.[40] The *Heroides* were valued as examples of epistolary rhetoric, promoted and extolled by Erasmus, and for this reason had an entrenched place in the school system. Although some unresolved unease was registered with regard to the possibly subversive content of letters by Phaedra or Medea, for example,[41] the prevailing approach turned the women of these letters into moral exempla; the frequently reprinted annotated edition by Guido Morillon included a commentary that emphasized the patience, fidelity, and devotion of the women.[42] This moral reading was also evident in the first French translation, produced in c. 1499 by Octavian de Saint-Gelais,[43] and in the two from the mid-sixteenth century by François Habert, including *Les Epîtres héroïdes, pour servir d'exemple Chrétien*.[44] The epistolarity of these letters was also key to their appeal—and we will see this come to the fore in the eighteenth century: imitations of the *Heroides*, often in the form of fictional 'responses' to the heroines, were used as examples of epistolary rhetoric in letter-writing manuals.[45]

And yet, for all that there seemed to be limited scope in the sixteenth century for women's engagement with Ovid, that is not to say that it was not present—however subtle this presence might be—or that a response which privileges 'properness' should be seen as a form of limitation. In her contribution to this volume, Emma Herdman examines how women negotiated the double challenge of Ovid's 'erotics of cruelty' and the prevalent allegorical interpretations of his work which were often at their expense by exploring uses of Ovid's portrayal of Aglaurus and Envy (*Met.* 2) by the mother and daughter pair, Madeleine and Catherine des Roches.[46] They resist the early modern

---

[40] White, *Renaissance Postscripts*.

[41] In 1509 Nole Bédier had banned the *Heroides* from the curriculum of the College de Montaigu. Lefèvre d'Etables also agreed that there was no place for *Heroides* in Christian education. See Ann Moss, *Ovid in Renaissance France: A Survey of Latin Editions and Commentaries Printed in France before 1600* (London: Warburg Institute, 1982), 9.

[42] Guido Morillon's translation of the *Heroides* was first printed in Paris by D. Roce in 1507; it was reprinted in Lyon in 1533 with additional notes by Joannes Baptista Egnatius and, according to Ann Moss, this edition, reprinted in both Paris and Lyon for the next fifty years, 'drives earlier commentaries from the market'. Moss, *Ovid in Renaissance France*, 12.

[43] Octavian de Saint-Gelais, *Les XXI Epîtres d'Ovide* (Paris: Verard, 1499).

[44] François Habert, *Les Epîtres héroïdes, très salutaires pour servir d'exemple à toute âme fidèle* (Paris: Fezandet, 1550); François Habert, *Les Epîtres héroïdes, pour servir d'exemple aux chrétiens* (Paris: Fezandet, 1560).

[45] See Marie-Claire Chatelain, 'Héroïde comme modèle épistolaire: l'exemple des *Lettres Amoureuses* de Malleville', *Littératures Classiques*, 71 (2010), 129–51. See also Sarah Ross and Rosalind Smith, eds, *Early Modern Women's Complaint: Gender, Form, and Politics* (Cham: Palgrave, 2020).

[46] Traub, 'Afterword', 266.

interpretation of this story in which Aglaurus is figure for women's curiosity, unlicensed knowledge, and indiscretion, to advocate instead for women's education and literary self-expression. Herdman thus suggests that by circumventing the obstacles deterring them from rewriting Ovid, the des Roches also challenge the norms that denied them access to, and expression of, various forms of knowledge. Jessica DeVos's chapter in this volume places translations of Ovid in the broader picture of translation as an act of nation building in sixteenth-century France, and challenges assumptions around the gendering of translation as feminine and inferior. She offers us a different example of a Renaissance women's response to Ovid: not one of oblique 'skirting' around the author, as in Herdman's study, but a direct, close, and intense engagement through precise translation, showcasing the translator's own talent and her own interpretation of Ovid—the translation of *Heroides* 2, Phyllis to Demophoon, by Madeleine de L'Aubespine (1546–96). It circulated in manuscript form in the late sixteenth century and this translation has received scant scholarly attention.

This negotiation of agency in the transformation of an Ovid 'suitable' for women was renewed in the seventeenth century. This was a time when women have been seen to come to unprecedented cultural prominence in France through their influence in salon culture. The salon was of central cultural importance during this period, and unlike the *Académie française,* established in 1634, its company included both men and women. Its early forms include the salon or 'chambre bleue' of Catherine de Vivonne, marquise de Rambouillet, in the 1620s, and from the early 1650s, the well-known novelist Madeleine de Scudéry, a member of the Rambouillet circle, hosted a regular Saturday salon, known as the *samedis.* Such salons have been seen as centres of sociable literary production: a range of literary genres were cultivated there, including poetry, the literary portrait, the conversation, and the novel. Indeed, the salon is considered to be largely responsible for the proliferation of female-authored novels and changing forms of culture and cultural practice (notably the shift from the dominance of classical models) which were contributing factors in the Quarrel of the Ancients and Moderns—a debate over the value and hegemony of ancient culture—at the close of the century.

However, that is not to say that interest in Ovid declined at this time, or that women—normally associated with the 'Modern' camp in this debate—lost a taste for Ovid. On the contrary, Ovid's poetry was almost everywhere and its influence far-reaching.[47] This can be seen in the widespread reception of

---

[47] White, *Renaissance Postscripts*; Stéphanie Loubère, *L'Art d'Aimer au siècle des lumières* (Oxford: SVEC, 2007).

12   INTRODUCTION

individual Ovidian myths from the *Metamorphoses*, such as Perseus and Andromeda,[48] Narcissus,[49] Arachne,[50] Iphis and Ianthe,[51] and Philomela;[52] and responses to Ovid by writers such as Jean Racine, Cyrano de Bergerac, Jean de La Fontaine, and Isaac de Benserade.[53] Ovid's mythology was used in royal architecture and art, key to the fabrication of Louis XIV as the 'Sun-King'.[54] There was a notable interest shown in the later part of the century in Ovid's love poetry: the focus on the sentimental and the social in shorter poetic forms was particularly appealing to salon communities and their emphasis on female taste (needless to say, the more erotic charge of Ovid's poems was moderated to suit this polite culture). Ovid thus proved fruitful for the modern aesthetic; likewise, many of the stories from the *Metamorphoses* were adapted for use in opera, another new genre.[55]

As recent scholars have begun to explore, a number of women turned to Ovid to advance their own positions as authors in the public sphere. Madeleine de Scudéry used her version of Ovid's *Heroides*, and particularly the letter from Sappho to Phaon, to promote her case for women's education;[56] Madame de Villedieu turned to the story of Ovid's life;[57] and Marie-Jeanne L'Héritier made Ovid the fictional go-between of Apollo and Mercury, chaperoning female authors to Parnassus in her fictional apotheosis: he is described as 'l'adorateur du beau sexe'.[58] In seventeenth-century England, women were the target readers of male translations of Ovid's *Heroides*, such as the 1636

---

[48] Benoît Bolduc, *Andromède au rocher: fortune théâtrale en France et en Italie 1587–1712* (Florence: Olschki, 2002).

[49] Pascale Auraix-Jonchière and Catherine Volpilhac-Auger, eds, *Isis, Narcisse, Psyché entre lumières et romanticisme: mythe et écritures, écritures du mythe* (Clemont-Ferrand: Presses Universitaires Blaise-Pascal, 2000).

[50] Sylvie Ballestra-Puech, *Métamorphose d'Arachné: l'artiste en araignée dans la littérature occidentale* (Geneva: Droz, 2006).

[51] Lise Leibacher, 'Speculum de l'autre femme: Les Avatars d'Iphis et Ianthe (Ovide) au XVII siècle', *Papers on French Seventeenth-Century Literature*, 59 (2003), 367–76.

[52] Terence Cave, '"Tu facto loquar": Philomela's Afterlives in Rabelais, Ronsard and Shakespeare', in Wes Williams and Neil Kenny, eds, *Retrospectives: Essays in Literature, Poetics and Cultural History by Terence Cave* (London: Legenda, 2009), 76–86.

[53] Georges May, *D'Ovide à Racine* (New Haven: Yale University Press, 1947).

[54] Jean-Pierre Néraudau, 'Ovide au château de Versailles, sous Louis XIV', in Raymond Chevallier, ed., *Colloque Présences d'Ovide* (Paris: Belles Lettres, 1982), 323–42; Henri Bardon, 'Sur l'influence d'Ovide en France au XVIIe siècle', *Atti del Convegno Internazionale Ovidiano*, 2 (1959), 69–83.

[55] See Helena Taylor, *The Lives of Ovid in Seventeenth-Century French Culture* (Oxford: Oxford University Press, 2017).

[56] Madeleine and Georges de Scudéry, *Les Femmes illustres ou Les harangues héroïques* (Paris: A. de Sommaville and A. Courbé, 1642), 431.

[57] Madame de Villedieu, *Ovide, ou Les Exilés de la cour d'Auguste* (Paris: Barbin, 1672–8). See Juliette Cherbuliez, *The Place of Exile: Leisure Literature and the Limits of Absolutism* (Lewisburg: Bucknell University Press, 2005).

[58] Marie-Jeanne L'Héritier, 'Le Parnasse reconnaissant', *Œuvres mêlées de Mlle L'H*** (1694; Paris: J. Guignard, 1696), 404–24 (p. 410).

version by Wye Saltonstall;[59] Aphra Behn contributed to the 1680 volume of multi-authored translations of Ovid's *Epistles*,[60] and influenced translations by other women, such as Anne Killigrew and Phillis Wheatley.[61] Some of these women were, on the one hand, responding to the polite, expurgated Ovid made suitable for their tastes, and thus were furthering this polite aesthetic; and yet, some were using Ovid more directly—and less politely—to engage in arguments about their status as authors.

In this collection Helena Taylor's chapter considers three female translators or 'versioners' of Ovid's *Heroides*; by examining *Heroides* 13, Laodamia to Protesilaus, she analyses the relationship between gender, translation, and fidelity, and charts divisions in Ovid's reception according to the different cultures of learning and taste the three authors analysed represent, pushing against the idea of a collective tradition. Océane Puche examines the first female-authored complete translation of Ovid's *Heroides* by Marie-Jeanne L'Héritier (1732), showing how she used her version of *Heroides* 4, Phaedra to Hippolytus, to assert her authorial position, and engage in the long-standing quarrels over women's cultural presence, the *querelle des femmes*. Like Madeleine de L'Aubespine, Marie-Jeanne L'Héritier's translation stands out from the versions by her male predecessors and contemporaries: where L'Aubespine's subtle reworking emphasized Phyllis' concern to rewrite the male-authored account of masculine heroic exploits, L'Héritier voices Phèdre in such a way as to defend her glory.

It is no surprise that the two contributions to this volume from the eighteenth century should also focus on versions of Ovid's *Heroides*: this text's popularity in this period is accounted for by the prevalence of the epistolary novel. From Gabriel Guilleragues's *Lettres Portugaises* (1669) through to Pierre Choderlos de Laclos's *Les Liaisons dangereuses* (1782), the epistolary novel, with its sentimental insights, can be seen as a continuation of the tradition established by Ovid's *Heroides*. Eighteenth-century France saw a significant number of translations of the *Heroides*, both of complete versions and of individual letters,[62] as well as a number of imitations, sequels, and 'spin-off' letters.[63] In this volume, Séverine

---

[59] Wye Saltonstall, *Ovid's Heroical Epistles Englished by W. S.* (London: W. Gilberston, 1636).

[60] Aphra Behn, 'Oenone to Paris', in *Ovid's Epistles Translated by Several Hands* (London: 1680).

[61] See Christopher Martin, 'Translating Ovid', in Peter E. Knox, ed., *A Companion to Ovid* (Oxford: Wiley-Blackwell, 2009), 469–84.

[62] Such as those of Jean Barrin (Paris: Marteau, 1703) and Marie-Jeanne L'Héritier (Paris: Prault, 1732).

[63] While there are too many to cite them all here, frequent translators were Claude-Joseph Dorat, Blin de Sainmore who contributed to the *Héroïdes ou lettres en vers* (Paris: Jorry and Delalain, 1767), Louis-Sébastien Mercier, contributing to *Héroïdes et autres pièces de poésie* (Paris, 1764), and Sébastien Gazon Dourxigné.

14 INTRODUCTION

Clément-Tarantino presents one such example of a 'spin-off' series in Charlotte de Bressey Lezay-Marnésia's *Lettres de Julie à Ovide* (1753), fictional letters from Julia, the emperor's daughter, to Ovid, presented playfully as historical documents. Clément-Tarantino examines how Lezay-Marnésia's *Lettres* reveal both Ovid's *Heroides* and his *Tristia* as subtle intertexts, allowing the French author to reconfigure Julia into an authoritative figure to rival the poet. Thea S. Thorsen then explores Ovid's reception in another genre popular in the eighteenth century, the *opéra comique*. Thorsen focuses on the now little-known but successful opera, *Sapho* (1794), by Constance de Salm, most recognized now for her feminist *Épître aux femmes* (1797). Thorsen shows her *Sapho* to be a reconfiguration of Ovid's *Heroides* 15; she places this in the context of two other Ovidian and 'courageous' moments that defined Salm's career: her 1788 poem *Le Bouton de rose*, Ovidian in its portrayal of metempsychosis, and her 1810 *Épître adressée à L'empereur Napoléon*, in which Thorsen shows Salm to cast herself as a new Ovid critical of Napoleon's (Augustus') new and misogynistic adultery laws. Across both the chapters by Clément-Tarantino and Thorsen we witness creative reworkings of Ovid's text into new genres and forms, presented as continuations or sequels of Ovid's work.

Ovid fell out of fashion in the nineteenth century: his reception in this period is, as Richard Jenkyns describes, 'an ungrateful topic'.[64] Norman Vance suggests that 'apart from questions of moral respectability and revulsion from Ovid the rake, there are perhaps two main reasons for this wilful and faintly unworthy suppression of Ovid. In a literary climate still dominated by romanticism he seemed to be merely facile and he was blamed for being derivative.'[65] This marginalization is confirmed by Isobel Hurst who shows him to be omitted from the university syllabus.[66] Ovid's reception in nineteenth-century France was also limited: scholars have traced some influence on writers as various as Sainte-Beuve and Victor Hugo,[67] and have explored the use of myths from the *Metamorphoses* in opera, but suggest that 'Ovid almost always disappears in the process'.[68]

---

[64] Richard Jenkyns, 'Review of *Ovid Renewed*, ed. by Charles Martindale', *Review of English Studies*, 41/161 (1990), 152.

[65] Norman Vance, 'Ovid and the Nineteenth Century', in Charles Martindale, ed., *Ovid Renewed: Ovidian Influences on Literature and Art from the Middle Ages to the Twentieth Century* (Cambridge: Cambridge University Press, 1990), 215–32 (p. 233).

[66] Isobel Hurst, *Victorian Women Writers and the Classics: The Feminine of Homer* (Oxford: Oxford University Press, 2006).

[67] See Fiona Cox, 'Ovid on the Channel Islands: The Exile of Victor Hugo', in Jennifer Ingleheart, ed., *Two Thousand Years of Solitude: Exile after Ovid* (Oxford: Oxford University Press, 2011), 173–88.

[68] Vance, 'Ovid and the Nineteenth Century', 233.

In among this apparent desert of reception, however, lie some interesting responses to Ovid: for instance, in 1842 the scholar Emma Garland provided the first female-authored full translation of Ovid's *Heroides* in English. As Fiona Cox shows in her chapter in this volume, Germaine de Staël's *Corinne ou l'Italie* (1807) is rich in Ovidian allusion and intertext (notably, the *Fasti*, the *Amores*, and the *Ars amatoria*). *Corinne ou l'Italie* is one of the most significant works about Rome penned by a woman: not only does Staël weave Ovidian intertexts throughout but she also casts her protagonist in a line of women intellectuals that harks back to the early modern *salonnières*, a line also linked by Ovidian reception. In his chapter, James Illingworth examines the centrality of the *Metamorphoses* and of metamorphosis to George Sand's œuvre. He moves beyond the critical tendency to focus solely on the Pygmalion and Narcissus myths and instead examines two playful metamorphic beings, the imaginary friend Corambé who features in Sand's autobiography, *Histoire de ma vie* (1854–5), and Gribouille of the *Histoire du véritable Gribouille* of 1850, which both bear Ovid's influence, in turn offering another means of under-standing Sand's own metamorphosis: from Aurore Dudevant to George Sand. Both these chapters attest to a cultural dispersal of Ovidian myths and themes: rather than rephrasing one particular work as we have seen happen thus far, they respond in more subtle ways to Ovid as mythographer.

The relation between metamorphic shape-shifting and fluid identity that Illingworth notes in Sand's work is a key theme in the two early twentieth-century responses to Ovid analysed here and which speak to each other productively: Claude Cahun's *Héroïnes* (1925) and Marguerite Yourcenar's *Feux* (1936), both subtle reworkings of Ovid's *Heroides*. Catherine Burke analyses Claude Cahun's response to Ovid, mapping this reception onto techniques found in Cahun's photographic self-portrait, in which themes of inversion and pluralistic identities are prominent, and placing it alongside Cahun's reception of Tiresias, as figure for non-normative gender identities. By tracing Ovid's influence on Cahun, Burke embraces the challenge to categorization posed by Cahun and argues for greater appreciation of this author-artist's contribution to surrealism. Studying another French version of Ovid's *Heroides*, published nine years after that of Cahun, Florence Klein interrogates Yourcenar's ambivalent feminism through analysis of her rework-ing of Ovid's *Heroides* in *Feux*, particularly the Achilles story from *Heroides* 3 and Sappho from *Heroides* 15. Klein argues that although these two tales seem to represent the possibility of transcending a limited, gendered space, and so also respond to the fluidity of identity espoused by the *Metamorphoses*, in fact they confirm fixed gendered identities.

16   INTRODUCTION

This interest in identity and the politics of identity resonates with the wider twentieth-century responses to Ovid (and continues to be a key area of focus in recent scholarship).[69] In his landmark study, *Ovid and the Moderns*, Theodore Ziolkowski demonstrates Ovid's appeal to modernist writers, including Pound and Joyce, stressing in particular the interest in the theme of transformation in his *Metamorphoses*, that we have seen to be prevalent in the works of Cahun and Yourcenar. In the late twentieth century, key English-language responses to the *Metamorphoses* came in the mid-1990s in the form of Michael Hoffman and James Lasdun's edited collection of poems, *After Ovid: New Metamorphoses* (1994), and Ted Hughes's *Tales from Ovid* (1997).[70] Interest in identity can also be traced in the uses of Ovid as figure for the exile. As Ziolkowski explores, Ovid as 'ur-exile' was a particularly prominent element of twentieth-century receptions of Ovid's work—evident both from his influence on Romanian writing (his place of exile, Tomis, being modern-day Constanta in Romania), and from his presence in writers exploring themes of exile, from Cold War Eastern Europe to 1980s Trinidad.[71] In many twentieth-century responses to Ovid, then, the *Metamorphoses* and *Tristia* emerge as prominent, with poems that had previously inspired much imitation, his love poetry and *Heroides*, all but receding from view—save for some important publications, such as Peter Green's translation, *Ovid: The Erotic Poems* (1982).[72]

Kathleen Hamel's chapter analyses the influence of Ovidian exile on the work of Julia Kristeva, Bulgarian-French theorist and novelist, who moved to France aged nineteen. Hamel focuses in particular on her autobiographical novel, *Le Vieil Homme et les loups* (1991), in which Kristeva thinks through experiences of exile, displacement, and the loss of her father. Kristeva draws on the fluidity, instability, and unpredictability of Ovid's *Metamorphoses* to portray 'un monde en mutation' (a changing world) and comment on society following the fall of the Berlin wall, using Ovid as an anti-establishment voice to condemn banality and homogenization of culture. In the penultimate chapter in this volume, Fiona Cox treats the phenomenon of migration narratives merging with tales of metamorphosis in the works of two writers exploring ideas of migration, displacement, and belonging. Cox analyses the French author Marie NDiaye's *Trois femmes puissantes* (2009), which recounts

---

[69] See Roynon and Orrells, eds, 'Ovid and Identity in the Twenty-First Century'.

[70] Michael Hoffman and James Lasdun, eds, *After Ovid: New Metamorphoses* (London: Faber and Faber, 1994); Ted Hughes, *Tales from Ovid* (London: Faber and Faber, 1997).

[71] Theodore Ziolkowski, *Ovid and the Moderns* (Ithaca: Cornell University Press, 2005), 99–139.

[72] Ovid, *The Erotic Poems*, trans. Peter Green (London: Penguin, 1982).

migration between France and Senegal from the perspective of three female characters and Linda Lê's *Les Trois Parques* (1997) and her essay *Par ailleurs (exils)* (2014). Ovid's understanding of loss and dislocation, developed in both the *Tristia* and the *Metamorphoses*, offers a powerful voice for the exploration of these themes in relation to France and its former colonies. Marie Cosnay's closing essay takes the political aspects of Ovidian reception in a new direction: she reads the ecological themes that pervade the *Metamorphoses* in the light of the global Covid-19 pandemic, offering a creative-critical response to an area of Ovid's work that has only recently begun to receive attention.[73]

One of the most powerful responses to Ovid in recent years in France is Céline Sciamma's 2019 *Portrait d'une jeune fille en feu*.[74] The film tells the story of an eighteenth-century painter, Marianne, travelling to an island off the coast of Brittany to paint the wedding portrait of the aristocratic Héloïse. Since Héloïse does not wish to marry, the portrait must be painted in secret and she believes that Marianne has arrived instead to be her companion. The more time the two women spend together, the closer they become, until eventually they fall in love with each other. Inevitably, in a film predicated upon falling in love and painting, there is much focus upon the ways in which the women gaze at each other. The film opens with one of Marianne's art students unearthing the 'Portrait d'une jeune fille en feu', a portrait of Héloïse, which prompts Marianne's memories of their love affair, now a long time in the past. The film moves from the painted seascape to Marianne travelling by sea to undertake her commission and meet Héloïse. The film is, therefore, haunted from the start by an awareness of loss—we know that the love story must entail the separation of the two lovers.

It is this space of loss that Ovid inhabits in the film. One evening Marianne and Héloïse, accompanied by the servant Sophie, sit together as Héloïse reads out loud the myth of Orpheus from Book 10 of Ovid's *Metamorphoses*. The scene reminds us that the film celebrates many different forms of traditionally-female creativity—as well as the painting that is foregrounded, the women also engage with embroidery, music, cooking, and reading. As they debate the meanings possible within Ovid's version of the myth, it is as if they have created their own mini salon. Sophie is appalled by the ghastly and cruel

[73] 'Ovid and the Natural World' was the subject of the 2022 International Ovidian Society-sponsored panel at SCS in San Francisco in 2022; and see Alison Sharrock, 'Ovid and the Ecological Crisis?' (2021), https://classicsforall.org.uk/reading-room/ad-familiares/ovid-and-ecological-crisis. See also Jill Da Silva, 'Ecocriticism and Myth: The Case of Erysichthon', *Interdisciplinary Studies in Literature and Environment*, 15/2 (2008), 103–16.

[74] Céline Sciamma, dir., *Portrait d'une jeune fille en feu* (Lilies Films/Hold-Up Films & Productions/Arte France Cinéma, 2019).

18   INTRODUCTION

trickery by which Orpheus loses Eurydice for a second time; Marianne, on the other hand, thinks it possible that Orpheus willed the loss, arguing that it is loss that gives the myth its poetic power. 'Il ne fait pas le choix de l'amoureux. Il fait le choix du poète' ('His choice is that of the poet rather than of the lover'), she argues.[75] The loss that is foregrounded at the start of the film is explicitly recognized by the lovers here. It is important, also, that the Orpheus myth is used to deepen the pathos of this lesbian love story. While the *Metamorphoses* is the Ovidian intertext that is overtly foregrounded, *Portrait d'une jeune fille en feu* also looks back to the *Heroides*, and it is no accident that the film is set at a time when the *Heroides* were enjoying especial recognition in France. The fifteenth letter in the *Heroides* is from Sappho to her male lover, Phaon, replete with the same burning passion and tenderness experienced by a woman for a woman that charges Sciamma's film. Furthermore, the importance of the sea within the film establishes a further connection with the *Heroides*.[76] As noted, Marianne's portrait of Héloïse at the start of the film metamorphoses into the seascape that sets the scene for her arrival at Héloïse's home. Marianne arrives at the island by boat and drenched, having had to dive into the sea to save her painting implements which had fallen overboard. At her first meeting with Héloïse she is alarmed when it appears that Héloïse is going to throw herself over a cliff into the sea; they exchange their first kiss by

---

[75] Translations are from the film's subtitles. For a sensitive reading of this scene see Benjamin Eldon Stevens, 'Not the Lover's Choice, but the Poet's: Classical Receptions in *Portrait of A Lady on Fire*', *Frontières. Revue d'Archéologie, Histoire et Histoire de l'art*, 2 (2020), https://publications-prairial. fr/frontiere-s/index.php?id=258. Rather than see this scene as a version of a French literary salon, Stevens suggests that with 'its emphasis on wine-drinking, the scene might recall a particular philosophical dialogue, Plato's *Symposium* or "Drinking-Party."' In both cases the topic is "love", and the *Symposium* makes reference to homosexual *eros*, including—unusually for ancient literature—love between women.' (Stevens refrains from pushing the Platonic connections too far). See also Sciamma's words about this scene: 'I (Sciamma) can't decide who's right, but I really wanted her (Héloïse) and Marianne to have strong intellectual debates and (for us) to see them think together, within their (artistic) collaboration but also at the heart of their love dialogue...I wanted to portray the intellectual process of falling in love, of feeling admiration and surprise at the mind of the person in front of you and how, suddenly, you create a language and sparks. And that's also why I can't choose in the Orpheus [*sic*] analysis.' Cited in Michèle Bacholle, 'For a Fluid Approach to Céline Sciamma's *Portrait of a Lady on Fire*', *French Cultural Studies*, 34/2 (2022), 147–60 (p. 153). Bacholle is citing Amy Taubin, ' "Here's looking at you": Céline Sciamma on the path of love and restoring lost histories', *Film Comment* (November/December 2019), https://www.filmcomment.com/article/interview-celine-sciamma-portrait-of-a-lady-on-fire/.

[76] See M. Catherine Bolton, 'Gendered Spaces in Ovid's *Heroides*', *The Classical World*, 102/3 (2009), 273–90: 'In the *Heroides*, the symbolic import of the sea figures large first in an erotic context, as the beloved (from Ulysses through Jason to Aeneas) most frequently departs and/ or arrives via the sea. The passion of love is therefore linked to the physical entity of water. In mythic terms, water itself has long been associated with female sexuality and the power of creativity; the birth of Venus from the foam of the sea is a Greco-Roman myth which speaks to this dual aspect of water and sexuality' (p. 273).

the sea and, of course, as for so many of Ovid's lovers, it is by the sea that they must ultimately take leave of each other.

In a recent study Emma Wilson argues that metamorphosis is a key theme throughout Sciamma's œuvre, observing that Sciamma 'draws from Ovid an interest in matter and substance, and specifically their mutability. Recalling Ovid in thinking about Sciamma reveals the ways in which her work, although strikingly original, is always in dialogue with a wider range of literary and artistic reference. Although its subject matter, up until *Portrait of a Lady on Fire,* is very contemporary, her themes are also immemorial.'[77] Wilson also movingly argues that the backward glance of *Portrait* is not just a reworking of the glance between Orpheus and Eurydice transposed to Marianne and Héloïse but is a device through which Sciamma looks back at the actress, her own former lover, Adèle Haenel:

> [Héloïse] is convulsed by the music, flooded with tears, like the Fates hearing Orpheus' singing in the Underworld. This last sequence testifies to the grief of Héloïse as she hears music, which has always been her passion, and as she remembers her love affair with Marianne. This is a portrait of Haenel as an actress. The film celebrates her beauty and her holding of intense emotion, whilst also looking back on her through art. The portrait is a tribute and also a new work of art, a new imagining of feminist filmmaking.[78]

We may have needed to wait for a twenty-first-century response to Ovid for some of these themes to be explored, namely an explicitly lesbian love story in which, at one point, Marianne paints a portrait of herself from a mirror propped against Héloïse's naked body;[79] but the film also looks back to key features of Ovidian reception by French women, such as the literary 'salon' and the eighteenth-century popularity of the *Heroides.*[80] Through the medium of film Sciamma celebrates the power of female creativity in different artistic realms, and reminds us that Ovid's reception is not confined to the world of literature.

---

[77] Emma Wilson, *Céline Sciamma – Portraits* (Edinburgh: Edinburgh University Press, 2021), 5–6.

[78] Ibid.,106.

[79] It is also quite radical that Marianne paints Sophie in her post-abortion condition.

[80] Bacholle emphasizes Sciamma's focus on fluidity, a concern which aligns Sciamma with several of the writers discussed in this book. She writes: 'In their final scene on the island, Héloïse and Marianne re-enacted the myth's conclusion: Marianne-Orpheus made the artist's choice when she obeyed Héloïse's injunction to turn around and the shutting door sent Héloïse-Eurydice, dressed in nuptial white, into darkness. Sciamma queer(ie)d the myth in three ways: by questioning it through the characters, by challenging its commonly accepted interpretation, and by reconciling what appeared to be two conflicting or, at least, diverging interpretations' (p. 153).

20   INTRODUCTION

The readings of Ovid analysed in this volume offer insights into Ovid's shifting reception across time alongside changes in women's cultural practice. We trace authors who explicitly and overtly engaged with Ovid and those who never named him as a source of influence but whose work bears traces of their engagement with his texts. We map a range of different means of reception from translation, to rewriting, to a more porous and diffuse influence and intertext. Running through some of the essays is the question, or the problem, of Ovid's representations of women: for some, responses that we can see as feminist or proto-feminist subvert or make new the original text (Thorsen, Herdman, Puche, DeVos, Taylor); for others, the problem of Ovid's representation of women is not resolved but rather retains its ambiguity in reworkings (Klein); and for others still, the gender ambiguity his work explores is a point of inspiration (Burke, Illingworth). Chapters on early modern sources have focused more on how women overcame the 'indecency' of reading and writing Ovid (DeVos, Herdman, Taylor), whereas different themes of exile and dislocation emerge as more prominent in twentieth- and twenty-first-century responses (Cox, Hamel). Autobiography and autofiction feature strongly in the chapters on the modern period (Illingworth, Burke, Hamel), but expressions of identity (gendered, professional, etc.) emerge as a strong motif of Ovidian reception across periods. Certain figures have surfaced as prominent—some expected, such as Sappho, but some perhaps less typical, such as Laodamia. This volume registers the *Heroides* as having a privileged influence on women's responses to Ovid—perhaps unsurprisingly given the place of women's voices in this text—but in many cases that influence cannot always be disentangled from the presences of other Ovidian works, particularly the *Metamorphoses* and also the *Tristia*. Our volume also opens a dialogue between 'critical' and 'creative' practice thanks to the reflective epilogue by Marie Cosnay, which gives this volume a hint of the generic hybridity so embraced by our polysemic point of influence: Ovid.

2

Women's Wit

Skirting Ovid in Renaissance France

Emma Herdman

Ovid's witty erudition, versatility, and consummate narrative artistry conspire with the rich mythological depth of his verse to make him one of the most widely read, published, and translated classical authors in Renaissance France. The tales of the *Metamorphoses*—one of the best known and most accessible classical texts in the early modern period, if not directly then via vernacular paraphrases—would have been familiar even to those who did not read Latin.[1] As a source of rich and readily recognized mythological material, and as a master of playful intertextuality, Ovid provides humanist writers with a wealth of opportunities for the intertextual allusions that confer valuable literary status upon their works.[2] That status is particularly valuable to women writing during the early modern *querelle des femmes*—a literary debate over the excellence or imperfections of women, leading to a practical debate over women's education—who are obliged to defend their appearance in print. Strategic allusions to Ovid offer women a way of obtaining and legitimizing their own poetic voice;[3] they

[1] Ann Moss, *Latin Commentaries on Ovid from the Renaissance* (Signal Mountain, TN: Library of Renaissance Humanism, 1998), 136.

[2] As Fritz Graf notes, there is more to Ovid's myths than his reputation for 'irreverent playfulness' might suggest: Fritz Graf, 'Myth in Ovid', in Philip Hardie, ed., *The Cambridge Companion to Ovid* (Cambridge: Cambridge University Press, 2002), 108–21 (p. 108).

[3] See for example the following studies of Ovidian myths in early modern French women's writing: Kirk D. Read, 'Poolside Transformations: Diana and Actaeon Revisited by French Renaissance Women Lyricists', in Anne R. Larsen and Colette H. Wynn, eds, *Renaissance Women Writers: French Texts/ American Contexts* (Detroit: Wayne State University Press, 1994), 38–54; Colette H. Wynn, 'Le Procès du même et de l'autre. Pernette Du Guillet et le mythe ovidien de Diane et Actaeon', in Evelyne Berriot-Salvadore, ed., *Les Représentations de l'autre: du Moyen Age au XVIIe siècle* (Saint-Etienne: Publications de l'Université de Saint-Etienne, 1995), 263–71; JoAnn Della Neva, ' "Mutare/Mutatus": Pernette Du Guillet's Actaeon Myth and the Silencing of the Poetic Voice', in Michel Guggenheim, ed., *Women in French Literature* (Saratoga: Alma Libri, 1988), 47–55; Carla Freccero, 'Ovidian Subjectivities in Early Modern Lyric: Identification and Desire in Petrarch and Louise Labé', in Goran V. Stanivukovic, ed., *Ovid and the Renaissance Body* (Toronto: University of Toronto Press, 2001), 21–37. Ovid tells the myth of Actaeon—whom Diana silences after he catches sight of her naked by turning him into a stag, and who is then eaten by his own hounds—in the *Metamorphoses*: Ovid, *Metamorphoses*, ed. R. J. Tarrant (Oxford: Clarendon Press, 2004), 3.138–252. All subsequent Latin

Emma Herdman, *Women's Wit: Skirting Ovid in Renaissance France* In: *Ovid in French: Reception by Women from the Renaissance to the Present*. Edited by: Helena Taylor and Fiona Cox, Oxford University Press.
© Oxford University Press 2023. DOI: 10.1093/oso/9780192895387.003.0002

22   WOMEN'S WIT: SKIRTING OVID IN RENAISSANCE FRANCE

also suggest a collective effort to wrest his valuable literary cachet from an exclusively male domain.[4]

Yet the large majority of Ovidian references in early modern women's writing are passing, superficial allusions to the familiar mythological framework of the *Metamorphoses* rather than signs of close intertextual engagement with Ovid's work.[5] For women reading and writing in the period, access to Ovid, whose often licentious wit is frequently at their expense, is neither straightforward nor desirable.[6] Early modern women wishing to engage with Ovid face two principal challenges. On the one hand, there is Ovid's 'erotics of cruelty'—a cruelty that seems to appeal to women as readers, but to deter them as writers—to which Valerie Traub attributes the absence of works by women in studies of early modern reception of Ovid.[7] On the other hand, there is a thriving early modern tradition, inspired by the *Ovide moralisé*, of allegorically interpreting Ovid's tales, frequently in ways that are invidious to women; Renaissance readings of Ovid thus keep him beyond women's easy reach.

This chapter focuses on Ovid's tale of Aglaurus, in Book 2 of the *Metamorphoses*, as a prime example both of how Ovid is harnessed to a misogynist moralizing tradition and of how that tradition is resisted. Aglaurus and her sisters are entrusted by Minerva with a casket containing the infant Erichthonius; Minerva forbids them from opening it, but Aglaurus disobeys. In retribution, Minerva instructs Envy to torment Aglaurus; when Aglaurus then enviously opposes her sister's marriage to Mercury, he turns her to stone (2.531–835).[8] The 'erotics of cruelty' are on display in both metamorphoses: Ovid lingers over descriptions that penetrate and pervade Aglaurus' helpless body, as her breath, blood, and bones are gradually permeated first with Envy's poison and then with the lifeless chill of cold, hard stone. This chapter starts by considering Ovid's portrayal of Aglaurus as a figure of opposition, whose

citations refer to this edition and will be indicated by book and line number. English translations are from Ovid, *Metamorphoses*, trans. Mary M. Innes (Harmondsworth, Middlesex: Penguin, 1955); for the Actaeon myth, see, 77–80. Ovid equates himself with Actaeon—punished (with exile) for having unwittingly seen something forbidden (he never reveals what)—in the *Tristia*: Ovid, *Tristia; Ex Ponto*, ed. and trans. Arthur Leslie Wheeler and G. P. Goold (2nd edn, Cambridge, MA: Harvard University Press, 1988; repr. 1996), *Tristia* 3.103–6.

[4] Heather James, 'Ovid in Renaissance English Literature', in Peter E. Knox, ed., *A Companion to Ovid* (Oxford: Wiley–Blackwell, 2009), 423–41 (p. 437).

[5] See for example the editor's comments in Hélisenne de Crenne, *Les Epistres familieres et invectives*, ed. Jerry C. Nash (Paris: Champion, 1996), 173. For a notable example of a woman engaging at a deeper level with an Ovidian myth, see Emma Herdman, 'Folie and Salmacis: Labé's Re-writing of Ovid', *Modern Language Review*, 108 (2013), 782–801.

[6] As Heather James explains, 'Ovid offered prestige. For women, however, he was also a liability.' 'Ovid in Renaissance English Literature', 437.

[7] Valerie Traub, 'Afterword', in Goran V. Stanivukovic, ed., *Ovid and the Renaissance Body* (Toronto: University of Toronto Press, 2001), 260–8 (p. 266).

[8] Innes, 64–72.

punishment for curiosity and disobedience towards the gods forms part of a sequence of tales on the dangers of possessing and revealing unlicensed knowledge.[9] Next it traces how her tale becomes an early modern fable, symbolizing women's curiosity and indiscretion, and warning of the need to keep women in silence and ignorance. The chapter then explores the ways in which two early modern writers, the Dames des Roches—Madeleine and her daughter Catherine—resist this interpretation and subtly use allusive references to Ovid to support their consistent advocacy of women's education and literary self-expression.[10] Their playful but morally corrective engagement with Ovid stands in sharp opposition to those who would deny women speech or knowledge, and who would use Ovid to do so, forming part of their wider resistance to the obstacles placed before educated and articulate women in early modern France.

The Dames des Roches rely on education and companionship to oppose the limitations that decorum imposes upon early modern women, summarized by the eighteenth-century literary historian Claude-Pierre Gouget as the 'préjugé trop ancien, qui condamne les femmes au silence, et presque à l'ignorance' (ancient prejudice that condemns women to silence and almost to ignorance).[11] Their own erudition and quick wit were celebrated by their contemporaries. The early literary historian La Croix du Maine describes them as 'toutes deux si doctes et si sçavantes' (both so learned and so knowledgeable),[12] and they were famed as much for their learning and their widely respected salon as for their works. One salon visitor, Estienne Pasquier, praises the richness of its improving conversation:

> Là l'on traite divers discours, ores de Philosophie, ores d'histoire, ou du temps, ou bien quelques propos gaillards. Et nul n'y entre qui n'en sorte, ou plus sçavant, ou mieux édifié.[13]

---

[9] On this rather overlooked sequence of tales about indiscreet tale-telling, see particularly A. M. Keith, *The Play of Fictions: Studies in Ovid's 'Metamorphoses' Book 2* (Ann Arbor: The University of Michigan Press, 1992); on the tales' critical reception and references to Ovid's own storytelling, see pp. 2–3.

[10] On the Dames des Roches, see George E. Diller, *Les Dames des Roches: étude sur la vie littéraire à Poitiers dans la deuxième moitié du XVIᵉ siècle* (Paris: Droz, 1936); see also the introductions to Madeleine and Catherine des Roches, *Les Œuvres*, ed. Anne R. Larsen (Geneva: Droz, 1993); Des Roches, *Les Secondes Œuvres*, ed. Anne R. Larsen (Geneva: Droz, 1998); Des Roches, *Les Missives*, ed. Anne R. Larsen (Geneva: Droz, 1999).

[11] Gouget's comment, from his *Bibliothèque Françoise* of 1752, is quoted in Des Roches, *Les Missives*, 384–5. Unless otherwise stated, all translations are my own.

[12] La Croix du Maine's assessments of the Dames des Roches, from his *Bibliothèque* of 1584, are quoted in Des Roches, *Les Missives*, 339–43 (p. 341).

[13] Pasquier's letters to Pierre Pithou, first published in 1586, are quoted in Des Roches, *Les Missives*, 343–9 (p. 348).

(Various subjects are discussed there: now philosophy, now history or the present times, or else there is lively conversation. And no one goes there who does not emerge either wiser or better informed.)

Lively and learned moral edification informs their works: the *Œuvres* of 1578, the *Secondes Œuvres* of 1583, and the *Missives*—a selection of their private correspondence, and the first such publication by women in France—of 1586. The jointly published volumes, containing first Madeleine's writing then Catherine's more extensive and varied works, including verse translations from Italian and Latin, are an exemplary display of their own creative versatility and literary culture.[14]

Yet erudition alone does not guarantee modesty: decorum requires early modern women to be accompanied when venturing into print. Through their joint publications and mutual dedications to each other of their works, the Dames des Roches each provide themselves with a literary chaperone, licensing their public appearance.[15] In this, they follow the example of Louise Labé's dedication of her 1555 *Euvres* to Clémence de Bourges: 'pource que les femmes ne se montrent volontiers en publiq seules, je vous ay choisie pour me servir de guide' (since women do not willingly appear in public alone, I have chosen you to act as my guide).[16] Again like Labé, Madeleine des Roches further extends this protective companionship by addressing her work to a female readership, defending her decision to write and to publish, and encouraging her readers to emulate her.[17] Thus the readerly companions who initially offer a writer decorous protection are enjoined to participate in a collective enterprise to promote women's learned and literary self-expression. A shared literary frame of reference strengthens this companionship and extends it to the authors in that frame, allying them to the promotion of women's learning and—if carefully chosen—the preservation of women's modesty.

Ovid's status as decorous company for women is ambiguous. In a playful example of an intervention in the *querelle des femmes*, the essayist Michel de Montaigne, writing at the same time as the Dames des Roches, objects to

---

[14] There are translations by Catherine of four epitaphs by Bernardo Accolti in *Les Œuvres*, 342–6, and of Claudian's 'De raptu Proserpinae' in *Les Missives*, 212–87. On Catherine's decision to translate Claudian's version of the myth, rather than Ovid's or Homer's, see Leah Chang, 'Catherine Des Roches' Two Proserpines: Textual Production and the "Ravissement de Proserpine" in the *Missives de Mesdames Des Roches* (1586)', *Symposium*, 58/4 (2005), 203–22.

[15] Des Roches, *Les Œuvres*, 81–4 and 181–5; *Les Secondes Œuvres*, 87 and 119–21; *Les Missives*, 84–7 and 146–7.

[16] Louise Labé, *Œuvres complètes*, ed. François Rigolot (Paris: Flammarion, 1986; repr. 2004), 43.

[17] Des Roches, *Les Œuvres*, 79–80; cf. Labé's addresses to the 'Dames Lionnoises', in Labé, *Œuvres complètes*, 108, 115, and 134.

women's engagement with scholarly disciplines for which they have no use, but allows intellectually ambitious women to engage with poetry:

> Si toutesfois il leur fache de nous ceder en quoy que ce soit, et veulent par curiosité avoir part aux livres, la poësie est un amusement propre à leur besoin: c'est un art follastre et subtil, desguisé, parlier, tout en plaisir, tout en montre, comme elles.[18]

> (If, however, it annoys them to concede to us in any matter, and if they want out of curiosity to partake in books, poetry is an amusement proper to their needs: it is a foolish and subtle art, disguised, talkative, all about pleasure and all about display, as are they.)

Montaigne here employs a form of rhetorical decorum, gallantly matching the style and qualities of poetry to those of its female readers (and writers).[19] In the process, he light-heartedly evokes a perennial battle of the sexes, in which women, stubbornly refusing to allow any superiority to men, are cast as superficial ('tout en montre'), deceitful ('desguisé'), indiscreet ('parlier'), and above all curious. In this sense, women and Ovid might seem to be well matched.

Yet while rhetorical decorum might allow women to engage with poetry and thereby with Ovid, social decorum does not. This is apparent from Montaigne's recollection of the thrill of pleasure he derived from reading Ovid in his youth, even if this reaction has altered over time:

> Je diray encore cecy, ou hardiment ou temerairement, que cette vieille ame poisante ne se laisse plus chatouiller, non seulement à l'Arioste, mais encores au bon Ovide: sa facilité et ses inventions, qui m'ont ravy autresfois, à peine m'entretiennent elles à cette heure.[20]

> (I shall add as well, whether boldly or recklessly, that this heavy old soul no longer allows itself to be tickled, either by Ariosto or even the good Ovid: his facility and his inventiveness, which ravished me in the past, scarcely divert me now.)

---

[18] Michel de Montaigne, *Les Essais*, ed. Pierre Villey and V.–L. Saulnier (Paris: Presses Universitaires de France, 2004), iii.3, 'De trois commerces', p. 823; cf. p. 822.

[19] Rhetorical decorum is 'the doctrine of suiting style to subject-matter and oration to audience'. Peter Mack, *A History of Renaissance Rhetoric 1380–1620* (Oxford: Oxford University Press, 2011), 331. Montaigne himself writes (partly) for a female readership.

[20] Montaigne, *Les Essais*, ii.10, 'Des livres', p. 410.

Montaigne is not simply ruing a change in literary taste brought about by old age. While he overtly attributes his youthful enjoyment of Ovid to literary appreciation, his air of boldly intimate confession and the sexually suggestive verbs 'chatouiller' and 'ravy' evoke an arousal that is not purely literary, one that a licentious author such as Ariosto or Ovid may readily inspire in a youthful reader but struggle to elicit from a reader weighed down by age.[21] In this sense, Ovid is far from an author with whom early modern women might decorously engage.

If social decorum limits the responses of women as readers, it also makes Ovid dangerous company for women as writers, who rely on their female readers or dedicatees as chaperones when venturing into print. Yet as the lively discussions of the Dames des Roches's literary salon show, modest decorum need not be completely humourless; nor need it skirt around Ovid. In a delicate balance, they wittily use Ovid to counter the prejudice against women that he has been used to bolster, allying him to their defence of women's education and virtuous self-expression, while maintaining their moral distance from the mutability and inconstancy that Ovid's flexible work represents. Thus they show their appreciation of Ovid and reclaim one of his more exclusively masculine prerogatives—his wit—which they ally with necessary womanly decorum to forceful argument. Handled with care, their Ovid becomes a suitable companion for women in print, wittily 'skirted' into an acceptably lady-like literary chaperone.

Ovid's Aglaurus: Telling Tales

Ovid's Aglaurus is a figure of opposition and forbidden knowledge: she is punished for disobedience and curious enquiry into divine mystery. Aglaurus and her sisters Pandrosus and Herse are entrusted by Minerva with a wicker casket and a strict injunction not to open it; Aglaurus inevitably does open it, and so discovers Erichthonius, the half-human, half-serpent son of Vulcan,

---

[21] On Montaigne's turn, nonetheless, to poetry for eroticism in old age, mingling poetic and sensual pleasure, see Jessie Hock, 'Voluptuous Style: Lucretius, Rhetoric, and Reception in Montaigne's "Sur des vers de Virgile"', *Modern Philology*, 118/4 (2021), 492–514. For more on Montaigne and the power of poetry to touch the imagination and the body, see Terence Cave, 'The Transit of Venus: Feeling Your Way Forward', in Neil Kenny, Richard Scholar, and Wes Williams, eds, *Montaigne in Transit: Essays in Honour of Ian Maclean* (Cambridge: Legenda, 2016), 9–18. See also Marc-André Wiesmann, 'Verses Have Fingers: Montaigne Reads Juvenal', *Journal of Medieval and Renaissance Studies*, 23 (1993), 43–67.

born of the earth from Vulcan's unsuccessful attempt to rape Minerva.[22] In earlier versions of the myth, Aglaurus and her sisters are either killed by the snake or snakes within the casket, or are driven mad and throw themselves from the top of the Acropolis to their death.[23] In Ovid's version, Minerva strikes Aglaurus with envy; this leads Aglaurus to a second act of divine betrayal, as she reneges on her bargain with Mercury and enviously attempts to thwart his marriage to her sister: in a second punitive metamorphosis, Mercury turns her to stone.[24] Envy—personified by Ovid in a ludic imitation of Virgil's Rumour—becomes the key and original feature of Ovid's Aglaurus.[25]

Ovid embeds the story of Aglaurus within a series of interwoven tales about the dangers of discovering or revealing secrets. The series tests the link between seeing and speaking of secrets, looked upon deliberately or inadvertently, with frank and direct curiosity or with envious and oblique hostility.[26] The first part of the story, in which Aglaurus illicitly opens the casket, is told only incidentally, as a narrative detail in the tale of the crow's metamorphosis from white to black as punishment for telling Minerva of Aglaurus' disobedience. The second part of Aglaurus' story, in which she is punished first by Minerva and then by Mercury, follows the related stories of Ocyrhoe and Battus: the fates silence the prophetic Ocyrhoe's revelation of their secrets by turning her into a mare, while Mercury tricks and bribes Battus into revealing the secret he had promised Mercury he would keep more silently than a stone,

[22] The sisters are the daughters of the Athenian king Cecrops, who is also half-human and half-serpent. See Simon Hornblower, Antony Spawforth, and Esther Eidinow, eds, *The Oxford Classical Dictionary* (Oxford: Oxford University Press, 2012), s.vv. 'Aglaurus', 'Erichthonius', and 'Cecrops'.

[23] See Hubert Cancik and Helmut Schneider, eds, *Brill's New Pauly: Antiquity* (Leiden; Boston: Brill, 2002), i, s.v. 'Aglaurus'; cf. Pausanias, *Description of Greece, Volume 1: Books 1–2 (Attica and Corinth)*, trans. W. H. S. Jones (Cambridge, MA: Harvard University Press, 1918), I.xviii.2, pp. 86–7; cf. Hyginus, *Fabulae*, ed. Peter K. Marshall (Munich; Leipzig: K. G. Saur, 2002), 166, pp. 138–9. The Pausanias version is summarized in Raphael Regius' commentary on the *Metamorphoses*, first published in 1493: *P. Ouidii Metamorphosis*, ed. Raphael Regius (Venice: Simon Bevilaqua, 1497), unpaginated.

[24] Ovid's source for the petrification of Aglaurus is Callimachus: see Keith, *The Play of Fictions*, 124.

[25] On Ovid's Invidia (Envy) as an echo of Virgil's literary personifications of Fama (Rumour) and the fury Allecto in the *Aeneid*, see Philip Hardie, 'The Word Personified: Fame and Envy in Virgil, Ovid, Spenser', *Materiali e discussioni per l'annalisi dei testi classici*, 61 (2009), 101–15 (pp. 102–5); see also Keith, *The Play of Fictions*, 127–31, who notes the thematic link as (Virgil's) Fama inspires (Ovid's) Invidia. See Virgil, *Opera*, ed. R. A. B. Mynors (Oxford: Clarendon Press, 1969), *Aeneid* 4.173–97 and 7.323–571, pp. 181–2 and 266–74; cf. Virgil, *The Aeneid*, trans. David West (London: Penguin, 1990), 86 and 172–80. On Ovid's other literary sources for Invidia, see Matthew W. Dickie, 'Ovid, *Metamorphoses* 2.760–64', *The American Journal of Philology*, 96 (1975), 378–90; Keith, *The Play of Fictions*, 127–8.

[26] On Invidia's oblique gaze and the etymological link to *in-videre* (to look askance, maliciously, or spitefully at; to cast an evil eye upon; to envy: see Charlton D. Lewis and Charles Short, *A Latin Dictionary* (Oxford: Clarendon Press, 1879), s.v. 'in-video'), see Hardie, 'The Word Personified', 106; William S. Anderson, *Ovid's 'Metamorphoses' Books 1–5* (Norman: University of Oklahoma Press, 1997), 324; Keith, *The Play of Fictions*, 125.

28 WOMEN'S WIT: SKIRTING OVID IN RENAISSANCE FRANCE

before duly turning him to stone.[27] When Mercury asks Aglaurus to favour his marriage to Herse, she coolly and shrewdly appraises his proposal in an echo of her earlier willingness to gaze steadily upon Minerva's divine secret, and demands payment for her services in an echo of the bribes through which Battus' silence and speech were bought and sold.[28]

Aglaurus' greed in selling her sister to Mercury reignites Minerva's anger over her earlier disobedience;[29] she overcomes her objection to Envy— 'quamuis tamen oderat illam' ('in spite of her loathing')[30]—sufficiently to order her to strike Aglaurus. Envy of her sister's marriage prompts Aglaurus to place herself obstructively on Herse's threshold in a direct physical and verbal challenge to Mercury:

> 'hinc ego me non sum nisi te motura repulso.'
> 'stemus' ait 'pacto' uelox Cyllenius 'isto'
> caelestique fores uirga patefecit.   (2.817–19)

('I shall not move from this spot until I have driven you away!' Swift-footed Mercury accepted her ultimatum. 'Let us keep to that agreement!' he said, and opened up the door with a touch of his magic wand.)[31]

Mercury binds Aglaurus to her pact by turning her, like Battus, and in a similar play upon her own words, to stone. Where Envy had tormented Aglaurus, metaphorically blackening her poisoned heart (echoing the blackening of the crow), her metamorphosis into similarly blackened stone makes her lifeless and cold, representing her opposition to love as she becomes a

---

[27] Ocyrhoe performs her loss not of knowledge but of voice, narrating her metamorphosis until she can speak no more; Battus is silenced but retains his deictic function as an 'index' or touchstone. On the intertextual allusions in Ovid's tale, see Sarah McCallum, 'Ego sum pastor: Pastoral Transformations in the Tale of Mercury and Battus (Ov. Met. 2.676–707)', The Classical Outlook, 92 (2017), 29–34.

[28] Critical sympathy for Aglaurus' venality can be limited: her moral ugliness is described by Carl Deroux, 'La métamorphose d'Aglauros (Ovide, Mét. II, 819–32)', Latomus, 74 (2015), 210–22 (p. 210); Anderson compares her unfavourably to Battus (for initiating the bargaining with Mercury and for setting her price: Anderson, Ovid's 'Metamorphoses' Books 1–5, 318), describing her and Mercury as 'two unappealing characters [who] deserve each other' (p. 323). Nevertheless, both pity her punitive metamorphoses (Deroux, p. 210; Anderson, p. 332); see also Charles Segal, 'Ovid's Metamorphic Bodies: Art, Gender, and Violence in the Metamorphoses', Arion, 5 (1998), 9–41 (p. 15).

[29] Regius' text of the Metamorphoses, taken as authoritative in the Renaissance, attributes Minerva's punishment of Aglaurus to her crimes against Mercury and Herse: 'Ingratamque deo fore iam: ingratamque sorori' (and now she would be ungrateful to the god and disagreeable to her sister): P. Ouidii Metamorphosis, 2.758, unpaginated. Renaissance commentators do not indicate whether Aglaurus' venality in selling her sister so dearly would make her disagreeable ('ingratam') to Herse for facilitating or for obstructing her marriage. In contrast, modern editions attribute Minerva's vengeance to something approaching divine envy: 'et gratamque deo fore iam gratamque sorori' ('Now this girl would be dear to Mercury and her sister'), Metamorphoses, 2.758; Innes, p. 70. On Minerva as envious, see Anderson, Ovid's 'Metamorphoses' Books 1–5, 323–5, commenting on ll. 752–5 and 765–7.

[30] Ovid, Metamorphoses, 2.782; Innes, p. 71.   [31] Innes, p. 72.

literal (if not moral) stumbling block, unmoving and unmoved.[32] Envy disrupts her cool dispassion, restored as she is turned to stone.[33]

Ovid highlights the narrative similarities between these interconnected tales to suggest their exemplarity, as the same actions lead to the same consequences. The blackened crow warns the still white raven against telling unwelcome truths, citing her own example:

> mea poena uolucres
> admonuisse potest ne uoce pericula quaerant.   (2.564–5)

(The punishment I suffered may serve as a warning to other birds, not to court danger by telling tales.)[34]

Yet Ovid undermines the moral lessons of his tales by demonstrating that in practice, exemplarity fails: the crow's warning does not deter the greedy raven, hoping for a reward, from telling Apollo about Coronis' infidelity and undergoing the same punishment.[35] Moreover, exemplarity falters before the key differences that Ovid discreetly introduces into his tales. Aglaurus may be narratively associated with a sequence of tale-tellers, but she herself never tells any tales. It is the crow who reveals Aglaurus' discovery of Erichthonius to Minerva; Aglaurus resists Envy's prompting to inform her father of Mercury's designs on Herse: 'uoluit... / saepe uelut crimen rigido narrare parenti' (2.812–13) (Often she planned to tell her stern father of the affair, as if it were some crime).[36]

---

[32] The deathly chill of Aglaurus' petrification contrasts with the lively heat of Mercury as he falls in love: Ovid, *Metamorphoses*, 2.827–8 and 727–9; Innes, pp. 72 and 69.

[33] Ovid's metamorphoses often function as metaphors, giving physical expression to a character trait: see Andrew Feldherr, 'Metamorphosis in the *Metamorphoses*', in Philip Hardie, ed., *The Cambridge Companion to Ovid* (Cambridge: Cambridge University Press, 2002), 163–79 (p. 176); they may be justified by etymological links or puns on characters' names: see Garth Tissol, *The Face of Nature: Wit, Narrative and Cosmic Origins in Ovid's 'Metamorphoses'* (Princeton, NJ: Princeton University Press, 1997), p. 173. Aglaurus, however, is fundamentally altered by Envy, as if by poison: see Segal, 'Ovid's Metamorphic Bodies', 14–15; Anderson, *Ovid's 'Metamorphoses' Books 1–5*, 332. On Aglaurus' petrification as a form of cancer, see Deroux, 'La métamorphose d'Aglauros', 210.

[34] Innes, p. 65.

[35] Keith (*The Play of Fictions*, 135), noting the lack of free speech under Augustus, suggests that the crow's warning against speech is the only practical use of storytelling; Keith nevertheless questions the story's narrative worth within the text, attributing the raven's refusal to heed the crow's warning to the narrative and onomastic similarities between Coronis—the criminal in the raven's tale—and the crow (p. 59).

[36] Innes, p. 71. Keith (*Play of Fictions*, 130) notes that Aglaurus' impulse to inform on Herse aligns her with the tale-tellers in this sequence, although as Hardie ('The Word Personified', 106) points out, the sequence is ended as that impulse remains unfulfilled. Nothing indicates that Aglaurus ever reveals the first secret (Erichthonius) that she discovers.

30 WOMEN'S WIT: SKIRTING OVID IN RENAISSANCE FRANCE

Nonetheless, she is perpetually silenced;[37] moreover, her petrification performs a narrative silence, covering the lacuna between Mercury stepping over Aglaurus' body to enter Herse's bedroom and returning to the heavens: what takes place in Herse's bedroom remains undisclosed. Ovid's Aglaurus, then, is a figure of opposition and of the human desire for knowledge; she negotiates with and challenges the gods she is willing to disobey, gazing with frank curiosity upon their secrets, but not explicitly revealing what she knows.

Ovid's caution against reading his tales as exemplary fables did not deter medieval and early modern commentators from interpreting his stories as moral allegories. The flexible moralizing tradition represented by Ovid's fourteenth-century Latin commentator, Petrus Berchorius, or Pierre Bersuire, whose allegorical interpretations of Ovid's tales continued to influence humanist commentators, becomes increasingly rigid, particularly in the illustrated editions intended to give their readers easy, educational access to Ovid, such as Johann Spreng's Latin *Metamorphoses Ovidii* of 1563 or Barthélemy Aneau's emblematic *Imagination poétique* of 1552, as Ovid's stories are condensed into a single woodcut image expounded by a lapidary piece of encapsulating verse.[38] These allegorical readings tend to separate Envy and Aglaurus, whose disobedience, greed, and curiosity are allied to indiscretion as her tale is used to warn against entrusting women with knowledge.

Berchorius reads the story of Aglaurus as an allegory that simultaneously warns against enquiry into divine mystery and shows that nothing is so well hidden that it will not be revealed. His spiritual allegory, equating Erichthonius, born of a virginal mother, with Christ and his casket with the Eucharist, to be given only to the virginally pure and holy, has the three sisters representing the three monastic vows of chastity, poverty, and obedience that protect the Christ child against luxury, avarice, and pride.[39] This spiritual allegory does not prevent Berchorius from moralizing about women's weakness. His discussion of a general human propensity to desire

---

[37] In contrast, the crow and raven—as harbingers of death—and the touchstone—as a cold indicator of a metal's worth—continue to tell potentially unwelcome truths.

[38] Petrus Berchorius, *Metamorphosis ovidiana moraliter explanata* (Paris: Ascensius, 1511). Berchorius offers the four traditional allegorical readings: physical, historical, moral, and spiritual or Christian; this last category is banned in 1559 by the Council of Trent: see Ann Moss, *Poetry and Fable: Studies in Mythological Narrative in Sixteenth-Century France* (Cambridge: Cambridge University Press, 1984), 6–16; Moss, *Latin Commentaries on Ovid*, 62–8. Raphael Regius' influential and widely reprinted text, which focuses on literary and philological questions, begins a turn away from allegory in sixteenth-century editions of Ovid: see Caroline Jameson, 'Ovid in the Sixteenth Century', in J. W. Binns, ed., *Ovid* (London & Boston: Routledge & Kegan Paul, 1973), 210–42 (pp. 210–11). As Jessica DeVos shows in the next chapter, this humanist preference for exegetical explanation of Ovid's text over anachronistic analogies introduces a move away from the often misogynist moralizing of Ovid's medieval readers, although this returns precisely in editions of Ovid made accessible to a female readership.

[39] Berchorius, fol. xxii[v].

the forbidden soon attributes this particularly to women, whose silence is dependent upon their ignorance:

> Si enim aliquid prohiberetur faciendum ad contrarium mens hominis amplius inclinatur: & potissimum mulieres: contra quas loquitur Theophrastus dicens. Garrulitati mulieris non est aliquid committendum: quia solum id tacere potest quod nescit.[40]

> (For if something is forbidden, the human mind is conversely more inclined to do it—this is especially so with women, of whom Theophrastus says 'nothing is to be entrusted to a chattering woman, for she can keep quiet only about what she does not know.')

Berchorius's Aglaurus moves from symbolizing virginal purity to representing a range of weaknesses attributed particularly to women: subjectivity to temptation; curiosity about the forbidden; and garrulous indiscretion. Similarly, Spreng's initially gender-neutral lament over the human propensity to desire the forbidden culminates in a specific attack upon women:

> Faemineo generi nemo concredere quicquam
>   Audeat, inconstans, et leve pectus habet.
> Omnia nosse cupit mulier, secreta revelat,
>   Et nisi quod nescit, nil retinere potest.[41]

> (May no one dare entrust anything to the female sex, which has an inconstant and light heart. A woman wants to know everything, she reveals secrets, and she can keep nothing quiet apart from what she does not know.)

Spreng's Aglaurus represents women's fickleness, curiosity, and indiscretion, while her deferred punishment for disobedience and greed warns that even hidden vices will eventually be punished.[42]

French versions of Aglaurus emphasize her unnatural venality in selling her sister to Mercury. The vernacular paraphrases of the *Metamorphoses*, the *Bible des poëtes* of 1493 and its revised replacement, the textually very similar *Grand Olympe* of 1532, both highlight the waywardness of Aglaurus, described as 'plus musarde des aultres' (more inclined to gaze than the others), and 'moult

---

[40] Berchorius, fol. xxii[v]. Similarly, he says of the sisters: 'Ille autem ex prohibitione magis temptate sicut mos est mulierum' (they were, however, more greatly tempted by the prohibition, as is the way with women) (fol. xxii[v]).

[41] Johann Spreng, *Metamorphoses Ovidii* (Paris: Hieronymus de Marnef & Gulielmus Cavellat, 1570), fol. 28[v].

[42] Spreng, *Metamorphoses Ovidii*, fol. 33[r–v].

32 WOMEN'S WIT: SKIRTING OVID IN RENAISSANCE FRANCE

orguilleuse et despite' (very proud and spiteful).[43] These paraphrases make Aglaurus more explicitly guilty of greed and of prostituting her sister, whose marriage to Mercury immediately follows his negotiations with Aglaurus. More accurately reflecting Ovid's text, Clément Marot's largely faithful 1543 French translation of the first two books of the *Metamorphoses* similarly emphasizes Aglaurus' disloyalty to Mercury and to her sister Herse through the introduction—perhaps for the sake of rhyme—of the adjectives 'ingrate' and 'perverse'.[44] In contrast, Barthélemy Aneau's *Imagination poétique*, with its woodcut illustrations of scenes from the *Metamorphoses*, focuses firmly on Aglaurus' curiosity and indiscretion.[45] Under the heading 'curiosité des femmes' (women's curiosity), a four-line summary of the three sisters' opening of Minerva's casket leads to the moralizing conclusion:

> Qu'est il R[i]en plus curieux que la Femme?
> Qu'est il Rien moins secret en cas infame?[46]

(Is there anything more curious than Woman? Is there anything less secretive about ignominy?)

The unanswerable questions highlight not only women's curiosity and indiscretion, but also their gossipy interest in secrets that are shameful. These readings of Aglaurus highlight her untrustworthiness; the curiosity that frankly challenges but remains silent in Ovid becomes dangerous to satisfy because of her indiscretion.

Madeleine des Roches's Aglaurus: Wisely Chosen Silence

It is against this backdrop that the Dames des Roches develop Ovid's opposition between wisdom (or Minerva) and envy. In this, they are perhaps influenced by the sixth-century Christian mythographer Fulgentius, who

---

[43] *Le Grand Olympe* (Lyons: Romain Morin, 1532), fols XXIX^r and XXXIII^v; cf. *La Bible des poëtes* (Paris: 1493–4), fols xvii^v and xxi^r. On these works, see Moss, *Poetry and Fable*, 6–7.

[44] Clément Marot, *Le Second Livre de la Metamorphose d'Ovide*, in Gérard Defaux, ed., *Œuvres poétiques de Clément Marot*, 2 vols (Paris: Bordas, 1993), ii, 452–93: ll. 1484 (p. 490), 1474 (p. 490), and 1377 (p. 487). 'Ingrate' is in the spirit of line 758 in Renaissance editions of Ovid's text: see n. 29 above.

[45] See Alison Saunders's introduction to the *Picta Poesis* in the French Emblems at Glasgow website: https://www.emblems.arts.gla.ac.uk/french/books.php?id=FANa; on the readership for these two works, see Brigitte Biot, *Barthélemy Aneau, régent de la Renaissance lyonnaise* (Paris: Champion, 1996), 282–6.

[46] Barthélemy Aneau, *Imagination poétique* (Lyons: Macé Bonhomme, 1552), 115; cf. the even more concise version in Barthélemy Aneau, *Picta Poesis* (Lyons: Macé Bonhomme, 1552), 87.

allegorically interprets Vulcan's desire for Minerva as the desire for wisdom, generating the struggle against envy (over worldly possessions) that he reads into Erichthonius' name; Fulgentius invites his readers to reflect on the strength of wisdom virtuously combined with chastity.[47] The theme of chaste wisdom, in opposition to the envy that it inspires but resists, is developed extensively in the Dames des Roches's writing. Similarly developed is the theme of mutability, again often opposed to the stability of wisdom. That theme does not preclude enjoyment of the frequent references to the myths and characters of the *Metamorphoses* that richly illustrate the Dames des Roches's works.[48] For the most part, but not always, these are only passing references; however, the elaborate and subtle Ovidian intertexts examined in the rest of this chapter demonstrate how fully the Dames des Roches are capable of engaging with Ovid in their works.

Madeleine des Roches's Sonnet XXIII in the *Œuvres* is on the theme of secrecy; its demonstration of wise discretion relies upon Ovid's Aglaurus myth. It opens with the poet rather tartly defending herself against her unnamed addressee's accusation of curiosity and, implicitly, indiscretion; this turns, in the tercets, to a more spiritual reflection on human frailty and dependence upon God. The opening quatrain hints at a narrative context to account for the vehemence of the initial interjection:

> Dea! si mon oeil a decouvert
> Cette trame tant demenée,
> Ay-je, d'une main profanée,
> Le corbillon d'ozier ouvert?[49]

(Well! If my eye discovered such a well-worn web, did I open the wicker casket with a profane hand?)

Aglaurus, who is not named in the sonnet, is obliquely identified by the 'corbillon d'ozier'—Ovid's 'Actaeo texta de uimine cista' ('chest woven from Actaean osiers')[50]—that she profaned; she is introduced as a point of contrast with the poet, who has looked only inadvertently on something that she should not have seen, and that has been so bandied about as to be barely a secret.

---

[47] Furius Publius Fulgentius, *Mythologiarum Liber II*, included in Hyginus, *C. Hygini Augusti Liberti fabularum liber* (Basel: Joannes Hervagius, 1535), 146. Erichthonius' name is usually taken to denote his birth from the earth: see Cancik and Schneider, *Brill's New Pauly*, s.v. 'Erichthonius'.

[48] The large majority of the Dames des Roches's references to Ovid are to the *Metamorphoses*; references to the *Fasti*, *Heroides*, and *Amores* are only very occasional.

[49] Des Roches, *Les Œuvres*, 142.   [50] Ovid, *Metamorphoses*, 2.554; Innes, p. 65.

34 WOMEN'S WIT: SKIRTING OVID IN RENAISSANCE FRANCE

In the second quatrain, the contrast with Aglaurus is used as evidence of the poet's lack of curiosity, while the accusation of indiscretion is turned back on her accuser:

> Je ne suis de fiel jaune et verd,
> Comme l'envie empoisonnée;
> Mais quoy! la colere est mal née
> Pour tenir un secret couvert.[51]

(I am not poisoned with yellow and green bile, like Envy; but really! anger is ill-born for keeping secrets.)

The textual echo of Ovid's Envy—'pectora felle uirent, lingua est suffusa ueneno' ('her poisonous breast [was] of a greenish hue, and her tongue dripped venom')[52]—further identifies Aglaurus; in contrast, the poet suffers neither from Aglaurus' envy nor from her accuser's anger, which she blames for revealing the secret the poet is implicitly accused of disclosing.[53] Des Roches's sonnet is initially playfully Ovidian, in content and in form: in performance of the poet's own silence, it requires the reader to recognize the allusion to Aglaurus in order to appreciate the contrast on which the poet's self-defence depends. Moreover, that self-defence relies light-heartedly on taking Ovid's Aglaurus to be as exemplary as his crow, and therefore on accepting that anyone who emulates her curiosity will be similarly punished by envy.

Yet the tercets represent a sharp change of tone, as defence and accusation give way to philosophical reflection and general moral instruction:

> Nous avons plustost l'oraison,
> Que l'usage de la raison,
> Compaigne de la modestie.
>
> Qui haut se veut en soy fier
> Est sujet à sacrifier
> A l'inconstance de Cynthie.[54]

(We have prayer, rather than the use of reason, as a companion for modesty. Anyone who deeply wishes to be self-reliant is liable to sacrifice to the inconstancy of Cynthia.)

---

[51] Des Roches, Les Œuvres, 142.   [52] Ovid, Metamorphoses, 2.777; Innes, p. 71.

[53] The quatrain's last two lines could be read as a warning—do not anger people with false accusations, for then they will reveal secrets—although Des Roches prefers to present herself as wisely free from such distorting passions.

[54] Des Roches, Les Œuvres, 142–3.

By asserting that modesty (be it the addressee's chastity or the poet's discretion) depends on prayer, the poet establishes her moral distance from Aglaurus and from Ovid. Ovid's Aglaurus disobeys and challenges the gods, gazing frankly upon the divine mystery they would cast over their lust, while Ovid himself delights in his own inconstancy (portraying the Envy-hating Minerva as envious; placing the non-tale-telling Aglaurus in a narrative sequence about tellers of tales). In contrast, the poet—equating the fickleness and petulance of the classical gods with the instability of human passions and reason—places her faith entirely in God.

The petrification of Ovid's Aglaurus, reflecting her opposition to the gods, is also in opposition to her earlier affliction with Envy. Similarly, Des Roches—as if playing on the connotations of her name—opposes the rock-like constancy she derives from her faith to envy and to her addressee.[55] In opposition to a Renaissance reading of Aglaurus that would condemn women to a silence born of ignorance rather than wisely chosen, the sonnet performs the poet's discretion, as she reveals only that there is a secret that she could be in a position to divulge. Like Ovid, she is willing to pique her readers' curiosity, although unlike the gossipy Ovid, who reveals what Minerva's casket contains, she refuses to gratify that curiosity by telling tales.[56] The tercets turn the poet into a moral stumbling block, standing in opposition to her addressee's anger, false accusations, and implicitly immodest secret. Where Aglaurus can rely only on the silent appearance of her petrified form to object and to accuse, the poet, having resisted curiosity, gossip, and envy, retains the ability to speak in her playful and morally edifying verse.

Catherine des Roches's Envy: Bodily Focus

Aglaurus, unnamed in this sonnet, makes no other appearance in the Dames des Roches's works. Envy, however, does—both generally, as the enemy of virtuous wisdom, and specifically, as personified in Ovid's tale of Aglaurus.[57]

---

[55] On the Dames des Roches's adoption of a name unalterable by marriage, reflecting land ownership not patrilinear succession, see Neil Kenny, *Born to Write: Literary Families and Social Hierarchy in Early Modern France* (Oxford: Oxford University Press, 2020), 114–15; on their playing with its connotations, see Kendall B. Tarte, 'Early Modern Literary Communities: Madeleine Des Roches's City of Women', *The Sixteenth Century Journal*, 35 (2004), 751–69 (p. 767). The rock, for Catherine, symbolizes the emotional support she gives to her mother and her unwavering determination not to marry; for Madeleine, it represents her general moral uprightness and constancy.

[56] The gossipy narrator of the *Metamorphoses* is in contrast with the Ovid of the *Tristia*, who does not reveal what he (inadvertently) saw, prompting his exile: Ovid, *Tristia* 2.103–6, pp. 62–3.

[57] On the subjection particularly of learned women to others' envy as a key theme in the Dames des Roches's works, see Anne R. Larsen's introduction to Des Roches, *Les Œuvres*, 57; cf. for example pp. 90 and 98. The capacity of poetry to inspire literary envy is itself a classical—and Ovidian—theme. The

36   WOMEN'S WIT: SKIRTING OVID IN RENAISSANCE FRANCE

Catherine des Roches's poem 'L'Agnodice', framed as a study of Envy, is the most sustained attack upon envy in their works. The tale of Agnodice—who disguises her sex in order to study and practise medicine, and so to restore both bodily health and intellectual freedom to the women of Attica—is taken from the very cursory account in Hyginus, which Catherine considerably elaborates.[58] She introduces it via the story of Phocion's burial, taken from Plutarch, as another example of a virtuous character being unjustly envied;[59] her personification of Envy, however, comes straight from Ovid.[60]

In Catherine's telling of the story, Envy's hatred of the virtuous Phocion leads her to take vengeance against the woman who honourably buries his body, flouting the Athenian oligarchs' vindictive decree 'that the body of Phocion should be carried beyond the boundary of the country, and that no Athenian should light a fire for his obsequies'.[61] Envy's vengeance will afflict all women, who will become the indirect victims of her attacks upon the Athenian men:

> Car en despit de toy j'animeray les ames
> Des maris, qui seront les tyrans de leurs femmes,
> Et qui leur deffendant le livre et le sçavoir,
> Leur osteront aussi de vivre le pouvoir.[62]

(For in my spite for you I shall incense the hearts of husbands, who will become tyrants over their wives, and who, denying them books and learning, will also take from them the power to live.)

The Athenian men enviously deprive their 'femmes doctes-belles' (learned-beautiful wives) of their beautiful learning and so of their pleasure; this mental

---

opening of *Amores* 1.15, showing the criticism Ovid faced as a full-time poet, is addressed to 'Liuor edax' (gnawing Envy): Ovid, *Amores I*, ed. and trans. John Barsby (Oxford: Oxford University Press, 1973; repr. 1995), 1.15.1, p. 156; see A. S. Hollis, 'The *Ars amatoria* and *Remedia amoris*', in J. W. Binns, ed., *Ovid* (London & Boston: Routledge & Kegan Paul, 1973), 84–115 (p. 88). The literary nature of Ovid's Invidia in relation to the risks and rewards of storytelling in the Aglaurus episode is noted by Keith, *Play of Fictions*, 131; see also Hardie, 'The Word Personified', 105–6.

[58] Hyginus, *Fabulae*, 274, pp. 196–7. On the celebration in Des Roches's poem of women's bodily knowledge and of the literal or metaphorical literary children to which it may give birth, see Kirk D. Read, 'Touching and Telling: Gendered Variations on a Gynecological Theme', in Kathleen P. Long, ed., *Gender and Scientific Discourse in Early Modern Culture* (Farnham: Ashgate, 2010), 259–77 (pp. 269–75).

[59] Plutarch, *Phocion*, in *Plutarch's Lives*, trans. Bernadotte Perrin (London: Heinemann, 1919), viii, 143–233: 37.2–3 (pp. 231–3).

[60] Des Roches's textual echoes of Ovid make his influence clear, although his own intertextual references, linking his Invidia to a long literary tradition, make it impossible to isolate Ovid as a source.

[61] Plutarch, *Phocion*, 37.2, pp. 230–1.

[62] Catherine des Roches, 'L'Agnodice', in *Les Œuvres*, 333–40 (p. 335).

deprivation leads to the women's physical suffering, which goes untreated as they are too modest to reveal their bodily ailments to their male doctors and no longer have the courage to offer each other their own help.

Catherine thus contextualizes the story of Agnodice, who must disguise her sex in order to gain (medical) knowledge and freedom, but then reveal it to demonstrate her innocence and propriety, showing first the women, refusing to be treated by a male doctor, and second the men, ready to condemn her to death for seduction of their wives, that she poses no sexual threat. Envy is responsible for the death sentence initially passed by the men on Agnodice:

> Aux hommes elle mist en soupçon la valeur
> De la belle Agnodice et ses graces gentilles.
> ...
> Eux, eprix de fureur, saisirent Agnodice
> Pour en faire à l'Envie un piteux sacrifice.[63]

(Envy made the men suspicious of the merit of the beautiful Agnodice and her gentle graces.... In their fury, they seized Agnodice in order to make her a pitiful sacrifice to Envy.)

By striking the men, Envy uses them as weapons with which to attack her actual target, which shifts from the woman who buried Phocion to the Athenian women generally and to Agnodice specifically, before broadening out again in the final lines of the poem:

> L'Envie, congnoissant ses efforts abbatus
> Par les faicts d'Agnodice et ses rares vertus,
> A poursuivy depuis d'une haine immortelle
> Les Dames qui estoient vertueuses comme elle.[64]

(Envy, realizing that her efforts had been defeated by Agnodice's deeds and by her rare virtues, has ever since pursued, with an undying hatred, women who are virtuous like her.)

Catherine's poem thus becomes an aetiological explanation—of the sort that fills the myths in Ovid's *Metamorphoses*—for why virtuous (and learned, and brave, and beautiful) women continue, unjustly, to be the victims of Envy.[65]

---

[63] Des Roches, *Les Œuvres*, 338.   [64] Ibid., 340.

[65] On the aetiological function of myth to explain the origins of natural and social phenomena, see Graf, 'Myth in Ovid', 115; on the *Metamorphoses* as a vast creation story, or collection of symbolically

38   WOMEN'S WIT: SKIRTING OVID IN RENAISSANCE FRANCE

Ovid takes the metaphor of biting, gnawing envy literally, as his embodiment of 'lean and wasted' Invidia ('macies in corpore toto')[66] feeds her malice on snakes' poison and eats away at herself: 'carpitque et carpitur una / suppliciumque suum est' ('gnawing at others, and being gnawed, she was herself her own torment'),[67] just as she does Aglaurus, faced with images of her sister's happiness: 'quibus inritata dolore / Cecropis occulto mordetur' ('So Cecrops' daughter was tormented by such thoughts, and the jealous anger she concealed ate into her heart').[68] Similarly, Catherine's Envie 'mangeoit son cueur' (ate away at her own heart), while snakes bite her bald head which they encircle in place of hair: 'Des viperes hideux... la mordoient tousjours' (hideous vipers bit her constantly).[69] Like Invidia, Catherine's Envie holds a 'branche espineuse' (thorny branch) and a 'furieux serpent' (furious snake), echoing her own 'ire serpenteuse' (snaking anger), with whose 'cruel venin' (cruel poison) she strikes her victims.[70] She is an 'ingrat' et fiere hotesse' (ungrateful and proud guest), who pays those who lodge and feed her with 'le dueil et la tristesse;... le chagrin et l'ennuy' (grief and sadness, chagrin and anguish).[71] Thus Catherine echoes Ovid's depictions of the bodily wasting away provoked by mental suffering, whether caused by Envy, as for Aglaurus, or by intellectual starvation, as for the women of Attica. Yet where Ovid focuses on Aglaurus' torments as a direct victim of Envy, Catherine focuses instead on the detrimental consequences suffered by Envy's indirect victims: the women in her narrative, unjustly and enviously denied access to education, are protected by their virtuous chastity from succumbing to the envy they inspire.

The corporeal imagery introduced by envy's gnawing tooth recurs in the poem's contrasting and detailed bodily descriptions of Agnodice, echoing

---

significant aetiological myths, see Tissol, *Face of Nature*, 192; on the links between aetiology, etymology, metamorphosis, and metaphor in Ovid, see Tissol, *Face of Nature*, 173; Segal, 'Ovid's Metamorphic Bodies', 14.

[66] Ovid, *Metamorphoses*, 2.775; Innes, p. 70.   [67] Ovid, *Metamorphoses*, 2.781–2; Innes, p. 71.

[68] Ovid, *Metamorphoses*, 2.805–6; Innes, p. 71. Invidia's self-consumption links her to the insatiable greed of another of the major personifications in the *Metamorphoses*, Fames (Hunger) in Book 8, who is similarly modelled on Virgil's Fama and Allecto: Ovid, *Metamorphoses*, 8.788–822; Innes, pp. 200–1; see Hardie, 'The Word Personified', 104–7; cf. 'Liuor edax' (gnawing Envy) in *Amores*, 1.15.1, p. 156. On Invidia as a wasting away, akin to rust or disease, see Dickie, 'Ovid, *Metamorphoses* 2.760–64', 378–80.

[69] Des Roches, *Les Œuvres*, 338.

[70] Ibid., 338 and 335; cf. Ovid, *Metamorphoses*, 2.789–90: 'baculumque capit quod spinea totum / uincula cingebant' ('then she took her staff, all encircled with thorny briars'); Innes, p. 71; cf. Ovid, *Metamorphoses*, 2.768–70: 'uidet intus edentem / uipereas carnes, uitiorum alimenta suorum, / Inuidiam' ('[Minerva saw] Envy within, busy at a meal of snake's flesh, the food on which she nourished her wickedness'); Innes, p. 70; cf. Ovid, *Metamorphoses*, 2.777: 'lingua est suffusa ueneno' ('her tongue dripped venom'); Innes, p. 71.

[71] Des Roches, *Les Œuvres*, 333.

Ovid's detailed descriptions of bodies undergoing metamorphosis, and justified by the poem's narrative (educating women about their own bodies) and by its argument (the close relationship between mental and bodily health). Agnodice's second bodily revelation of her sex, to prove her sexual innocence to the Athenian men, focuses chastely on her hair, and on the abstract qualities that are symbolized by her physical breast: 'monstrant son sein beau, aggreable sejour / Des Muses, des vertus, des graces, de l'amour' (baring her beautiful breast, the delightful seat of the Muses, the virtues, the graces, and of love).[72] The men react equally chastely, falling silent to listen to Agnodice with 'une humble reverence' (a humble mark of respect).[73]

Agnodice's first revelation of her sex, to the women, similarly involves her showing them her hair and her breast, described on this occasion more physically and, potentially, erotically as the site of 'les blanches pommes rondes' (her round, white apples), inviting touch and taste as well as the gaze.[74] Yet the sensuous invitation of these apples is to the female body as the site not of eroticism but of the knowledge—bodily and general—unjustly denied to the Athenian women. This is seen in the quasi-religious devotion inspired in the women who gaze at length upon Agnodice's statuesque body as a symbol of her virtue:

> Les Dames admirant ceste honte naïsve,
> Et de son teint doüillet la blanche couleur vive,
> Et de son sein poupin le petit mont jumeau,
> Et de son chef sacré l'or crepelu tant beau,
> Et de ses yeux divins les flammes ravissantes,
> Et de ses doux propos les graces attirantes,
> Baiserent mille fois et sa bouche et son sein,
> Recevant le secours de son heureuse main.[75]

(The women, admiring her true modesty, and the light white colour of her soft complexion, and the two little mounds on her dainty breast, and the beautiful wavy gold of her sacred head, and the ravishing flames of her divine eyes, and the alluring grace of her gentle speech, bestowed a thousand kisses on her mouth and her breast, receiving help from her blessed hand.)

The detailed focus upon Agnodice's body—licensed by the (supposedly) unlascivious single-sex context—reflects the bodily knowledge that she has

---

[72] Ibid., 338–9.   [73] Ibid., 339.   [74] Ibid., 337.   [75] Ibid., 337.

40   WOMEN'S WIT: SKIRTING OVID IN RENAISSANCE FRANCE

acquired while studying medicine and that she passes on to the women she treats. The extended listing of her bodily traits resembles the form of a poetic blazon, but rewrites its function: where the erotic blazon itemizes body parts in order to linger over and imaginatively possess them, the listing of Agnodice's bodily features serves to separate and depersonalize them. The itemized Agnodice—frozen and motionless in the narrative as the description lingers on her body—resembles an unmoving and unmoved statue; the religious vocabulary ('sacré', 'divin', 'graces') portrays the kisses showered upon her mouth and breast by the women of Athens not as erotic but as devotional, as if bestowed upon a statue of the Virgin in gratitude for divine succour and blessing.[76] Like the similarly statuesque Aglaurus, Agnodice has wilfully acquired forbidden knowledge, leading to envy; yet unlike Aglaurus, Agnodice puts that forbidden but helpful knowledge to good use, firstly by practising medicine, and secondly by restoring women's access to books and learning.

Coda: Sparring with Ovid—Bodily Deflection

Agnodice is not the only example of Catherine des Roches's ability to play with a potentially erotic bodily description in the model of Ovid and to elevate it to something more chaste and spiritual. Her contribution to the poetic contest inspired by the flea that supposedly landed on her breast during the Grands Jours in Poitiers in 1579 is a superlative example of female ingenuity in response to a situation remarkably similar to that of the girl at the Circus, in Book I of Ovid's *Ars amatoria*, with the speck of (fictive) dust upon her dress. Ovid's advice to the studious reader of his mock manual of seduction includes a lesson on the amorous possibilities offered by a visit to the Circus, with its opportunity to sit, in forced proximity, next to a neighbour of the opposite sex:

> utque fit, in gremium puluis si forte puellae
> deciderit, digitis excutiendus erit;
> etsi nullus erit puluis, tamen excute nullum.[77]

---

[76] See Cathy Yandell, 'Iconography and Iconoclasm: the Female Breast in French Renaissance Culture', *The French Review*, 83 (2010), 540–58.

[77] Ovid, *Ars amatoria: Book I*, ed. A. S. Hollis (Oxford: Clarendon Press, 1977; repr. 1992), ll. 149–51. Ovid had already put his own recommendations into practice in the *Amores*, as Hollis notes: 'Compare *Am.* iii. 2. 41–2 "dum loquor alba leui sparsa est tibi puluere uestis: / sordide de niueo corpore puluis abi!"' (as I speak, a speck of dust has landed on your white dress: dirty dust, be gone from this snowy body!) (p. 61).

(If by chance a speck of dust falls, as it will fall, into the girl's lap, you must brush it off with your fingers; and if it doesn't, brush it off anyway.)

Ostensibly, such sedulous attentiveness—whether necessary or gratuitous—will win the girl's gratitude and, ultimately, her favour; less overtly, it creates an opportunity for erotically charged physical contact between the seducer's fingers and the girl's lap, licensed by the innocence of the ostensible intention of preserving the immaculate purity of the girl's dress.

Ovid's readers are invited to laugh straightforwardly at the transparency of the ploy and the gullibility of the girl, with its enticing promise that she will soon prove easy prey to the seducer. They may also laugh at the wit of the narration: the confident prediction 'utque fit' pre-empts the chance occurrence ('si forte') that an artificially engineered circumstance ('etsi...tamen...') will in any case render unnecessary. Ovid's narrator demonstrates a comically excessive ingenuity—this is a seducer who has thought of absolutely everything. Ovid's more knowing readers may also laugh at the whole concept of the mock manual, whose fictive reader earnestly and urgently consults its pages in order to learn what ought to come naturally.

The heavily one-sided sexual sparring of the *Ars amatoria* contrasts with the more evenly matched literary sparring of the playfully combative conversation in the Dames des Roches's salon, described by Estienne Pasquier:

Estant doncques là avecques elles, je commençay à m'en escrimer au moins mal qu'il me fut possible; et croyez qu'à beau jeu, beau retour; cela s'appelle une heure et demie pour le moins: et comme nous estions en ces discours, mon bonheur voulut que j'aperceusse une Pulce qui s'estoit parquée au beau milieu de son sein: je vous dy par exprés mon bonheur; car peut-estre eusse-je esté bien empesché à poursuivre ma premiere route, aprés un si long entretien, sans ce nouveau sujet; tellement que je m'en sens fort redevable à ceste petite bestiole.[78]

(As I was there with them, I began to skirmish as well as I could, and believe me gave as good as I got; this went on for an hour and a half at least: and as we were in conversation, it was my good fortune to notice a flea that had settled right on the middle of her breast: I say specifically that this was my

---

[78] Pasquier, quoted in Des Roches, *Les Missives*, 344–5. On the competitive, noble, and masculine sporting pursuits evoked by Pasquier's description, see Anne R. Larsen, 'On Reading *La Puce de Madame Des-Roches*: Catherine des Roches's *Responces* (1583)', *Renaissance and Reformation*, 22 (1998), 63–75 (pp. 64–5).

good fortune, for I might well have found it difficult to keep going on my original course, after such a long conversation, without this new subject; so much so that I feel greatly indebted to this little creature.)

The flea that offers a welcome new topic of discussion, after such sustained conversational jousting, belongs to a long literary tradition of desiring to be metamorphosed into something inconsequential that thereby has proximity to the beloved; it gives rise to a set of encomiastic poems by the salon visitors, published in 1582 as *La Puce de Madame Des-Roches*.[79] Madeleine and Catherine both engage in the poetic contest—showing their willingness to share and enjoy its wit—while simultaneously correcting the focus on Catherine's physical body that it inevitably encourages. Madeleine invites the poets in the collection to support the flea in its desire for a neo-platonic ascent from the 'Roche' (rock) of Catherine's breast to 'le ciel' (the heavens).[80] Catherine presents the flea's wise focus upon her breast not as erotic (even though the flea is 'fretillarde', frisky) but as a source of 'nourriture et enseignement' (nourishment and learning) and a place of refuge.[81]

If the sight of a flea offers the *Puce* poets an excuse to focus on Catherine's breast, she redirects that focus on her body towards a philosophically and spiritually higher sphere, elegantly extracting herself from the position in which these eager readers of the *Ars amatoria* try to put her.[82] Ovid's seduction manual highlights—and uses to its advantage—the impossible position in which women are placed by the double standards that govern the sexes. The girl on whom the would-be seducer preys cannot admit to seeing through his strategies: such knowingness would be incompatible with the decorum that depends on her (actual or feigned) naivety, which in turn helps the seducer's strategy to succeed. Women reading Ovid in early modern France are placed in an equally impossible predicament: to enjoy Ovid's wit is, in this instance,

---

[79] See Marcel Françon, 'Un motif de la poésie amoureuse au XVIᵉ siècle', *PMLA*, 56 (1941), 307–36, who highlights the influence on the *La Puce* collection of the pseudo-Virgilian *Culex* and the pseudo-Ovidian *Carmen de Pulice* (attributed to the medieval neo-Latin poet Ofilius Sergianus), itself modelled on the *Culex*. On the *Culex*, see K. Sara Myers, 'The *Culex*'s Metapoetic Funerary Garden', *The Classical Quarterly*, 70 (2021), 749–55; on its influence, see Emily Gowers, 'Lucan's (G)natal Poem: Statius' *Silvae* 2.7, the *Culex*, and the Aesthetics of Miniaturization', *Classical Antiquity*, 40 (2021), 45–75. On the *La Puce* collection, see Larsen's introduction in Des Roches, *Les Secondes Œuvres*, 21–4 and 68–9.

[80] Des Roches, *Les Secondes Œuvres*, 108.

[81] Ibid., 335–6; see Yandell, 'Iconography and Iconoclasm', 553–4.

[82] Larsen, 'On Reading *La Puce*'; see also Ann Rosalind Jones, 'Contentious Readings: Urban Humanism and Gender Difference in *La Puce de Madame Des-Roches* (1582)', *Renaissance Quarterly*, 8 (1995), 109–27. Just as Ovid distinguishes between the direction of Aglaurus' frank gaze and the indirection of Envy's sidelong glances, so Catherine distinguishes between the open invitation to look directly at Agnodice's educative body and this deflection of any erotic focus on her own body.

to be both knowing about and complicit in seduction; to resist his playful immorality is to be tight-lipped, straight-laced, and unamused. Thus it seems early modern women must sacrifice either their virtue or their sense of humour if they are to read Ovid or to engage with him in their work. Yet the Dames des Roches's willingness, in their salon and in their writing, to engage in well-matched sparring forms a pointed contrast with the *Ars amatoria*; Catherine's resistance to any erotic focus on her breast offers her and her opponents a different pleasure from the easy acquiescence Ovid's mock seduction manual goes to such lengths to achieve.

Madeleine des Roches's sonnet engages playfully and obliquely with Ovid, testing her reader's intelligence, with the challenge to recognize the veiled allusion to Aglaurus and to accept its exemplarity, and testing her reader's wisdom, with the challenge to resist curiosity over the scurrilous secret that she hints at but never reveals. In its wise and constant resistance, informed by faith, to gossip and to envy, Madeleine's sonnet is an example of the consistent advocacy of women's virtuous and educated literary self-expression in the Des Roches's works. Similarly, Catherine's 'L'Agnodice' portrays educated and virtuous women as victims of others' envy rather than subject to it themselves. Catherine's poem is Ovidian in its personification of Envy and its detailed focus upon the itemized female body; far from Ovidian, though, is Catherine's insistence upon that quasi-religious body as chaste and educative, rather than sexual.

Similarly, the potentially erotic focus on the female body in the *Puce* collection is wittily adjusted by Catherine to something more high-minded and decorous. She thereby asserts not only her unwavering chastity, even in the face of playful attacks that could have come straight out of the *Ars amatoria*, but also her right and her ability to be both decorous and witty as she parries those attacks and answers back.[83] Like her mother, she shows that the moral high ground need not be a humourless sphere. Thus the Ovid that emerges from the Dames des Roches's works has himself been metamorphosed— the playfully inconstant tale-teller and authority on seducing women is changed from the friend of those who would deny women access to education or self-expression into an equal sparring partner, subject to their witty moral correction but nonetheless an engaging and suitable companion for women appearing in print and defending their right to do so.

---

[83] On critical debate over the playfulness of the *Ars amatoria*, taken either as serious or parodic, see Patricia Watson, 'Praecepta amoris: Ovid's Didactic Elegy', in Barbara Weiden Boyd, ed., *Brill's Companion to Ovid* (Leiden: Brill, 2002), 141–65 (pp. 148–9).

3

Madeleine de L'Aubespine's Translation of *Heroides* 2

Jessica DeVos

In *La Défense et illustration de la langue française* Joachim Du Bellay urged his fellow poets to domesticate foreign models in order to graft them onto their own nascent, blossoming national literature. While he warned that the translation of Greek and Latin poetry into French could only produce verse that was inferior to the original, he nevertheless advised those who wished to engage in this endeavour of *translatio studii et imperii* to begin by carefully studying and imitating classical models before attempting to pen their own original works in the vernacular. In addition to this pedagogical purpose, translating classical works facilitated the importation of culture from Greece to Rome and now from Rome to Paris. Du Bellay conceived of translation in its broadest sense. It was not a form of coding by which individual words or phrases in one language were replaced by their closest equivalents in another, but rather a painstaking and often frustratingly difficult quest to unearth and revive the literary past in order to breathe new life into the present. Highlighting the indispensable role of translation as a vehicle for the transfer of culture, Karen Newman and Jane Tylus ask the fundamental question, 'Would there have been a Renaissance without translation?', and respond on behalf of the authors in their edited collection (with whom Du Bellay would agree) that 'the answer is a resounding no'.[1]

Yet despite the centrality of translation to the very existence of the Renaissance, little attention has been given to the role played by French women in this crucial endeavour of linguistic and literary nation building. Translation has long been considered inferior to 'original' literary creation and discourse surrounding the activity frequently highlights its inadequacy or derivative nature in descriptions that employ gendered language and

---

[1] Karen Newman and Jane Tylus, 'Introduction', in Karen Newman and Jane Tylus, eds, *Early Modern Cultures of Translation* (Philadelphia: University of Pennsylvania Press, 2015), 1.

Jessica DeVos, *Madeleine de L'Aubespine's Translation of* Heroides *2* In: *Ovid in French: Reception by Women from the Renaissance to the Present.* Edited by: Helena Taylor and Fiona Cox, Oxford University Press. © Oxford University Press 2023. DOI: 10.1093/oso/9780192895387.003.0003

metaphors.[2] Deborah Uman argues that this emphasis on the subservient status of translation thus paralleled the social and legal status of women to men during the Renaissance and suggests that this relegation may have offered creative possibilities to women:

> For women, who were supposed to be defined in relation to their husbands, fathers, and sons, translation may have presented them not with a vehicle that facilitated clear self-expression but rather with a strategy of articulation that accurately mirrored their own complicated positions in the public and private spheres.[3]

The heroines of Ovid's elegiac epistles, who creatively subvert canonical male-focused epic narratives, provided Renaissance women translators with one such 'strategy of articulation'. Yet if the gendering of translation may have offered opportunities in the sixteenth century, Marie-Alice Belle has observed how it has hindered scholarship in the twenty-first: 'the perceived inferiority of translation as a literary practice, and its traditional association with women in the early modern period, have lately been identified as the greatest critical pitfalls when approaching early modern women's translations.'[4] Citing foundational texts that brought attention to two overlooked dimensions of cultural participation and production—Joan Kelly's *Becoming Visible: Women in European History* and Lawrence Venuti's *The Translator's Invisibility: A History of Translation*—Belle argues that the work of Renaissance women translators has suffered from a compounded lack of visibility. While Belle's introductory essay explores the intersection of gender and translation, Brenda M. Hosington similarly pairs the study of translation with a second phenomenon. Identifying their shared objective of making texts, authors, and ideas available to a wider audience, the contributions to her edited volume examine the links between translation and the advent of printing.[5] Tania Demetriou and Rowan Tomlinson pair the same two countries presented in Belle's volume in order to explore the cultures of translation in early modern

---

[2] For a concise overview of these related phenomena during the early modern period, see Deborah Uman, '"This Defective Edition": Gender and Translation', in *Women as Translators in Early Modern England* (Newark: University of Delaware Press, 2012), 1–16.

[3] Ibid., 5.

[4] Marie-Alice Belle, 'Locating Early Modern Women's Translations: Critical and Historiographical Issues', *Renaissance and Reformation/Renaissance et Réforme*, 35/4 (2012), 5–23 (p. 8) [special issue: *Women's Translations in Early Modern England and France*].

[5] Brenda M. Hosington, 'Introduction: Translation and Print Culture in Early Modern Europe', *Renaissance Studies*, 29/1 (2015), 5–18.

46 MADELEINE DE L'AUBESPINE'S TRANSLATION OF *HEROIDES* 2

France as well as the crucial role played by French as both an original and an intermediary language in the shaping of English translation culture.[6]

These collections of essays reflect the burgeoning scholarly interest in Renaissance translation as well as its general 'rehabilitation' as a legitimate area of literary study over the past decade. They focus on diverse national literatures both within and beyond traditional geographical boundaries and adopt an array of methodological approaches that 'range from biographical to multimodal, linguistic to literary, cultural to historiographical'.[7] Such diversity is appropriate when considering the wide range of functions served by translation. In addition to its most familiar role of making accessible texts, authors, and knowledge to a wider audience, Hosington reminds us that during the Renaissance translation also contributed to 'creating or perfecting national languages'.[8] This is how Du Bellay and his fellow members of the Pléiade understood the activity and, as linguistic and literary archaeologists, the poets who heeded the call to pillage the past did so in order to ensure its renewal in the present. Ann Moss explains that they 'regarded themselves first and foremost as discoverers, restorers, and interpreters of ancient culture'[9] and Paul White similarly states that 'humanists knew that ancient literature was always written *for them*, and that they were the rightful heirs to the classical tradition' [White's emphasis].[10] In the specific case of the *Heroides*, these Renaissance readers considered themselves the rightful *destinataires* of Ovid's epistles and their responses took a variety of forms: commentaries, imitations, *risposte*, and, of course, translations.

However, as Emma Herdman illustrated in the preceding chapter, women writers encountered particular challenges when engaging with the Latin author. They were often on the receiving end of Ovid's celebrated wit, or were the objects of what Valerie Traub has labelled his 'erotics of cruelty'.[11] As a result, some women found creative ways to 'skirt' the author while engaging with select elements of his texts from a distance. Madeleine de L'Aubespine's translation of *Heroides* 2 is an exception to this trend since it reveals intense and sustained engagement with even the subtlest details of her Ovidian

---

[6] Tania Demetriou and Rowan Tomlinson, eds., *The Culture of Translation in Early Modern England and France, 1500–1660* (Basingstoke: Palgrave Macmillan, 2015).

[7] Hosington, 'Introduction', 18. [8] Ibid., 5.

[9] Ann Moss, *Ovid in Renaissance France: A Survey of the Latin editions of Ovid and Commentaries Printed in France before 1600* (London: Warburg Institute, University of London, 1982), 1.

[10] Paul White, *Renaissance Postscripts: Responding to Ovid's* Heroides *in Sixteenth–Century France* (Columbus: Ohio State University Press, 2009), 11.

[11] Valerie Traub, 'Afterword', in Goran V. Stanivukovic, ed., *Ovid and the Renaissance Body* (Toronto: University of Toronto Press, 2001), 260–8 (p. 266).

source—the approach prescribed by Leonardo Bruni required to produce a 'perfect translation':

> sic in traductionibus interpres quidem optimus sese in primum scribendi auctorem tota mente et animo et voluntate convertet et quodammodo transformabit eiusque orationis figuram, statum, ingressum coloremque et liniamenta cuncta exprimere meditabitur. Ex quo mirabilis quidam resultat effectus.[12]

> (Thus, in translating, the best translator projects themselves into the original author of the text, with all their mind, soul, and will, and in a certain way transforms themselves, and in their work will seek to express the form, the posture, the pace, and the colour, and all of the features of the original. In this way a truly miraculous effect is produced.)

Fully investing herself—'tota mente et animo et voluntate'—in Ovid and his text, Madeline de L'Aubespine exemplifies the ideal translator as envisioned by Bruni.

Yet, as Anna Klosowska reminds us:

> Ironically, our contemporary critics may be inclined to stress that in her translations of the *Heroides*, l'Aubespine participated in the elaboration of the theme of female masochism. By contrast, l'Aubespine's contemporaries focused on the fact that as an author of contemporary French versions of some of the most popular texts of the Latin canon, she 'surpassed the most learned French men'.[13]

It is not coincidental that Klosowska uses the speculative 'may be inclined' when referring to potential modern reactions to L'Aubespine's translations of Ovid: to date, there have been no published studies analysing her translations. The aim of this chapter is to give long overdue critical attention to her translation of *Heroides* 2, an exemplary poetic work that does indeed surpass the work of her French male contemporaries who were also translating Ovid's epistles. In this poem, the Thracian princess Phyllis is writing to her absent beloved, Demophoon, the son of Theseus and Phaedra. Following the Trojan

---

[12] Leonardo Bruni, *Sulla perfetta traduzione*, ed. Paolo Vitti (Naples: Liguori, 2004), 84. Unless otherwise noted, all translations are my own.

[13] Anna Klosowska, 'Introduction' in Anna Klosowska, ed., *Madeleine de l'Aubespine: Selected Poems and Translations* (Chicago: University of Chicago Press, 2007), 31.

War, he arrived in Thrace where they fell in love and were married. He subsequently departed for Greece and when the two are not reunited by the promised date, Phyllis commits suicide. According to some sources, Demophoon later returns, only to find his wife has been transformed into a leafless tree, which blossoms upon his embrace of the trunk.

L'Aubespine's translation was never printed, but circulated in manuscript form. As testified by La Croix du Maine (see below), the medium of publication appears to have been the author's choice. It granted her greater control over the reception of her works, allowing her to share her poetry with an erudite, elite, proto-salon circle whom she envisioned as her ideal audience. Her readers were also Latinists who could read and appreciate the *Heroides* in the original and were thus well equipped to assess her ability as both a translator and a poet. In her translations she was not seeking to make Ovid's work accessible to a larger audience, but rather to showcase her own talents. Although she has been largely forgotten by modern literary scholars,[14] her male contemporaries considered her an equal participant in the ambitious project of forging a new national literature in the vernacular. In this chapter I seek to elucidate the literary qualities of L'Aubespine's translation while situating it within the historical context of sixteenth-century French translations of Ovid. Thus, after a brief introduction presenting an overview of the place of Ovid's *Heroides* in sixteenth-century French literary culture, the remainder of this study is dedicated to a close analysis of key passages in L'Aubespine's poem, examined alongside the work of her male contemporaries, in order to illustrate why Ronsard concluded that this 'femme a vaincu les plus doctes françois' ('woman surpassed the most learned French men').[15]

* * *

---

[14] Klosowska is a notable exception to this trend. In addition to her bilingual edition of L'Aubespine's works, she has published several essays examining questions of sex, gender, and subjectivity in L'Aubespine's verse from the theoretical perspectives of queer and cultural studies. See, for instance, Anna Klosowska, 'Madeleine de l'Aubespine: Life, Works, and Auto-Mythography: An Exchange with Ronsard, ca. 1570–80', *French Forum*, 32 (2007), 19–38; Anna Klosowska, 'Erotica and Women in Early Modern France: Madeleine de l'Aubespine's Queer Poems', *Journal of the History of Sexuality*, 17 (2008), 190–215. Perrine Galand Willemen has convincingly argued that L'Aubespine authored the Latin poem *Cantilupum*. Her scholarship and insightful readings provide further evidence of L'Aubespine's exceptional abilities as a Latinist. Perrine Galand Willemen, 'Les jardins de Chanteloup (*Cantilupum*, 1587): promenade poétique et itinéraire moral sous la plume d'une grande dame du XVIe siècle, Madeleine de Villeroy', in Lucia Bertolini, Donatella Coppini, and Clementina Marsico, eds, *Nel cantiere degli umanisti: per Mariangela Regoliosi* (Florence: Edizione Polistampa, 2014), 533–54.

[15] Klosowska, *Madeleine de l'Aubespine: Selected Poems and Translations*, 58 and 59.

The start of the sixteenth century witnessed a domestication of Ovid's *Heroides* both in the original language as well as in translations into the vernacular. While the Latin poems had been available previously as imports from Italy, the first editions printed in France appeared in the final decade of the fifteenth century.[16] In 1500 Jodocus Badius Ascensius, a Belgian working in Lyon, added an introduction and supplementary material to a version containing the commentaries of two famous fifteenth-century Italian humanists, Antonius Volscus and Ubertinus Clericus Crescentinas. This annotated version was reprinted fifteen times before 1536,[17] when it was superseded by the edition of Guido Morillo (Guy Morillon) and Johannes Baptista Egnatius (Giovanni de' Cipelli). Although an edition by Morillo alone was first published in Paris in 1507, according to Moss, 'it is only after 1533, when it was printed at Lyons for the first time, in conjunction with the *observationes* of Egnatius, that it becomes popular, and drives the earlier commentaries from the market within five years.'[18] Subsequent editions were reprinted first in Lyon until 1567, then in Paris until 1585,[19] making this the standard edition at the moment when L'Aubespine was translating Ovid's poems.

During the same time period, demand for French translations was also on the rise. In addition to the numerous manuscript versions that continued to circulate, Octavian de Saint-Gelais's translation was printed at least nineteen times between 1500 and 1550,[20] before being supplanted by Charles Fontaine's translation of the first ten poems in 1552. The 1580 edition of Fontaine's work presents a complete translation of Ovid's elegiac epistles by incorporating Saint-Gelais's versions of the remaining poems. In the 'Petit avertissement aux lecteurs' Fontaine justifies his reasons for undertaking a new translation. After acknowledging the existence of other French translations (in particular

---

[16] The University of St Andrews' *Universal Short Title Catalogue* and the British Library's *Incunabula Short Title Catalogue* ascribe tentative publication dates of 1490 to the *Epistolae Heroides* published by Pierre Levet in Paris and 1498 to the *Epistolae Heroides* published in Paris by Antoine Denidel. The first Latin edition printed in France for which publication details can be firmly established is Publius Ovidius Naso, *Epistolae Heroides. Auli Sabini responsiones ad epistolas Ovidii* (Paris: Michel Le Noir, 1499/1500).

[17] Publius Ovidius Naso, *Epistolae heroides et Sappho et Ibis* (Lyon: Jean de Vingle for Etienne Gueynard, 1500). For additional information on reprints of this edition see Moss, *Ovid in Renaissance France*, 8–11, and White, *Renaissance Postscripts*, 88–91.

[18] Moss, *Ovid in Renaissance France*, 12.

[19] For additional details regarding the Morillo/Egnatius edition, see Moss, *Ovid in Renaissance France*, 12–15, and White, *Renaissance Postscripts*, 93–5.

[20] Publius Ovidius Naso, *Epistolae Heroides*, trans. Octavian de Saint-Gelais (Paris: Michel Le Noir, 1500). The earliest editions of Saint-Gelais's translations do not all carry publication dates and there is some disagreement among scholars as to the exact number of publications that appeared. For the conservative figure adopted by the present study, see White, *Renaissance Postscripts*, 147.

50   MADELEINE DE L'AUBESPINE'S TRANSLATION OF *HEROIDES* 2

those of Saint-Gelais whom he could hardly ignore since he incorporated his predecessor's work into his own publication), he explains:

> En quoy disant je n'enten le blasmer, ains plutôt le vueil je excuser, et prendre en bonne part ce qu'il ha fait lors que notre langue Françoise n'estoit pas encor bien avant sortie de son enfance, ny n'estoient les arts et sciences tant esclarcies, ny les esprits si prompts, vifs et agus comme de present.[21]
>
> (In so saying, I do not intend to blame, but rather I wish to excuse and welcome what he did while our French language had not yet grown out of its infancy, and neither were the arts and sciences so enlightened, nor the intellects so quick, lively, and sharp as at present.)

Fontaine's description of a youthful, immature language that could only be brought to its perfected maturity by the current generation of 'esprits' who possess greater intellectual dexterity than their predecessors echoes Du Bellay's calls to action expressed throughout *La Défense*.[22] Indeed, in his translation of Ovid's *Heroides* Fontaine situates himself among those praised by Pléiade member Pontus de Tyard for having contributed to the 'mutation du stile Poëtique' (change in poetic style) and 'le progrez et avancement qu'a fait nostre langage François' (progress and advancement that our French language has made).[23]

Madeleine de L'Aubespine's contemporaries included her among those 'esprits si prompts, vifs et agus' who contributed to the progress and perfection of the French language and her poetic prowess was well known. In his 1584 *Bibliothèque*, La Croix du Maine praises her literary talents, singling out her exemplary translations of the *Heroides*:

> Mad. Madelene de l'Aubespine, fille de monsieur le Secretaire de l'Aubespine, et femme de messier Nicolas de Neufuille, seigneur de Villeroy, premier Secretaire d'estat, etc. (duquel nous avons fait mention cy devant à la lettre N.) cette dame est si heureuse à composer en prose et en vers, et a l'esprit et le judgment si rares, qu'elle attire un chacun à la contemplation de tant de vertuz qui reluysent en elle, lesquelles elle a comme par succession de ceux desquels elle a pris origine, et pour faire preuve de ce que j'ay dit touchant son sçavoir et

---

[21] Charles Fontaine, *Les XXI épitres d'Ovide* (Paris: Hierosme de Marnef et la Veufve Guillaume Cavellat, 1580), 439.

[22] For an overview of how Fontaine's conception of translation both agrees with and differs from that of Du Bellay, see White, *Renaissance Postscripts*, 151–7.

[23] Pontus de Tyard, *Erreurs amoureuses*, ed. John A. McClelland (Geneva: Droz, 1967), 90.

doctrine, j'allegueray sa traduction des Epistres d'Ovide lesquelles elle n'a encores fait imprimer, non plus qu'une infinité de poëmes de son invention, lesquelles sortiront en lumiere quand il luy plaira.[24]

(Madame Madeleine de l'Aubespine, daughter of Monsieur the Secretary de l'Aubespine and wife of Monsieur Nicolas de Neufville, Lord of Villeroy, First Secretary of State, etc. (of whom we made mention above under the letter "N") this woman is so inspired in her writings, both in prose and in verse, and has such rare talent and intellect, that all are drawn to contemplate the rare gifts and virtues that she exhibits, which she has inherited through her noble lineage, and as proof of my claims regarding her intellect and study, I propose her translations of Ovid's Epistles, which she has not yet published, as well as a plethora of poems of her own composition, which will see the light when it pleases her.)

In his assessment of L'Aubespine's work, La Croix du Maine clearly did not consider her translations subservient to her 'original' works. Her selection of *Heroides* 2 was particularly auspicious. While the plight of Phyllis captivated the imagination of medieval authors, there are few literary antecedents to Ovid's version and Renaissance commentators were unaware of any sources prior to his elegiac epistle.[25] *Heroides* 2 therefore differs from other poems in the collection as Renaissance readers were more likely to receive it as an 'original' pronouncement by Phyllis, rather than the heroine's version to be read against a dominant, canonical, hypotext. This ambiguity and liberty offered creative possibilities to Renaissance authors such as Madeleine de L'Aubespine who adeptly exploits them at key moments in her translation. When considering French versions of *Heroides* 2 it is often difficult to distinguish between imitation, translation, and original literary production. Of all Ovid's abandoned heroines, Phyllis is perhaps the most concerned with rewriting male-authored accounts of masculine exploits and it is within this context of gendered and competing discourses that we shall begin examining the opening lines of *Heroides* 2.[26]

*　*　*

---

[24] François Grudé, sieur de La Croix du Maine, *Premier volume de la bibliotheque du Sieur de la Croix-du Maine* (Paris: A. l'Angellier, 1584), 497.

[25] White, *Renaissance Postscripts*, 95.

[26] For discussions of the early modern reception of other particular Heroides epistles, namely *Heroides* 4, Phaedra to Hippolytus, and *Heroides* 13, Laodamia to Protesilaus, see the chapters by Océane Puche and Helena Taylor respectively in this volume (Chapters 5 and 4).

52 MADELEINE DE L'AUBESPINE'S TRANSLATION OF *HEROIDES* 2

Phyllis begins her epistle by addressing Demophoon in the following manner:

> Hospita, Demophoon, tua te Rhodopeia Phyllis
> > Ultra promissum tempus abesse queror. (2.1–2)

(I, your Phyllis, who welcomed you to Rhodope, Demophoon, complain that
the promised day is past, and you [are] not here.)[27]

In the Latin original, the first person is only evoked in the final word of the
couplet with the deponent verb 'queror'. Like many French and English translators, Fontaine immediately introduces a first-person speaker in his translation:

> De toy *me plains ie* Phyllis ton hostesse
> O Demophon, qui ne me tiens promesse
> Ayant laissé passer le temps ainsi,
> Que tu devoys de retour etre ici.[28]
>
> > [my emphasis]

(Of you, I lament, Phyllis, your hostess / Oh Demophoon, who is not keeping
the promise made to me / The time thus having passed / You ought to be here
returned.)

This is not a surprising solution as the syntax in both French and English
favours such constructions. For White, the chiasmus formed by the semantic
units in Fontaine's version (you–I–I–you) reminds us that while 'Ovid's Phyllis
had been able to embrace Demophoon grammatically if not in reality, Fontaine's
version projects Demophoon as embracing Phyllis'.[29] Yet L'Aubespine's translation highlights some of the troubling elements of White's astute observation:

> Ceste tienne Phillis, que trop d'amour deceut
> Lors que dedans son port, douce, elle te receut,
> Se plaint, o Demophon! d'une plainte eternelle
> Qu'outre le temps promis tu sois esloigné d'elle.[30]
>
> > (vv. 1–4)

---

[27] Ovid, *Heroides and Amores*, trans. Grant Showerman (1977; Cambridge, MA: Harvard University
Press, 1996), 19, 21. All subsequent Latin citations and English translations of the *Heroides* refer to this
edition and will be indicated by verse number within the text.

[28] Fontaine, *Les XXI épitres d'Ovide*, 31.   [29] White, *Renaissance Postscripts*, 181.

[30] Marguerite de Valois, *Album de poésies*, ed. Colette Winn and François Rouget (Paris: Classiques
Garnier, 2009), 76. All subsequent citations refer to this edition and will be indicated by verse number
within the text.

(This Phyllis of yours, who was deceived by too great a love, / When she received you sweetly within her port, / Laments, Oh Demophoon! An eternal lament / That you remain apart from her beyond the promised time of return.)

Throughout these four verses L'Aubespine's Phyllis follows Ovid in the opening line of *Heroides* 2 by speaking of herself in the third person as 'elle'. L'Aubespine also faithfully translates the Ovidian original by preserving the Latin possessive: 'tua...Phyllis' as 'Ceste tienne Phillis' in French. While Fontaine's version generally privileges subject and indirect pronouns, he too includes one possessive: 'ton hostesse'. In such constructions, it is difficult to determine who is embracing whom. When one individual 'possesses' another, subjecthood and agency become blurred in a fashion that modern psycho-therapists might label dysfunctional 'fusion'. Within a philological context more familiar to L'Aubespine and her contemporaries, Lawrence Lipking reminds us of the etymology and literary history of female 'abandonment':

The term goes back to Latin, *ad*, 'to,' *bandon*, 'power or control' (cognate with English 'ban'). Originally it signified a submission to power, as in bowing to the will of a monarch; the person who owns you can also toss you away. But the same etymology, with a slight adjustment of the prepos-ition, allows a totally opposite meaning: freedom from bondage. The exile or outlaw makes her own laws. Hence those who are abandoned may be *banished* by the one who controls them (given up *by*) or they may take the reins entirely into their own hands (given up *to*). This verbal duplicity hints at the roots of power beneath the desolation of abandoned women—are they chattels or do they belong to themselves?—as well as the uneasiness with which most cultures regard them. Those who are banished are also let loose; utter surrender resembles utter freedom.[31]

L'Aubespine seizes upon and exploits this etymological complexity through-out her poem. She concludes her translation of the first ten lines of the Latin poem with a significant and original addition:

Spes quoque lenta fuit ; tarde, quae credita laedunt,
         credimus. invita nuc es amante nocens.   (2.9–10)

---

[31] Lawrence Lipking, *Abandoned Women and Poetic Tradition* (Chicago: University of Chicago Press, 1988), xvii.

54 MADELEINE DE L'AUBESPINE'S TRANSLATION OF *HEROIDES* 2

(Hope, too, has been slow to leave me; we are tardy in believing, when belief brings hurt.)

> Tousjours nous croyons tard ce qui nous est contraire,
> Mais je m'en voy trahie, et fault que, maulgré moy,
> Le desespoir tout seul me donne ores la loy.   (vv. 16–18)

(We are always late to believe what goes against us / But I see I am betrayed, and it must be, that in spite of myself / Despair alone henceforth will govern me.)

Phyllis' declaration that henceforth she will be governed by 'le desespoir tout seul' is L'Aubespine's invention and the choice of wording is both semantically and poetically rich as 'ores la loy' is a homonym for 'hors la loi'. L'Aubespine thus suggests that her heroine, governed solely by despair, will also henceforth be operating outside of the law.

Indeed, aware that she has transgressed social conventions, Ovid's Phyllis redirects her hopes for redress to the domain of the divine. She implores the gods to return Demophoon to her, offering them prayers and incense while on bended knee: 'saepe deos supplex, ut tu, scelerate, valeres, / cum prece turicremis sum venerate sacris' (2.17–18) ('Oft, bending the knee in prayer that you fare well—ah, base, base man!—have I venerated the gods with prayer or with burning of holy incense'). L'Aubespine slightly alters the pagan practices of the original as her Phyllis does not genuflect or offer sacrifices: 'Sur les autelz des dieux, en diverses manieres / J'offre d'un cueur devot mes pleurs et mes prieres' (vv. 31–2) (On the altars of the gods, and in various manners / From a devout heart I offer tears and prayers). While imploring the gods solely through prayers and tears resonates with contemporary orthodox 'offerings', she addresses the pagan pantheon of gods throughout the poem. When god is evoked in the singular it designates a specific classical deity (Cupid, v. 51; Venus, v. 59; Ceres, v. 62; Juno, v. 63; Bacchus, v. 124), with one significant exception: the final direct address to 'Dieu' in verse 101. It is at this point in the French poem that L'Aubespine's Phyllis begins her transformation from a supplicant into a prophetic poet. In Ovid's original elegiac epistle, after detailing the suffering caused by Demophoon's departure, Phyllis invokes collectively the gods she has previously mentioned: 'di faciant, laudis summa sit ista tuae!' (2.66) ('May the gods grant that this be your crowning praise'). Saint-Gelais weakens her words by transforming them from a pronouncement into a prayer that simply expresses her desire: 'Si prie aux dieux que tant il[s] veuillent faire, / Que cecy soit de ton loz le sommaire' (Thus I pray to the gods that they make it so / That this be the epitome of your praise).[32] Similarly, Fontaine reconstructs the syntax as an exhortation: 'O Demophon, facent les Dieux parfaits, / Que ce soit là le chef de tes beaux faits' (O Demophoon, may the perfect gods see to it / That this be the foremost of your beautiful deeds).[33] L'Aubespine's Phyllis, on the other hand, does not wish for a particular outcome or plead with the gods that they make it so. She is an oracle who simply pronounces what God has ordained: 'Dieu veille que ce soit le plus clair de tes faicts' (v. 101) (God desires that this be the brightest of your deeds).

At this critical juncture, Phyllis shifts the focus away from her own predicament as well as the canonical narrative away from Demophoon's epic exploits, focusing instead upon his role as an unfaithful lover. Both the original Latin passage and L'Aubespine's French translation present an ekphrastic interlude that underscores a family lineage of infidelity. While the Latin poem describes a pair of statues erected in the centre of Athens: 'inter et Aegidas, media statuaris in urbe, / magnificus titulis stet pater ante suis' (2.67–8) ('In the midst of your city, even among the sons of Aegeus, go let yourself be statued, and let your mighty father be set there first, with record of his deeds'), L'Aubespine's Phyllis envisions an entire family gallery depicting Demophoon and Theseus, as well as an unspecified number of his ancestors: 'Et qu'entre tes ayeulx elevez et portraictz / Il paroisse en la place orné de cette gloire!' (vv. 102–3) (And among your exalted ancestors and portraits / May he appear in his place, gilded in glory). She enumerates Theseus' glorious triumphs that will be eternally preserved: his victories over Sciron, Procrustes, Sinus, the minotaurs and centaurs, as well as his escape from Hades. With more than a hint of sarcasm, she explains that Demophoon's image will follow that of his father, but that the son's inscription will simply read 'Celuy que vous voiez, pour preuve genereuse, / Trompa soubz beau semblant son hostesse amoureuse' (vv. 115–16) (He whom you see, as ample ordeal / Deceived under false pretences his enamoured hostess). Manipulative amorous treachery is the only trait Demophoon shares with his father:

> Ha! de tant de beaux faicts par ton pere achevez,
> Il n'en reste en ton ame aucuns traicts engravez,
> Fors de ses trahisons: Ariadne laissée
> Est le seul acte sien vivant en ta pensée[.]
>
> (vv. 117–20)

---

[32] Octavian de Saint-Gelais, *Les Vingt et Une Epistre* [*sic*] *d'Ovide* (Paris: Nicolas du Chemin, 1546), 10ᵛ.

[33] Fontaine, *Les XXI épitres d'Ovide*, 35.

56 MADELEINE DE L'AUBESPINE'S TRANSLATION OF *HEROIDES* 2

(Ah! Of the many great deeds achieved by your father / There remains not a single trait engraved in your soul / Except for his betrayals: Ariadne abandoned / Is the only one of his acts alive in your mind.)

Just as Theseus abandoned Ariadne, Demophoon, 'legitime heritier de l'infidelité' (v. 121) (true heir of infidelity), has emulated his father by deceiving Phyllis.

In their elegiac epistles, nearly all of Ovid's heroines accuse their beloveds of fickleness and infidelity, yet Phyllis is the most concerned with the rewriting of his-stories. In addition to revising Demophoon's narrative, she reframes those of Theseus and Ariadne as well. She also exhibits the greatest awareness of the stories of other abandoned women and, as Laurel Fulkerson has argued, is so imbued with the plights of these heroines that she misreads her own predicament. In the specific case of the Carthaginian queen, Phyllis

> is too empathetic a reader of Dido's story, and, given a few external similarities, cannot help but insert herself into it. That is why she uses vocabulary similar to Dido's, and why she so easily convinces herself to commit suicide. Phyllis, like other women of the *Heroides*, reads the poems of the corpus, and bases her reading—and writing—of the events in her own life on them.[34]

Although Fulkerson here speaks of Phyllis as if she were an independent author, the preceding passage eloquently and insightfully explains the complex relationship between Ovid and his heroine:

> Yet perhaps we look too quickly behind the mask of Phyllis to find Ovid, for she can be seen as the alluding author, even altering her own story to fit better into the mold of the abandoned woman; she belongs in the *Heroides* simply because she has already decided that she has been abandoned. Phyllis, then, is not similar to Dido solely because Ovid sees her that way, but because he has constructed a Phyllis who sees *herself* that way.[35]

Renaissance readers also identified similarities between Ovid's Dido and Phyllis and interpreted them in a variety of fashions.[36] As we shall see,

---

[34] Laurel Fulkerson, *The Ovidian Heroine as Author: Reading, Writing, and Community in the Heroides* (Cambridge: Cambridge University Press, 2005), 29.

[35] Ibid., 29.

[36] For some of the ways Renaissance writers and printers highlighted the similarities between the two epistles, see White, *Renaissance Postscripts*, 96–105.

Fontaine glosses Phyllis' textual 'confusion' by transforming her into an early modern prototype of Emma Bovary who is incapable of understanding her own situation. L'Aubespine's relationship with Phyllis, on the other hand, is similar to Ovid's: the abandoned heroine is a ventriloquized vehicle through which the author is able to showcase her own poetic gifts.

These differing visions of Phyllis' 'agency' and 'awareness' are captured in the translation of three words that generated significant disagreement among Renaissance commentators and translators, 'exitus acta probat', which occur in line 85 of *Heroides* 2. Much like another famous Renaissance misquotation—Machiavelli's alleged 'the ends justify the means'[37]—both passages deal with the relationship between a ruler's intent and the outcome of their actions as well as how these actions will be judged by their subjects. White reminds us that when inscribed in commonplace books and *florilegia*, the Latin saying was usually removed from the surrounding passage. In order to fully appreciate L'Aubespine's translation, it must be returned to its original context in which Phyllis responds to the criticisms she predicts her countrymen will address to her:

> atque aliquis 'iam nunc doctas eat,' inquit, 'Athenas;
> > armiferam Thracen qui regat, alter erit.
> exitus acta probat.' careat successibus, opto,
> > quisquis ab eventu fact notanda putat!   (2.83–6)

> (And someone says: 'Let her now away to learned Athens; to rule in armour-bearing Thrace another shall be found. The event proves well the wisdom of her course.' Let him come to naught, I pray, who thinks the deed should be condemned from its result.)

The added speech marks in the Loeb edition remind us that, in this passage, Phyllis is citing the words of others. Without the aid of modern punctuation it

---

[37] Towards the conclusion of Chapter 18 of *Il Principe*, Machiavelli states, 'Facci dunque uno principe di vincere e mantenere lo stato; è mezzi saranno sempre iudicati onorevoli e da ciascuno laudati; perché il vulgo ne va sempre preso con quello che pare, e con lo evento della cosa; e nel mondo non è se non vulgo.' This is not a moral or political argument justifying the use of any means necessary to achieve a desired end result, but rather an observation about the fickle and ignorant populace who will always judge based upon appearances. This unflattering depiction of the masses is often smoothed over in English translations, but Robert M. Adams's version captures something of the original tone: 'Let a prince, therefore, win victories and uphold his state; his methods will always be considered worthy, and everyone will praise them, because the masses are always impressed by the superficial appearance of things, and by the outcome of an enterprise. And the world consists of nothing but the masses.' Niccolò Machiavelli, *The Prince: A Revised Translation, Backgrounds, Interpretations, Marginalia*, trans. and ed. Robert M. Adams (New York: Norton, 1992), 49.

58   MADELEINE DE L'AUBESPINE'S TRANSLATION OF *HEROIDES* 2

was a more challenging passage and Renaissance commentators disagreed over its meaning.[38] Ubertinus Clericus (the Italian Ubertino Clerico da Crescentino) gets it right when he acknowledges that even the best-laid plans might go awry and proposes two possible interpretations for the verses. The first asserts that Phyllis is arguing that she should be judged by her intentions, by the desired result of her course of action, not the actual outcome. The second is influenced by the two ensuing lines—'at si nostra tuo spumescant aequora remo, / iam mihi, iam dicar consuluisse meis' (2.87–8) ('Ah, but if our seas should foam beneath your oar, then should I be said to have counselled well for myself, then well for my countrymen'). In this instance, Phyllis warns that potential critics should refrain from judgement as everything may still turn out for the best and they will be forced to change their tune. Both Clericus and Volscus specify in their commentaries that Demophoon does indeed return.

Clericus also extracts from Phyllis' predicament a general moral principle, which he then applies to contemporary clandestine marriages between unequal parties. Highlighting the peculiarity of such an appropriation, White reminds us that it was probably driven by the intended audience of Clericus's commentary:

> [H]e wrote not for a schoolroom readership, but for the upper classes of Casale. The case described by Clericus would have been more likely a matter of concern to this readership than to the schoolboys or students the other commentators write for; and indeed the question of clandestine marriage was hotly debated in the sixteenth century.[39]

Many of the Latin editions printed in France and abroad were accompanied by commentaries, and, as is typical of sixteenth-century humanist exegesis, these commentaries moved away from the moralizing tendencies of their medieval predecessors, serving instead a philological and pedagogical purpose. Renaissance commentaries glossed difficult words and passages, explained obscure geographical references, and provided useful historical and mythological information. Unlike many of his contemporaries who intended their commentaries to be used by schoolboys, however, Clericus published his text for a more general, bourgeois audience whom he clearly felt might benefit from his moral guidance as well as his clarifications of the text and aids to comprehension. The French writers who translated Ovid into their vernacular

---

[38] White, *Renaissance Postscripts*, 116–24.   [39] White, *Renaissance Postscripts*, 119.

envisioned an even wider audience than Clericus and other commentators who wrote in Latin. As we shall see, when women readers are explicitly included among the intended public, the misogynistic medieval moralizing tendencies, which Renaissance Latin commentators had largely abandoned, resurface. Phyllis is reduced, once again, to the counter-exemplum of *amor stultus*.

Saint-Gelais's translation of Ovid's text guides the reader towards his intended reading and moral judgement:

> Maint en y a qui aussi dit et compte,
> Ores voyez que la fin faict le compte.
> Certes Phyllis trop à vn se tenoit,
> C'est à bon droict si pis lui aduenoit,
> Ainsi de moy chascun la fin regarde[.][40]

(Many are those who say and believe / Now you see that it is the outcome that counts / Certainly Phyllis was too attached to this one / It is right that it go worse for her / This is how each regards my fate.)

Within these lines of reported speech, it is sometimes unclear who is speaking—Phyllis, her Thracian subjects, or Saint-Gelais himself. Rather than referring to the common practice of judging actions according to their outcome, Saint-Gelais transforms the passage into personal criticism and punishment of Phyllis, which do not appear in the original: 'Certes *Phyllis* trop à vn se tenoit / C'est à bon droict si pis *lui* aduenoit' [my emphasis]. When Saint-Gelais's Phyllis then concludes 'Ainsi de moy chascun la fin regarde', she articulates that this censure is both universal ('chascun') and personal ('de moy'). While she does not grammatically include herself among her critics, it is unclear whether she shares their perspective. Thus, rather than introducing a general philosophical and moral discussion about the relation of outcomes to intentions, Saint-Gelais's translation simply punishes Phyllis for her act.

Fontaine's translation, however, explicitly incorporates Phyllis' self-censure: 'On dit bien vray, la fin approuue l'œuvre' (They speak the truth, a work is justified by its outcome).[41] Here, the reproach that Phyllis anticipates will be lodged against her is spoken by a general 'on' that transcends time and place. This anticipated public repeats an eternal truth and, by adding that it 'dit bien

---

[40] Saint-Gelais, *Les Vingt et Une Epistre [sic] d'Ovide*, 11^r.
[41] Fontaine, *Les XXI épitres d'Ovide*, 36.

vray', Fontaine's Phyllis also suggests that those who would judge her actions by their outcome are justified. In both the original and Fontaine's French translation, Phyllis continues by entertaining the possibility that Demophoon may still return and by contemplating how this would affect her subjects' judgement. Instead of a viable possibility however, Fontaine views such musing as evidence of Phyllis' delusional state. Rather than a skilled orator or writer, Fontaine's Phyllis is reduced to the stereotypical woman scorned, blinded by passion who is incapable of accepting reality or comprehending her own situation. Should this transformation have escaped the notice of his readers, Fontaine includes the following explanation among the annotations found at the end of the elegiac epistle:

> Elle repond maintenant au propos precedent comme disant et confessant qu'il est bien vray que lon iuge des faits par la fin et issue mais toutesfois elle ne veut confesser que la fin et issue de son fait soit mauuaise, et qu'elle soit ia auenue, à savoir que Demophon l'ait du tout deliassee, et qu'il ne vueile plus retourner vers elle: ains au contraire elle presuppose que quelque cas, empeschement, ou infortune luy est auenue qui le retient et retarde de venir.[42]

> (She now responds to the preceding remarks stating and confessing that it is true that one judges acts by their end and outcome but nevertheless she does not want to admit that the end and outcome of her act might be bad and that it has already occurred, that is to say that Demophoon has abandoned her and that he no longer wishes to return to her: rather to the contrary she presumes that some event, impediment, or misfortune has occurred and prevents and delays him from coming.)

Fontaine thus returns to the medieval reading by which Phyllis is the *exemplum ex negatiuo* of *amor stultus* and serves as a moral warning to all women. Indeed, in the paratextual material, Fontaine makes explicit the connection between the poetic predicament of a classical heroine and the lived realities of his female contemporaries. In the *Preface svr l'epitre de Phyllis a Demophon*, Fontaine directly warns his women readers: 'toute femme doit bien ici prendre vn bel exemple, de ne mettre son amour trop ardemmment et folement en vn homme, quel qu'il soit: car la fin de folle amour iamais n'en fut bonne' (All women ought to heed this excellent example, not to love a man too

---

[42] Ibid., 44.

passionately or foolishly, whoever he may be: as the result of foolish love is never good).[43]

Madeleine de L'Aubespine, on the other hand, need not rely upon paratextual proselytizing to prop up her art. Her literary gifts suffice. Here is how she tackles the prickly passage surrounding *Heroides* II.85:

> On dict que par sa fin l'ouvrage est couronné,
> Mais celui puisse avoir succez mal fortuné
> Sans que jamais le ciel ses deseins favorise,
> Qui par l'evenement veult juger l'entreprise.

(vv. 133–6)

(They say that a work is crowned by its result / But he might have an unfortunate outcome / Without the heavens ever favouring his plans / He who wishes to judge a course of action by its outcome.)

L'Aubespine's translation shares similarities with Fontaine's. Both poets opt for the ambiguous French 'fin' as a translation of the Latin 'exitus'. Adopting the pronoun 'on', L'Aubespine's Phyllis also acknowledges that judging a work by its outcome is common practice. She does not, however, concede that this is correct. Instead, she presents a counter argument, introduced by the conjunction 'Mais'. Her choice of the adjective 'couronné' to conclude line 133 highlights her talents as a poet. She could just as easily have translated the line as 'On dict que par sa fin l'acte est toujours jugé' (They say that acts are always judged by their outcomes), but the construction concluding with 'couronné' is an elegant alternative since the outcome of Phyllis taking Demophoon as her husband was that he became King of Thrace. The use of the subjunctive 'puisse' in the following line echoes Ovid's subjunctive 'careat', but the erasure of the first-person 'opto' allows Phyllis (as well as L'Aubespine as author) to claim the role of a prophetic poet. It is a universal reminder that even the best-laid plans might go awry. This translation would certainly resonate with L'Aubespine's French contemporaries who were living at a time of shifting political landscapes punctuated by the unpredictable violence of civil war. Indeed, Montaigne was similarly reflecting upon an individual's inability to determine the outcome of actions in his contemporary essay, *Divers evenemens de mesme conseil*. Theirs was an audience sensitive to the

---

[43] Ibid., 29.

whims of Fortune, to the precariousness not just of love, but also of life and death.

Phyllis concludes her epistle by dictating the inscription that will appear on her tomb. The tension between love and the threat of self-effacement and loss of agency that lurked throughout the elegy now manifests itself in its most brutal form in her epitaph:

> PHYLLIDA DEMOPHOON LETO DEDIT HOSPES AMANTEM;
> ILLE NECIS CAUSAM PRAEBUIT, IPSA MANUM. (2.147–8)
> (DEMOPHOON 'TWAS SENT PHYLLIS TO HER DOOM;
> HER GUEST WAS HE, SHE LOVED HIM WELL.
> HE WAS THE CAUSE THAT BROUGHT HER DEATH TO PASS;
> HER OWN THE HAND BY WHICH SHE FELL.)

In these final two lines, Ovid's poetic talents and linguistic dexterity are on full display. The chiasmus in the first line (Phyllis—Demophoon—Demophoon—Phyllis) is inverted in the second with the evocation of 'ille' and 'ipsa'. This grammatical criss-crossing is further underscored by the verb 'praebuit', which governs two objects: the abstract 'causam' preceding it and the concrete 'manum' that follows. A further, semantic complexity is introduced due to the double meanings of 'hospes' as both guest and host. Ovid's epitaph thus implicates both Demophoon and Phyllis in the heroine's death.

Whereas Fontaine created a chiasmus enabling Demophoon to embrace Phyllis grammatically in the opening lines of the poem, L'Aubespine disentangles Ovid's syntax in the concluding epitaph in order to underscore clear subjecthood and agency:

> Demophoon fist mourir Phillis la malheureuse,
> Luy, fugitif estranger, son hostesse amoureuse.
> Il fut coupable seul de ce meurtre inhumain,
> Bien que pour l'accomplir elle y prestast la main.
>
> (vv. 239–42)

(Demophoon killed ill-fated Phyllis / He, a fleeing foreigner, his enamoured hostess / He alone was guilty of this barbaric murder / Although in order to carry it out she lent her hand.)

Demophoon and Phyllis are thrice mentioned, always in that order: first by their proper names, then under the guise of their elegiac roles ('fugitif estranger' and 'hostesse amoureuse'), and finally with the pronouns 'il' and 'elle'. The repeated evocation of Demophoon ('Demophoon', 'Luy', 'Il') at the beginning of three subsequent lines of verse creates a forceful indictment. Indeed, he is accused of bearing sole responsibility for the heroine's death: 'Il fut coupable *seul* de ce meurtre inhumain' [my emphasis]. The only mention of Phyllis' role in her suicide is introduced with a concessive conjunction in the final line, where it appears as an insignificant detail or afterthought.

The device of the epitaph creates the illusion that Phyllis is reading words inscribed on her tomb, lending this final verdict an air of authority. This is not the opinion of an embittered woman, but rather an impersonal, eternal pronouncement carved in stone. By erasing his epic exploits and rewriting his story, Phyllis ensures that Demophoon will be remembered by posterity as an unfaithful lover and murderer. She has thus inscribed herself within the long literary tradition of abandoned heroines. Yet, as Fulkerson has argued, Ovid's Phyllis becomes an abandoned heroine not 'solely because Ovid sees her that way, but because he has constructed a Phyllis who sees *herself* that way'. Throughout L'Aubespine's poem, the francophone Phyllis also rewrites her story, perhaps most significantly by recasting herself as a victim of homicide in the final couplet of the poem. These poetic and thematic innovations are, however, the creations of the historical author behind the fictitious heroine who sought to showcase her talents as a translator, Latinist, and poet.

* * *

Gargantua's letter to his son in François Rabelais's *Pantagruel* is often cited as an example of how women's intellectual accomplishments were considered a source of national pride during the Renaissance. Beyond the fictional Rabelaisian universe, in sixteenth-century Italy, 'exemplary learned women were widely viewed as an asset to cities and communities, extolled by local humanists and brought out to make speeches and recite in classical languages when visiting dignitaries passed through, as a means of demonstrating the general exemplarity of a location.'[44] To be a truly advanced and cultured civilization, a nation must count at least a few women among its literary elite. As Du Bellay himself explains in *La Deffence*: 'Voyla pourquoy les femmes mesmes aspiroint à ceste gloire d'eloquence et erudition, comme Sapho, Corynne, Cornelie, et un milier d'autres, dont les noms sont conjoings avecques la memoire des Grecz et Romains' (This is why even women aspired

---

[44] Abigail Brundin, 'Vittoria Colonna in Manuscript', in Abigail Brundin, Tatiana Crivelli, and Maria Serena Sapegno, eds, *A Companion to Vittoria Colonna* (Leiden: Brill, 2016), 39–68 (pp. 50–1).

64 MADELEINE DE L'AUBESPINE'S TRANSLATION OF *HEROIDES* 2

to this glory of eloquence and erudition, such as Sappho, Corinna, Cornelia, and a thousand others whose names are married to the memory of Greeks and Romans).[45]

In his 1587 sonnet dedicated to Madeleine de L'Aubespine, 'Sur les vers de Callianthe', Desportes singles out two of the three exemplary women writers cited by Du Bellay.[46] The first two quatrains contain the familiar praise employed several decades earlier by the male poets of the Pléiade in order to promote themselves, their verse, and one another:

> Myrtis, Corinne, et la Muse de Grece
> Sapphon, qu'Amour fist si haut soupirer,
> Tous leurs escrits n'oseroyent comparer
> A ces beaux vers qu'a chantez ma maistresse.
>
> Qui veut sçavoir de quels traits Amour blesse,
> Sans voir vos yeux trop prompts à martyrer,
> Lise ces vers qu'habile il sceut tirer
> De vostre esprit digne d'une deese.[47]
>
> (Myrtis, Corinna, and the Muse of Greece,
> Sappho, whom Love made sigh so loud,
> All their writings would not dare compare
> To the beautiful verse that my mistress has sung.
>
> Whoever wants to know with what arrows Love wounds,
> Without seeing your eyes, too quick to inflict pain,
> Let him read the verse that clever Love drew
> From your mind, worthy of a goddess.)[48]

The etymology of καλλιανθη (Callianthe) contains both beauty (kalé, kalós) as well as floral blossoms (anthé) and the Greek pseudonym was an apt choice for

---

[45] Joachim du Bellay, *La Deffence et illustration de la langue françoyse*, ed. Henri Chamard (1948; Paris: Société des Textes Français Modernes, 2000), 81–2.

[46] Prior to L'Aubespine's death in 1596, printed versions of this poem bore the more opaque title, 'Sur les vers d'un[e] Dame'. For an overview of how 'Callianthe' became identified as Madeleine de L'Aubespine, see Roger Sorg, 'Une fille de Ronsard, la bergère Rozette', *Revue des deux mondes* (1 January 1923), as well as Roger Sorg, ed., *Les Chansons de Callianthe, fille de Ronsard* (Paris: Léon Pichon, 1926), 8–9. See also Jacques Lavaud, *Un poète de cour au temps des derniers Valois: Philippe Desportes* (Paris: Droz, 1936), 308–11, 501–20, and, more recently, Isabelle de Conihout and Pascal Ract-Madoux, 'Ni Grolier, ni Mahieu: Laubespine', *Bulletin du Bibliophile*, 1 (2004), 63–88.

[47] Philippe Desportes, *Diverses amours et autres œuvres meslées*, ed. Victor E. Graham (Geneva: Droz, 1963), 161.

[48] Klosowska, *Madeleine de l'Aubespine: Selected Poems and Translations*, 58–59. Klosowska's translation.

a woman whose family name meant hawthorn and whose verse circulated in *florilegia*.[49] The inclusion of the Greek female poets Myrtis, Corinna, and Sappho in the first lines of the poem is significant in several respects. After giving Madeleine de L'Aubespine a Greek name, Desportes places her in the company of three illustrious historical women writers. Instead of comparing his beloved to mythological characters or allegories of physical beauty, he emphasizes that her literary prowess surpassed that of her ancient poetic predecessors. Moreover, Desportes's mention of Corinna evokes the fabled literary relationship between a Greek woman poet and her male competitor, the illustrious composer of odes, Pindar, with whom Ronsard himself invited comparisons. Summarizing a now-lost sonnet by Ronsard that was part of an exchange with L'Aubespine, Bernardino Peyron explained that the male poet assigned to her the role of Corinna: 'Ronsard replica con un'altra poesia in cui afferma che tale poetessa emula Corinna.'[50] Anna Klowsowska discovered the final tercet of the sonnet to which Peyron alludes and included it in her 2007 publication of L'Aubespine's works. These three verses contain Ronsard's praise of L'Aubespine cited in the introduction to this chapter:

> Si vollant vous tombez pour me vouloir trop croire
> Au moings vous acquerez pour tombe ceste gloire
> Q'une femme a vaincu les plus doctes françois.

> (If you fall in your flight, too willing to believe me,
> At least you will have earned this glory for your tomb
> That a woman surpassed the most learned French men.)[51]

While the other eleven lines of Ronsard's concluding poem have been lost, his sonnet initiating the exchange as well as L'Aubespine's *risposta* have survived. In these two poems, Ronsard and L'Aubespine engaged in collaborative self-fashioning. The figures of Icarus, Phaethon, and Apollo are central to the construction of their poetic personae in these sonnets, yet Peyron's mention of Corinna underscores the importance of the Greek poetess in the now-lost quatrains and first tercet of Ronsard's sonnet. Below the Italian word 'poetessa', Peyron subscripted 'poetriam' in parentheses and the inclusion of the Latin term may have served to underscore classicizing elements present in

---

[49] I wish to thank two of my favorite philologists, Ned Duval, for sharing with me the etymology of 'καλλιανθη', and Greg Mellen, for remarking upon the cleverness of l'Aubespine's pseudonym.
[50] Turin, Biblioteca Nazionale Universitaria, MS 8 Peyron Franc.
[51] Klosowska, *Madeleine de l'Aubespine: Selected Poems and Translations*, 58–9. Klosowska's translation.

Ronsard's lost verses. As such, Peyron's notes resemble the exegesis of Renaissance humanists who sought to clarify the poetics of Ovid's *Heroides*.

Returning to Desportes's sonnet, we encounter additional evidence of how L'Aubespine was inscribed by her contemporaries within literary culture. The second quatrain adds to the French imitations of *Canzoniere* 248 and further highlights the affinity between Ronsard and l'Aubespine. Petrarch sends 'Chi vuol veder quantunque po Natura / e'l Ciel' (Whoever wishes to see all that Nature and Heaven can do)[52] to contemplate Laura's beauty and virtue, while in *Les Antiquitez de Rome*, Du Bellay introduces the element of artifice and redirects 'Qui voudra voir tout ce qu'ont pu nature / *l'art* et le ciel' [my emphasis] (5.1–2) (Whoever wishes to see all that Nature, Art, and Heaven can do) to contemplate the ruins of Rome.[53] In a more narcissistic vein, Ronsard begins his *Amours* by instructing 'Qui voudra voyr comme un Dieu me surmonte' (1.1) (Whoever wishes to see how a god overcomes me) and 'Qui voudra voir une jeunesse prompte / A suyvre en vain l'object de son malheur' (1.5–6) (Whoever wishes to see a youth eager / To fruitlessly follow the source of their misfortune) to take a long hard look at the lovesick poet himself.[54] It is Ronsard's adaptation that appeals most to Desportes in his praise of L'Aubespine. He does not cast her as a beautiful passive object of contemplation in the tradition of Petrarch or Du Bellay, but rather compares her to Ronsard who chooses to make a spectacle of himself by exposing his versified amorous suffering to his readers. In her version of *Heroides* 2, Madeleine de L'Aubespine successfully showcased her talents as a Latinist, translator, and poet. Her erudition and literary gifts were praised by Desportes, Ronsard, and others who considered her an equal participant in the ambitious project of forging a new national literature in the vernacular. As I have argued elsewhere, when cast as Ronsard's *fille d'alliance*, L'Aubespine is granted the most prestigious poetic paternity imaginable in Renaissance France.[55] Thanks to Peyron's description of Ronsard's lost sonnet, we can now add to her list of literary avatars that of Corinna to Ronsard's Pindar.

---

[52] Francesco Petrarca, *Petrarch's Lyric Poems: The* Rime sparse *and Other Lyrics*, trans. and ed. Robert M. Durling (Cambridge, MA: Harvard University Press, 1976), 410–411. Durling's translation.

[53] Joachim Du Bellay, *Les Antiquitéz de Rome et Les Regrets* (Geneva: Droz, 1960).

[54] Pierre de Ronsard, *Oeuvres complètes*, ed. Jean Céard, Daniel Ménager, Michel Simonin (Paris: Gallimard, 1993).

[55] Jessica DeVos, 'Ronsard's Poetic Progeny: Fashioning Madeleine de l'Aubespine's Poetic Persona', *Yale French Studies*, 134 (2018), 126–44.

4

Belle and *Fidèle*? Women Translating Ovid in Early Modern France

Helena Taylor

Ovid's *Heroides* was one of the most influential Latin texts in the early modern period. It was appropriated for narratives of female virtue in the sixteenth century and is credited with influencing the rise of the epistolary novel in the eighteenth century.[1] In the seventeenth century the *Heroides* has been seen as significant in terms of its impact on the development of epistolary rhetoric, notably in the early decades;[2] its continued influence on catalogues of exemplary women, or *femmes fortes*;[3] and, later in the century in particular, its place in the *galant* literary culture that foregrounded sentimental expression and sociability, in which Ovid's other poems of sentiment, especially the *Amores*, also played a significant role.[4] The changing reception of the *Heroides* can be mapped onto the wider shift in Ovid's reception occurring across the seventeenth century in France whereby his work went from being predominantly part of an erudite 'savant' culture to being appropriated into the sociable, mixed-gender literary salon culture that dominated the second half of the century.[5] This was a culture in which women were prominent and in which contemporary—and national—taste took precedence over the hegemonic sway that ancient culture had enjoyed during the Renaissance.[6] This shifting

---

This chapter was written with the support of the Leverhulme Trust, which I gratefully acknowledge.

[1] For an example of the relation between the eighteenth-century epistolary novel and Ovid's *Heroides*, see the chapter by Séverine Clément-Tarantino in this volume (Chapter 6).
[2] Marie-Claire Chatelain, 'L'Héroïde comme modèle épistolaire: l'exemple des *Lettres Amoureuses* de Malleville', *Littératures Classiques*, 71 (2010), 129–51.
[3] On the *femmes fortes*, see Ian Maclean, *Woman Triumphant: Feminism in French Literature, 1610–1652* (Oxford: Clarendon Press, 1977).
[4] Delphine Denis, *Le Parnasse galant: institution d'une catégorie littéraire au XVII siècle* (Paris: Champion, 2001), 289–304.
[5] See Marie-Claire Chatelain, *Ovide savant, Ovide galant: Ovide en France dans la seconde moitié du XVII siècle* (Paris: Champion, 2008).
[6] On the Quarrel of the Ancients and Moderns, see Joan DeJean, *Ancients against Moderns: Culture Wars and the Making of a Fin de Siècle* (Chicago: University of Chicago Press, 1997) and Larry F. Norman, *The Shock of the Ancient: Literature and History in Early Modern France* (Chicago: University of Chicago Press, 2011).

Helena Taylor, Belle *and* Fidèle? *Women Translating Ovid in Early Modern France* In: *Ovid in French: Reception by Women from the Renaissance to the Present*. Edited by: Helena Taylor and Fiona Cox, Oxford University Press.
© Oxford University Press 2023. DOI: 10.1093/oso/9780192895387.003.0004

68 WOMEN TRANSLATING OVID IN EARLY MODERN FRANCE

literary landscape in turn had a considerable effect on translation theory and practice, as interpretative versions—close to what Lawrence Venuti would call 'domesticating', known as 'belles infidèles' at the time—became the fashion.[7]

In this chapter I want to explore the translation by women of one single letter, *Heroides* 13, from Laodamia, the faithful young Greek bride, to her husband, Protesilaus; I will examine what the translations reveal about translation theory, literary taste, and the aesthetic and ethical demands placed on women in the public sphere within this changing cultural context. To do so, I shall consider translations by three women: Marie de Gournay, whose *Epistre de Laodamie, traduicte d'Ovide*, first published in 1626, is her only translation from Ovid's *Heroides*, and indeed of Ovid, although she translated Virgil, Tacitus, Sallust, and Cicero;[8] Madeleine de Scudéry (and her brother, Georges), whose co-authored *Femmes illustres* (1642) includes seven Ovidian heroines, one of whom is Laodamia;[9] and Marie-Jeanne L'Héritier, mostly known now for her fairy tales in the late seventeenth century, who published the first female-authored complete translation of Ovid's *Heroides* in 1732, two years before her death.[10] Although there were a number of translations of Ovid's *Heroides* in England,[11] including the best-known multi-authored *Epistles* by Dryden and others (for which Aphra Behn translated the letter from Oenone to Paris), the appeal of these letters to women translators seems to be a French phenomenon.[12]

Laodamia, immortalized briefly in English by Wordsworth's nineteenth-century poem,[13] is not the best-known figure from the *Heroides* or from the

---

[7] Lawrence Venuti, *The Translator's Invisibility* (London: Routledge, 1995).

[8] Marie de Gournay, 'Epistre de Laodamia à Protesilaus', in Jean-Claude Arnould, Évelyne Berriot, Claude Blum, Anna Lia Franchetti, Marie-Claire Thomine, and Valerie Worth-Stylianou, eds, *Œuvres complètes*, 2 vols (Paris: Champion, 2002), ii, 1455–64. All references hereafter are to this edition, with page numbers given in the body of the text. Unless otherwise stated, all translations of this and other French sources are my own.

[9] Georges [and Madeleine] de Scudéry, *Les Femmes illustres ou les harangues héroïques* (Paris: A. de Sommaville, 1642). All references hereafter are to this edition, with page numbers given in the text.

[10] Marie-Jeanne L'Héritier, *Les Epîtres héroïques d'Ovide* (Paris: Brunet fils, 1732). All references hereafter are to this edition, with page numbers given in the text. See the chapter by Océane Puche for further discussion of L'Héritier's translation (Chapter 5).

[11] See Stuart Gillespie and Robert Cummings, 'A Bibliography of Ovidian Translations and Imitations in English', *Translation and Literature*, 13 (2004), 207–18.

[12] See Katherine Heavey, 'Aphra Behn's *Oenone to Paris*: Ovidian Paraphrase by Women Writers', *Translation and Literature*, 23 (2014), 303–20 (p. 315); and Sarah Annes Brown, 'Women Translators', in Stuart Gillespie and David Hopkins, eds, *The Oxford History of Literary Translation in English* (Oxford: Oxford University Press, 2005), 111–20.

[13] On Wordsworth's Laodamia, see Philip Hardie, 'Wordsworth's Translation of *Aeneid* 1–3 and the Earlier Tradition of English Translations of Virgil', in Susanna Braund and Zara Martirosova Torlone, eds, *Virgil and his Translators* (Oxford: Oxford University Press, 2018), 318–30.

Greek myths which inspired Ovid: Natalie Haynes feared Laodamia's marginal story would not survive the edits of her novel *A Thousand Ships* (2019).[14] This was also the case in the early modern period: Laodamia does not feature in, for instance, Boccaccio's *De mulieribus claris* [Concerning Famous Women] (1361–2), or in the majority of early modern exemplary manuals for women;[15] nor is she the most frequently translated heroine in selected versions of Ovid's epistles by male translators in the seventeenth century.[16] However, Laodamia proves an important object of study firstly because she is the *only* female figure translated by all the seventeenth-century women who translate some or any of Ovid's epistles;[17] and secondly, and relatedly, because the French Laodamia poses specific questions about the relationship between female virtue, translation practice, and gendered notions of literary taste.[18] This is a period that saw, from roughly the middle of the seventeenth century, the coining of the gendered term 'belles infidèles' (unfaithful beauties) as a contested but vaunted translation practice;[19] the feminizing of taste and of proper and modest writing with the rise of salon culture; and the development of the gendered concept of 'belles lettres', a definition of literary writing that separated it from 'learned' and religious writing and proved both enabling and restrictive for women writers.[20] What is the relationship between Laodamia as a figure of fidelity, such changing literary practices, and the way in which these women chose to translate this particular epistle? How might feminist translation theory, which has attended to the gendering of translation metaphors, enhance our analysis

---

[14] Natalie Haynes, interview on 'Women's Hour', BBC Radio Four, 2 May 2019. https://www.bbc.co.uk/programmes/m0004mc9.

[15] She is not mentioned in Jacques Du Bosc's *L'honnête femme* (Paris: Billaine, 1623), which uses a number of women from Ovid's *Metamorphoses*; nor is she in Pierre Le Moyne's influential *Galerie des femmes fortes* (Paris: Compagnie des libraires du Palais, 1663).

[16] She does not feature in the selective translations by L.-J. Bellefleur, *Les Amours d'Ovide, avec . . . les Épistres de Sapho à Phaon et de Canacé à son frère Macarée* (Paris: J. Petit-Pas, 1621); Claude Gaspard Bachet de Mézeriac, *Les Epistres d'Ovide* (Bourg-en-Bresse: J. Tainturier, 1626); Nicolas Renouard, *Les Métamorphoses d'Ovide avec . . . quelques epistres d'Ovide* (Paris: Vve. Langelier, 1619); Thomas Corneille, *Pièces choisies d'Ovide* (Paris: G. de Luynes, 1670); [Jean Barrin], *Les Epistres et toutes les élégies amoureuses d'Ovide* (Paris: C. Barbin, 1676).

[17] Chatelain shows the influence of the Medea and Canace letters on the poetry of the Comtesse de Suze, Mme de Lauverge, and Mme de la Sablière: Chatelain, *Ovide savant*, 561–75.

[18] For a discussion of Marguerite Yourcenar's rewriting of Laodamia in her 1936 novel, *Feux*, see Florence Klein's chapter in this volume (Chapter 11).

[19] When Perrot Ablancourt published his translation of Lucian in 1654, Gilles Ménage is said to have observed: 'Lorsque la version de Lucien de M. d'Ablancourt parut, bien des gens se plaignirent de ce qu'elle n'était pas fidèle. Pour moi je l'appelai la belle infidèle, qui était le nom que j'avais donné étant jeune à une de mes maitresses' (When M. d'Ablancourt's version of Lucian was published, many people complained that it was not faithful. I call it the 'unfaithful beauty' which is a name I gave to one of my mistresses when I was younger). *Menagiana*, 4 vols (Paris: F. Delaulne, 1715), ii, 186. See Roger Zuber, *Les 'Belles Infidèles' et la formation du goût classique* (Paris: Armand Colin, 1968).

[20] Myriam Dufour-Maître, 'Les "Belles" et les Belles-Lettres: femmes, instances du féminin et nouvelles configurations du savoir', in John D. Lyons and Cara Welch, eds, *Le Savoir au XVIIe siècle* (Tübingen: Gunter Narr, 2003), 35–64.

70 WOMEN TRANSLATING OVID IN EARLY MODERN FRANCE

of the early context of such a phenomenon?[21] What does comparison of translations from three different moments across the seventeenth and early eighteenth centuries reveal about Ovidian reception in relation to the status of antiquity, 'national taste', and the context for women writing in this period?

* * *

Laodamia's letter to Protesilaus is the thirteenth epistle of Ovid's *Heroides*, written shortly after their wedding, once Protesilaus has left for Troy with the Greek fleet and is stationed en route at Aulis, where unfavourable winds are preventing the troops from setting sail. It is characterized by premonitions and a suspicious fear of the oracle which states that the first to set foot on Trojan soil would be the first to die: the letter is primarily a warning that Protesilaus not hasten ashore and, more generally, that he avoid the worst of combat and return home unscathed (needless to say, the letter is also characterized by its irony as this warning is little heeded: he is the first to alight and his early death is mentioned briefly by Homer in the *Iliad* 2.695). In the final section of the letter, Laodamia explains that she has made a wax statue of Protesilaus which she will love in his place; this extends the themes of dreams, visions, and substituted presence which punctuate the letter. The statue substitute also, as Philip Hardie shows, redoubles the letter's irony as the story beyond Ovid's version has it that after Protesilaus died, he was allowed to return from the Underworld to be with Laodamia again briefly in the liminal state of living death;[22] she could so little endure his death a second time that she stabbed herself.[23] Laodamia's fidelity and the innocence of their love are contrasted implicitly throughout the letter with the infidelity of Helen, whom Laodamia describes as 'turpis adultera' (shameful adulterer) (13.133). As Hardie argues, Laodamia stands out from the other *Heroides* because 'unlike most of [the letters], Laodamia's letter contains no trace of suspicion or jealousy' and she and Protesilaus are 'the perfectly matched couple'.[24]

Laodamia's story was primarily conveyed to early modern readers through Ovid's version, but other depictions also shaped how she was seen, in turn affecting the translations of Ovid's epistles; in all these depictions, her fidelity and innocence are emphasized.[25] Her story is told in Catullus 68, where the

---

[21] Lori Chamberlain, 'Gender and the Metaphorics of Translation', in Lawrence Venuti, ed., *The Translation Studies Reader* (New York and London: Routledge, 2000), 314–42.

[22] Philip Hardie, *Ovid's Poetics of Illusion* (Cambridge: Cambridge University Press, 2002), 132.

[23] This resurrection is thought to have been the subject of the lost play by Euripides, *Protesilaus*, and is mentioned in Propertius 1.19.7–10 and in Pliny the Elder, *Naturalis Historia*, 16.88.

[24] Hardie, *Ovid's Poetics of Illusion*, 132.

[25] See James Reeson, *Ovid Heroides 11, 13, & 14: A Commentary* (Leiden: Brill, 2001), 162.

Laodamia and Protesilaus story is an example of true love, as Catullus makes a 'wishful comparison', to quote Oliver Lyne, between his own girlfriend and the Greek bride (in Catullus 68.131–2).[26] She features briefly in Virgil's *Aeneid*, where she is in the Mourning Fields of the Underworld with those, including Dido, 'consumed' by 'stern Love' (6.442). Hyginus, an important reference in France from the early sixteenth century onwards, includes Laodamia along with Penelope and Hecuba, under the heading 'quae castissimae fuerunt' (the most faithful women).[27] Singling Laodamia out for her fidelity occurred in later works: for instance, Jean de Vives in his influential *The Education of a Christian Woman* (1523) lists Laodamia in the chapter detailing 'How a woman should behave towards her husband'.[28] She also features as an example of fidelity in the mid-seventeenth-century novel about salon culture, *La Précieuse; ou le mystère de la ruelle* (1658), by cultural critic, Michel de la Pure;[29] and her distinctive faithfulness is echoed in the preface to the 1697 translation of the *Heroides* by Etienne de Martignac: she and Penelope are singled out as two who 'ont aimé fidèlement leurs maris pendant une longue absence' (faithfully loved their husbands during a long absence).[30] Laodamia, therefore, with her fidelity and innocence, proves an exemplary figure, both in her own right and compared to the other women of the *Heroides*.

Despite her presence in Catullus and Hyginus, Laodamia was primarily known to French readers through Ovid's *Heroides*; a brief account of its translations, and the changes in taste and practice they demonstrate, is useful here to contextualize the versions by Gournay, Scudéry, and L'Héritier. After the two major verse translations in the sixteenth century, that of Octavian de Saint-Gelais (1499), which saw at least nineteen editions between 1500 and 1550, and of Charles Fontaine (1552), who only translated the first eleven letters and not Laodamia's epistle,[31] the translations of the seventeenth and early eighteenth centuries fall into two broad categories. The first are the interpretative and sometimes selective verse translations, including those produced in the early decades of the seventeenth century by a group known

---

[26] See R. O. A. M. Lyne, 'Love and Death: Laodamia and Protesilaus in Catullus, Propertius, and Others', *The Classical Quarterly*, 48 (1998), 200–12 (p. 206).

[27] Hyginus, *Fabulae*, ed. Peter K. Marshall (Munich; Leipzig: K. G. Saur, 2002).

[28] Jean de Vives, *The Education of a Christian Woman*, ed. and trans. Charles Fantazzi (Chicago: Chicago University Press, 2000), 189.

[29] Michel de Pure, *La Précieuse ou le Mystère de la Ruelle* (1656–1660), ed. Myriam Dufour-Maître (Paris: Champion, 2010), 475.

[30] Etienne de Martignac, *Les Œuvres d'Ovide*, 9 vols (Lyon: H. Molin, 1697), i.

[31] Octavian de Saint-Gelais, *Les espistres de Ovide translatées de latin en français* (Paris: Verard, 1499); Charles Fontaine, *Les Epistres d'Ovide* (Lyon: Rollet, 1552). For a discussion of these translations, see Jessica DeVos's chapter in this volume (Chapter 3).

72 WOMEN TRANSLATING OVID IN EARLY MODERN FRANCE

as the 'illustres bergers', among which is the multi-authored version by Du Perron, de Lingendes, de La Brosse and Hédelin (1616), as well as a number of fictional responses by the male heroes;[32] the selective *galant* versions by Thomas Corneille (1670) and Jean Barrin (1676), neither of whom translates Laodamia's letter; and Henri Richer's 1723 verse translation of eight letters, including Laodamia's, and his composition of two responses (from Hippolyte and Protesilaus).[33] The second are the prose translations: by Michel de Marolles (1661); by Etienne de Martignac (1697), as part of his translation of Ovid's complete works; and by Jean-Baptiste de Bellegarde who included ten prose epistles, including Laodamia's, in his translation of Ovid's *Metamorphoses* of 1701.[34]

In general terms, the verse versions tend to prioritize contemporary aesthetics and the use of French, and the prose versions usually function as supplements to the original and contain helpful commentary and notes (indeed, Marolles and Martignac include a parallel Latin text). Broadly, although not always perfectly, the different approaches can be mapped onto the major 'culture war' of seventeenth-century France, the Quarrel of the Ancients and Moderns, with the Ancients advocating the supremacy of classical culture and the Moderns that of French culture.[35]

This debate is also played out across the versions by the three women studied here: Gournay's prose translation reacts against modernizing linguistic and poetic practices, and contrasts with the Modern stance present in the version by the Scudérys and L'Héritier. All three female authors adopt self-conscious ideological positions; but they also inject into this cultural debate the vexed question of their positions as female translators and writers. As Danielle Clarke has argued, translation was paradoxically both a 'culturally authoritative form of literary production' and a 'seemingly acceptable activity for women'; far from the modern (contested) concept of the translator as 'invisible', translators and translation were lauded aspects of early modern intellectual life.[36] As Jessica DeVos explores in the previous chapter, female

[32] Du Perron and others, *Les Epîtres d'Ovide* (Paris: Du Bray, 1616). See Paul White, *Renaissance Postscripts: Responding to Ovid's 'Heroides' in Sixteenth-Century France* (Columbus: Ohio State University Press, 2009), 215–23.

[33] Henri Richer, *Epistres choisies des Héroïnes d'Ovide* (Paris: E. Ganeau, 1723).

[34] Michel de Marolles, *Les Epistres Heroides d'Ovide* (Paris: Veuve P. Lamy, 1661); Jean-Baptiste de Bellegarde, *Les Métamorphoses d'Ovide* (Paris: P. Emery, 1701).

[35] On the nuanced positions of these translators, see Chatelain, *Ovide savant*, 40–61. On the contemporary version of this translation debate in France, see Séverine Clément-Tarantino, 'The *Aeneid* and "Les Belles Lettres"', in Susanna Braund and Zara Martirosova Torlone, eds, *Virgil and his Translators* (Oxford: Oxford University Press, 2018), 209–23.

[36] Danielle Clarke, 'Translation', in Laura Lunger Knoppers, ed., *The Cambridge Companion to Early Modern Women's Writing* (Cambridge: Cambridge University Press, 2010), 167–80.

translators had a key role to play in the nation-building endeavour of Renaissance translation in France (albeit one less recognized by scholarship). And yet, as I will explore, for all this acceptability, translation of classical texts in particular, with the male-gendered knowledge this ostensibly reveals, posed specific challenges for women in a culture that increasingly valued female modesty in print. Building on recent work by Hilary Brown which stresses the need to challenge the notion of a 'female tradition' of translation, pushing against the premise that women translate according to their gender identity and that their work is coloured by marginalization and subversiveness, in what follows I demonstrate that while the three women examined here were all negotiating expectations of their sex in print, they take a wide range of positions.[37] I will use Laodamia as a case study to track the changing ethos of women's writing practice across the century, and stress the importance of ideology, taste, and poetics over allegiances based on gender: while there may be an alternative, non-male history of early modern Ovidian reception, it was not constructed as such at the time.

Maire de Gournay's 'Faithful' Laodamia

Laodamia's letter is the only Ovidian text translated by Marie de Gournay; but translation was a central part of her intellectual practice. Not only did she translate the best part of four books of the *Aeneid* and selections of Tacitus, Sallust, and Cicero, but she also produced translations of the Latin quotations in Montaigne's *Essais*, of which she was the first posthumous editor.[38] Her discussions of translation theory in the long prefaces that accompany her translations, and its implementation in her practice, were also central to her arguments about poetics and language, which were the subjects of a number of her essays.[39] Gournay's version of Laodamia's epistle and its accompanying preface are no exception to her practice.[40] Her translation

---

[37] Hilary Brown, *Women and Early Modern Cultures of Translation: Beyond the Female Tradition* (Oxford: Oxford University Press, 2022), 8. For other recent studies on the intersection between feminism, gender, and translation, see Luise von Flotow and Hala Kamal, eds, *The Routledge Handbook of Translation, Feminism and Gender* (London: Routledge, 2020); and Helen Vassallo, *Towards a Feminist Translator Studies: Intersectional Activism in Translation and Publishing* (London: Routledge, 2022).

[38] Michel de Montaigne, *Les Essais de Michel de Montaigne, édition nouvelle: enrichie d'annotations en marge, du nom des Autheurs citez, de la version du Latin d'iceux* (Paris: Sevestre, 1617).

[39] For instance, Gournay, 'Sur la version des poètes antiques, ou des metaphores', *Œuvres complètes*, i, 930–62.

[40] On the importance of prefaces, see Marie-Alice Belle, 'Locating Early Modern Women's Translations: Critical and Historiographical Issues', *Renaissance and Reformation*, 35/4 (2012), 5–23.

74   WOMEN TRANSLATING OVID IN EARLY MODERN FRANCE

is dedicated to her cousin, Madame de Peray, Marie de Saint Mesmin, and is dated 1608; it was first published in 1626 in the first edition of her complete works, *L'Ombre de la Damoiselle de Gournay*, after her cousin had died, as an additional note of homage explains. In the two-page dedication addressed to her cousin while she was still alive, it becomes clear why Gournay chose the Laodamia letter: Gournay's homage goes beyond simply dedicating the work to her cousin; it is embedded within the translation itself. She has chosen Laodamia's letter because of the example of fidelity that she represents; this is paralleled with the fidelity and trust of Gournay's friendship with Peray:

> La raison qui m'a conviée à faire choix de cette Piece et la vous offrir, c'est que vous et moy nous sommes tousjours aymées, sinon de mesme ardeur et mesme sorte, au moins de mesme constance et sincerité que Protesilaus et cette Infante.   (p. 1456)
>
> (The reason I decided to translate this letter and offer it to you is that you and I have long loved each other, if not with the same ardour or in the same way, at least with the same constancy and sincerity as Protesilaus and this young woman.)

Laodamia's innocence, her 'constancy' and 'sincerity', make her a perfect model with which to praise the friendship between Gournay and her cousin.

If compared to the prefaces Gournay writes to accompany her translation of the *Aeneid* or the Latin prose texts, the intimacy of this letter and the importance placed on friendship is all the more striking. The dedicatees of other translations are male translators (Du Perron; Berthaut) or public figures (the prelate, Monseigneur de Gélas), resulting in a public tone and the author's self-conscious position and ethos. These prefaces tend to be dominated by statements about Gournay's translation practice and poetics, as well as assertions of her own role as a translator—the 'moy traductrice'—which are diffident but also defiant in the face of male authority.[41] In contrast, as we have just seen, her dedication to her cousin is marked by intimacy and a private voice. However, that is not to suggest that the difference in prefatory tone makes for a difference in translation; on the contrary, this translation is a further example of the accurate translation practice so consistently and fervently championed by Gournay: Laodamia's 'fidelity' to Protesilaus becomes a clear guiding principle for Gournay's 'fidelity' to Ovid's original text. Such

---

[41] See Jean-Philippe Beaulieu, '"Moy Traductrice": le façonnement de la figure auctoriale dans le paratexte des traductions de Marie de Gournay', *Renaissance and Reformation*, 35/4 (2012), 119–34.

'fidelity' or accuracy was central to Gournay's legitimizing of her role as translator: it acted as proof of her knowledge of Latin.

Like that of Madeleine de L'Aubespine examined in the previous chapter, Gournay's translation is marked by a precise closeness to the original text and a related defence of her ability as a woman to read Latin. Such a defence occurs explicitly a number of times across her work.[42] Her version of Ovid was also a chance for her to demonstrate principles of translation of which she was a fervent defender: namely, accuracy, and maintaining the original context and specific terminology (even if considered unseemly, unfashionable, or specialist). This defence is part of her larger embattled and fervent championing of linguistic practices—such as particular rhyme forms and the use of foreign words—which were, as she saw it, under threat by the influential poet François de Malherbe and the modernizing and nationalizing aesthetics of linguistic purification that he and his circle espoused. Her views on translation are aired in a number of her other prefaces. In the *Avis sur la traduction de la seconde Philippique de Ciceron*, which directly follows her Ovid letter in her complete works, she deplores translators who add interpretative explanations; she also resists the trend of adapting ancient texts according to contemporary taste (a version of 'domestication' in Venuti's terms) and blames these tendencies on accommodations aimed at female readers, resisting such 'feminine' civilizing of language.[43]

With this in mind, it is no surprise that Gournay's translation of Ovid demonstrates accuracy and a frank approach: accuracy was proof of her ability; frankness was her rejection of such polite aesthetics. This approach sets her work apart from the verse versions of Laodamia's letter by Octavian de Saint-Gelais and by Du Perron et al. who make no attempt to offer a line-by-line account.[44] Gournay's frankness is particularly evident in her approach to the erotic elements of this epistle; its striking nature will become apparent as we explore the versions from later in the century. Gournay establishes this subtle eroticism in her summary that precedes the translation; here, unlike any other French version, she emphasizes the suddenness of Protesilaus' departure on their wedding night: 'Protesilaus...se desroba du lict de Laodamia la propre nuict de leurs nopces' (p. 1458) (Protesilaus left Laodamia's bed the very night of their marriage). There are two particularly erotic moments in Laodamia's letter, in which their physical relationship is emphasized: 'nox

---

[42] In the 'Lettre à Monseigneur de Gélas, Sur la version de deux Oraisons Latines' and in the 'Copie de la Vie de la Damoiselle de Gournay', in Gournay, *Œuvres complètes*, ii, 1436, 1862.

[43] See also Dufour-Maître, 'Les "Belles" et les Belles-Lettres', 60.

[44] Octavian de Saint–Gelais, *Les vingt et une epistres d'Ovide* (Paris: Nicolas du Chemin, 1546).

76 WOMEN TRANSLATING OVID IN EARLY MODERN FRANCE

grata puellis / quarum suppositus colla lacertus habet' ('the night which is welcome to young women whose lovers place an embracing arm under their necks') (vv. 104–5), and:

> Quando ego, te reducem cupidis amplexa lacertis
> languida laetitia solvar ab ipsa mea?
> quando erit, ut lecto mecum bene iunctus in uno
> militae referas splendida facta tuae
> quae mihi dum referes, quamvis audire iuvabit
> multa tamen capies oscula, multa dabis
>
> > (*Heroides* 13.115–22)

(When will I clasp you, having returned safely,
in my eager arms and lose myself in a languishing embrace?
When will you join me again close on the couch,
telling me of your glorious deeds in the field?
And while you are telling me about them, though it will be a delight
  to hear
You will snatch many kisses and give me many in return.)[45]

Gournay translates the first as 'nuict si plaisante aux jeunes espouses, qui jettent les bras espandus à l'entour d'un col chery' (p. 1462) (the night so pleasant to newlyweds who throw arms around a cherished neck), transposing with moral correctness 'espouses' for 'puella' but maintaining the physical reference. She translates the second description line for line, and she even makes the kisses more explicit by repeating the word 'baiser' (p. 1462), where the Latin version does not. This uncompromising and accurate approach is evident throughout her translation; her closeness to Ovid's version is also evidenced by her attempts to replicate not only the content but also the style of the translation. She keeps the alliteration of 'vertite vela' ('reverse your sails') (134), adding repetition for emphasis: 'tournez, tournez les voiles vers Inachie' (p. 1463), and where she slightly loses the inauspicious force of 'mali' (86) in her translation as 'desastre' (p. 1461) she then makes up for it with 'sinistre augure' (p. 1461) for 'offenso... signa' (88).

For all its closeness, her translation also contains subtle developments of Laodamia's character and an emphasis that is lost in later versions. This is

---

[45] Ovid, *Heroides and Amores*, trans. Grant Showerman (1977; Cambridge, MA: Harvard University Press, 1996). All subsequent Latin citations and English translations of the *Heroides* refer to this edition and will be indicated by verse number in the text.

particularly evident in the final sequence of the epistle. Where a participle, 'amplexus' (154), is used to describe the wax model of Protesilaus being embraced in Ovid's version, Gournay uses an active verb: 'je luy feray des caresses' (p. 1464) (I will caress him). Gournay translates the term 'comitem' ('companion') (163) as 'je te veux estre compaigne par tout' (p. 1464) (I want to be your companion wherever you go), where later translators give Laodamia a less equal position with the verb *suivre* (to follow). Finally, where Ovid's final line closes with an emphasis on Protesilaus: 'si tibi cura mei, sit tibi cura tui!' ('if you care for me, then care for yourself') (166), Gournay inverts this: 'Prends soucy de toi, si tu le prends de moy' (p. 1464) (Take care of yourself if you have any care for me). While subtle, Gournay's nuanced insistence on Laodamia's agency, where possible within the bounds of her own translation practice, chimes with her *De l'Égalité des hommes et des femmes* (1622), an essay on the importance of women acquiring equal education and their equal ability to do so; her 'faithful' translation of Ovid's faithful heroine is also a chance to champion women's education and linguistic abilities by demonstrating her own.

This notion of fidelity, and Gournay's own stake in it, is echoed in her other literary use of Laodamia, in the *Envoy de l'Epistre de Laodamie, version d'Ovide*, dedicated to the Queen Regent, Marie de Medici, published in the 1626 edition of her work and dated to 1610–14. Laodamia here becomes a figure for Marie de Medici, widowed in 1610 following the assassination of Henri IV. Addressed to Laodamia/Medici, the *envoi* is used to praise the Queen Regent's fidelity: 'vous pleurez un mary perdu...Et le Ciel veut que vous viviez / Pour un miroir d'amour constant' (p. 1829) (you grieve for a lost husband...and the heavens wish you to live on as a mirror of constant love). Just as in the *Epistre*, Laodamia's fidelity is mapped onto that of Gournay's female dedicatee, but it also implicates Gournay herself: as faithful subject to her Queen Regent, as faithful friend to her cousin, and as faithful translator of Ovid.

Rhetoric and Gender in the *Femmes illustres*

Where Gournay's female dedicatee was a specific individual, the Scudérys' *Femmes illustres*, a series of some forty *harangues* by mythical and historical women, published nearly twenty years later, is dedicated 'aux dames' (to ladies). Seven of the forty figures come from the *Heroides*: Sapho, Pénélope, Briseis, Œnone, Didon, Laodamie, and Hélène, and the debt of these letters,

78 WOMEN TRANSLATING OVID IN EARLY MODERN FRANCE

and the collection as a whole, to Ovid has been noted by critics.[46] The authorship of this text is much less clear than in Gournay's case: published in 1642, under the name of Georges de Scudéry, it is attributed to both Georges and his sister, Madeleine,[47] who co-authored with Georges a long novel, *Artamène ou la grand Cyrus* (1649–53), ten years later, also published under his name. Where Gournay emphasized the personal fidelity and morality of Laodamia, the Scudérys turn all the women into moral examples, drawing on both the traditional reception of this text and the contemporary interest in catalogues of illustrious or powerful women.[48] They also, crucially, emphasize their eloquence and rhetoric as the *harangues* are oral, not epistolary.[49]

The preface casts these letters as models of female rhetoric, developing an influential notion of feminine literary style. This rhetoric is characterized by its 'naturalness' and non-learned nature and is explicitly distinguished from that of the university or classroom:

J'ay tasché de faire mes Heroines eloquentes; mais je n'ay pas jugé que l'eloquence d'une Dame deust estre celle d'un Maistre aux Arts. Les ruelles et les classes, les Colleges et le Louvre, la Cour et l'Université ont des manieres aussi differentes que si c'estoient des peuples fort éloignez, et quiconque feroit voir une Demoiselle du pais Latin aux jeunes Gens de la Court, ils la regarderoient comme un Monstre et la traitteroient de ridicule. (n.p.)

(I have tried to make my heroines eloquent; but I do not think that a woman's eloquence should be that of a school master. The salon and the classroom, schools and the Louvre, the court and the university have such different manners that they seem to be occupied by entirely different people; if anyone showed a young woman from the Latin land to the young people of the court, they would regard her as a monster and ridicule her.)

---

[46] Donna Kuizenga, 'L'Arc de triomphe des dames: Héroïsme dans *Les Femmes illustres* de Madeleine et Georges de Scudéry', in Alain Niderst, ed., *Les Trois Scudéry* (Paris: Klincksieck, 1993), 301–10; Marie-Claire Chatelain, 'L'Héroïde chez Mademoiselle de Scudéry', in Delphine Denis and Anne-Elisabeth Spica, eds, *Mlle de Scudéry: une femme de lettres au XVIIe siècle* (Arras: Artois Presses Université, 2002), 41–58. See also Helena Taylor, '"L'Adorateur du beau sexe": Madeleine de Scudéry et Marie-Jeanne L'Héritier, lectrices d'Ovide', in Stefania Cerrito and Marylène Possamaï-Pérez, eds, *Ovide en France du Moyen Âge à nos jours* (Paris: Classiques Garnier, 2020), 243–63.

[47] See Kuizenga, 'L'Arc de triomphe', 301.

[48] An extreme example of this moralizing approach is François Habert's mid-sixteenth-century Christian rewriting of the letters, changing authors and recipients to biblical figures. François Habert, *Les Epistres héroïdes, tres salutaires pour servir d'exemple à toute ame fidele* (Paris: M. Fezandet, 1550).

[49] On the orality of Ovid's *Heroides*, see Howard Jacobson, *Ovid's Heroides* (Princeton, NJ: Princeton University Press, 1974).

Throughout the *Femmes illustres* this feminine rhetorical space is also explicitly one of authority and influence. This is evident from the Sapho letter, which is the best known and thought to be by Madeleine de Scudéry alone.[50] In this much commented upon letter, Sapho urges Erinne, a female friend, rather than her lover, Phaon, as in the Ovidian tradition, to cultivate writing skills because beauty is fleeting and suggests that 'on pourroit mesme dire que si les choses estoient ordonnées comme il faut, l'estude des belles lettres, devroit plustot estre permise aux femmes qu'aux hommes' (p. 431) (one could even say that if things went as they should, the study of *belles lettres* should be permitted to women rather than men).[51] That Erinne should cultivate 'belles lettres' rather than make herself 'belle' is representative of what Myriam Dufour-Maître describes as the dominant feminine *ethos* in this period, characterized by modesty and discretion, which Madeleine de Scudéry played an influential role in developing; it also highlights the female-gendering of certain forms of literary production and the related 'civilized' French language.[52] We can already see a shift from Gournay's practice and aesthetics.

Scudéry extends the discussion of female eloquence and 'belles lettres' present in the *Femmes illustres* in her other representations of Sapho: Sapho is the figure for the ideal female intellectual, as elaborated in the 'Histoire de Sapho', in *Artamène ou le grand Cyrus* (1649–53):

En effet on peut savoir quelques Langues Estrangères; on peut avouer qu'on a lu Homère, Hésiode, et les excellents Ouvrages de l'illustre Aristée, sans faire trop la savante: on peut même en dire son avis d'une manière si modeste, et si peu affirmative, que sans choquer la bienséance de son Sexe, on ne laisse pas de faire voir qu'on a de l'esprit, de la connaissance, et du jugement.[53]

(She may speak several languages; she may confess to having read Homer, Hesiod, and the excellent works of the illustrious Aristaeus without seeming a pedant; she can even offer her opinion of them in a modest way, without being aggressive, so that without transgressing what is appropriate for her sex, she can let it be known that she is a woman of wit, knowledge, and judgement.)

---

[50] Joan DeJean, *Fictions of Sappho: 1546–1937* (Chicago: University of Chicago Press, 1987), 60–78.
[51] On the later influence of Scudéry's Sapho in the French tradition, see the chapter in this volume by Thea S. Thorsen analysing the eighteenth-century *opéra*, *Sapho*, by Constance de Salm (Chapter 7).
[52] Dufour-Maître, 'Les "Belles" et les Belles-Lettres', 64.
[53] Madeleine and Georges de Scudéry, 'Histoire de Sapho', *Artamène ou le Grand Cyrus* (Paris: Courbé, 1656), x, 355–608 (p. 401).

80 WOMEN TRANSLATING OVID IN EARLY MODERN FRANCE

Not only does Scudéry sketch a modest female intellectual, in an authorial strategy that makes far more compromises than that of Gournay, but she also explicitly uses representations of antiquity to explore present concerns, a practice Gournay so disliked; the *Femmes illustres* thus mark an important shift in Ovidian reception and women's writing.

The Scudérys' translation of Laodamia's letter also models the rhetorical practice championed in the preface. Laodamia's letter occurs in the second volume of the *Femmes illustres* in which all the letters are preceded by a 'moral': Laodamia's is 'que l'on doit se conserver pour la personne aimée' (p. 118) (that one must preserve oneself for one's beloved). The epistle is structured around this moral, reinforcing its qualities as a rhetorical exercise, and so making it an instructive example of polite eloquence for (female) readers; the moral also identifies the importance of the ethical example provided by the illustrious heroines. Despite the many changes in the epistle to Ovid's Laodamia—for instance, the timing is changed so that Protesilaus has not yet left and is present as Laodamia's interlocutor—there are a number of direct echoes, making Ovid's influence unmistakable; indeed, Laodamia's *harangue* stands out for its closeness to Ovid's version.[54] These similarities include Laodamia's visions of Hector; the warning that Protesilaus should hasten not to leave but to return; Laodamia's fantasies about the joy of his return, followed by her despair. There are a number of direct semantic echoes: 'ventus erat nautis aptus, non aptus amanti' ('the wind was suited to sailors, not lovers') (11) becomes 's'il est favorable aux grecs, il est contraire à Laodamie' (although the wind is favourable to the Greeks, it is not so to Laodamia). The oppositions between Menelaus and Protesilaus (and Laodamia and Helen) are emphasized: 'et que parce qu'elle a quité son mary, il faille que mon Mary me quite?' (p. 123) (because she left her husband, is it necessary that my husband leave me?); 'car si Menelas doit combatre en desesperé, pour reconquerir Helene, vous devez combatre avec prudence, pour conserver Laodamie' (p. 126) (for if Menelaus has to fight desperately to recover Helen, you should fight carefully to conserve Laodamie). It is striking that many of these textual similarities expand on the explicit binaries present in Ovid's text, which the 'moral' also echoes: such oppositions are purposefully exposed and amplified in the Scudérys' version in an exemplary exercise of rhetorical consistency and precision, so much so that the eloquence of the *harangue* is sometimes at the mercy of this rhetoric.

This Laodamia has more courage and authority than Ovid's young bride. The Scudérys develop her reactions to the futility of this war: 'quid petitur

---

[54] Kuizenga, 'L'Arc de triomphe', 156.

tanto nisi turpis adultera bello?' ('what do you seek with such great a war but a shameful adulterer?') (133) becomes 'mais de penser que vous n'ayez autre interest en cette affaire que de ramener une fugitive et une inconstante, à Menelas son Mary, c'est ce qui vient à bout de toute ma patience et de toute ma raison' (p. 123) (but to think that you have no other interest in this affair than to bring home an unfaithful fugitive to her husband, Menelaus: that tests my patience and my reason). A long section is added towards the end of this *harangue* (pp. 130–41), in which the Scudérys elaborate on Laodamia's grief, all the while affording her a rhetorical dignity which keeps her from desperation. Laodamia's fantasies combine with the duality of the 'moral' to create persuasive rhetoric: 'J'ay à vous dire que Laodamia est dans votre cœur; c'est là qu'il faut la deffendre du poignard d'Hector' (p. 134) (know that Laodamia is in your heart; that's where you must defend her against Hector's sword) and 'quoy que je connoisse assez, que vous separer de moy, c'est vous separer de la plus chere partie de vous mesme' (p. 138) (although I do know that if you separate yourself from me, you separate yourself from the most cherished part of yourself). The full extent of her command (and indeed, her rhetoric), however, is conveyed by the emphasis placed on her premonitions and almost divine oracular powers. Laodamia states: 'c'est un Dieu qui m'inspire...ne m'écoutez donc plus comme une femme affligée, mais comme une personne que le Ciel vous envoye pour votre conservation' (p. 139) (I am inspired by a God: listen to me no longer as a afflicted woman, but as a person sent to you by the heavens for your own preservation). In the concluding 'effet de cette harangue' which explains how Protesilaus died, Laodamia's own death is not described; instead, she is sorrowful but shown as having been justified in her premonitions: 'Laodamie connût...que les pre-sentiments que nous avons quelques-fois ne sont pas toûjours à negliger' (p. 142) (Laodamia discovered that the presentiments we sometimes have should not always be ignored). With the authority conferred by the Scudérys, Laodamia seems to develop from the helpless and fearful young bride she is in Ovid to a powerful semi-divine figure whose knowledge is presaging rather than anxious, and whose rhetoric, although ineffective, marks her dignity and self-control.

Marie-Jeanne L'Héritier's Unfaithful Beauty

Separated by two generations, Marie-Jeanne L'Héritier and Madeleine de Scudéry are, on the whole, united by their Modern stance and their acceptance of *galant* culture: L'Héritier was writing very much in the wake of Scudérian

82 WOMEN TRANSLATING OVID IN EARLY MODERN FRANCE

strategies of modesty and properness. In the next chapter, Océane Puche explores in greater detail L'Héritier's translation and its relation to this culture. The connections between L'Héritier and Scudéry were also personal, as L'Héritier had frequented Madeleine de Scudéry's salon. By the time L'Héritier came to translate the *Heroides* in 1732, there had been three complete translations of this text (Marolles, Martignac, and Bellegarde) and a number of selected editions (Corneille, Barrin, and Richer). All of these versions explicitly or implicitly targeted female readers; with an insistence on clarity for those who might not otherwise know these myths (Corneille, Marolles, Bellegarde), or emphasis on the morality of the heroines (Marolles, Martignac), Ovid's verse was translated according to the polite, *galant*, and proper aesthetics associated with the feminine (Corneille, Marolles, Martignac, Richer). Marie-Jeanne L'Héritier continues this approach with her translation. It is dedicated to the Countess of Verteillac and in the preface L'Héritier makes it clear that she intends this text for a female reader: 'J'espere du moins que les Dames me tiendront quelque compte de leur donner en vers des traductions qui n'avoient point paru depuis une si longue suite d'années' (x) (I hope, at least, that women will acknowledge me for giving them a translation in verse of a text which has not been translated for a good number of years). In this preface she also shows her debt to Scudéry by casting herself very much in the mould of the modest intellectual: 'il semblera qu'il y ait eu bien de la témérité à moi d'entreprendre un Ouvrage, où n'ont pas voulu s'engager tant d'habiles gens qui ont paru dans notre siécle' (viii) (It will seem that I have been very bold in undertaking a work which has put off many capable minds of our time), thanking certain 'capable men' (ix) and in particular the 'Messieurs Boivin' (ix) for having encouraged her in her translation.

However, this posture is not entirely governed by a strategy of modesty. Like Gournay, she navigates the fine line between association with male counterparts and an insistence on her distinction from them. In the typical practice of translation prefaces, she gives a detailed account of all the translations that have preceded hers and places her own version within this line. It is noteworthy that this line is all male: the absence of the *Femmes illustres* from this list is not striking given that it was not a translation in the strict sense. But Gournay's absence is more provocative. It is possible that L'Héritier may not have been aware of Gournay's translation given that it is of a single letter, and is included within her complete works, unlike some of her other translations which were also published separately;[55] her complete works were also not

---

[55] Marie de Gournay, *Versions de quelques pièces de Virgile, Tacite et Salluste* (Paris: Fleury Bourriquant, 1619); *Eschantillons de Virgile* (Paris: 1620).

reprinted after 1641. The absence might also be accounted for by the general lack of recognition Gournay achieved for her translation of Ovid's epistle and the tendency to narrate her out of the canon. Indeed, L'Héritier had earlier written two texts with catalogues of women writers, which celebrate figures such as Christine de Pizan as well as contemporaries, in which Gournay is somewhat sidelined, even in this community.[56]

The account of previous translations of Ovid's *Heroides* that L'Héritier includes in her preface is an updated version of the one included in the dedicatory letter by François Ogier, which introduces Marolles's edition of the *Heroides* (1661). In Ogier's letter Gournay is not mentioned for her translation, but she *is* referred to, anecdotally, and Ogier describes her to Marolles as 'vostre bonne amie et la mienne' (n.p.); we know that Marolles frequented her salon and thought very highly of her.[57] In the *remarques* dedicated to the Laodamia letter in this 1661 edition, where Gournay might have been mentioned, Marolles replicates this absence and states explicitly: 'M. de Lingendes est le seul qui ait traduit cette Epistre en prose' (p. 288) (Mr de Lingendes is the only person to have translated this letter into prose). We cannot know whether Marolles and Ogier were aware of Gournay's translation, but given that in her own writing she mentions discussing her translation of Cicero with Ogier, and we know she, Ogier, and Marolles frequented each other's company, it seems possible, making her absence more striking.[58] Furthermore, given that L'Héritier was also aware of Gournay's work in general, and given the importance L'Héritier places on being a female translator, Gournay's absence in L'Héritier's preface also poses questions: it suggests the importance of both male approval and of shared aesthetic practice over 'female solidarity', thus subtly challenging the enduring critical tendency to read 'early modern women' as a collective entity.

Marie-Jeanne L'Héritier's translation differs from the close translation of Gournay and the moralizing, rhetorical version of the Scudérys: she offers a verse translation that owes much to the *galant* versions by Corneille, Barrin (who did not translate Laodamia's letter), and Richer, in terms of attention to the lyricism of the French, but she prioritizes decorum. L'Héritier's version of Laodamia's letter can be seen as typical of her approach to Ovid's text as a whole, as is discussed by Océane Puche in the next chapter; its main characteristics are the *bienséance* with which she approaches the erotic aspects of the text,

---

[56] See Helena Taylor, 'Marie de Gournay et le Parnasse des femmes', in M. Roussillon, S. Guyot, D. Glynn, and M.-M. Fragonard, eds, *Littéraire—pour Alain Viala* (Arras: Artois Presses Université, 2018), 227–37.

[57] Michel de Marolles, *Mémoires de Michel de Marolles*, 2 vols (Paris: Sommaville, 1656), i, 58.

[58] Marie de Gournay, *Œuvres complètes*, ii, 1469, fn C.

84   WOMEN TRANSLATING OVID IN EARLY MODERN FRANCE

her selective approach, and her simplification of Ovid's language: she makes Laodamia more direct, French, and of the translator's own time and place.[59]

Compared not only to Gournay, but also to the major translations of this epistle that punctuate the near one hundred years between these two women's versions (those of Marolles, Martignac, Bellegarde, and Richer), L'Héritier's approach to the erotic and intimate moments of this epistle is the most censoring and modest. Even the 'oscula' of line 7, which is translated as 'baiser' in most other versions is rendered in the terms of *galant*, polite courtship: 'marques de tendresse' (p. 184) (marks of tenderness) (it is also 'tendresse' in Richer's version).[60] The description of Laodamia's night-time longing, in which Gournay maintained the physical references, is rendered less erotic in the versions by Marolles, Martignac, Bellegarde, and Richer who show restraint regarding this intimacy, all removing the explicit reference to the neck, replacing it with a less sexual 'embrace in arms'. L'Héritier takes this suppression further still: in her version, nights are difficult only because of phantoms and nightmares:

> Ma peine est pourtant plus cruelle
> Dans l'horreur de la nuit que dans l'éclat du jour;
> Avec plus de rigueur l'ombre me renouvelle
> Les sujets de trembler que trouve mon amour.
>
> (p. 192)

> (My pain is more cruel
> In the horror of the night than in the light of day;
> With more rigour do the shadows renew
> The dreadful situations that confront my beloved.)

Similarly, the scene in which Laodamia imagines her lover narrating his exploits in bed while being interrupted with kisses is also modified. Marolles, Bellegarde, and Richer suppress the reference to the couch but keep Laodamia's description of her languishing delight; Martignac translates the entire sequence; L'Héritier excises not only the reference to the couch but also the languishing delight and she uses 'des tendres amitiés' (p. 193) (tender marks of affection) for kisses.

This modest language presents Laodamia as young and somewhat naïve; this is also borne out in L'Héritier's representation of Laodamia's character, in which she amplifies her sensitivity. For instance, the description of the

---

[59] For a discussion of L'Héritier's text as a whole, see Taylor, ' "L'Adorateur du beau sexe" '.

[60] Richer, *Epistres*, 61.

moment of separation in lines 13–14 of Ovid's text is extended over three stanzas in L'Héritier's text (p. 184); likewise, the description of Laodamia gazing after Protesilaus' departing ships (lines 17–18 in Ovid) is narrated over two stanzas. L'Héritier also simplifies Laodamia's language and highlights her inexperience. For 'Parcite, Dardanidae, de tot, precor, hostibus uni, / ne meus ex illo corpore sanguis eat!' ('O ye sons of Dardanus, spare, I pray, from so many foes, at least one, so that my blood does not flow from his body') (79–80), she writes, 'Vous Troyens! Soyez-moi propices, / Parmi tant d'Ennemis un seul homme n'est rien / Epargnez mon Epoux, il fait seul mes délices, / Vous répandrez mon sang si vous versez le sien' (p. 190) (You, Trojans! Act favourably towards me! / One single man among so many enemies is nothing: / Spare my husband, he alone is my delight, / You spill my blood with his). By emphasizing her stake in this request ('mes délices', 'soyez-moi', etc.), L'Héritier dwells on Laodamia's single-minded perception of Protesilaus as her husband before all else, and her lack of appreciation of the stakes of war. Her translation of the final section, in which, instead of the verb *suivre*, employed by the male translators, or the 'compaigne' of Gournay's version, she has 'épouse fidèle' (p. 197) (faithful wife), strengthens this picture of Laodamia as a youthful, innocent bride. L'Héritier writes in her prefaces that 'je l'ai un peu adouci dans les endroits où les bienséances auroient pû être blessées' (ix) (I have softened the text a little where it offended decorum): Laodamia's innocence allows L'Héritier to create a stylistic coherence between the Greek bride's ethics and the aesthetic practice she cultivates as a translator.

Coda: *Belles Infidèles?*

Analysis of the different versions of Laodamia's letter proves a valuable way of highlighting a paradox at the heart of the expectations of the woman writer in this period: fidelity should only ever be ethical; in translation, a level of 'infidelity' was the dominant fashion. For women writers, 'fidelity' in translation was the opposite of 'beautiful' because it entailed an improper, or even pedantic, demonstration of knowledge, far from the so vaunted discretion, and it risked resulting in work that was not morally correct; it was also 'ugly' because too much time spent on study implied a neglect of one's personal attributes, according to the satirical *topos*.[61] Ugliness was a charge laid against a number of female writers in this period (Scudéry included), but Gournay,

---

[61] For a discussion of the 'indecency of knowledge' in relation to Ovid, see Emma Herdman's contribution to this volume (Chapter 2).

86 WOMEN TRANSLATING OVID IN EARLY MODERN FRANCE

who did not follow the *ethos* of the modest writer, was the most attacked and vilified.[62] This was not, of course, just because of her Ovid letter; but her resistance to current fashions in translation and literary practice, which this letter reveals, account for some of that scorn. In contrast, Scudéry and L'Héritier cultivated a perfect marriage between moral correctness and 'beautiful infidelity' in their writing practice. The difference, as has been noted, is one of a feminism of equality versus a feminism of difference:[63] Gournay uses Laodamia's fidelity to legitimize her own place in the male-dominated field of classical translation; by the time of Scudéry, and particularly L'Héritier, Laodamia's fidelity symbolizes these women's espousal of the modest and moralizing role they must play to be recognized.

Attention to the gendering of literary terms, such as 'belles infidèles' and 'belles lettres', is, as Dufour-Maître has argued, crucial for understanding the complexities of women's place in this emerging literary field: one in which they at once had a recognized, even foundational, position, but in which their authority was delimited and their practice restrained.[64] Much of this 'gatekeeping'—as in the setting of rigid standards of modesty for women who wanted to enter the literary field—was conducted by women. It also confirms the slippage noted by Lori Chamberlain between gendered metaphors for translation and a patriarchal system, even though we have now moved away from the notion of translation as a secondary act.[65] Ovid's *Heroides* lend themselves to an exploration of the women's place in the public sphere because of their perceived combination of ethics and aesthetics: the history of the reception of the heroines as morally exemplary means they were instrumentalized ethically, and the first-person nature of these women's voices made them exemplars of female rhetoric and eloquence, and so of aesthetic practice. Laodamia is a particularly fruitful figure not only because of her innocence and fidelity, but also because, as a female Pygmalion, she is a figure for the female artist, whose work, a model of Protesilaus, emblematizes the imitative and relational nature of translation, which makes a new work out of something else. The stark contrast between the two translations by Gournay and L'Héritier shows the influence of the regulating practices of polite language, promoted to no small degree by Scudéry, and how far women had to uphold

[62] For a brief discussion, see Taylor, 'Marie de Gournay et le Parnasse des femmes'.

[63] Karen Green, 'Women's Writing and the Early Modern Genre Wars', *Hypatia*, 28 (2013), 499–515 (p. 504).

[64] Myriam Dufour-Maître, 'Les "antipathies": académies des dames savantes et ruelles des précieuses, un discours polémique dans l'espace des Belles-Lettres', in Claudine Poulouin and Jean-Claude Arnould, eds, *Bonnes lettres/Belles lettres* (Paris: H. Champion, 2006), 271–92 (p. 290).

[65] Chamberlain, 'Gender and the Metaphorics of Translation', 307.

such practices to be recognized and successful. L'Héritier received great praise by members of the *Academie française* for her translation and eventually a pension; Gournay's translation, as explored, went all but unnoticed. The shift in Ovid's reception documented across the seventeenth century and into the early eighteenth century, whereby his work became much more assimilated into mixed-gender circles and was adapted to suit contemporary tastes—part of a shift dubbed as the democratization of knowledge—was thus double-edged for women readers and writers. Just as Ovid's reception over the seventeenth century became at once more pronounced, social and accessible to women, it also became more regulated and codified.

5

Defending Phaedra's Glory

The Corrective Translation of *Heroides* 4 by Marie-Jeanne L'Héritier in *Les Epîtres héroïques* (1732)

Océane Puche

Marie-Jeanne L'Héritier de Villandon is best known as the author of short stories and fairy tales from the end of the seventeenth century.[1] She is particularly renowned for her literary relationship with Charles Perrault, her uncle, but also for her friendship with well-known female writers of her time, such as Antoinette Deshoulières and Madeleine de Scudéry, who was her mentor.[2] Her fiction and poetry were published between 1690 and 1716, in the context of the two major literary quarrels which animated France at that time, opposing ancients against moderns. The 'ancients' in this debate, sometimes thought of as reactionary, argued that ancient literature was a perfect model to be imitated; the 'moderns', with a more progressive sense of society and literature, defended a teleological notion of progress, praising ancient culture but recognizing its limitations. As Eliane Viennot has shown, this quarrel was not limited to literary questions, but had a 'gendered aspect', notably its intersection with the 'querelle des femmes' and its interrogation of women's place in society and literary culture.[3] It is in this context that L'Héritier produced her translation of Ovid's *Heroides*, the *Epîtres héroïques d'Ovide*, the first complete version by a woman; it was published in 1732, two years before her death.[4]

---

[1] The most well known of these are *L'Adroite Princesse ou les Aventures de Finette* and *Marmoisan ou la fille en garçon*.

[2] I refer here to the work of U. Heidmann and J.-M. Adam who have emphasized the literary connections between L'Héritier and Perrault. Jean-Michel Adam and Ute Heidmann, eds, *Textualité et intertextualité des contes. Perrault, Apulée, La Fontaine, Lhéritier…* (Paris: Classiques Garnier, 2010).

[3] Eliane Viennot, 'Revisiter la "Querelle des femmes": mais de quoi parle-t-on?', in *Revisiter la Querelle des femmes. Discours sur l'égalité/l'inégalité des femmes et des hommes, de 1750 aux lendemains de la Révolution* (Saint-Étienne: Publications de l'Université de Saint-Étienne, 2012), 1–20.

[4] Marie de Gournay translated a single letter 'Laodamia à Protésilaus', published in 1626, and the Scudérys modelled some of their *harangues* from *Les Femmes illustres* (1642) on Ovid's *Heroides*. See Helena Taylor's chapter in this volume (Chapter 4).

Océane Puche, Defending Phaedra's Glory: The Corrective Translation of Heroides *4 by Marie-Jeanne L'Héritier in* Les Epîtres héroïques *(1732)* In: *Ovid in French: Reception by Women from the Renaissance to the Present.* Edited by: Helena Taylor and Fiona Cox, Oxford University Press. © Oxford University Press 2023. DOI: 10.1093/oso/9780192895387.003.0005

L'Héritier chose to translate the *Heroides*, which was in fact her only translation, for two likely reasons: firstly, it was the best-known work by Ovid in this period, as is evidenced by the number of its translations.[5] L'Héritier was familiar with Ovid: he is a significant character in two texts she composed on the occasion of the death of Antoinette Deshoulières in 1694 and of Madeleine de Scudéry in 1701.[6] In the two texts she imagines that Ovid escorts these women to Mount Parnassus to join Apollo and the Muses and have literary glory conferred upon them. Ovid, therefore, is a poet she considers favourable to women; and this is borne out in her translation. Her choice of the *Heroides* was also most likely motivated by the fact that this text constitutes the first space, in Western literature, in which female characters were given such a prominent voice.[7] In the dedicatory epistle addressed to her young friend, the Countess of Verteillac, also a poet, L'Héritier aligns her work with the wider movement celebrating women's glory, which can be dated to the early seventeenth century. The roles played by Marie de Médicis and Anne d'Autriche in political and cultural life in France prompted, according to Ian Maclean, a literary movement which celebrated the 'triumphs' of women's virtue and courage.[8] This is the context in which Madeleine de Scudéry published the two volumes of her *Harangues des femmes illustres*, in 1642, as analysed by Helena Taylor in the previous chapter, and Pierre Le Moyne his 1647 *Gallerie de femmes fortes*.[9]

However, choosing the *Heroides* as a means of celebrating female glory was also problematic since its female characters are either unhappy in love or, worse, desperate to the point of no return. The fourth epistle, Phaedra to Hippolytus, which will form the subject of this chapter, is of particular interest in this respect: Ovid imagines that Phaedra confesses her illicit love for her stepson and develops a detailed argument for why he should share her feelings, coming up with strategies for avoiding detection. It would seem, therefore, difficult to speak of 'feminine glory' in relation to this fourth epistle. Phaedra's

---

[5] There are many translators of Ovid in the seventeenth century: Pierre Deimier (1612), Lingendes, Du Perron, et Hédelin (1616), Méziriac (1616), Renouard (1616), Michel de Marolles (1661), Thomas Corneille (1669), Jean Barrin (1676), Martignac (1697), and Morvan de Bellegarde (1701).

[6] Marie-Jeanne L'Héritier, 'Le Parnasse reconnoissant ou Le triomphe de Madame Des-Houlières : A Mademoiselle de Scuderi', *Œuvres mêlées de Mlle L'H**** (1694; Paris: Guignard, 1696), 404–24, and Marie-Jeanne L'Héritier, *L'Apothéose de Mademoiselle de Scudéry* (Paris: Moreau, 1702).

[7] There is of course Ovid's model: Propertius 4.3. Women are given voice in tragedy, but this is often lost among other male voices.

[8] Ian Maclean, *Women Triumphant: Feminism in French Literature 1610–1652* (Oxford: Oxford University Press, 1977).

[9] The volumes were signed by Georges de Scudéry, but have been attributed to them both. See Donna Kuizenga, 'L'Arc de triomphe des dames: Héroïsme dans Les Femmes illustres de Madeleine et Georges de Scudéry', in Alain Niderst, ed., *Les Trois Scudéry* (Paris: Klincksieck, 1993), 301–10 (p. 301).

90   DEFENDING PHAEDRA'S GLORY

passion for Hippolytus was a well-known story in France in this period, particularly thanks to the two theatrical versions from 1677: the now famous *Phèdre* by Jean Racine, and the all but forgotten version by Jacques Pradon, *Phèdre et Hippolyte*. Their versions gave rise to a quarrel over the question of imitation of the ancient sources.[10] Pradon, as a 'modern' in this debate, had refused to follow the ancient models and had radically changed the plot of the story to eliminate the incest: Phèdre is no longer Hippolyte's stepmother. In contrast, Racine was celebrated by the ancients for conserving this element of the plot and exploring in detail the complexity of Phèdre's passion. As I will show, L'Héritier's translation reveals her modern position in this debate, albeit using different methods to Pradon: while she does not exactly celebrate Phèdre's 'glory', she does, at least, defend her.[11] In order to do this, she needs to correct not only the translations she has inherited—as she does in her translation and the prefatory summary, or 'argumentum'—but also Ovid's original. To explore this, I will first compare the summary that L'Héritier used to preface her letter, which she calls the 'sujet de l'épître' (the subject of the epistle), with similar 'argumenta' of Pierre Deimier, Gaspar Bachet de Méziriac, Daniel Crispin, and Jean Barrin, all translators or editors of the *Heroides*.[12] This comparison will reveal the heuristic that our translator imposes on Ovid's text to prime the readers to her interpretation of the heroine, an interpretation I will examine in the second part of the chapter. L'Héritier does not follow Ovid and offers a new version of Phèdre's epistle in order to present her as less guilty and to preserve, as she does across her translation, the heroine's reputation.

The 'Argumentum' or 'Subject of the Epistle'

The prefatory 'argumenta' or 'subjects' that introduce each of the *Epîtres héroïques* are rhetorical: here L'Héritier is not Ovid's translator but rather an author who contextualizes the letter that follows. These texts, written in the 'argumenta' tradition, are generally based on the stories they introduce and are

---

[10] These models include Euripides' *Hippolytus* and Seneca's *Phaedra*.

[11] For discussion of a Renaissance translation of Ovid's *Heroides*, see Jessica DeVos's chapter in this volume on Madeleine de L'Aubespine's translation of *Heroides* 2, Phyllis to Demophoon (Chapter 3).

[12] These translations were all known to L'Héritier and most are referenced in her *Avertissement*. Marie-Jeanne L'Héritier, *Les Epîtres héroïques d'Ovide traduites en vers françois* (Paris: Brunet fils, 1732), vii–viii. Subsequent page references for L'Héritier's translation will be given in the text. Unless otherwise stated, all translations from French are by Helena Taylor.

pedagogical in that they are written to explain the mythology. In the prefatory *sujet* that introduces Phèdre's epistle to Hippolyte, L'Héritier initially reviews the situation in which the heroine finds herself, as she does for the other twenty epistles, situating the character in her family line: 'Phèdre étoit fille de Minos, roi de Crête' (Phèdre was the daughter of Minos, King of Crete) and 'femme de Thésée' (p. 45) (wife of Thésée).[13] L'Héritier then describes Thésée, who is defined by his ambivalent reputation as a hero and a womanizer, which leads her, subtly, to allude to the circumstances of Phèdre's and Thésée's meeting in Crete: she refers to his 'noire ingratitude' (p. 45) (base ingratitude). This recalls the background story: Phaedra's sister, Ariadne, had helped Theseus find his way out of the labyrinth after he had killed the Minotaur, only to be abandoned on an island after he reneged on his promise to marry her. This suggestive phrase shows that this *sujet* was not simply written with an objective pedagogical purpose in mind: it has the intention of presenting events in such a way as to justify Phèdre's behaviour and to denigrate Thésée. This is also evident in the following passage when L'Héritier describes the early years of their marriage as being one of unequal affections. Phèdre's passion for her husband is contrasted with his absence, indifference, and infidelity, which justifies her waning interest in him and, potentially, her new and illicit feelings for Hippolytus.

The first half of this *sujet* consists of addressing the events which surrounded the birth of Phèdre's passion for her stepson. L'Héritier presents an attenuating picture of these circumstances and emphasizes Phèdre's innocent record: she was not 'habituée au crime' (used to crime). She is also aware of the immoral character of her passion: 'elle vit toute l'horreur' (she saw it in all its horror) and 'honteusement' (p. 45) (shamefully) capitulated. This adverb could be interpreted objectively to show that she ceded to the passion in a shameful manner, that is, as others would judge it; or it could be interpreted subjectively to signify that Phèdre suffered shame, so that L'Héritier uses it to inspire her readers' pity. The *sujet* closes with a description of the more immediate circumstances of the letter. Phèdre writes to her stepson because she is 'pas encore assez hardie' (p. 45) (not bold enough): by this, L'Héritier implies that she was *prudent* enough not to articulate her love to him in person. This phrase resonates with the adverb, 'shamefully', of the previous

---

[13] All the other 'subjects' start with a similar geneaology: particularly interesting here is the eleventh letter, that of Canacé to Macarée. She is the other incestuous heroine of this collection as she falls for her brother. I have shown elsewhere how L'Héritier purged this epistle of all the terms connoting family relations to suppress the incest. Océane Puche, 'Les Epîtres héroïques de Marie-Jeanne L'Héritier: traduction et réception d'Ovide au XVIIe siècle', PhD thesis, Université de Lille SHS, 2020, 336–40.

92 DEFENDING PHAEDRA'S GLORY

sentence, and contributes to making the heroine a woman tortured by a passion that she recognizes as immoral and criminal. The end of the *sujet* is coloured by terms which express her fault, but they are tempered by the way L'Héritier describes her heroine's rhetoric. She is presented as an oracle, which is perhaps no surprise given the place of 'suasorius' or rhetoric in Ovid's education.[14] She is also presented as having a significant amount of 'art' and has recourse to tools of rhetoric as she uses 'des maximes et des plaintes… ingénieuses' to 'donner de la compassion' and 'chercher à le persuader' (pp. 45–6) (clever maxims and appeals to her stepson to elicit compassion and to try to persuade him). In this *sujet*, then, L'Héritier not only characterizes Phèdre, but also emphasizes Thésée's lack of love and her own shame. While her presentation might not seem to be particularly remarkable, it becomes more so when compared with the *argumenta* of recent translators, Pierre Deimier (1612), Claude Gaspar Bachet de Méziriac (1626), and the 1702 re-edition of Jean Barrin's translation, as well as that which accompanies the Daniel Crispin *Ad usum Delphini* Latin edition of the text (1689)—*argumenta* which L'Héritier had certainly read because she mentions them in her *Avertissement* and uses them throughout her translation.[15] Read alongside this tradition, L'Héritier's *sujet* stands out as defending Phèdre's glory.

L'Héritier counters, I suggest, the way in which Phèdre's letter has been introduced in these previous *argumenta*. This opposition is particularly evident in relation to the character of Thésée. Deimier[16] and Méziriac[17] define him factually in relation to Phèdre: she is his wife. Deimier adds that he is the King of Athens and that he was deceived by Phèdre into invoking Neptune against his son; thus, he is a victim of our heroine. Méziriac only mentions him in relation to Hippolyte and the latter's mother. The *argumenta* of Crispin[18] and of Barrin[19] open with a description of Thésée and his exploits in Crete, explaining that Bacchus made him abandon Ariane and marry Phèdre. These details show what L'Héritier missed out: she chose a version of the myth that

---

[14] Ovid mentions this education in *Tristia* 4.10.

[15] Her primary intertext is the pirated edition of the *Epîtres* published by Pierre Marteau in Cologne in 1702. As I have argued elsewhere, this edition is notable because it brings together the translations by Jean Barrin published in 1676, and completed by Thomas Corneille. Each letter is preceded by an *argumentum* which L'Héritier follows closely.

[16] Pierre Deimier, *Lettres amoureuses non moins pleines de belles conceptions que de beaux discours* (Paris: G. Sevestre, 1612), 66.

[17] Claude Gaspar Bachet de Méziriac, *Les Epistres d'Ovide traduites en Vers françois avec des commentaires fort curieux* (Bourg en Bresse: J. Tainturier, 1626), 338.

[18] Ovid, *Epistularum Heroidum Liber: interpretatione et notis illustravit D. Cripinus Helvetius; jussu Christianissimi Regis ad Vsum Serenissimi Delphini* (1689; London: Bye and Law, 1795), 29.

[19] [Jean Barrin], *Les Epitres amoureuses d'Ovide traduites en François, nouvelle édition augmentée et embellie de figures* (Cologne: P. Marteau, 1702), 177–8.

did not involve the Bacchus explanation in order to present Thésée in a more negative light than her predecessors.

The portrayal of Thésée's absence is also key to how the pair are presented. In Deimier's translation Thésée's absence is used as a chance for Phèdre to plot and satisfy her guilty passion. This is emphasized as Phèdre is described as 'spying on' her husband's departure; his voyage is described as long and dangerous, in the service of aiding a dear friend. Méziriac affords Thésée all the qualities of a hero—courage and generosity—further highlighting Phèdre's vice. In Crispin's notice, the absence is described with an ablative absolute, *absente Theseo*, which can have a temporal meaning ('while Theseus was away') or a causal one ('because Theseus was away'). Unlike Méziriac, he allows for some ambiguity in terms of Thésée's responsibility for Phèdre's passion. In contrast, the *argumentum* of the 1702 Barrin edition takes a different approach and proves more of a model for L'Héritier: Thésée's absence and Phèdre's ennui are shown to cause Phèdre's passion. This comparison with other versions highlights how far L'Héritier with her negative portrait of Thésée and compassion for Phèdre tries to shift some of the fault for Phèdre's guilty love onto Thésée.[20]

This attempt to shift the responsibility is also present in the way L'Héritier represents Hippolyte in comparison to her predecessors. Having offered reasons to blame Thésée, suggesting Phèdre's love for her stepson was caused by his absence, she uses an apparently simple formula to describe his son: 'et elle prit un coupable penchant pour Hippolyte fils de ce Prince' (p. 45) (she felt a guilty attraction to Hippolyte, son of this prince). L'Héritier describes Hippolyte in relation to Thésée, but the latter is not described as Phèdre's husband here. And yet, in all the other *argumenta*, the incestuous character of her love is made explicit: Deimier stresses the family relations—'estant devenuë Amoureuse d'Hippolyte fils de son mary' (having fallen in love with Hippolyte, son of her husband); Méziriac does the same and condemns this love as a detestable 'incest'. Crispin uses the term *privigni* which means 'stepson', which is also present in the 1702 text: 'Hippolyte son beau-fils' (Hippolyte, her stepson). In this way, L'Héritier deliberately avoids naming the family ties which unite Phèdre and Hippolyte, which shifts the attention towards her passion and away from its object, and which serves as part of Phèdre's defence.

---

[20] This criticism of military glory can be placed in the broader criticisms of epic values advanced by the Moderns and evident in the second volume of Charles Perrault's *Parallèle des Anciens et des Modernes*, 4 vols (Paris: Coignard, 1688–97), a point I will not develop here.

94   DEFENDING PHAEDRA'S GLORY

The differences in how the *argumenta* close make L'Héritier's intentions even more evident. The first two translators, Deimier and Méziriac, evoke Hippolyte's death as a consequence of the violence of Phèdre's passion. They both describe her in such a way so as to condemn her: for Deimier she is the seductress; for Méziriac, she is a manipulator. Her suicide is presented by both as justice for her crimes; and while Deimier affords her some repentance, suggesting she was overcome with regret, Méziriac makes her an *exemplum* of female vice (her actions leave a 'memorable example') in contrast to the positive, virtuous example set by Hippolyte. Crispin ends his *argumentum* with the immediate context of the letter and its contents: Phèdre's confession of her love. He says little about Hippolyte save to mention that his penchant for celibacy and hunting made him unavailable to Phèdre: it would seem that Crispin is not out to condemn Phèdre in his text. With her closing sentences, L'Héritier follows quite closely the *argumenta* for the 1702 Barrin edition, which also omits to mention the deaths of Phèdre and Hippolyte, but she adds a new dimension. She repeats the 1702 descriptions of Phèdre combatting her passion, succumbing to it with shame, but modifies the language to amplify the representation of Phèdre as a victim of her love and not an incarnation of vice: as mentioned earlier, she stresses that she was not 'habituée au crime' (used to crime) and that her love was horrifying and odious to her. L'Héritier also stresses that Phèdre's letter demonstrates significant rhetorical skill by adding this qualification: that Phèdre possesses 'beaucoup d'art' (p. 45) (much skill). L'Héritier thus affords Phèdre a literary talent which is not directly connected to her passion. This bold addition combined with the efforts of our author to present a heroine overcome by her conscience overturn the interpretations by Deimier and Méziriac which stress Phèdre's lubricity. In her introductory *sujet*, therefore, L'Héritier offers a new version of the heroine, defending her glory.

Phèdre to Hippolyte: L'Héritier's Translation

In the translation of Ovid's text, L'Héritier develops the position sketched in her *sujet* and attempts to present the heroine as less guilty in order to defend her glory. The tools she uses for this become apparent through a comparison of her translation with Ovid's original. As a translator with modern tastes, L'Héritier replaces the Latin couplet with a verse form that works in French: the quatrain. In so doing, she was engaging with the second phase of the Quarrel of the Ancients and Moderns (the Homer quarrel of the early eighteenth century), following the recommendations of Houdar de la Motte to privilege the style of the receiving culture and, in particular, to use verse. In the Phèdre epistle, the quatrains are composed of two Alexandrines, one octosyllable and one decasyllable. This both allows her to capture in French (which is less economical than Latin) Ovid's original and to make her mark on that adaptation of that original.[21] I will show that L'Héritier, as a 'modern', defends the idea that progress has produced a more polite, civilized society and literature: she is particularly bold in the way she does this, excising a whole section of Ovid's text to show Phèdre in this light and to present her as less guilty. I will also examine the elements she *adds*, notably in relation to Thésée's guilt and Phèdre's victimization, to show how this too defends Phèdre's glory.

The edition itself of L'Héritier's translation could be seen as 'modern' as, unlike Michel de Marolles and Etienne de Martignac (previous translators of Ovid's work), L'Héritier does not include a parallel Latin text. This allows the reader to forget the origin of these epistles and to reinscribe them in the contemporary sociocultural context. This editorial decision enables, in particular, dissimulation of her excisions which reconfigure Phèdre. A direct comparison with Ovid's version reveals that she has removed 23 verses from a total of 176.[22] The verses she has suppressed are lines 123–46, in which Phaedra invites Hippolytus to succumb to her passion, and plots their secret union. In this section Phaedra explains the plan she has devised and also uses a number of terms which emphasize her family ties with Hippolytus: for instance, 'cognato' ('relation') (4.138); 'fida noverca' ('trustworthy stepmother') (4.140); 'par privigno meo' ('towards my stepson') (4.140), which are juxtaposed with the term for embrace ('amplexos') (4.139). The lexical field used in this section stresses fault ('licet peccemus', 'culpa') and dissimulation ('celare', 'tegi', and 'decipiendus'), revealing that she has abandoned herself to her secret passion and documenting her furtive attempts to ensnare her stepson. Furthermore, in lines 125–26, she regrets that her own children did not die when they were born: 'O utinam nocitura tibi, pulcherrime rerum, / in medio nisu viscera rupta forent!' ('Ah, would that the bosom which was to

---

[21] L'Héritier explains in her *Avertissement* that she has translated this text in such a way to suggest that Ovid wrote it in French: 'I tried to make sure that Ovid did not speak Latin in French, and all the while conserving his thoughts, I did all I could to give my verses a natural and original inflection.' L'Héritier, *Les Épîtres héroïques*, ix.

[22] The text for Ovid's original that she was using is that established by Helvetius in the *Ad usum Delphini* edition edited by Crispin. In this chapter, all Latin quotations and translations come from Ovid, *Heroides and Amores*, trans. Grant Showerman, ed. G. P. Goold (Cambridge, MA: Harvard University Press, 2014). They will subsequently be referenced with line numbers in the text.

96 DEFENDING PHAEDRA'S GLORY

work you wrong, fairest of men, had been rent in the midst of its throes!')
(125–6). This line is treated in an interesting way by Crispin in his commentary: focusing on the term 'viscera', he corrects the interpretation proposed by
Hubertinus (and the twentieth-century Loeb translation quoted here) that
Phaedra is praying for herself, regretting that she did not die in childbirth.[23]
Crispin, in contrast, explains that 'viscera' is a metonym to describe Phaedra's
children and confirms her guilt when he glosses this passage to suggest that
'she would have preferred that her sons died at birth rather than harm
Hippolytus'.[24] The heroine is not simply guilty of incest but also of designs
to infanticide.

L'Héritier assures her reader in her *Avertissement* that she has 'toûjours
suivi avec une grande exactitude' (always followed [her author] with great
exactitude) and that she has only 'adouci dans les endroits où les Bienséances
auroient pû être blessées' (p. ix) (softened him where he might offend
bienséance). However, it can hardly be said that she has suppressed this
passage out of respect for *bienséance*: it was kept by all the translators prior to
L'Héritier, also constrained by such *bienséance*;[25] it is also commented upon
by Crispin in his edition for the *Ad usum Delphini* collection, which, as
Catherine Volpihac-Auger has shown, was used for pedagogical purposes
and was known for its expurgated versions of classical texts.[26] Instead, this
suppression can be seen in relation to the dialogue L'Héritier has opened
with her predecessors in her *sujet*: it reinforces her presentation of Phèdre
as less guilty and more likeable. Her removal of both Phèdre's reflections
on infanticide and her delight in her vice can be seen as a correction of
Ovid's text.

The verses which frame the passage omitted by L'Héritier have also been
changed to disguise the omission and to incriminate Thésée, who is presented
as the truly guilty figure in this episode:

---

[23] See Ubertino da Crescentino who published a commentary in the sixteenth century of the
Heroides and Cicero's *Epistulae ad familiares*.

[24] Ovid, *Epistularum Heroidum Liber*, 38.

[25] I will note here the references for the relevant passages from other translators: Deimier, *Lettres
amoureuses*, 79–83; Claude Gaspar Bachet de Méziriac, *Les Epistres d'Ovide* (La Haye: H. de Sauzet,
1616), 312–14; Michel de Marolles, abbé de Villeloi, *Les Epistres Heroides d'Ovide* (Paris : Vᵛᵉ P. Lamy,
1661), 31–2; Estienne d'Algay de Martignac, *Les Œuvres d'Ovide traduction nouvelle avec des
remarques, contenant les XXI Epistres d'Ovide* (Lyon: H. Mollin, 1697), 65–8; Morvan de Bellegarde,
Les Epistres choisies d'Ovide (Paris: David, 1701), 548–51.

[26] See Catherine Volpilhac-Auger, 'La Collection *Ad usum Delphini*: entre érudition et pédagogie',
Les Humanités classiques, 74 (1997), 203–14 [special issue: *Histoire de l'éducation*], particularly
pp. 211–12. See also Catherine Volpilhac-Auger, ed., *La collection Ad usum Delphini. L'Antiquité au
miroir du Grand Siècle* (Grenoble: ELLUG, 2000), 23–4 and 163–71.

Qui jamais auroit cru qu'un si précieux gage
N'eût pas mis contre lui sa vie en sûreté,
  Et qu'elle eût dû craindre la rage
   Par qui le fer dans son sein fut porté?

Point d'Hymen avec elle, afin qu'à la Couronne
Aucuns droits s'il mouroit ne vous fussent acquis:
  Il vous hait, il vous abandonne,
   Quel naturel d'un père pour un fils!

Après tant de rigueurs respectez-vous un père
Qui n'a jamais fait voir de tendresse pour vous?
  Qui me quitte, et qui s'ose faire
   Un déshonneur du nom de mon Epoux!

             (p. 58)

(Who would have thought that so precious a promise
Would not have guaranteed safety
  And that instead she [Hippolyte's mother] should fear his rage
  And that he would plunge a sword in her breast?

He did not marry your mother; so that to the crown,
you have no claims if he died.
  He hates you; he has abandoned you
  What feelings a father for his son!

[lines 123–46 which she has omitted]

  After such trials will you respect a father
  Who has shown so little affection for you?
   Who also abandons me and dares to
   Dishonour his role as my husband?)

These newly configured verses underscore how Phèdre's rhetoric is targeted at Thésée as she exaggerates his faults. He is characterized by a violence which is implicit in Ovid's version when he suggests that Theseus murdered Hippolytus' mother. L'Héritier develops this further: he is full of hubris because of his 'rage' and does not know what love is. In the first two verses of the quatrain, L'Héritier reprises lines 119–20 of Ovid's original—'ne nupta quidem taedaque accepta iugali' ('Yes, and she was not even wed to him and taken to his home with the nuptial torch')—to emphasize that Thésée never married Hippolyte's mother and to stress his manipulation. The last two verses of the quatrain enable her to add a series of three juxtaposed propositions,

98   DEFENDING PHAEDRA'S GLORY

which, by an effect of amplification, accuse Thésée of not feeling fatherly love: 'Il vous hait, il vous abandonne / Quel naturel d'un père pour un fils!' L'Héritier thus substitutes her omission of lines 121–46 with a new argument. She emphasizes this in the following quatrain when Phèdre reiterates the point that Thésee never had any affection for his son and thereby affords Phèdre a rhetorical strategy, already evident in Ovid's text, which consists of establishing common ground with Hippolyte. L'Héritier then continues with two propositions which further characterize Thésee, but this time in relation to Phèdre, which strengthens her common ground with Hippolyte: just as he does not love his bastard son, he does not love Phèdre. Furthermore, the prepositional expression which opens the quatrain, 'after so many trials', is an anaphora which repeats the previous line and, because it seems superfluous, constitutes a trace of the verses 121–46 which L'Héritier has omitted. She substitutes for Phèdre's strategies to seduce Hippolyte the 'trials' of Thésée which make him detestable to both his son and L'Héritier's readers. These additions to the verses which frame the section she has omitted amplify, therefore, Thésée's guilt, so that the attention of both the intended reader—Hippolyte—and L'Héritier's readers is placed less on Phèdre's forbidden love and more on Thésée's cruelty.

L'Héritier cannot purge this fourth epistle of incest because this mythological aspect is too well-known, although she does remove the incest from her translation of the letter from Canacé to Macarée.[27] Therefore, L'Héritier must, in addition to suppressing the most compromising passage, as described, inflect Phèdre's letter in other more subtle ways. She does so with a process of re-lexicalization: that is, she introduces terms in her translation which serve to modify the heroine's character so that she no longer abandons her 'pudor' as the letter continues, as she does in the original.[28] L'Héritier does this by adding elements which reinforce an idea that is already present in Ovid's text: that Phèdre is a victim of love. Having reminded her reader that the women in her family are all victims of the wrath of Venus, the heroine places herself, in lines 61–4, in a line of descendants from the sun (against whom Venus has a vendetta for revealing her love for Mars to her husband, Hephaistos): Phaedra's

---

[27] There had been, as discussed, the *querelle* between Racine and Pradon on this point. In his article 'Racine en Querelles', P. Fièvre demonstrates the importance of this dispute between Racine and Pradon, showing how its reach went beyond literature. Perrault took part in it. However, the story of Phèdre was so well known that L'Héritier could not cut out the incest. Paul Fièvre, 'Racine en querelles', *Littératures classiques*, 81/2 (2013), 199–210.

[28] On this point, see J. Fabre-Serris on the term 'pudor' from the fourth epistle, read through an intertextual nexus with Gallus and Sulpicia. Jacqueline Fabre-Serris, 'Sulpicia, Gallus et les élégiaques. Propositions de lecture de l'épigramme 3.13', *EuGeStA*, 7 (2017), 115–39.

mother, Pasiphae, was doomed to fall in love with a bull, producing the monstrous Minotaur, Phaedra's half-brother. In L'Héritier's translation we encounter, as is to be expected, elements of the Latin as she places herself in this ill-fated line; however, L'Héritier modifies this to emphasize Phèdre's inability to defend herself: the first couplet of 'en, ego nunc, ne forte parum Minoia credar, in socias leges ultima gentis eo!' ('Behold, now I, lest I be thought too little a child of Minos' line, I am the latest of my stock to come under the law that rules us all!') (61) becomes 'J'aime enfin à mon tour et ne puis m'en défendre' (p. 52) (Now it is my turn to love, and I cannot defend myself against it).

L'Héritier takes further liberties with Ovid's text: she reintroduces two images which serve to emphasize Phèdre's status as victim. The next line of Ovid's couplet 'in socias leges ultima gentis eo!' becomes 'Ce penchant marque en moi la fille de Minos / C'est un tribut qu'il me faut rendre / Au fier Amour qui trouble mon repos' (p. 52) (these feelings prove that I am the daughter of Minos; it is a tribute I must offer to fierce love who has troubled my tranquillity). Here L'Héritier recalls the Cretan episode—emphasized further with the mention of her sister, Ariane, in the next couplet—and makes Phèdre a sacrificial victim offered to the god of love who is presented as a new Minotaur, described as 'fier' in the Latin sense of the term, 'ferus': savage and fierce. The phrase 'who troubled my tranquillity' takes on a euphemistic quality which highlights the violence against Phèdre, against which she is defenceless. L'Héritier's translation of verses 63–4—'Hoc quoque fatale est: placuit domus una duabus / Me tua forma capit, capta parente soror' ('This, too, is fateful, that one house has won us both; your beauty has captured my heart, my sister's heart was captured by your father') (63)—furthers this perspective. She does not repeat the polyptoton, 'capit/capta', through which Phèdre identifies with Ariane, but rather introduces an asymmetry: 'Ma soeur s'aveugla pour le Père / C'est pour le fils que je perds la raison' (p. 52) (My sister fell for the father, I am losing my wits over his son). This semantic variation on the verb 'capere'—which means here 'capture'—makes Phèdre a victim of love, and thus a more sympathetic figure. The fact that she is described as losing her wits proves she is no longer her own mistress, and no longer responsible for her own actions.

The reconfiguration of the heroine's character is also demonstrated by L'Héritier's treatment of the motif of shame in this letter. In Ovid's version Phaedra gradually transitions from being consumed by shame to embracing her forbidden love by planning ways to realize it, as we have seen. In contrast, L'Héritier makes it clear that Phèdre remains overwhelmed by guilt. This is particularly evident in the way she translates lines 41–50. Here the heroine attempts to show Hippolyte that they share the same interests: hunting and

100 DEFENDING PHAEDRA'S GLORY

chariot-racing. She conveys to him that in these pursuits she is taken over by an agitated state of pleasure and acts the Bacchante. It is at the moment when Phèdre regains her senses that L'Héritier's translation differs from the original which reads: 'namque mihi referunt, cum se furor ille remisit, Omnia; me tacitam conscius urit amor' ('For they tell me of all these things when that madness of mine has passed away; and I keep silence, conscious 'tis love that tortures me') (51–2). L'Héritier amplifies this couplet:

> Quand de cette fureur un peu moins tourmentée,
> J'apprends ce que j'ai dit et tout ce que j'ai fait,
>> J'ai honte de m'être emportée
>> J'en sçai la cause et l'on en voit l'effet.

(p. 51)

> (When a little less tormented by this fury
> I realize what I said and all that I did
>> I am ashamed of being so carried away
>> I know the cause of this and see its effects.)

In Ovid's version she remains silent, overcome with love: L'Héritier translates differently the temporal proposition 'cum se furor ille remisit', using instead a passive form: 'Quand de cette fureur un peu moins tourmentée', which presents Phèdre as a victim of such fury. L'Héritier removes the metaphor of fire and reinterprets Phèdre's silence; she is stupefied both by the power of her love and by shame: 'J'ai honte de m'être emportée'. The term 'conscius' which grammatically qualifies 'amor', but in terms of sense relates to 'me tacitam', that is, to Phèdre, is developed by L'Héritier in the decasyllable which closes the quatrain: 'J'en sçay la cause'.[29] The shame that L'Héritier has added to this passage derives from this 'cause', her guilty love. Thus, the translation of this couplet confirms what the author announced in the *sujet*: that Phèdre is not used to crime. This interpretation enhances the reconfiguration of the heroine's character as she seems more overcome and ashamed than in Ovid's version, unable to find strength in her love.

At the end of the epistle, in lines 155–6, after having abandoned herself to this forbidden love and plotted her successful seduction, Ovid's Phaedra frees herself of shame: 'depudui, profugusque pudor sua signa relinquit. / Da veniam fassae duraque corda doma!' ('My modesty has fled, and as it fled it left

---

[29] This is also how Crispin understands this clause in the note to his *Ad usum Delphini* edition: 'Conscius Cujus ego sum conscia'. Ovid, *Epistularum Heroidum Liber*, 33.

its standards behind. Forgive me my confession, and soften your hard heart!')
(155–6). In this couplet, Ovid once again uses polyptoton and varies the motif
of sexual shame by employing the verb 'depudui'—with its notable prefix
'de'—in the perfect tense which signifies the completed nature of the action.
The verb is echoed in the substantive, 'pudor', qualified by 'profugus', 'in
flight'. In addition, the poet employs a military image ('sua signa relinquit')
which also suggests abandonment: Phaedra's resistance has crumbled as she
composes this letter. L'Héritier, however, does not follow Ovid: there is no
equivalent for this 'pudor' in retreat:

> La raison cherche en vain à retenir ma flamme;
> Elle cède au penchant qui vous livre mon cœur:
>> Voyez le trouble de mon âme
>> Et bannissez votre injuste froideur.
>
> (p. 58)
>
> (Reason seeks in vain to retain my passion
> it surrenders to my desire to offer you my heart
>> Witness the trouble in my soul
>> and banish your unjust coldness.)

The quatrain opens in a significant way with the term 'raison' which
suggests that the heroine combats her own Minotaur: love. The erotic/
military vocabulary ('flamme', 'penchant', 'trouble', and 'cœur'), as well as
the use of the present tense, gives the impression that the bitter fight waged
against her passion is not over, even though it is in vain. L'Héritier removes
from her text all predilection for crime and instead offers a portrait of
a woman at war with herself, heroically trying to resist, as much as she
can, her forbidden passion. Her treatment of 'pudor' in the translation
consists of showing, as she announces in the *sujet* of her epistle, that
Phèdre surrendered 'shamefully', in the subjective sense of this adverb,
aware of her crime.

Conclusion

In her *Épîtres héroïques* L'Héritier maintains a complex and ambivalent
relationship with Ovid. Although her decision to translate this text (and
only this one) suggests a taste for Ovid, she was also willing to challenge
his representation of Phaedra. In her translation L'Héritier responds to

102 DEFENDING PHAEDRA'S GLORY

the way Phèdre has been characterized by Ovid, his seventeenth-century translators, and even perhaps by Racine. She composes a new framework for interpretation in which she modifies the representation of Phèdre's character as it is presented in the previous *argumenta*. This modification takes two forms: first, she develops the representation of Thésée by connecting his exploits in Crete to his abandoning of Ariane. Instead of valorizing his heroism, she highlights his violence, his negligence as a husband, and his infidelity, which is used to explain why Phèdre should turn to Hippolyte for affection. Secondly, she contradicts Meziriac's representation of Phèdre as an *exemplum* of feminine lubricity: she plays down the incestuous nature of Phèdre's love by deliberately not mentioning the family ties which unite her to Hippolyte. L'Héritier insists on the fact that incestuous and adulterous behaviour is not customary for Phèdre, showing how much she struggles against her passion. This new interpretation necessarily entails modifications to the Latin text, given that in Ovid's version, Phaedra progressively abandons her feelings of shame to give herself over to her passion, plotting strategies of dissimulation which underscore her crime. L'Héritier, by contrast, has removed the most compromising passage of this letter and has painted a negative portrait of Thésée, stressing that Phèdre is a victim of love. It is particularly L'Héritier's use of vocabulary connoting shame and the madness of love which makes Phèdre a tortured figure, showing no delight for her criminal passion: she is ashamed and a victim, facing her own Minotaur. With her bold adaptation of Ovid's text, L'Héritier makes Phèdre one of the *femmes fortes* who people the catalogues of Scudéry and Le Moyne. Even if her glory is not fully celebrated—after all, she remains guilty of a forbidden love—it is, at least, defended by the author.

What of L'Héritier's insistence on the literary quality of Phèdre's letter? One might suggest that this demonstration of the 'ars' of the letter is a final strategy on behalf of the heroine, able to manipulate Hippolyte and come across as a victim to enhance her seduction. But this would be to overlook the context of Phèdre's letter in the wider collection, the intention of which was to celebrate women's glory. Phèdre's literary talents can be compared to those of Sappho, whose letter is the last in L'Héritier's translation: Sappho and Phèdre are both heroines guilty of forbidden passions—one for her stepson, the other for women. However, in both cases, L'Héritier emphasizes their literary talents and, for the most part, plays down the elements that make them guilty of immoral behaviour. In so doing, she goes further than Scudéry who aligns women's glory with their moral or sexual behaviour. L'Héritier, with these modifications, subtly asserts her heroines' morality in order to invite her readers to admire their artistic talents in celebration of women's literary glory.[30]

Translated by Helena Taylor

[30] I have explored elsewhere the way in which L'Héritier's celebration of literary prowess meant that she aligned herself with Anne Dacier, an 'ancient' in the Quarrel, and the translator of Sappho. Puche, 'Les Epîtres héroïques de Marie-Jeanne L'Héritier', 603–35 (pp. 624–35).

6

The *Letters from Julia to Ovid*, by Charlotte Antoinette de Bressey, Marquise of Lezay-Marnésia

Séverine Clément-Tarantino

Les *Lettres de Julie* ont eu beaucoup d'éditions, et se trouvent dans plusieurs recueils; cependant, l'auteur n'a pas de célébrité. La raison en est bien simple: on n'a jamais pu vaincre sa modestie et forcer cette femme si ingénieuse, si aimable et si douce à avouer son ouvrage; son secret n'étoit connu que de son fils et de deux ou trois amis: ce fils le révèle, bien assuré qu'il rend service à sa mémoire. Que de larmes il a versé sur cet écrit charmant! Combien n'en verseroit-il pas encore s'il ne voyoit que le jour est prochain où il rejoindra la plus aimable, la plus aimée des mères![1]

(The *Letters from Julia* have had many editions, and are found in several collections; however, the identity of the author has remained unknown. The reason for this is quite simple; it has proven impossible to overcome her modesty and to force this most ingenious, amiable, and sweet woman to acknowledge her work. Only her son and one or two friends knew her secret: this son now reveals her identity, assured that in so doing he pays tribute to her memory. What tears he has shed over this charming text! How many more would he yet shed, if he did not see the day drawing near when he will once again be with the kindest, most beloved of mothers!)

This is how Claude-François-Adrien de Lezay-Marnésia (1735–1800) reveals to the world that his late mother, Charlotte Antoinette de Bressey, marquise of Lezay-Marnésia (1707–85), was the author of the *Lettres de Julie à Ovide*

---

[1] C. F. A. de Lezay-Marnésia, *Plan de lecture pour une jeune dame, seconde édition augmentée d'un Supplément et de divers morceaux de Littérature et de Morale* (Paris: Louis, 1800). The quotation is found on p. 101, which belongs to a 'Supplement' added in this edition. Unless otherwise stated, all translations from French are by Eleanor Hodgson.

Séverine Clément-Tarantino, *The* Letters from Julia to Ovid, *by Charlotte Antoinette de Bressey, Marquise of Lezay-Marnésia* In: *Ovid in French: Reception by Women from the Renaissance to the Present.* Edited by: Helena Taylor and Fiona Cox, Oxford University Press. © Oxford University Press 2023. DOI: 10.1093/oso/9780192895387.003.0006

[Letters from Julia to Ovid],[2] a work that he highly recommends in his *Plan de lecture pour une jeune dame* [Advised Reading for a Young Lady] (1800). Although Claude-François-Adrien de Lezay-Marnésia was recognized as an author, best remembered today for the two articles that he wrote for the *Encyclopédie* and his recently re-edited *Lettres écrites des rives de l'Ohio* [Letters Written on the Banks of the Ohio],[3] his mother was known only as a *salonnière*, and not as an author in her own right. Lezay-Marnésia affirms that his mother's *Lettres* (published as the real correspondence between Julia, daughter of Augustus, and the poet Ovid[4]) is as worthy of being read as the other female-authored works he discusses at the end of his *Plan de lecture*, including texts by Mme Necker, and novels by Mme de Flaan and Mme de Montolieu. The pages dedicated to the *Lettres* focus on their 'grâce' (grace), 'pureté' (purity), 'piquant' (wit), and, through a comparison with Pliny the Younger and Mme de Sévigné, the moderation and self-control of the work.[5] In particular, Lezay-Marnésia highlights his mother's 'truthful' description of the court of Emperor Augustus and its characters, and contrasts her portrait of Tiberius with Tacitus' description, presenting his mother's work as a skilful and informative example of the art of 'nuance'.[6] Moreover, the concern shown by this respectful son for urgent reform of France's morals[7] is likely to have

---

[2] Unless otherwise stated, Bressey's *Lettres de Julie à Ovide* (1753) will hereafter be referred to by the short title *Lettres*.

[3] C. F. A. Lezay-Marnésia, *Lettres écrites des rives de l'Ohio* (Paris: Garnier, 2019).

[4] According to tradition, Julia the Elder, daughter of Augustus, had been exiled in the year 2 BC due to her debauchery and adultery. This date makes the story and the amorous correspondence with Ovid (banished in AD 8) unlikely from an historical point of view. This mistake is part of the ancient tradition: in his *carmina*, Sidonius Apollinaris makes Ovid's relationship with a *puella Caesarea* (v. 160) one of the reasons for Ovid's banishment (23.158–61), and the 'young girl of Caesar' who used the name Corinne (v. 161) could be identified as Augustus Caesar's daughter. For further information, see R. J. R. Hexter, 'The Poetry of Ovid's Exile', in S. J. Anderson, ed., *Ovid: The Classical Heritage* (London: Routledge, 1995), 43–4. The text has been read in this way and the confusion has continued between Julia *maior* and Julia *minor*, the granddaughter of Augustus who was exiled in the same year as Ovid (AD 8). See H. Taylor, *The Lives of Ovid in Seventeenth-Century France Culture* (Oxford: Oxford University Press, 2017), 31. In several notable seventeenth-century works written by women and involving Ovid, it is clearly the relationship between Ovid and Julia, daughter of Augustus, that is in question. See the texts cited by Taylor, *The Lives of Ovid*, including *Clélie*, by Madame de Scudéry (1654–60, pp. 87–8), and *Les Exilez de la cour d'Auguste* (1672–78; Utrecht: 1684) by Madame de Villedieu (p. 92 ff.).

[5] C. F. A. de Lezay-Marnésia, *Plan de lecture pour une jeune dame*, 100. He notes that where Mme de Sévigné 'laissoit aller sa plume' (let her pen run away with her) by being swept up in maternal love, Julia 'guid[e]' (guides) her own by remembering at all times to whom she is writing, and by being mindful of her flaws.

[6] Ibid., 101.

[7] For Lezay-Marnésia, the education of women had to play a central role in this reform. In the last chapter of his *Plan de lecture* dedicated to a work he admired the most, Isabelle de Montolieu's *Caroline de Lichtfield* (ibid., 103 ff.), Lezay-Marnésia engages in a tirade on the need to (re)educate women in order to restore morals and religion. The final lines reflect this belief (p. 114): 'Qu'on parvienne, avec plus d'instruction, à rendre les Françoises ce qu'elles étoient avant le règne de François Premier, qui, en les détournant de la vie de famille, a détruit les vertus domestiques et perverti les mœurs publiques;

106 THE *LETTERS FROM JULIA TO OVID*

made him sensitive to any moral connection between his mother, now identified as an author, and the classical poet whom she addresses through Julia: Publius Ovidius Naso.[8]

The *Lettres de Julie à Ovide* have recently received renewed critical attention thanks to Michel Delon, an eminent specialist of eighteenth-century French literature.[9] As he has noted, Charlotte Antoinette de Bressey's work enjoyed remarkable success until the middle of the nineteenth century, following the anonymous publication of its first edition in Rome in 1753. In my analysis of the text, I will focus for the most part on the first edition of the work (which contains only the letters from Julia to Ovid), since the responses from Ovid to Julia inserted into later editions were almost certainly not written by Charlotte Antoinette de Bressey.[10] Incidentally, other writers also brought attention to the genre of the *héroïde* through other epistolary works based on the relationship between the daughter of Augustus and the poet considered to be 'the most amiable man of his time.'[11] This is the case for Claude-Joseph Dorat, who, in 1759, published a letter from Julia to Ovid (*Julie, fille d'Auguste à Ovide, Héroïde*), a letter in verse that draws more on *Tristia* and *Epistulae ex Ponto*,

---

qu'on les rende ce qu'elles sont en Angleterre, en Allemagne, chez les Américains, et nous trouverons dans nos ménages la paix et le bonheur; et le Gouvernement sentira combien il est plus facile de régir un peuple sensé, tranquille, doux, aimable, qu'un peuple sans principes, sans morale et sans Religion' (May we succeed, with more learning, in making French women what they were before the reign of François I, who, in turning them away from family life, destroyed domestic virtues and corrupted public morals; may we make them like women in England, in Germany, and in America, and thus find peace and happiness in our households; and the Government will see how much easier it is to rule over a sensible, tranquil, sweet, and amiable people than over a people without principles, without morals, and without Religion).

[8] Ovid features in Lezay-Marnésia's *Plan de lecture* through discussion of his *Metamorphoses*, which the author regrets have not yet been translated well into French, unlike Virgil's *Georgics* (translated by Delille) (ibid., 33). The *Metamorphoses* are seen as useful due to their inclusion of 'le système complet' (the complete system) of mythology, though Lezay-Marnésia freely criticizes Ovid for having too much wit and not enough character, comparing him unfavourably to Virgil (p. 32).

[9] M. Delon, 'Les *Lettres de Julie à Ovide* (1753): de l'implicite à l'amplification', lecture given at the Université de Rouen-Normandie, 25 April 2017 (seminar by S. Provini), https://webtv.univ-rouen.fr/videos/les-lettres-de-julie-a-ovide-1753-de-limplicite-a-lamplification-par-michel-delon-professeur-emerite-a-paris-sorbonne_50849/.

[10] See, for example, J.-M. Quérard, *Les supercheries littéraires dévoilées: Galerie des auteurs apocryphes, supposés, déguisés, plagiés, et des éditeurs infidèles de la littérature française, pendant les quatre derniers siècles* (Paris, 1850), iii, 199. With regards to his entry on Marmontel, he clarifies that the 'Lettres amoureuses de Julie et d'Ovide' [Love Letters from Julia and Ovid] by Marmontel are in fact by Mme de Marnésia. The other significant information (regarding the same book, edited in 1797) is that the 'Réponses d'Ovide à Julie' [Responses from Ovid to Julia] are 'by Cailleau'. Then we learn that this same Cailleau had also been responsible for a re-edition of the *Lettres de Julie à Ovide* under the title *Lettres de tendresse <et d'amour>* [Letters of Tenderness <and Love>], with no date given, although we know that these were published in 1808. On p. 285 of 'Le Congrès de Cythère (septième édition), et Le Jugement de l'amour sur le Congrès' (Pisa and Paris, 1789), M. C** is noted as the author of Ovid's responses.

[11] Preface to the *Lettres de Julie à Ovide et d'Ovide à Julie, précédées d'une notice sur la vie de ce poète et suivies d'une Epître en vers de Julie à Ovide* (Paris: Delaunay, 1809), iv.

as Julia writes to the poet after his banishment.[12] In his preface, Dorat says nothing about Charlotte Antoinette de Bressey's *Lettres de Julie à Ovide*; however, his letter appears at the end of one of the early nineteenth-century editions of her work.[13] Another letter written in verse was published in 1767, although this time it was written from Ovid to Julia, and was preceded by a prose letter addressed to Diderot. The author of this letter is recognized as Alexandre-Frédéric-Jacques Masson, marquis of Pezay. His opening letter (addressed to Diderot) explains why he has written his Ovidian letter, even though he disapproves of the genre of the *héroïde*, and mentions two authors who have engaged with this genre, one of whom is Dorat.[14] One of the criticisms Masson makes of this genre of poetry is its improbability (how can we imagine that someone suffering from violent turmoil would be able to compose verse?), and he resolves this by choosing to write as a poet, and indeed as the poet to whom we know the act of writing verse came most easily.[15] However, neither Masson nor Dorat mentions the *Lettres de Julie à Ovide*. Thus, although the work certainly met with some success, it appears to have been overlooked by contemporary authors who were more concerned with writing other Ovidian letters. Moreover, as Bressey's work comprises letters written in prose and various plotlines, it might be best to locate her collection more in the tradition of the epistolary novel than the genre of the *héroïde*.

This chapter will begin with a short presentation of the contents of the work, focusing on the *Lettres de Julie à Ovide*, and not the later added responses from Ovid, with the aim of highlighting in particular the author's skill in narrative construction. The discussion that follows will pay particular attention to the way in which Ovid has been appropriated in the *Lettres*, questioning the extent to which they explicitly use and rewrite Ovid's work, analysing the image of Ovid that prevails within them, and exploring their depiction of Julia as an author. Whatever the preface of the *Lettres* may say, it would be difficult to consider the work as anything other than a 'mensonge imprimé' (publishing hoax),[16] given the distance between the French context

---

[12] Claude-Joseph Dorat, *Julie, fille d'Auguste à Ovide, Héroïde* (The Hague: 1759).

[13] *Lettres de Julie à Ovide et d'Ovide à Julie* (1809), 186–92.

[14] [Masson de Pezay], *Lettre d'Ovide à Julie, précédée d'une lettre en prose à M. Diderot* (n.p., 1767), 3; Dorat's *Julie, fille d'Auguste à Ovide, Héroïde* (see note 12) is not the work in question here, but *Zeïla*.

[15] See [Masson de Pezay], *Lettre d'Ovide*, 12. On the implausible nature of the *Heroides* conceit, see also Florence Klein's and Thea S. Thorsen's chapters in this volume (Chapters 11 and 7). More generally, on the influence of the *Heroides* in early modern France, see the chapters by Jessica DeVos, Helena Taylor, and Océane Puche (Chapters 3, 4, and 5).

[16] *Lettres de Julie à Ovide*, preface, vi : 'Il se trouvera quelque Sçavant qui niera que ces Lettres soient de Julie...' ('There may perhaps be found amongst the Litterati, some inclined to deny these Letters to

108   THE *LETTERS FROM JULIA TO OVID*

and Ovid. Nevertheless, it would seem that this did not prevent Julia (and Charlotte de Bressey through her) from immersing herself in the poet's work such that she could, in some way, ensure its continuation.

'The more I love you, the more I fear. What would become of me if I should lose you?' The Successful Creation of a Romantic *Suspens*

Charlotte de Bressey had Ovid's inexorable banishment to Tomis in mind as she wrote the *Lettres*. In other words, when reading Julia's forty-three letters, the reader knows that this relationship will not last: this sense of a foregone conclusion is also a feature of the *Heroides*. Nevertheless, the heroine's expression of her sentiments is given the same intensity by the author as one would expect of such a love affair, irrespective of its inevitable conclusion. At the same time, the author succeeds in extending the narrative created by the series of letters such that interest is maintained throughout and intensified on several occasions until the tragic ending. The reader is swept along emotionally by the narrative, and so feels the fluctuation in emotions expressed (or at least in the attention given to them) in a similar manner to the two lovers.

In letters I to X, Julia writes as an anonymous author—as does Charlotte de Bressey herself—hiding her identity as she begins to confess her love to Ovid, all the while testing his ability to share this emotion. In the letter following the revelation of her identity, Julia offers precautionary words, and shares her prophetic fears: 'Tout serait perdu, Ovide, si notre secret était découvert' (p. 19) ('Should our secret be discovered, Ovid, all is lost') (p. 13). Letters XI to XXII cover a period of happiness, before the tension that leads to the lovers' fateful separation begins to develop in letter XXIII. This tension is subtle at first, expressed in Julia's initial fears regarding the power that Livia exerts over Augustus and relating to Tiberius' attentions towards her, yet builds significantly after Tiberius leaves his wife Agrippina (letter XXVII), and increases further still following failed attempts to dissuade Augustus from marrying

---

have been of Julia's writing...') (p. ix). Charlotte-Antoinette de Bressey, *Letters from Julia, the daughter of Augustus, to Ovid. A manuscript discovered at Herculaneum. Translated from a copy of the original. To which is annexed, The lady and the sylph. A visionary tale* (London: Lockyer Davis, 1753). No translator name given. Please note all translations of the *Lettres* are taken from this edition, although at times have been adapted where necessary. Page references are given in the text to both the French original (1753) and this translation (1753).

Julia to Tiberius.[17] Letter XXXII sees the dénouement of the events leading to the heroine's unhappiness, as Julia sorrowfully announces this forced marriage. The prospect of this union casts doubt and disapproval over their relationship, followed by increased fear and cautiousness regarding the possibility of being discovered. However, in spite of this, the lovers still find ways to communicate, to see one another, and to continue their love affair after Julia's marriage. Letters XXXV to XL thus see the development of a new period of happiness, and although the attention given to Tiberius in letter XLI may raise suspicions about impending danger, letter XLII rather abruptly announces Julia's painful waking to the news of his banishment, as she learns that she has lost Ovid forever. Letter XLIII is the final letter that she writes, once he is perhaps already in Tomis, and she sees death as the only way out of her despair.

I–X	Julia tests Ovid by refusing to reveal her identity...until she finally gives in.
XI–XXII	The two lovers enjoy their relationship and their mutual feelings. '[P]lus je vous aime, plus je crains. Que deviendrais-je si je vous perdois?' (XII, p. 23) ('The more I love you, the more I fear. What would become of me if I should lose you?') (p. 14).
XXIII–XXXII	Julia is forced to marry Tiberius. 'Tout est perdu, Ovide. Le temps des persécutions est arrivé. Tibère vient de répudier l'aimable Agrippine....Vous voyez, Ovide, tous les malheurs que cette aventure m'annonce' (XXVII, pp. 74–6) ('All is lost, Ovid; the time of persecution is at length arrived. Tiberius has just divorced the lovely Agrippina...You must see, Ovid, what miseries this adventure threatens me with') (pp. 47–8).[18]
XXXIII–XL	After Julia's marriage, the two lovers resume their relationship and experience more happy moments together.
XLI–XLIII	After a happy trip to Baiae, the couple find the return to Rome difficult: Julia is unable to see Ovid, and Tiberius becomes insistent. The unexpected news of Ovid's exile arrives. 'Quel réveil, grands Dieux! Ovide, que viens-je d'apprendre? je vous perds pour jamais' (XLII, p. 123) ('Good Gods! what tidings! Ovid, what is it I have just heard? I am to lose you for ever') (p. 79).[19]

[17] The marriage of Julia and Tiberius was arranged in 11 BC. Tiberius had to first separate from Vipsania Agrippina Minor, one of Agrippa's daughters from his first marriage. According to Suetonius (*Tiberius* 7), Livia's son was forced unwillingly into this second marriage, as he loved Agrippina and disapproved of Julia's morals. Charlotte de Bressey appears to follow Tacitus more closely, whose discussion of Julia's exile to Pandateria (*Annales* 1.53) focuses on the young woman's dislike of Tiberius. Julia's first two husbands, Marcellus (here 'Marcel') and Agrippa, are both mentioned in the *Lettres de Julie à Ovide*: the letter writer acknowledges that even though she may not have loved these chosen spouses, she had nevertheless respected both men (letter XXIII, p. 55; English, p. 35).
[18] The published translation has been adapted here for clarity.
[19] The published translation has been adapted here for clarity.

110   THE *LETTERS FROM JULIA TO OVID*

The summary above shows some examples of the sense of foreboding expressed by Julia in the *Lettres*, which create enough suspense to satisfy the reader. Tragic irony is employed alongside these premonitions, such as in letter XXXII in which Julia reveals the awful news of her marriage to Tiberius, before briefly dreaming of escaping to a foreign land with Ovid.[20] Her words herald the poet's exile in Tomis, where we know he will go alone. However, as the heroine is aware that she is dreaming,[21] the passage in fact has another effect: it reignites the narrative and sparks the reader's interest by marking the beginning of the last period of happiness in the lovers' story.

Another narrative device used effectively by the author is the development of subplots in the *Lettres*. The first of these runs throughout the first happy phase of the love affair (from letter XIV to letter XIX) and concerns Sulpicia, who is going to be forced to marry a (different) man called Tiberius even though she loves Silvanus. Sulpicia begs Julia to speak to the emperor on her behalf, although the details of this intercession are not given. Nevertheless, in letter XVIII Julia gives details of Sulpicia's wedding with Silvanus: explaining to Ovid why she was forced to unwillingly accompany Octavia, Augustus' sister, on an excursion to the countryside, Julia states that she cannot join him, since she had received the good news of Sulpicia's marriage to her beloved Silvanus, and goes on to describe the joyful wedding in the following letter (XIX). This story serves as a counterpoint to the plight of Julia and Ovid. Later, Julia's plea to escape her own forced marriage falls on deaf ears when she attempts to tell her father that she will not marry another, more important Tiberius, namely Livia's son and Augustus' future successor.[22]

Another subplot occurs just before the upheaval triggered by letter XXVII in the third 'section' of the novel (letters XXIII–XXXII, as indicated in the table above). This is the story of Cornelia, a vestal virgin, who, as permitted by religious law, decides to return to society after thirty years spent almost against her will in the service of Vesta. Almost instantly, she becomes enamoured with Ovid, to whom she wishes to give her heart and her fortune, and Julia finds herself in the position of matchmaker. Since Ovid responds with a harsh letter

---

[20] 'Hélas, que ne puis-je aller vivre avec vous dans une terre étrangère, où ignorée du monde entier je n'emporte avec moi que le plaisir de vous plaire et de vous rendre heureux!' (pp. 98–9) ('Alas! Why cannot I be permitted to live with you in some distant foreign land, unknown to all the world? I should carry with me the transporting joy of pleasing you, and making you happy') (p. 63).

[21] 'Que mon état est différent de ce que je viens de peindre! j'en connois toute l'horreur...' (p. 99) ('But ah! how different my condition is from that I've been describing! I know too well the horror of it') (p. 63).

[22] See letters XXVIII to XXXI, and particularly the last of these (XXXI) for Julia's expression of the extreme suffering caused by the inflexibility of her once amiable father, who has become so strict under Livia's influence.

to decline Cornelia's offer, Julia takes it upon herself to communicate this rejection to Cornelia in the least hurtful way possible. Thus, she tells Cornelia that the main reason for Ovid's rejection centres on the poet's horror of the word 'engagement'.[23] A few letters later, the unhappy Julia takes up a similar argument to refuse her marriage with Tiberius, but to no avail.[24] After the happiness she experienced in response to Cornelia's new-found freedom, and after having helped Ovid to retain his own freedom from Cornelia, Julia soon loses the only thing in her possession that she truly values: *her* freedom.

A third and final story is outlined from letter XXXVI onwards, and concerns the relationship between Augustus and Terentia, wife of Maecenas.[25] While Julia and Ovid succeed in meeting one another 'chez la fille de Cicéron [*sic*]' ('at Cicero's daughter's'), their evening is somewhat disturbed by the unexpected arrival of Augustus, who comes to see his mistress. Far from criticizing her father's behaviour, Julia is envious, and lauds the lovers' freedom. Julia at first contrasts this affair with her own relationship, yet, in a similar manner to her dreams of a life in a foreign land in the letter announcing her marriage to Tiberius (letter XXXII), the passages praising her father's liaison in fact trigger a positive momentum within the main plot. In the later passages of letter XXXVI, Julia reaffirms her faith in the love that binds her to Ovid, and in their loyalty to one another. In the *Lettres*, the relationship between Augustus and Terentia is not fully developed,[26] such that the only story in real focus from this moment on and until the end of the work is that of the two main protagonists. This relationship takes on a different shape when one considers the responses intertwined within these letters. While Charlotte de Bressey's *Lettres* suggest that Ovid is exiled as a result of Tiberius' suspicions (and the subsequent revelation of the lovers' affair), her anonymous 'continuator'[27] favours involuntary indiscretion on the part of Ovid in the responses added

---

[23] Letter XXVI, pp. 72–3 (English, pp. 44–6).

[24] Letter XXVIII, p. 83 (English, pp. 52–3); see also letter XXIX, p. 88 (English, pp. 55–6) (Octavia speaks for Julia before Augustus, echoing Julia's words as Ovid's spokesperson to Cornelia).

[25] This relationship, or rather Augustus' passion for Terentia, is attested by Dio Cassius (54, 19, 3). R. Verdière, who suggested a rivalry of lovers between Augustus and Ovid as the reason for the latter's banishment, made Terentia the subject of this rivalry, and the woman behind the figure of 'Corinna': R. Verdière, 'Un amour secret d'Ovide', *L'Antiquité classique*, 40–2 (1971), 623–48 (pp. 641–6). In *Les Exilez* by Mme de Villedieu (1684), Terentia also contributes unwillingly to Ovid's punishment: by seeking to prevent Ovid's relationship with Julia, daughter of Augustus, from angering the emperor, she makes Crassus jealous; he loves Terentia and wrongly thinks that Ovid has seduced her. A duel ensues, Julia betrays her secret love affair, and Ovid is soon exiled. Villedieu, *Les Exilez*, 13–34; cf. Taylor, *The Lives of Ovid*, 92, for a reflection on the reading practices used and interrogated.

[26] The trip to Baiae towards the end of the volume is firstly suggested as a health cure for Augustus, who no doubt wanted to take his mistress there without preventing Livia from also travelling there (letter XXXVIII).

[27] See n.10 above.

112   THE *LETTERS FROM JULIA TO OVID*

from Ovid to Julia, perhaps influenced by what Ovid himself says about his exile when he suggests he saw something he should not have seen (*Tristia* 2.103–6). Indeed, when he goes to Maecenas' home in search of his lover, Ovid claims to have found Augustus not only with his mistress, Terentia, but also with a young Georgian slave girl.[28] In contrast, the heroine's despair in Bressey's *Lettres de Julie à Ovide* is greatly increased by her belief that she is the cause of her lover's banishment (letter XLII). This despair appears to be all-consuming in the last letter (XLIII), in which the theme of Ovid's dreaded fickleness briefly returns, and in which Julia shuts herself off in solitude, awaiting death.

Which Ovid?

Ovid is anything but fickle in this work, and Julia is similarly constant.[29] Although the author 'plays' with the reputation of her two main characters for much of the collection, the story that she weaves and develops between them is a real love story based on sincerity and fidelity. Ultimately, there is some distance between the image of Ovid that Julia makes reference to on several occasions at the start of the *Lettres* and the side of his character (and perhaps of Ovid's real personality) that is revealed through his affair with Augustus' daughter. The first ten letters, in which Julia hides her identity and pretends not to be Julia, allow her to freely yet cautiously confess her love for the poet, all the while testing him. These tests, through which he proves that he is gallant, that he writes well, and that he is curious and insistent,[30] also show his 'dissipation' ('volatility') and his lack of 'pénétration' ('insight'), as well as an excessive 'esprit' ('mind'), so that he appears to be all wit and no feeling.[31]

---

[28]   *Lettres de Julie à Ovide et d'Ovide à Julie* (1809), 182.

[29]   This point is particularly stressed in the preface to *Lettres de Julie à Ovide et d'Ovide à Julie* (1809), iv. One of the advantages of this collection is that it is able to 'pallier un peu les torts de cette Julie si maltraitée par ses contemporains et surtout par une postérité sévère' (address some of the faults of this Julia so mistreated by her contemporaries, and certainly by a harsh historical legacy). Even though we witness first-hand her 'emportements' (outbursts), she nevertheless remains 'maîtresse d'elle-même' (mistress of her emotions). While her love affair with Ovid makes her culpable, this adultery is justified by several circumstances (including the violence with which she is forced to marry Tiberius, p. v).

[30]   See in particular letter I—'Le galant Ovide', p. 1; 'The gallant Ovid', p. 1, the opening line of the collection, letter II—'la réputation et les ouvrages d'Ovide m'étoient connus et je sçavois que personne n'écrivoit aussi bien que lui' (p. 3) ('had I not heard your fame, and seen your works, and knew that no man writes so well as Ovid') (p. 3) and 'Votre curiosité ne me surprend pas davantage' (p. 3) ('Nor am I more surprised at your curiosity') (p. 3), and letter VI—'Que vous devenez pressant!' (p. 9) ('How pressing do you grow!') (p. 6).

[31]   See letter III in particular. This letter opens with playful criticisms from Julia who, during a party held by her father, was able to look at Ovid while his 'dissipation' ('volatility') prevented him from seeing her and discovering her secret. She continues: 'Je le vois bien, Ovide entend mieux le langage de

The concealment of Julia's identity forces Ovid to rid himself of these flaws little by little, letting his feelings be expressed so that he can gain access to the woman whom he undoubtedly holds in sincere affection. An important step is taken when the two lovers speak for the first time (letter VII). Julia observes and recognizes the giddiness that colours the poet's words: 'Que j'ai eu de plaisir hier! Je vous ai vu, je vous ai parlé! Cet heureux désordre, enfant du sentiment, régnoit dans tous vos discours' (p. 10) ('How great the transport which I yesterday enjoyed! I have seen, I have conversed with you. That agreeable confusion, ever the child of love, reigned through your whole discourse') (p. 7).[32] The decisive step is then taken when she once again reproaches Ovid for his lack of depth, his recklessness, and his preference for charm over emotion. Yet, in reality, by daring to approach Julia during an evening at Livia's (letter IX), he unknowingly succeeds in getting her to reveal her identity. The sincerity that he shows in recognizing his mistake and in asking Julia for a 'préservatif' ('antidote') against Julia[33] is what makes her decide to reveal her identity: 'Oui, vous me verrez, & c'est à votre sincérité que vous devez cette démarche' (letter X, p. 16) ('Yes, you shall see me; and to your own sincerity it is you stand indebted for this step of mine') (p. 11). As a result of the strategy initially adopted by Julia, once the 'charme est enfin rompu' (letter XI, p. 17) ('charm at length is broken') (p. 11) and she reveals her identity to her lover, we also discover an Ovid in part stripped of the prejudices that his reputation and tradition had placed upon him. 'Le galant Ovid' ('the gallant Ovid') and indeed the 'plus aimable mais aussi [le] plus volage des mortels' (letter I, p. 1) ('most fickle, though the most amiable of men') (p. 2) are thus replaced by an Ovid capable of real and lasting emotions.[34]

Nevertheless, the *magister Amoris* still has his hour of glory. The second phase of the love story between Julia and Ovid culminates in the lovers'

---

l'esprit que celui du cœur & sa pénétration ne s'étend pas jusques-là' (p. 5) ('I perceive full well, that Ovid better knows the language of the mind than of the heart; and that his penetration reaches not so far as to the latter') (p. 3). This draws on one of the recurrent criticisms levelled at the poet (and each other) by members of erudite and gallant society in the eighteenth century; see S. Loubère, *L'Art d'aimer au siècle des Lumières* (Oxford: Voltaire Foundation, 2007), 6–7, with, in particular, a quotation from Fréron that closely aligns with Julia's words.

[32] The published translation has been adapted here for clarity.

[33] 'Vous me demandez un préservatif contre les charmes de Julie' (p. 15) ('You ask of me an antidote against the charms of Julia') (p. 10), incipit of letter X.

[34] Only his excess of wit continues to plague Ovid: 'je vous l'avoüe, je crains que vous ne parliez que le langage de l'esprit, & que vos yeux ne me trompent' (p. 26) ('I admit to you, I fear you only speak the language of your wit, and that your eyes deceive me') (p. 16), writes Julia in letter XIII, after having stressed the pertinence of Ovid's words during their meeting the previous day, and their convincing effect at that time.

114   THE *LETTERS FROM JULIA TO OVID*

triumph and in the discreet celebration of an unforgettable night together (letter XV). Julia, however, calls this her 'défaite' ('defeat'), and writes to Ovid of the cradle of *his* joys, rather than hers (p. 32; English, p. 21).[35] Later, in letter XXIV, where Julia praises the persuasive power of Ovid's words (he has succeeded in calming her on the subject of Tiberius), she goes on to state clearly: 'C'est vous qui m'avez appris le véritable culte que l'on doit à l'amour. C'est encore vous qui m'avez fait sentir cette volupté si pure qui prend sa source dans le cœur et qu'une tendre délicatesse accompagne toujours' (p. 59) ('it is you who taught me first the proper worship which is due to love. It is you who have made me feel that pure delight, which takes its first foundation in the heart, and ever is accompanied with the most tender delicacy') (p. 37). While the idea of sensual pleasure may perhaps be at play here, the similarity of this passage with a previous letter on the question of 'volupté' ('pleasure') leads the reader to believe that Julia in fact attaches most importance to spiritual pleasure. This is letter XVII, which closely follows the letter telling of the lover Ovid's 'triomphe' ('triumph'). (It also makes us think of letter 2.12 of the *Amores*, although it is hard to know whether the author had this in mind.) In letter XVII, Julia is set on expressing the intense pleasure that she experienced even when she was not with Ovid; she proclaims her own triumph which occurred when she was at Octavia's and the conversation turned to the poet, whose works were read aloud and praised by many:

> Non, mon cher Ovide, rien n'est si flatteur que de voir honorer son choix par les hommages que l'on rend à celui qui en est l'objet. J'ai partagé votre triomphe, ou plutôt c'est moi qui ai triomphé. J'ai goûté cette volupté si pure où le cœur seul a part.   (letter XVII, p. 36)

> (Oh! my dear Ovid, nothing can give so high a satisfaction as to perceive one's choice honoured by the homage paid by others to the object of it. I shared your triumph, or rather I am the one who triumphed. I tasted to the height that pure pleasure in which the heart alone is sharer.)   (p. 23)[36]

---

[35] In *Les Exilez de la cour d'Auguste* by Mme de Villedieu, Julia had resisted Ovid's advances: 'la Princesse, quoy qu'il plaise à la médisance de publier, s'est toûjours conservée le droit de réprimer mon audace' (the Princess, whatever slanderers may say, always maintained the right to resist my bold advances) (p. 15). In *Les Lettres de Julie à Ovide*, without a doubt Julia allows him to 'repaistre d'alimens plus solides' ('nourish himself with substantial nutrients'), or to 'soulager' ('relieve') the ardour of his desire through 'les remedes qui luy sont propres' ('the remedies at his disposal'). However, this is not the principle focus of their relationship, and the lover's 'cradle' of pleasures does not become the 'grave' of their love (I am paraphrasing the phrase with which Julia concludes letter XV, p. 32; English, p. 21).

[36] The published translation has been adapted here for clarity.

SÉVERINE CLÉMENT-TARANTINO   115

In other passages, Julia herself praises her lover as being the most amiable man, who need not fear rivals, and has no reason to be jealous (see letter XXXVI, p. 69). On several occasions, Ovid is almost likened to the god of Love,[37] which perhaps explains better than his status as a poet the reason why he is so knowledgeable about the subject.

It is noteworthy that when Julia makes reference to what Ovid knows, believes, or may have said about love, this does not necessarily trigger an intertextual allusion to the poet's works.[38] Of course, we can identify several *topoï* and motifs from Roman elegiac poetry, as practised by Ovid, and we could perhaps suggest some more targeted allusions to the *Amores* and the *Ars amatoria* within the *Lettres*. Examples include the importance of frustration and desire (letter XIII), the primacy of the sight of the beloved in a spectacle or a festive celebration (the end of letter XXIV),[39] the use of a slave as a go-between (established in a *post scriptum* to the first letter),[40] and the search for excuses and strategies to overcome obstacles or avoid being separated (letter XVIII).[41] However, fiction appears to dominate on the whole, and the

---

[37] This is very clear at the start of the work in letter IV, when Julia plays the game of seduction and illusion: 'Sçavez-vous quelle a été mon occupation pendant tout le temps qu'a duré le sacrifice? J'ai élevé un Autel dont vous étiez le Dieu; mes vœux, mes soupirs tenoient lieu d'encens, & mon cœur de victime' (pp. 6–7) ('What think you was my business during the sacrifice? Raising an altar, whereof yourself alone was the divinity; my vows and sighs supplied the place of incense, and my heart the victim') (pp. 4–5). Later, Ovid and love are closely linked: 'L'amour qui brillait dans vos yeux me perçoit de mille traits' (letter XIII, pp. 25–6) ('The love which shone forth in your eyes, shot a thousand arrows to my heart') (p. 16); 'et l'Amant et l'Amour' (letter XIV, p. 27) ('love himself…[and] the lover') (p. 17), 'trop foible contre Ovide et l'amour' (letter XV, p. 32) ('how weak I was…against love and Ovid') (p. 20).

[38] This is hardly surprising, if, like Loubère (*L'Art* d'aimer, 40), we consider the importance accorded to translations of Ovid in the seventeenth century, particularly for authors who went on to propose new 'arts of love' in the eighteenth century. See also M.-C. Châtelain, *Ovide savant, Ovide galant. Ovide en France dans la seconde moitié du XVIIᵉ siècle* (Paris: Champion, 2008), 11.

[39] At p. 60 (English, p. 38). Cf. *Ars amatoria* 1.495–6. In a translation by Cuers de Cogolin (1751) roughly contemporaneous to the *Lettres de Julie à Ovide*, the translation of these verses gives even greater space to the language of the eyes: 'Le langage des yeux est celui des Amans. / Et leurs troubles confus font des aveux charmants.… Insensible aux plaisirs que vous offrent ces lieux, / N'y goutez que celui d'admirer ses beaux yeux.' (p. 22) (The language of the eyes is that of Love. / And their confused troubles make charming confessions.… Unaware of the pleasures that these places offer, / Do not taste any others than that of admiring her beautiful eyes). On this subject, see also letters XXII and XXIII in the *Lettres de Julie à Ovide*.

[40] Cf. *Ars amatoria* 1.351–2. In the *Lettres*, Flora, the freed slave, is Julia's faithful accomplice, and there is no question of the lover trying to corrupt her.

[41] At pp. 38–9 (English, pp. 24–5). The passage is amusing, as the identity of Julia, *puella elegiaca* and Augustus's daughter, means that Augustus himself has become part of the motifs involved: consider how the author 'corrects' Ovid—'Je n'ai rien oublié… occupation, santé, enfin j'ai eu recours à Auguste, dont j'espérois que l'autorité me serviroit mieux que les prétextes qui me réussissaient si mal' ('I omitted nothing… business, health, and lastly I pleased the Emperor [Augustus], whose authority I was in hopes would have stood me in better stead than the other excuses which had been of so little service to me'). In the circumstances, Julia fails all the same, as the trip to Latium organized by Octavia is also designed to surprise her with the knowledge of Sulpicia's marriage to the man she loves. Typical motifs, such as a preference for love over war or the state, are also found throughout the *Lettres*.

116 THE *LETTERS FROM JULIA TO OVID*

reader can well imagine that it is the fictional 'real' Ovid who converses with Julia (the real-life author, such as he has been imagined, and not the author as he presents himself within his own works, often known as Naso). So it is this Ovid who declares that love is fearful (letter VII, p. 11; English, p. 7), and who states that love is never satisfied, as he pressures Julia for another meeting in private (letter XII, p. 22; English, p. 14). Julia later builds on statements Ovid has made to her in person or in his letters: 'je crois comme vous, mon cher Ovide, qu'il n'y a que la médiocrité de l'amour qui puisse le faire condamner et que son ardeur seule le justifie toujours', (letter XXV, p. 61) ('I think with you, my dearest Ovid, that only mediocrity in love can make it blameable, and ardour in it always is a sufficient vindication of it') (p. 38).

The strongest intertextual references to Ovid's works are found in the mythological allusions made by Julia in the *Lettres*. These are mostly in the early part of the collection and, interestingly, question the carelessness of Ovid, who has apparently forgotten the lessons taught by these tales. There are two of interest: one is less relevant and alarming than the other; both nevertheless add to the ever-growing number of bad omens that plague the two protagonists. The first is a reference to Cupid and Psyche. According to Julia, when Ovid insists on lifting the veil and knowing her real identity, he is forgetting the unhappiness that was caused by Psyche's great curiosity when she decided to look upon her husband's real face.[42] Although Ovid does not explicitly address this myth in his work, we cannot rule out its 'migration' into collections of Ovid's texts at some stage in their reception history, as has been the case for other myths.[43] This hypothesis is further strengthened by the

See, for example, letter IV, where Julia substitutes the god of Love/Ovid in the place of Mars and letter XXXIII, p. 99 (English, p. 63), where Julia states that reigning over Ovid's heart is the only 'empire' that could 'please me'.

[42] Letter VI, p. 10 (English, p. 6).

[43] Cf. G. Huber-Rebenich and S. Lütkemeyer, 'Non Ovidian "Immigrants" in Printed Illustration Cycles of the Metamorphoses', in K. A. E. Enenkel and J. L. de Jong, eds, *Pictorial and Literary Transformations in Various Media, 1400–1800* (Leiden: Brill, 2020). 'Cupid and Psyche' appear in a large, illustrated volume of Ovid's works by Crispijn de Passe in 1602, although it is their wedding that features, used to signify the Golden Age, and in the form of an engraving by Goltzius (Huber-Rebenich and Lütkemeyer, 'Non Ovidian "Immigrants"', 18–20). A key example of such 'migration' in the reception history of Ovid's works is that of the 'Judgement of Paris' which, in the seventeenth century in particular, is found in editions of the poet's complete works, as well as in illustrations referring to this work (ibid., 22–6); see also the page 'Traductions en tous genres' in the digital exhibition '*Lire les Métamorphoses d'Ovide*': https://nubis.univ-paris1.fr/web/lire-les-metamorphoses/traductions-en-tous-genres.html. See also S. Clément-Tarantino, 'Les Cabinets de Bailleul ornés de scènes mythologiques ou le triomphe d'Ovide', in R. Poignault and H. Vial, eds, *Présences ovidiennes* (Clermont-Ferrand, Collection Caesarodunum LII-LIIIbis, 2020), 485–19 (pp. 492–3). A recent example of the use of Apuleius' fable of Cupid and Psyche in a version of Ovid's work is found in Mary Zimmermann's theatrical reproduction of the *Metamorphoses*: Metamorphoses: *A Play*, based on D. R. Slavitt's translation of the *Metamorphoses* of Ovid (Chicago: Northwestern University Press, 2002).

fact that Apuleius indicates his knowledge of Ovid in the passages of his *Metamorphoses* which relate this tale.[44] The second mythological reference shares a similar context: when Julia reproaches Ovid for having got too close to Julia (before she has revealed her identity), she reminds him of Phaethon's misfortune when he goes too close to the sun. These two allusions (which, as it so happens, show the heroine in a positive light) interestingly draw attention to a flaw which, according to accounts of the reasons for the poet's exile, was central to his 'crime': curiosity, whether deliberate, innocent or unintentional, as mentioned above.[45] Indeed, Phaethon is explicitly associated with the poet's punishment at the start of the *Tristia* (1.1.79–80).[46] It is interesting to note that so few references to mythology appear later on in the *Lettres*, as Bressey instead turns to real or credible historical figures (notably, as we have seen, by using these as examples or counterexamples in her subplots). Did she therefore seek to be the historian that her son claimed her to be? It seems very unlikely. We shall justify this position as we now conclude with a discussion of the role and voice that Charlotte de Bressey gives to Julia in the *Lettres*.

The Triumph of Julia, a New Ovid

If Ovid is depicted in the *Lettres* as being truly faithful and in love, the portrayal of Julia, daughter of Augustus, also corrects the traditional image of this figure. While she may boldly demand her freedom, she makes such a demand in particular at the moment when she feels herself caught in the trap of her marriage to Tiberius. Thus, her claim for freedom is not part of her general behaviour, or an indication of the loose morals that she is alleged to have had.[47]

As she herself highlights in the *Lettres*, Julie is the true unhappy victim of the story: she is forced to marry a man whom she hates (p. 93; English, p. 59),

---

[44] E. J. Kenney, *Cupid & Psyche* (Cambridge: Cambridge University Press, 1990), 23–4, 29–30, *passim*.

[45] Cf. *Tristia* 2.103–6, where Ovid tells of having seen something that he should not have seen, likening himself to Actaeon unwittingly stumbling upon Diana while bathing.

[46] Were he ever to come back to life, Phaethon would avoid the sky. This *exemplum* features in a passage in which Ovid recommends that his book does not find its way onto Palatine Hill.

[47] The only exception is found at the start of letter XXXIX. There, Julia expresses her happiness at being in Baiae, as a result of the great freedom that she experiences there, particularly with regards love: 'Ovide, que ce séjour me plaît! l'on y jouit d'une liberté que l'on ne connoit point à Rome, l'amour brille dans tous les yeux, point de surveillants, point de jaloux. L'on aime, on se le dit...' (p. 117) ('Oh Ovid! How delightful is this dwelling! Here we enjoy that liberty which is not known at Rome: love shines in every eye; no spies, no jealousy dares enter here. We love, and we declare it...') (p. 75).

118   THE *LETTERS FROM JULIA TO OVID*

and to suffer his company; in contrast, when Ovid is separated from Julia, he is free to think about their love and recall the happy moments they shared together (p. 103; English, p. 66). Besides, shortly after having gone out of her way to save her friend Sulpicia from a forced marriage, Julia must suffer the same fate, the horror of which makes her wish for death (letter XXX, p. 94; English, p. 61). The account of this devastating event leads to a negative depiction not only of Tiberius, but also of Livia: she holds Livia responsible for having lost everything, including her father's affection, and hopes to receive a fatal blow from her (letter XXXI, p. 96; English, p. 61).

However, once the terrible moment of her 'sacrifice' has passed, Julia picks herself up again. Her hope and energy are renewed by an angry outburst, triggered by Ovid's jealousy, and we appear to witness a role reversal between the two figures. At the start of letter XXXVI, Julia, who says that she forgives Ovid for his doubts, finds herself reassuring him of her sincerity, and reminding him that her 'cœur est incapable de feindre' (p. 108) ('heart [is] incapable of all dissimulation') (p. 69). Letter XXXIX is the true turning point in Julia's taking on Ovid's role and characteristics, particularly his wit, even if she resists him complimenting her for doing so, in order to insist on her sincerity of sentiment. In the opening lines of the letter (the first to have been written from Baiae), Julia insists on the similarities between their emotions which lead them to see things with the same eyes. She then goes on to reprimand her lover for having complimented her on her wit: 'Comment, Ovide, vous me faites des compliments? est-ce à moi que vous devriez les adresser? rendez toujours justice à mon cœur, mais ne louez jamais mon esprit' (p. 118) ('How many compliments, my dearest Ovid, do you make me! Is it to me you would address them? Do justice always to my heart, but do not praise my wit') (p. 76). As we have seen, Julia criticizes Ovid for having more wit than sentiment at the start of the *Lettres*, and this reproach provides a clear allusion to the criticism traditionally levelled at Ovid for being too fond of his *ingenium* or wit.[48] In the story told within the *Lettres*, Ovid must rid himself of some of this wit in order to be with his beloved. Yet, at the end of the collection it is Julia who becomes the inventive one, using her *mens* as a means of continuing to exert her freedom and to relive in her imagination the sweet moments that she spent with Ovid (letter XXXVII, p. 71). Julia thus acquires, or reacquires, part of the freedom that Ovid still enjoys as a man, and the lack of which deepens her own misfortune (as discussed above).

---

[48] It is the Ovid *nimium amator ingenii sui* who is described by Quintilian (10.1.88). See also n. 28 above.

Above all, and perhaps most clearly in the last letters of the collection,[49] Julia appears to take on the qualities of Ovid, along with some of his behaviours and ways of speaking. In particular, she reminds the reader of Ovid's writings in exile, in which he affirms that even Augustus has no power over his *ingenium*, which remains unfettered and allows him to see those close to him and to revisit the places and moments of joy that he holds dear.[50] The more that we sense the impending event of Ovid's banishment, or rather his disappearance, the more Julia appears able to take on his role and integrate aspects of Ovid's exile. While the brutal ending and Julia's final goodbye prevent us from imagining a future for this feminine Ovid, the transformation of Julia in the *Lettres* remains no less remarkable.

Conclusion

The *Lettres de Julie à Ovide* should not be read as an example of the 'master of love' successfully training one of his disciples. As we have seen, the role of *magister* is certainly alluded to on several occasions, yet in this work language is centred not on the instruction of *eros*, but rather on the discovery of a form of love synonymous with 'tenderness'.[51] It can be argued that Julia converts Ovid to this form of love, to which he will remain true.[52] Moreover, after having fallen in love with the poet almost instantly (letter XXV, p. 38), Julia did not naively undertake her task of seduction: she decided to use illusion and concealment in order to disarm Ovid in this seductive game. Later, after the terrible event of her forced marriage, she remains cautious and shows her strength, or indeed superiority.

---

[49] Earlier in the *Lettres*, the focus given to the themes of illusion and, even more significantly, to the relationship between art and nature gives further weight to this form of Ovidian consecration of Julia as an author. See pp. 11, 13, and 41–2 (English, pp. 7, 9, and 26)—'et si l'art y entre pour quelque chose, il est si bien caché qu'on ne le reconnaît pas' ('and if ever art is introduced, she is so much disguised that she cannot be known') (p. 26) regarding the charms of the stay in the countryside with Octavia.

[50] *Tristia* 3.7.47–8. See also *Tristia* 3.4.56; and 4.2.57–60.

[51] This is also a feature of some of the seventeenth-century female versions of Ovid's love story as they seek to convert him to a 'good' sort of gallantry. See Helena Taylor, 'Ovid, Galanterie and Politics in Madame de Villedieu's Les Exilés de la cour d'Auguste', *Early Modern French Studies*, 37/1 (2015), 49–63.

[52] We can turn to the figure of Saint-Preux in *Julie ou la Nouvelle Héloïse* here. After the lovers' second sexual encounter, Saint-Preux not only declares his love to Julia, but also his belief that she knows how to 'mieux aimer que [lui]' (love better than [him]), and that she alone knows the 'félicité suprême' (supreme happiness), the 'volupté si pure' (pure delight) that is 'le sentiment dont [s]on cœur se nourrit' (the sentiment which feeds [his] heart). J.-J. Rousseau, *Julie ou la Nouvelle Héloïse*, Leborgne et Lotterie, 2018; letter 55, p. 187. There are certainly several similarities between the two Julias (and also several differences, particularly concerning marriage). This question warrants further study, given that Rousseau's novel was first published in 1761.

120   THE *LETTERS FROM JULIA TO OVID*

It is possible that Charlotte de Bressey did not try to compete directly with Ovid, whose works are present in faint intertextual allusions through which the author shows her knowledge of the important questions that run through his work, as well as the principal elements of his erotic elegies. This gives a mark of authenticity to the figure of Julia that Bressey creates, who, in fact, could claim to compete with the poet. Julia does this by establishing new codes in her relationship with Ovid, while making it clear that she remains aware of those set by her lover. After first joining Ovid in his arena, she goes on to highlight their similarities through their shared sentiments, and is praised by Ovid for her own wit and ingenuity.

Close analysis of the authoritative figure of Julia in the *Lettres* leads us to suggest that she aligns with the tradition that identifies her as the *puella* named in the *Amores* as Corinna. It is undoubtedly to this tradition that Dorat alludes in his letter from Julia to Ovid, in which the heroine notes that 'Seule, je l'inspirai, je ne m'en défends pas; / Les leçons qu'il vous donne, il les prit dans mes bras' (I alone inspired him, I do not deny it; The lessons that he teaches you, he learned in my arms).[53] Yet the Julia created by Charlotte de Bressey is more than just a muse: Ovid inspired her to write letters in which she dares to say and reaffirm the sincerity of her love, and to enjoy briefly the freedom that elsewhere escapes her.

Translated by Eleanor Hodgson

[53] Dorat, *Julie, fille d'Auguste à Ovide*, 6.

7

Metempsychosis, Sappho, and Adultery Laws

Ovidian Moments in the Career of Constance de Salm (1767–1845)

Thea S. Thorsen

This chapter argues that three moments may be identified as 'Ovidian' in the career of Constance de Salm and that these moments are each represented by a specific work. One of these works is Salm's poem *Le Bouton de rose*, whose main Ovidian quality lies, as will be argued, in the poem's 'metempsychosis'; the next is Salm's play *Sapho*, where the Ovidian reverberations are extensive, as it echoes Ovid's *Heroides* 15, and further connections are traced between the literary careers of Salm and Ovid. The final work I will investigate is Salm's *Épître adressée à L'empereur Napoléon* [Letter Addressed to the Emperor Napoleon], written in the very same year that she was commissioned to compose the Emperor's wedding cantata, yet in which she criticizes the sovereign for allowing laws against adultery that strongly promoted inequality between the sexes; in this case, it will be argued, the Emperor Napoleon strikingly mirrors Augustus, and Salm Ovid.

The French woman author at the centre of this chapter went by many names during her career, which saw a rich and varied output that was produced during some of the most extraordinary moments in world history. Her birth name was Constance (or rather Constance-Marie) de Théis, under which she published her first poetry in the 1780s.[1] When she subsequently married, her name changed to Madame Constance Pipelet de Leury. The marriage took place in the revolutionary year of 1789, and her name was

---

I would like to thank Professor Martin Wåhlberg and Dr Maxime Margollé for their advice while I was researching this chapter.

[1] M. L. Barbier, 'Notice biographique sur Madame la princesse Constance de Salm-Dick [*sic*]', *Biographie Universelle*, 81 (1847), 3–8 (p. 4).

Thea S. Thorsen, *Metempsychosis, Sappho, and Adultery Laws: Ovidian Moments in the Career of Constance de Salm (1767–1845)* In: *Ovid in French: Reception by Women from the Renaissance to the Present*. Edited by: Helena Taylor and Fiona Cox, Oxford University Press. © Oxford University Press 2023. DOI: 10.1093/oso/9780192895387.003.0007

122   METEMPSYCHOSIS, SAPPHO, AND ADULTERY LAWS

naturally trimmed down to 'Citoyenne Pipelet'[2] when her first play, *Sapho*,[3] was staged in 1794, immediately after the Terror.[4] The play was staged in one of the most central theatres in Paris, which at the time was called the *Théatre des Amis de la Patrie*,[5] and to the music of one of the most renowned composers of Salm's time: Jean-Paul-Égide Martini (1741–1816).[6] The performance of this work in the new medium of *opéra comique*,[7] which had gradually been eclipsing the *grands opéras* of the *ancien régime*,[8] was a huge success.[9] Salm's second play, *Camille, ou Amitié et Imprudence*, was staged at the *Comédie française* in 1799, the very same year she divorced her first husband.[10] In 1803 she remarried, thus becoming first 'Comtesse' and then 'Princess Madame Constance de Salm-Dyck'. This denomination she again trimmed down to 'Madame la Princesse Constance de Salm' when she published her *Œuvres complètes* in four volumes in 1842, only three years prior to her death in 1845. These collected works included letters and discourses (volume 1), different kinds of poetry, including her opéra, *Sapho*, written in verse (volume 2), the novel *Vingt-quatre heures d'une femme sensible*, plus a collection of essays entitled *Pensées* (volume 3), as well as the *Éloges, rapports, notice* and the autobiography *Mes soixante ans: ou mes souvenirs politiques et littéraires* (volume 4).[11] I refer in

---

[2] S. Y. H. Law, 'Composing *Citoyennes* through *Sapho*', *The Opera Quarterly*, 32/1 (2017), 5–28.

[3] For the sake of coherence throughout, I will render the names of ancient characters according to UK spelling, even where Salm and other authors employ the French; the exception will be in titles of works.

[4] C. de Salm, *Œuvres complètes*, 4 vols (Paris: Librairie de Firmin Didot Frères et Arthus Bertrand, Libraire, 1842), i, pp. xiii–xiv.

[5] See the libretto by J. P. A. Martini, *Sapho, tragédie en trois actes et en vers, par la C[itoyen]ne Pipelet, mise en musique... Représentée pour la 1re fois, sur le théâtre des amis de la Patrie rue de Louvois, le 22 frimaire l'an 3e de la République (14 xbre 1794 v. s.)... gravé par le C[itoye]n Lobry* (Paris: n.p., 1795). The theatre, which carried many names before it was demolished in the nineteenth century, stood on the spot which today is Square Louvois in Paris.

[6] Martini was from Freystadt in Germany but had a long career in France. He composed for Marie Antoinette, produced various pieces throughout the French Revolution, and became a professor at the Conservatoire de Paris, as well as, after the restoration of the Bourbon regime, *surintendant de la musique du roi*. His romance 'Plaisir d'amour' (1784) lives on in Elvis Presley's adaptation 'Can't Help Falling in Love' from 1961.

[7] Law, 'Composing *Citoyennes* through *Sapho*'. For more about the specificities of this medium, see below.

[8] M. Margollé, 'Aspects de l'opéra-comique sous la Révolution: L'évolution du goût et du comique aux théâtres Favart et Feydeau entre Médée (1797) et L'Irato (1801)', PhD diss., University of Poitiers, 2013, 39.

[9] See e.g. Salm, *Œuvres complètes*, i, p. xiv. See Law, 'Composing *Citoyennes* through *Sapho*', 6.

[10] Salm's second play was not well received due to, according to Salm herself, a pioneering 'dénoûment tragique de ce drame, qui était alors une chose toute nouvelle' (tragic plot of this drama, which at the time was an entirely new thing) (Salm, *Œuvres complètes*, i, p. xiv). Unless otherwise stated, all translations are my own.

[11] Despite the title, this four-volume publication does not contain all Salm's works. See N. Berenguier, 'Publish or Perish! Constance de Salm's Identity Crisis and Unfulfilled Promise', *Dix-Neuf*, 21/1 (2017), 46–68.

this chapter to Constance de Salm in accordance with the name she chose for her complete works: 'Salm'.[12]

To the extent that Salm is known today, it is primarily for her *Épître aux femmes* (1797), an incisive feminist retort to the openly misogynistic *Ode aux belles qui veulent devenir poëtes* by Ponce-Denis Écouchard-Lebrun (1729–1807). Écouchard-Lebrun thus initiated a 'querelles des femmes auteurs' that was largely settled by Salm's decisive contribution.[13] One of the brilliant strategies Salm employs in this letter is not to address Écouchard-Lebrun explicitly, but rather her fellow women.[14] The community of women authors in France extends beyond Salm's own contemporary times, and among the precursors who have been evoked as an inspiration of the *Épître aux femmes* in scholarship is Madeleine Scudéry (1607–1701).[15] In Salm's

[12] In this regard I follow e.g. M. Bercot, M. Collot, and C. Seth, eds, *Anthologie de la poésie française XVIIIe siècle, XIXe siècle, XXe siècle* (Paris: Gallimard, 2000); C. Seth, 'L'Épître aux femmes: textes et contextes', *Cahiers Roucher-André Chénier*, 29 (2010), 41–64; and C. Seth, 'La Femme Auteur, stratégies et paradigmes—L'exemple de Constance de Salm', in A. Del Lungo and B. Louichon, eds, *La littérature en Bas-Bleus* (Paris: Garnier, 2010), 195–214; and E. M. Hine, *Constance de Salm, her influence and her circle in the aftermath of the French Revolution: 'A Mind of No Common Order'* (New York: Peter Lang, 2012).

[13] See Seth, 'L'Épître aux femmes', and P. Blanchard, 'De la querelle des femmes à la guerre des satires: Les combats de Constance de Théis', in Laurance Vanoflen, eds, *Femmes et philosophie des Lumières: De l'imaginaire à la vie des idées* (Paris: Garnier, 2020), 305–22.

[14] The *Épître aux femmes* arguably addresses all the arguments presented against women authors that came up during the *querelle* and also, implicitly, targets Écouchard-Lebrun, especially through the couplet: Insensés! Vous voulez une femme ignorante, / Eh bien! soit; confondez l'épouse et la servante (Fool! You want an ignorant woman, oh well! So be it; confound your wife with the servant), Salm, *Œuvres complètes*, i, p. xiii. Écouchard-Lebrun was ridiculed for having been divorced his wife, allegedly due to maltreatment, after which he instead married his servant; see Blanchard, 'De la querelle des femmes', 318.

[15] M. Sharif, 'La Révolution française et le Théâtre de propagande: l'exemple de *Sapho* (1794) de Constance Pipelet', *Recherches en langue et littérature françaises*, 9/14 (2015), 43–74 (p. 44). Other influences that have been suggested include those of Olympe de Gouges (1748–93) and, though not a woman, Nicholas de Caritat, Marquis de Condorcet (1743–94), who frequented the same *lycée* as Salm and strongly supported women's rights; Blanchard, 'De la querelle des femmes', 310–11, 321. Notably, both died during the Terror, Gouges by the guillotine and Condorcet during imprisonment, awaiting his execution. Along with Madeleine de Scudéry's section on Sappho in her novel *Artamène ou le Grand Cyrus* (1649–53), the following were also centred on Sappho and may have influenced Constance de Salm: Nicholas Berner, *Sapho*, a cantata (1723); Bernard Burette, *Sapho, à Phaon* ode, 'performed in concert at Versailles in 1730' (Law, 'Composing *Citoyennes* through *Sapho*', 24); Thomas L'Afflichard (music) and Adrien-Joseph Valois d'Orville (text), *La nouvelle Sapho* (1735); Louis Lemaire, *Sapho*, 'cantatille'; Louis Antoine Le Febvre, *Sapho, cantatille à voix seule avec symphonie* (1763); La Jonchère, *Sapho, opéra* (the libretto was published in 1772); Claude-Louis-Michel Sacy, *Les Amours de Sapho et de Phaon* (1775); Alessandro Verri, *Le avventure di Saffo* (1780), which was influential beyond Italy. The list is not exhaustive; see also H. Rüdiger, *Sapho: Ihr Ruf und Ruhm bei der Nachwelt* (Leipzig: Dieterische Verlagsbuchhandlung, 1933); J. DeJean, *Fictions of Sappho* (Chicago: Chicago University Press, 1989), *passim*, but esp. pp. 313–15; K. Newman, ed. and trans., *Madeleine de Scudéry: The Story of Sappho* (Chicago: University of Chicago Press, 2003); H. Krief, *La Sapho des Lumières: Mlle de Scudéry, Fontenelle, Gacon, Voltaire, Rousseau, Pesselier, Moutonnet de Clairefort, Barthélemy, Lantier, Mme de Staël* (Saint-Étienne: Publications de l'Université de Saint-Étienne, 2006); Law, 'Composing *Citoyennes* through *Sapho*', *passim*, esp. p. 24, and D. Loscalzo, *Saffo, la hetaira*, Syncrisis 4 (Pisa and Rome: Fabrizio Serra Editore, 2019), 21–4.

124 METEMPSYCHOSIS, SAPPHO, AND ADULTERY LAWS

Épître aux femmes, she evokes references to her own play *Sapho*.[16] Sappho, the iconic woman poet from archaic Lesbos (seventh century BC),[17] is a natural point of contact between Salm's *Épître aux femmes* and her play *Sapho*, but also alludes to Scudéry's *Sapho à Erinne, Vingtiesme harangue* from her *Les Femmes illustres ou Les harangues héroïques* (1642), and the so-called *l'histoire de Sapho* narrated in the second part of the tenth and final volume of her massive novel *Artamène ou Le grand Cyrus* (1649–53).[18] Scudéry's *harangue*, which is purportedly penned by Sappho, vindicates women's capacity to be intellectuals and criticizes marriage as a form of slavery, as does Salm in her *Épître aux femmes*. Moreover, Scudéry's Sapphic *harangue* is addressed to Erinna, whom we re-encounter, along with Damophyle, a character in Scudéry's *l'histoire de Sapho*, as figures in Salm's play *Sapho*.[19]

However, in the preface of Salm's published play, she does not refer explicitly to Scudéry or any other authors who could have had the role as mediators of the high esteem that she herself bestows upon Sappho, with one exception: Ovid (43 BC–AD 17/18).[20] Pointing out that little remains of Sappho's output in her own day and age, Salm explains:

> mais l'hommage que lui rend Ovide, L'Hymne à Vénus par Denys d'Halicarnasse, et L'Ode que Boileau a traduite d'après Longin, suffisent pour donner une idée de ses grands talents.
>
> (but the homage that Ovid offers her, the Hymn to Venus by Dionysius of Halicarnassus and the Ode which Boileau has translated from the text given in Longinus, suffice to provide an idea of her great talents.)[21]

'L'Hymne' and 'L'Ode', for which Dionysius of Halicarnassus (first century BC), Boileau (1636–1711), and Longinus (or Pseudo-Longinus, first century AD) are mentioned mainly as agents of transmission, are among the most enduring examples of Sappho's sublime mastery,[22] namely those compositions that are

---

[16] Salm, *Œuvres complètes*, i, 19.   [17] See n. 53 below.

[18] On Scudéry's *Les Femmes illustres* as reception of Ovid, see Helena Taylor's chapter in this volume (Chapter 4).

[19] I will return to both Erinna and Damophyle in the context of Salm's play *Sapho* below.

[20] The only works Salm does mention explicitly are Jean-Jacques Barthélemy, *Voyage du jeune Anarcharsis en Grèce* (1788), and Ennio Quirino Visconti, *Iconographie grecque*, which was published in 1808 in Paris. She mentions these only to modify their points; see Salm, *Œuvres complètes*, ii, 6 n. 1.

[21] Salm, *Œuvres complètes*, ii, 7.

[22] For the history of editions and translations of these and other poems in France, see DeJean, *Fictions of Sappho*, 313–14, Krief, *La Sapho des Lumières*, 7–26, and J. Fabre-Serris, 'Anne Dacier (1681), Renée Vivien (1903): Or What Does It Mean for a Woman to Translate Sappho?', in Rosie Wyles and Edith Hall, eds, *Women Classical Scholars: Unsealing the Fountain from the Renaissance to Jacqueline de Romilly* (Oxford: Oxford University Press, 2016), 78–103.

now known as poem 1 and Fr. 31. '[T]the homage that Ovid offers her' may be represented by several instances in his output,[23] but especially the epistolary elegy referred to as *Heroides* 15, *Sappho Phaoni* [Sappho to Phaon], also known as the *Epistula Sapphus* [Sappho's Letter] (*c.*19 BC–AD 2), to which I will return below.[24] One point of intersection, which needs elucidating first, is that of their parallel careers.

Ovid and Salm's careers share a remarkable number of features, even though they lived some eighteen centuries apart, one a man and the other a woman, in very different contexts. Even so, both expressed a strong urge to write literature from a young age,[25] and consequently made their literary debuts in public as teenagers;[26] they also both composed plays in their twenties that feature heroines,[27] and both continued to produce works where female

---

[23] See J. Ingleheart, '*Vates Lesbia*: Images of Sappho in the Poetry of Ovid', in Thea S. Thorsen and Stephen Harrison, eds, *Roman Receptions of Sappho* (Oxford: Oxford University Press, 2019), 205–26; and C. Elisei, 'Sappho as a Pupil of the *praeceptor amoris* and Sappho as *magistra amoris*: Some Lessons of the *Ars amatoria* Anticipated in *Heroides* 15', in Thea S. Thorsen and Stephen Harrison, eds, *Roman Receptions of Sappho* (Oxford: Oxford University Press, 2019), 227–48.

[24] The 'Ur-biography for Sappho', DeJean, *Fictions of Sappho*, 42. *Heroides* 15 as both a work by Ovid and a homage to Sappho has been challenged by two strands in scholarship. In one of these strands, critics have questioned the poem's authenticity: K. Lachmann, 'De Ovidii *Epistulis*', in J. Vahlen, ed., *Kleinere Schriften zur Klassischen Philologie von Karl Lachmann* (Berlin: Reimer, 1974); R. Tarrant, 'The Authenticity of the Letter of Sappho to Phaon (*Heroides* XV)', *Harvard Studies in Classical Philology*, 85 (1981), 133–53; C. Murgia, 'Imitation and Authenticity in Ovid's *Metamorphoses* 1.477 and *Heroides* 15', *American Journal of Philology*, 106 (1984), 456–74; P. E. Knox, ed. *Ovid, Heroides, Select epistles* (Cambridge: Cambridge University Press, 1995); and O. Zwierlein, *Die Ovid- und Vergil-Revision in tiberischer Zeit* (Berlin: De Gruyter, 1999). See Thea S. Thorsen, *Ovid's Early Poetry: From his Single* Heroides *to his* Remedia amoris (Cambridge: Cambridge University Press, 2014), 93–123. In the other strand, critics have questioned the extent to which the poem is a homage to Sappho: see E. D. Harvey, 'Ventriloquizing Sappho: Ovid, Donne, and the Erotics of the Feminine Voice', *Criticism*, 31 (1989), 115–38; P. Gordon, 'The Lover's Voice in *Heroides* 15: Or, Why Is Sappho a Man?', in Judith Hallett and Marilyn B. Skinner, eds, *Roman Sexualities* (Princeton: Princeton University Press, 1997), 274–91; S. H. Lindheim, *Mail and Female: Epistolary Narrative and Desire in Ovid's* Heroides (Madison: Wisconsin University Press, 2003); and J. Hallett. 'Catullan Voices in *Heroides* 15: How Sappho Became a Man', *Dictynna*, 2 (2005), 1–15. For arguments in favour of the poem being both authentic and a homage to Sappho, see G. Rosati, 'Sabinus, the *Heroides* and the Poet–Nightingale: Some Observations on the Authenticity of the *Epistula Sapphus*', *The Classical Quarterly*, 46 (1996), 207–16; V. Rimell, 'Epistolary Fictions: Authorial Identity in *Heroides* 15', *Proceedings of the Cambridge Philological Society*, 45 (1999), 109–35; J. Hallett, 'Ovid's Sappho and Roman Women Poets', *Dictynna*, 6 (2009), 1–12; Thorsen, *Ovid's Early Poetry*; Thorsen, 'The Newest Sappho (2016) and Ovid's *Heroides* 15', in Thea S. Thorsen and Stephen Harrison, eds, *Roman Receptions of Sappho* (Oxford: Oxford University Press, 2019), 249–64; and Elisei, 'Sappho as a Pupil'.

[25] Salm presents writing as an undertaking 'où c'est difficile de s'arrêter' (it is difficult to stop oneself) (*Œuvres complètes*, ii, 4); compare Ovid's 'sponte sua carmen numeros ueniebat ad aptos/et quod temptabam scribere uersus erat' (yet all unbidden song would come upon befitting numbers and whatever I tried to write was verse), *Tristia* 4.10.25–6.

[26] Ovid claims that he had only shaved once or twice ('barba resecta mihi bisue semelue fuit', *Tristia* 4.10.58) when he first recited his love poems publicly, and Salm published her first poetry in the 1780s, when she too was just a teenager.

[27] It is generally believed that Ovid's (almost entirely) lost tragedy *Medea* was composed in the earlier phase of his literary career; probably when he was in his twenties (see Theodor Heinze, ed., *Der XII. Heroidenbrief: Medea an Jason. Mit einer Beilage: Die Fragmente der Tragödie Medea* (Leiden: Brill, 1997)), and Salm saw the staging of her *Sapho* when she was only twenty-seven.

126 METEMPSYCHOSIS, SAPPHO, AND ADULTERY LAWS

figures are centre stage throughout their literary careers.[28] These careers lasted until the respective authors' deaths, and for their literary accomplishments they both received great, if not unanimous, appraisal.[29] Both Ovid and Salm also lived through some of the most dramatic revolutions in human history, and from the debris of the massive societal upheavals both saw an emperor rise to supreme power.

Not only that, but both directly addressed these emperors, combining literary celebrations of their powers with attempts to influence their politics. Importantly, both Ovid and Salm link the affairs of the heart with the affairs of the state, and they do so under circumstances which are almost eerily similar: for even if Ovid, like Salm, also engaged in the praise of the emperor (Ovid most notably so with his *chef-d'œuvre* the *Metamorphoses*),[30] both were also critical of these emperors. Salm's criticism, to which I will return below, promotes an idea of equality between the sexes as a solution to the tensions between love and politics, which she time and again stresses in her work. As she says, addressing men in her *Épître aux femmes*: 'Laissez-nous plus de

---

[28] Among which Ovid's *Heroides* is paramount. The chronological order of Ovid's early poetry is notoriously hard to establish (Thorsen, *Ovid's Early Poetry*, 1–8), but even so, Ovid's *Heroides* must be among the first works he composed. The *terminus post quem* remains the publication of Virgil's *Aeneid*, which was issued only after his death in 19 BC, since Ovid alludes to this work in his *Heroides* 7, from Dido to Aeneas, the central figures in Virgil's *Aeneid* Books 2–4. Moreover, in addition to her *Sapho*, Salm wrote the play *Camille* (see above), whose title is the name of a woman; for the prominence of female figures in her output, see the brief survey of her *Œuvres complètes* above.

[29] Ovid was immediately and widely popular, a fact he himself attests to (*Tristia* 4.10.55–6), as does his massive reception history from the poet Martial (first century AD), as well as quotations from his poetry on the walls of Pompeii; see A. W. Van Buren, 'A Pompeian Distich', *The American Journal of Philology*, 80/4 (1959), 380–2; J. Miller, and C. Newlands, eds, *The Handbook to the Reception of Ovid* (Chichester: Wiley and Sons, 2014), 38; and K. Milnor, *Graffiti and the Literary Landscape in Roman Pompeii* (Oxford: Oxford University Press, 2014). In fact, very few ancient poets can rival his global influence on post-classical art, literature, and culture (see e.g. Miller and Newlands). It seems safe to assume that the very popularity of Ovid must have contributed to the discontent of the emperor Augustus, who finally banned him from Rome, which was also a form of criticism. A less political and more literary kind of criticism of Ovid, already in his contemporary times, was that he was 'too great a lover of his own talent' ('nimium amator ingenii sui', Quintilian, *Institutio Oratoria* 10.1.98, cf. Seneca the elder, *Controuersiae* 2.2.12). Salm, on the other hand, while less influential after her death, was in her lifetime the first woman to be accepted to the *Lycée des Arts* in Paris and she was later also made a member of the *lycées* of Toulouse and Marseille, and of *La Société des Belles-Lettres de Paris*, all in recognition of her literary achievements, see *Dictionnaire Fortunée Briquet*, s.v. 'Constance-Marie de Théis'. Further recognition is also evident from the fact that she was known as a 'Boileau des femmes' (Boileau of Women) and 'Muse de la Raison' (Muse of Reason). Louis Tisseron and De Quincy attribute the first saying to 'a poet' and the second to André Chénier, 'Notice biographique sur la vie et les écrits de Mme la princesse Constance de Salm-Dyck', *Fastes nobiliaires* (Paris: Imprimerie d'Amédée Saintin, 1845), 3–20 (p. 4). See also J. Letzter, 'Making a Spectacle of Oneself: French Revolutionary Opera by Women Author(s)', *Cambridge Opera Journal*, 11 (1999), 215–32 (p. 230).

[30] The work outlines the history of the world from its creation to its pinnacle under the reign of Augustus.

droits, et vous en perdrez moins' (let us have more rights, and you will lose less).[31] Ovid, who has a similar focus on tensions between love and politics in his output, is perhaps less clear regarding a feminist solution, and so scholarship still debates the mixed messages of sexism and feminism in his works.[32] However, as I will argue, when Ovid is regarded from the vantage point of Salm's reception of him, his feminist qualities become more conspicuous.

As already pointed out, Salm explicitly mentions Ovid in the preface to her play, *Sapho*. This play was also dedicated to her father, from whom Salm received an excellent education, which included classical literature.[33] Nevertheless, the moments that will be framed as 'Ovidian' in this chapter do not necessarily reflect Salm's intention to evoke Ovid in each discussed case of her career. Rather—in line with the reception studies approach—I argue that these 'Ovidian' moments become strikingly visible to the reader, who is familiar with crucial details in both authors' careers.[34]

Metempsychosis

Salm's poem, *Le Bouton de rose*, which she composed at the behest of some unnamed acquaintances to an old tune known as the *Baronne*, was first published in the *Almanach des Grâces* in 1788, and about ten years later made 'almost popular' with a new tune by the composer Louis Barthélémy Pradher (1782–1843).[35] It is a remarkable poem, which dwells on the pending transformation of a rosebud into a rose, simultaneously evoking the transformation of a girl into a woman. The poem is filled with erotic imagery—in the traditional erotic vocabulary, the rosebud evokes both breasts and the clitoris[36]—and the poetic 'I' claims that if she were such as rosebud, she would 'not die but of pleasure in the bosom of the rose', which readily evokes

---

[31] Salm, *Œuvres complètes*, ii, 11.

[32] A place to start to gain an overview of this complexity might be the review by S. E. Seidler (https://bmcr.brynmawr.edu/2021/2021.06.43/) of Melanie Möller, *Gegen/Gewalt/Schreiben: De-Konstruktionen von Geschlechts- und Rollenbildern in der Ovid-Rezeption. Philologus. Supplemente*, xiii (Boston: De Gruyter, 2020).

[33] See e.g. Tisseron and De Quincy, 'Notice biographique', p. 4, and Bercot, Collot, and Seth, *Anthologie*, 1380. Salm dedicates her play *Sapho* to her father through a brief poem, where she thanks him also for her education. Salm, *Œuvres complètes*, ii, 2.

[34] As summarized e.g. by C. Martindale and L. Hardwick, 'Reception', in S. Hornblower, A. Spawforth, and E. Eidinow, eds, *Oxford Classical Dictionary* (4th edn; Oxford: Oxford University Press, 2015).

[35] Salm, *Œuvres complètes*, ii, 309–10.   [36] Seth, in Bercot, Collot, and Seth, *Anthologie*, 1381.

128   METEMPSYCHOSIS, SAPPHO, AND ADULTERY LAWS

orgasm and pubescent anxiety; the final prayer expresses a wish to halt the development into maturity. And all this is described not in an objectifying fashion, but as emerging from an inner conflict of the poetic persona of a young woman author:

Bouton de rose,	Rosebud
Tu seras plus heureux que moi;	you will be more fortunate than I;
Car je te destine à ma Rose,	for I intend you for my rose,
Et ma Rose est ainsi que toi	and my rose is like you,
Bouton de rose.	rosebud.
Au sein de Rose,	In the bosom of the rose,
Heureux bouton, tu vas mourir!	happy bud, you will die!
Moi, si j'étais bouton de rose,	I, if I were a rosebud,
Je ne mourrais que de plaisir	would not die but of pleasure
Au sein de Rose.	in the bosom of the rose.
Au sein de Rose	In the bosom of the rose
Tu pourras trouver un rival;	you can find a rival;
Ne joute pas, bouton de rose.	do not escape, rosebud,
Car, en beauté, rien n'est égal	for in beauty nothing is equal
Au sein de Rose.	to the bosom of the rose.
Bouton de rose,	Rosebud,
Adieu, Rose vient, je la vois:	goodbye, the rose is coming, I see her:
S'il est une métempsycose,	If there is metempsychosis,
Grands dieux! par pitié rendez-moi	Great gods! For pity's sake, turn me into
Bouton de rose.	a rosebud.[37]

The poem is also remarkably evocative of several features that are found in, and typical of, Ovid. For example, the exclamation 'Grands dieux!', which evokes a pagan rather than a Christian context, fitting for the Enlightenment's distance to the Church, echoes Ovid's own employment of the phrase *di magni* on several occasions in his poetry.[38] Moreover, as already pointed out, to 'die of pleasure' easily recalls the climax of an orgasm, and whether this was the intention of Salm's phrasing or not, Ovid, the self-professed

---

[37] Translation by Jane Burkowski.
[38] See *Amores*, 2.19.18, *Fasti*, 6.187, and *Heroides*, 18.102. This is not a very common expression in Latin literature, but in fact is otherwise only found in Plautus (*Truculentus* 701) and three times in Catullus (14A.12; 53.5; 109.3).

magister amoris, is actually one of very few ancient authors who recommends that women should enjoy sexual arousal and have orgasms (he also attributes one to Sappho, precisely in *Heroides* 15, although this could not have been known to Salm due to the state of the transmitted text at the time).[39] Furthermore, Salm aligns the poetic 'I' with different stages in the floral life of a rose, which is evocative of Ovid's more mature masterpiece the *Metamorphoses*, in which numerous transformations of humans into animal and even vegetal life forms take place. And in this context, Salm's evocation of metempsychosis is particularly evocative,[40] as it goes straight to the heart of Ovid's masterpiece, where the idea is formulated through the mouthpiece of the ancient master of metempsychotic philosophy, Pythagoras, in the dictum 'all changes, nothing perishes' ('omnia mutantur nihil interit', *Metamorphoses*, 15.153).[41]

Sappho

Metempsychosis is a strongly metapoetic concept, which in Roman literature is initiated by the dream vision of Ennius (239–169 BC) where the soul of Homer is claimed to have transmigrated to the body of Ennius himself (after an intermediate stage as a peacock).[42] Assuming the soul, or qualities, of a model poet is an important part of being an author in ancient Rome, where Sappho is one such model of increasing importance, culminating in Ovid's *Heroides* 15, which is both a portrait of Sappho and a cross-dressed

---

[39] See esp. *Ars amatoria* 2.686 and 3.793–4, Thorsen, *Ovid's Early Poetry*, 143–6, esp. n. 37. The orgasmic reading of *Heroides* 15.139 could not have been known to Salm, as it was retrieved from a medieval manuscript at a later point in time; however, the passage at *Heroides* 15.47–50, which basically also recounts sexual embraces that end in climax, was available in Salm's time. See A. P. Palmer, ed., *Ovid: Heroides*, vol. 1, with the Greek translation of Planudes, and a new introduction by Duncan Kennedy (1898; Bristol: Bristol Phoenix Press, 2005).

[40] The concept was in vogue at the time she wrote her poem, as seen e.g. in the novel *Sopha* by Claude Prosper Jolyot de Crébillon (1707–1777), where the main character is transformed into the shape of a sofa; cf. Seth, in Bercot, Collot, and Seth, *Anthologie*, 1381.

[41] See C. Segal, 'Myth and Philosophy in the *Metamorphoses*: Ovid's Augustanism and the Augustan Conclusion to Book XV', *American Journal of Philology*, 90 (1969), 257–92; and C. Segal, 'Intertextuality and Immortality: Ovid, Pythagoras and Lucretius in *Metamorphoses* 15', *Materiali e discussioni per l'analisi dei testi classici*, 46 (2001), 63–101; J. F. Miller, 'The Memories of Ovid's Pythagoras', *Mnemosyne*, 47 (1994), 473–87; P. Hardie, 'The Speech of Pythagoras in Ovid *Metamorphoses* 15: Empedoclean epos', *Classical Quarterly*, 45 (1995), 204–14; P. Hardie, *Ovid's Poetics of Illusion* (Cambridge: Cambridge University Press, 2002), 10, 95; and M. Beagon, 'Ordering Wonderland: Ovid's Pythagoras and the Augustan Vision', in Philip R. Hardie, ed., *Paradox and the Marvellous in Augustan Literature and Culture* (Oxford: Oxford University Press, 2009), 288–309.

[42] Persius 6.9–11.

130   METEMPSYCHOSIS, SAPPHO, AND ADULTERY LAWS

self-portrait of Ovid.[43] This poem has conditioned the reception history of Sappho, and in this history the role of Ovid has often been eclipsed by that of his female precursor.[44] In the following, I will therefore strike a different course than that which is commonly taken in studies involving the reception history of *Heroides* 15, by focusing on Ovid and Salm, rather than on how the figure of Sappho emerges in both authors.[45]

Approaching *Heroides* 15 from the point of view of Salm's play allows us to better appreciate the drama of the Ovidian poem.[46] Such drama derives first and foremost from its suspense. All of Ovid's *Heroides*, or 'letters of heroines', capture specific moments in complex plots.[47] Given the epistolary mode of the genre, the first-person singular of the letter writer has limited knowledge of future events, which may be better known to a reader familiar with established versions of specific stories.[48] The specific moment in the complex plot that is captured in *Heroides* 15 is the immediate aftermath of Sappho's secret abandonment by her beloved Phaon who had eloped from the island of Lesbos to Sicily. The elegiac letter of *Heroides* 15 is thus Sappho's attempt to persuade Phaon to return to her, or at least to send her a letter confirming that he has indeed left her, so that she may know that it is not all just some misunderstanding (*Heroides* 15.217–20).

Very early on in her letter, Sappho reminds Phaon of how her supreme poetic talent is indistinguishable from her erotic prowess,[49] and how he used to

---

[43] Especially prominent examples of poets who resort to Sappho as their model prior to Ovid are Catullus and Horace; see Thorsen and Harrison, eds, *Roman Receptions of Sappho*. On the representations of Sappho in Claude Cahun's 1925 *Héroïnes*, see Catherine Burke's chapter in this volume (Chapter 10); for Marguerite Yourcenar's reworking of Ovid's Sappho in *Feux* (1936), see the chapter by Florence Klein in this volume (Chapter 11).

[44] See n. 23 above.

[45] For excellent interpretations of the figure of Sappho *per se* and in the context of the revolution in Salm's play, see Law, 'Composing *Citoyennes* through *Sapho*', and P. Perazzolo, 'Un "animal sans pareil" sous la Révolution: la Sapho ambiguë de Constance de Salm', *Revue italienne d'études françaises*, 8 (2018).

[46] Sappho has been a prominent name in the context of drama since antiquity. According to Strabo (*Geographica* 10.2.99), the New Attic Comedy playwright Menander referred to Sappho's leap from the Leucadian cliffs in his play *Leukadia* (see below), and the playwright Diphilus (frr. 69, 70 Kock) is referred to as having written a play entitled *Sappho*, as is the playwright Ephippus (fr. 20 Kock), whereas e.g. the playwright Plato Comicus (fr. 1) is reported as having composed plays with the title *Phaon*. These are just some examples.

[47] Kennedy is pioneering in appreciating this crucial quality of the work. Duncan Kennedy, 'The Epistolary Mode and the First of Ovid's *Heroides*', *The Classical Quarterly*, 34 (1984), 413–22.

[48] This dynamic was dubbed the 'future reflexive' in a famous article by Barchiesi. See also the chapters addressing this feature by Séverine Clément-Tarantino and Florence Klein in this volume (Chapters 6 and 11).

[49] Sappho's reception history has a problematic entanglement with prostitution, as seen e.g. in Loscalzo, *Saffo, la hetaera*, and my review of that book (Thea S. Thorsen, 'Review of D. Loscalzo, *Saffo, la hetaira* (Pisa: Fabrizio Serra editore, 2019)', in *Journal of Hellenic Studies*, 141 (2021), 246–7). It is therefore notable that, according to *Heroides* 15, being an expert lover does not make one a prostitute, which Ovid's Sappho makes clear since she boasts of her erotic expertise while despising her brother's

appreciate both (15.21–50). Sappho thus implies that Phaon has been exceptionally lucky to experience her brand of *amoris opus* (making of love-(poetry)) (15.46), as she recalls that she used to love many girls and women, whom she then rejected for him alone (15.12–20; 199–204). Consequently, Phaon, whom Sappho has now chosen as her true love, is displaying a striking ingratitude by abandoning her, she implies. To demonstrate her grief at this abandonment, she describes, among other things, how she has been wandering around, longing, grieving, and singing, alone in the woods where Phaon and she used to make love (15.137–56).

At one point during these wanderings, Sappho explains, a naiad suddenly appeared to her. This naiad then gave her a curious piece of advice (15.161–2), which, as we shall see, resonates particularly strongly with Salm's *Sapho*. To cure her lovesickness, the naiad claims, Sappho must go to the cliffs of Leucas, where the lovesick who throw themselves from the cliff not only survive but are also cured of their heartache (15.163–72). The naiad's advice thus offers a pretext for the climactic closure of Sappho's letter, where her proclaimed intention to follow this advice is combined with her expressed fear of jumping to her death from the Leucadian cliff, thus intensifying her final appeal to Phaon to come back, or at least to write back, so that she will know whether she will have to jump or not. Importantly, Sappho does not depict herself as explicitly suicidal in *Heroides* 15: her plan to jump from the Leucadian rock, which might of course be regarded as a veiled threat to kill herself,[50] is rather presented as an attempt to mend a broken heart, for which, after all, the requited love of Phaon remains the best medicine, as Sappho explicitly and repeatedly reminds him (15.185–94).

The drama of *Heroides* 15 is thus open-ended: we cannot really know what happens next; Phaon might return, or he might confirm his rejection through a *crudelis epistula* (cruel letter) (15.219). Similarly, Sappho might be cured of her lovesickness by jumping off the Leucadian cliffs, or she might die. And

---

prostitute girlfriend (cf. *Heroides* 15.63, 'frater meretricis captus amore' (brother taken by the love of a whore)); cf. also Herodotus, *Historiae* 2.135, and Posidippus 22 (Austin and Bastianini). In her *Précis de la vie de Sapho*, which precedes her play, Salm mentions that Sappho was the subject of slander (Salm, *Œuvres complètes*, ii, 4–5), which may refer to prostitution as readily as homoeroticism, since it is the former aspect of Sappho's reception history that she criticizes Visconti for promoting by referring to the two Sapphos in his book; see Salm *Œuvres complètes*, ii, n. 1. The ancient reference for the idea of 'Sappho the hetaira' as opposed to 'Sappho the poet' is Aelian, *Varia Historia* 12.18–19; the reference to Nymphis = Nymphodorus for the same claim, is highly problematic; see T. Thorsen and R. Berge, 'Receiving Receptions Received: A New Collection of *testimonia Sapphica* c.600 BC–AD 1000', in Thea S. Thorsen and Stephen Harrison, eds, *Roman Receptions of Sappho*, 290–402 (pp. 296–7). See also Perazzolo, 'Un "animal sans pareil"', 1–2.

[50] Sappho's prayers to several powers and deities to soften her fall convey that she doubts the claim of the naiad that it is safe to jump off the cliffs; see 15.177–84.

132   METEMPSYCHOSIS, SAPPHO, AND ADULTERY LAWS

precisely because this is all unknown as Sappho pens her letter, her plan to go to Leucas, rendered more likely to be realized through her employment of the future tense, helps to stress the gravity of her present predicament: 'Ibimus... monstrataque saxa petemus' (I shall indeed go... and I shall find the rocks that have been pointed out) (15.175).

The narrative of *Heroides* 15 thus ends in a cliffhanger, which is echoed strikingly in Salm's play. In many ways Salm's play unfolds as *Heroides* 15's sequel:[51] while Ovid's Sappho promises to go to Leucas (cf. 'ibimus...', above), but remains on Lesbos for at least the time it takes to write her letter, Salm's Sappho has left her native island and arrived on that of Leucas.[52] At the same time, we see that Salm relies also on other sources than Ovid, especially regarding the persons Sappho is surrounded by in the play. The cast of *Sapho* includes, alongside Sappho and Phaon, Stesichorus, 'a Greek poet and old man who is a friend of Sappho',[53] Damophyle, 'false friend of Sappho',[54] Cleis, 'student of Sappho and in love with Phaon',[55] Erinna,[56] 'Sappho's first student', and the high priest of Apollo's temple, in addition to more priests, more students of Sappho, Leucadians, male and female, children, and further men.[57] Except for Sappho and Phaon, none of these others features in *Heroides* 15, while Erinna and Damophyle feature prominently in Scudéry's two works involving Sappho, which do not, however, include Stesichorus.[58] Salm thus makes her own mix of Sappho's entourage in her play.

In the play's first act we meet Sappho surrounded by her students, whom she has brought with her to her new abode. And whereas Sappho knows only that Phaon has abandoned her, not why or with whom, as she pens her letter of *Heroides* 15, Salm's Sappho has just discovered that Phaon left for Sicily with her student Cleis. She is deeply upset and indeed claims that she wants to

---

[51] Like many other 'fictions of Sappho'; see Rüdiger, *Sapho*, DeJean, *Fictions of Sappho*, and Loscalzo, *Saffo, la hetaera*, 21–4.

[52] Cf. also Scudéry and La Jonchère, in n. 15 above.

[53] Under the first entry for 'Sappho' in the Byzantine encyclopaedia known as the *Suda* (Σ 107 Adler), we read: 'Sappho:... a lyric poetess; flourished in the forty-second Olympiad [= 612–608 BE], when Alcaeus, Stesichorus and Pittacus were also alive.'

[54] First attested in Philostratus of Athens, *Life of Apollonius of Tyana* 1.30.5.

[55] Cleis is mentioned in the same entry, see above, of the *Suda* (Σ 107 Adler), as the name both of mother and daughter of Sappho. *Heroides* 15.70, 120 mentions her daughter (*filia*), but does not offer her name.

[56] In the *Suda* (E 521 Adler), the poet Erinna is said to have been 'a companion and contemporary of Sappho'. Erinna's date, and consequently connection with Sappho, has been questioned only in recent scholarship; see especially M. L. West, 'Erinna', *Zeitschrift für Papyrologie und Epigraphik*, 25 (1977), 95–119.

[57] 'STÉSICHORE, poète grec, vieillard ami de Sapho', 'DAMOPHILE, fausse amie de Sapho', 'CLÉIS, élève de Sapho et amante de Phaon', 'ÉRINNE, première élève de Sapho'. Salm, *Œuvres complètes*, ii, 8.

[58] Ibid.

commit suicide by throwing herself from the Leucadian cliffs. Erinna and Stesichorus try to make Sappho change her mind, while Damophyle reveals—through asides to the audience—that she wants Sappho to jump, since her own love interest, the poet Alcaeus, only has eyes for Sappho. Soon Cleis arrives to tell Sappho that she has left Phaon and begs Sappho's forgiveness for having fallen in love with her teacher's beloved. Sappho forgives Cleis. Erinna then announces that Phaon too has just arrived at Leucas, and Sappho is overjoyed.

The setting of the second act is at the temple of Apollo by the cliff. Here, the high priest addresses the other priests, and explains that they need someone to jump from the cliff on the oracular command of Apollo to maintain their power.[59] Conveniently, Damophyle arrives and persuades the priests to target Sappho as their next victim. To achieve a common goal, Damophyle suggests to the priests that she will make Phaon break Sappho's heart again, so that Sappho will throw herself into the sea, and thus, by committing suicide, become the victim that the priests need. Damophyle starts to unfold her plan, but it does not all turn out as she has foreseen, for Sappho intervenes unexpectedly, and Phaon chooses (however reluctantly) to marry her, and not Cleis.

In the third act, night has come, and Damophyle, now fearing that her plan will be entirely overturned, has gathered some men, and is waiting in hiding for Cleis and Phaon, who have planned to meet for a last farewell and renounce their love for each other out of respect for Sappho. However, at the very instant that they do so, both are kidnapped by Damophyle and the men, and taken aboard a boat. Morning dawns, and everything is prepared for the wedding between Sappho and Phaon at the temple of Apollo. Naturally, Phaon never shows up (as he has been kidnapped), and thunder begins to sound from above as Sappho's anxiety grows. Soon she sees the boat with Phaon, Cleis, and Damophyle on it, and mad with grief at what she believes to be the betrayal of her lover and her student, Sappho is now bent on jumping from the Leucadian cliffs. Stesichorus tries to persuade her not to do it but is stopped by the high priest. And so, as the thunder increases, and lightning also begins to strike, Sappho declares that she forgives Phaon, and jumps to her death. In the final scene Stesichorus prays to the gods to vindicate the wrongs Sappho has had to endure, and the boat with Cleis, Phaon, and Damophyle on it sinks, while the temple of Apollo ignites and crumbles as the lightning becomes a rain of fire.

---

[59] Salm thus cleverly exploits the ancient rite of jumping from the cliff of Leucas as mentioned by Strabo (63/64 BC–AD 23) in his *Geography* (10.2.29) and as used by the naiad in Ovid's *Heroides* 15; see above and Salm, *Œuvres complètes*, ii, 6, n. 1.

134   METEMPSYCHOSIS, SAPPHO, AND ADULTERY LAWS

Thus, Salm's *Sapho* represents a narrative continuum with Ovid's *Heroides* 15 in which the former work brings Sappho to a tragic death, which is sealed not by her unrequited love of Phaon, nor the murderous scheme of the false friend Damophyle, but by the hypocritical priests, whose self-serving machinations are immediately avenged, seemingly by divine powers.

Ovid's *Heroides* and Salm's *Sapho* may be said to be revolutionary in more than one sense. Not only were both works written under (post-)revolutionary political circumstances, but they are also revolutionary in aesthetic terms. Indeed, Ovid's *Heroides* are perhaps the author's most innovative work, as the poet himself suggests. For, in the third book of his *Ars amatoria*, Ovid imagines that a future admirer will recommend his *Heroides* precisely by heralding the work's innovative qualities: 'ignotum hoc aliis ille nouauit opus' (he created that work/genre, as entirely new/unheard of to all others) (*Ars amatoria* 3.346). Certainly, several features make this work unprecedented in ancient literary history. That said, Ovid's *Heroides* does not appear to emerge from nothing.[60] The genre of Latin love elegy offers the most conspicuous mould for this fifteen-poem collection.[61] The most important hallmarks of this mould are the metrical form of the elegiac couplet and the theme of unhappy love.[62] These hallmarks are present, yet at the same time transformed in Ovid's *Heroides*. Here, the elegiac couplet is merged with the epistolary form, and unhappy love, which in conventional elegy is set in the poet's contemporary Rome, is here moved to the realm of legendary literature. The most innovative feature of Ovid's *Heroides* remains, however, as discussed in the chapters by Jessica DeVos, Helena Taylor, Océane Puche, and Florence Klein in this volume (Chapters 3, 4, 5, and 11), the female perspective, which allows Ovid to retell—and usurp—the entire literary history that precedes him, from Homer to Virgil, afresh. When Ovid seals such an innovative enterprise with a portrait of an actual poet, Sappho, she arguably assumes the qualities of his *altera ego*.

Salm's *Sapho* mirrors Ovid's *Heroides* in its combination of form and content, which includes important elements pertaining to the tradition, yet also contributes to its transformation. Much like Ovid's *Heroides*, Salm's *Sapho* is hard to pin down in terms of genre.[63] However, in the same way as

---

[60] F. Spoth, *Ovids Heroides als Elegien* (Munich: Beck, 1992) is a key source on the interplay between the genre of Latin love elegy and Ovid's *Heroides*.

[61] See also Thea S. Thorsen, 'Ovid the Love Elegist', in Thea S. Thorsen, ed., *The Cambridge Companion to Latin Love Elegy* (Cambridge: Cambridge University Press, 2013), 114–32 (pp. 117–20).

[62] Ibid., *passim*.   [63] Law, 'Composing *Citoyennes* through *Sapho*', 16.

the literary genre of elegy offers a basic form for Ovid's work, the theatrical genre of opera offers a similar foundational scheme for *Sapho*. As already touched upon, in the decades before Salm composed her play, the *grands opéras* of the *ancien régime* had long been in crisis, and opera's traditional shape had progressively been challenged by new and innovative forms, most notably represented by the medium of *opéra comique*.[64] Salm contributes to this development by adhering to the emerging medium's distinctive features. Her *Sapho* employs the required combination of sung and spoken dialogue, a hallmark of the *opéra comique*, and unfolds over the course of three acts, rather than the classical number of five, typical of the *grands opéras*. At the same time, Salm arguably appropriates and innovates on the preceding operatic legacy. Firstly, she chooses a theme from antiquity, which is typical of the traditional opera; next, she casts her theme in the shape of a tragedy, which is naturally (but not exclusively) at home in that same operatic tradition. Notably, the theme for the plot is not only taken from antiquity, but also displays a romantic, novelistic character;[65] it is, in the words of Salm herself, 'moitié Romanesque, moitié historique'.[66] This combination appears less traditional. Finally, the play is written entirely in verse, which would be more common in traditional opera than in the novel form of the *opéra comique*, where prose and poetry are often mixed. Thus, Salm conspicuously plays with form and content in her *Sapho*, as does Ovid in his *Heroides*.

Among the further parallels between *Heroides* 15 and *Sapho* is the fact that Salm implicitly suggests some generic fluidity, if not innovation (cf. *Ars amatoria* 3.346, above), by variously referring to her work as a *tragédie mêlée de chants* (tragedy mixed with songs), a *tragédie lyrique* (lyric tragedy), or *L'Opéra de Sapho*.[67] There is also the female perspective;[68] and just as the epistolary mode privileges the direct speech of the first person singular in Ovid's *Heroides*, so the play *Sapho* also promotes the direct speech of the female protagonist. Naturally, the figure of Sappho shares the stage with other characters, who also speak in the first person singular. And, in this regard, it may be noteworthy that while a gender balance is observable in *Heroides* 15, since the purported 'I' is female and the poet behind the poem is male, Salm

---

[64] Margollé, 'Aspects de l'opéra-comique', 9–120.

[65] Cf. esp. Scudéry, Sacy, and Verri (n. 15 above), which are all novels.

[66] Salm, *Œuvres complètes*, ii, 7.

[67] The first of these designations is found in the 1842 publication of the play (Salm, *Œuvres complètes*, ii, 9); the other two are both given in her collection of poetry, Constance de Salm, *Poésies de Madame la Comtesse de Salm* (Paris: De l'Imprimerie de F. Didot, À sa Librairie, 1811), 1.

[68] Not to mention the female authorship, of course, which is a point of contrast with Ovid; see, however, Law, 'Composing *Citoyennes* through *Sapho*'.

136   METEMPSYCHOSIS, SAPPHO, AND ADULTERY LAWS

establishes a similar gender balance through the characters in the plot, in which the heroine Sappho is paired with the female villain Damophyle and the irresponsible (yet not profoundly ill-willed) Phaon is placed in contrast with Sappho's steadfast and caring protector Stesichorus. The way in which the poetic 'I' of Sappho in her craft and calling reflects on the poet behind the work is also a shared feature of *Heroides* 15 and *Sapho*.

There is another issue that merits some attention, one which is often neglected in classical scholarship, but which Salm's reception of *Heroides* 15 renders more central: namely, the question of the relevance of performance for Ovid's *Heroides*. Surely, one of the seemingly greatest differences between *Heroides* 15 and *Sapho* is the performative aspect, which in the latter case is an undeniable part of the work as it was initially conceived, and in the former is less obvious.

However, many of the performative and, indeed, musical aspects of ancient poetry are presently little understood, although the two forms of art often appear hard to disentangle.[69] It is therefore notable that, in the passage from the third book of the *Ars amatoria* referred to above, where Ovid imagines that a future admirer will recommend his poetic output thus far to a potential readership, he applies the verb 'cantetur' (let it be sung) and the phrase 'composita uoce' (with modulated, trained voice)[70] to his *Heroides*, which he simply dubs, in the singular, as 'a letter', thus: 'uel tibi composita cantetur EPISTVLA uoce' (or let some *Letter* be sung with practised voice) (*Ars amatoria* 3.345). Indeed, all the *Heroides*, Sappho's epistle to Phaon included, are performable, and through the possibility embedded in Ovid's choice of words in the passage quoted above, most notably represented by the passive verb form, 'cantetur', and the specification of a trained voice, 'composita uoce', one might glimpse the contours of another parallel between *Heroides* 15 and *Sapho*, namely that of performance.[71]

Adultery Laws

The tension in the play *Sapho* between Sappho's love and the Apolline priesthood's politics, as it were, is typical of much of Salm's output. And the same

---

[69] But some light has recently been shed on the connection in Tosca Lynch and Eleanor Rocconi, eds, *A Companion to Ancient Greek and Roman Music* (Chichester: Wiley-Blackwell, 2020).

[70] R. Gibson, *Ovid, Ars amatoria, Book 3* (Cambridge: Cambridge University Press, 2003), 239, and Jacqueline Dangel, 'Réécriture topique en réception polyphonique: Sapho lyrique revisitée par Ovide élégiaque (Héroïde XV)', *Latomus*, 67 (2008), 114–29.

[71] This prompts further thoughts about Ovid's lost tragedy, *Medea*, which was certainly also intended for performance accompanied by music.

tension between the theme of love and that of politics is also a hallmark of Ovid's works. Notably, this tension is increased in both cases due to the introduction of laws regarding adultery by their respective emperors.

When the emperor Augustus (63 BC–AD 19) began to introduce laws against adultery,[72] Ovid famously composed his handbook for non-marital love, the *Ars amatoria*. Marriage was not based on love in ancient Rome and therefore, if someone were to pursue love, it was likely to be of an extramarital kind. Augustus' laws applied only to sex with the mothers, daughters, and wives of Roman citizens. Sex with slaves and sex workers was not criminalized. So, if you could be sexually satisfied without committing adultery according to the law, for what other reason would you break it if not for love? In Ovid's contemporary Rome, to defend love therefore readily equals defending adultery, however bizarre this may seem from the perspective of our day and age.[73] And as a retribution for writing the *Ars amatoria*, Augustus famously relegated Ovid to the shores of the Black Sea. I have argued elsewhere that the punishment of adulterous wives with death is subtly criticized in the final book of the *Ars amatoria*, which stages the husband Cephalus' killing of his adulterous wife Procris,[74] adding significant gravity to a work that too often has been interpreted as purely frivolous.[75]

It is therefore striking, in the context of the present chapter, that Ovid's more oblique criticism of the Emperor's laws against adultery is reflected in Salm's direct confrontation with the Emperor Napoleon concerning the same issue. In her versified *Épître adressée à L'empereur Napoléon*, which was written in opposition to two new laws that were part of the Penal Code of 1810, she protests against a husband's now-acquired right to kill a wife who has been apprehended *in flagrante delicto*. Notably, the Penal Code and Salm's criticism were issued in the same year she had been commissioned to compose, and composed, a cantata for the wedding of Napoleon and the

---

[72] These laws are most often referred to as *lex Iulia de maritandis ordinibus*; *lex Iulia de adulteriis coercendis*; *lex Iulia theatralis*; *lex Fufia Caninia* and *lex Aelia Sentina*; see 'section S' in M. G. L. Cooley and B. W. J. G. Wilson, eds, *The Age of Augustus* (London: London Association of Classical Teachers, 2013).

[73] Ovid's criticism of Augustus and defence of (extramarital) love could not be explicitly expressed in the face of Augustus' programme against adultery, and in *Tristia* 2, his apology addressed to the emperor from exile, he explicitly claims that his *Ars amatoria* was written for prostitutes only (*Tristia* 2.1.303), who were exempt from the adultery laws, but this claim is arguably tongue-in-cheek. See J. Ingleheart, *A Commentary on Ovid, Tristia Book 2* (Oxford: Oxford University Press, 2010), *ad loc.*

[74] See Ovid, *Remedia amoris*, 453.

[75] Thea Thorsen, 'The Second Erato and the Deeper Design of Ovid's *Ars amatoria*: Unravelling the Anti-Marital Union of Venus, Procris and Romulus', in Luis Rivero and others, eds, *Vivam! Estudios sobre la obra de Ovidio. Studies on Ovid's Poetry* (Huelva: University of Huelva, 2018), 141–68.

138 METEMPSYCHOSIS, SAPPHO, AND ADULTERY LAWS

archduchess Marie-Louise, again to the music of Martini.[76] In her 1842 publication of her *Œuvres complètes* she adds the following note to her letter to the emperor:

> 'dans le cas d'adultère, prévu par l'art. 336, *le meurtre commis par l'époux* sur son épouse, ainsi que sur le complice, à l'instant où il les surprend en fragrant délit dans la maison conjugale, est excusable.' Art. 339. '*Le mari qui aura entretenu une concubine dans la maison conjugale*, et qui aura été convaincu sur la plainte de la femme, *sera puni d'une amende de cent francs à deux mille francs.*' Lorsque ces deux articles furent adoptés, ils devinrent, dans la société, le sujet de beaucoup de discussions, ce qui m'inspira cette Épître à L'Empereur, que je fis en peu d'heures, et que je lui adressai à l'instant. Il trouva mes réclamations justes; car, quelques jours après, dans un de ces cercles qui avaient lieu deux fois par semaine aux Tuileries, il vint à moi, et me dit: '*J'ai lu vos vers; vous avez raison; c'est bien, très-bien.*'[77]

> ('in the case of adultery, covered by art. 336, *murder committed by a husband* against his wife, at the moment that he discovers them *in flagrante delicto* in the marital home, is pardonable.' Art. 339. '*A husband who has taken a concubine in the marital home*, and who has been convicted following a complaint by his wife, *is to be punished by a fee of one hundred to two thousand francs.*' When these two articles were adopted, they became the subject of a great deal of discussion in society, which inspired me to pen this *Epistle to the Emperor*, which I completed in a matter of hours, and which I addressed to him at once. He found my protestations fair; for, a few days afterward, at one of the gatherings that were held twice a week at the Tuileries, he approached me, and said: '*I have read your verses; you are right; it is good, very good.*')[78]

The cruel asymmetry that these laws established between husband and wife meant in practice that capital punishment was introduced—without trial— for adulterous wives caught in the act, while murderous husbands of such wives were not considered criminals according to the law. Moreover, these husbands, if they themselves committed a similar offence, and had extra-marital affairs, only had to pay a fine. In essence, these laws, and especially art. 336, did not differ much from Roman laws concerning adultery, and so Salm is right to point out that history should have come further in

---

[76] Salm, *Œuvres complètes*, ii, 106–13.   [77] Ibid., ii, 20–1.

[78] Translation by Jane Burkowski.

this regard, when she closes her letter to the emperor with the following powerful couplet:

Mais qu'il ne soit pas dit, qu'en ce siècle si grand
L'assassin d'une femme a droit d'être innocent.[79]

(But it should not be said, in a time so great, / that the murderer of a woman has the right to be innocent.)

Conclusion

Salm is rightly heralded as a 'feminist *ante litteram*'.[80] No doubt, the solution she envisaged for the tension between affairs of the heart and affairs of the state was a kind of feminism that could facilitate gender equality. Her appraisal of men whom she regarded or represented as helpful in that regard, such as her own father or the figure of Stesichorus in her play *Sapho*, and even her employment of her different surnames (which indeed reflects her relation to men—again, the father, and her husbands)[81] have been interpreted as indicative of her dependence on patriarchal structures,[82] and at best a kind of cautiousness or, worse, a kind of cowardice, compared to bolder feminists of her time.[83]

However, as the comparison between Ovid and Salm in this chapter should suggest, men and women, perhaps especially male and female authors, might indeed have very much in common. And if Salm not only champions women's rights, but also points out that men should contribute to establishing such women's rights, and that they themselves would benefit from that, then this may be regarded as neither too cautious nor cowardly.

Indeed, I hope to have shown in this chapter that the 'Ovidian' moments of Salm's career outline a trajectory of different kinds of courageousness throughout her entire output, and that this courageousness resonates strikingly with that of Ovid, who in turn appears more conspicuously feminist as we follow him—with Salm!—from rare appreciations of female pleasure and grand concepts of metempsychosis, via dramatic (and metempsychotic) representations of the greatest of love poets, Sappho, to poetic attempts to replace institutionalized inequalities between men and women with equality and justice.[84]

---

[79] Salm, *Œuvres complètes*, i, 230.   [80] Bercot, Collot, and Seth, *Anthologie*, 1380.
[81] Law, 'Composing *Citoyennes* through *Sapho*'.   [82] DeJean, *Fictions of Sappho*, 192.
[83] Berenguier, 'Publish or Perish!'.
[84] See I. Ziogas, *Law and Love in Ovid: Courting Justice in the Age of Augustus* (Oxford: Oxford University Press, 2021).

8

Corinne at the Capitol

Fiona Cox

In a famous analysis of *Aeneid* 8 (306–61) James Zetzel observed that the word 'olim' can look both to the past and ahead into the future, so that the moment of prophecy stretches not only from Aeneas' vision to the Augustan present, when Virgil was writing, but beyond that again to the fall of the Roman empire.[1] Perhaps it is unsurprising that in Mme de Staël's *Corinne ou l'Italie* (1807) the reader is first introduced to the protagonist (whose function is, in part, to represent Rome)[2] at this most sacred and symbolically charged site. This is also where Lord Nelvil, the man with whom she has a doomed love affair, lays eyes upon her for the first time as one of the audience of her musical and poetical performances, having heard much about her fame and accomplishments. Mme de Staël gestures towards the long and potent history of the Capitol's symbolism as she depicts Corinne's progress towards the site: 'L'admiration du peuple pour elle allait toujours en croissant, plus elle approchait du Capitole, de ce lieu si fécond en souvenirs' (p. 52). (The people's admiration for her grew and grew the more she approached the Capitol, this place so replete with memories.)[3] She is, of course, looking back to these potent lines of Virgil (and an article examining the extensive and significant network of Virgilian allusion within *Corinne* demands to be written), but she is looking back to Virgil through Ovid, whose *Fasti* also lead us to this site and,

---

[1] 'The *nunc/olim* figure in 348 is itself ambiguous since *olim* can refer to past or future: either "golden now, once densely wooded" or "golden now, one day to be densely wooded". So it is not only a matter of whether we prefer woods or gold; the trajectory of history is itself unclear, either from gold to woods or vice versa, and the lines might allow us to see beyond Augustan grandeur to a return to the wild. *Nunc* may introduce a further wavering, since it could mean "now in Virgil's day" or "now in Aeneas' day", and "golden" could be literal or metaphorical, "belonging to a golden time" or "made of gold, gilded".' Charles Martindale, ed., *The Cambridge Companion to Virgil* (Cambridge: Cambridge University Press, 1997), 5.

[2] See Catharine Edwards, *Writing Rome: A Textual Approach to the City* (Cambridge: Cambridge University Press, 1996), 131: 'a novel which at once became required reading for all educated visitors to Rome, presents as its principal character a woman who may be interpreted as standing for Rome itself (even though she is not as Italian as she seems at first).'

[3] Madame de Staël, *Corinne ou l'Italie* (Paris: Gallimard, 1985). All references to the work are from this edition, with page numbers given in parentheses in the text. Unless otherwise stated, all translations of *Corinne* and of other French texts are my own.

Fiona Cox, *Corinne at the Capitol* In: *Ovid in French: Reception by Women from the Renaissance to the Present.* Edited by: Helena Taylor and Fiona Cox, Oxford University Press. © Oxford University Press 2023. DOI: 10.1093/oso/9780192895387.003.0008

significantly, lead us there on a day of processions and celebration, such as the day on which Corinne first appears:

> vestibus intactis Tarpeias itur in arces
>> et populus festo concolor ipse suo est,
> iamque novi praeeunt fasces, nova purpura fulget,
>> et nova conspicuum pondera sentit ebur. . . .
> Iuppiter arce suo totum cum spectat in orbem
>> nil nisi Romanum, quod tueatur, habet.
>
> (1.79–83, 85–6)

(In spotless garments the procession goes to the Tarpeian heights and the People itself is coloured to match its festal day. And now new *fasces* go in front, new purple gleams, new weight is felt on the bright ivory. . . . When Jupiter from his citadel looks out over the whole earth, he has nothing to gaze on but what belongs to Rome.)[4]

Furthermore, when we are introduced to Rome's ideal woman, the embodiment of the city, it is apparent that 'Corinne, poète, écrivain, improvisatrice et l'une des plus belles personnes de Rome' (p. 49) (Corinne, poet, writer, improviser and one of the most beautiful people in Rome) is not only a paragon for her own times, but also meets Ovid's criteria for an ideal Roman woman, as set out in his *Ars amatoria*. In Book 3 (329–52) Ovid advises women to ensure learned conversation, and skilful song and dance, talents that Corinne possesses to an unusual degree and for which the Romans fête her at the start of the book, even going so far as to liken her to a nymph:

> Oswald se promenait dans les rues de Rome en attendant l'arrivée de Corinne. A chaque instant on la nommait, on racontait un trait nouveau d'elle, qui annonçait la réunion de tous les talents qui captivent l'imagination. L'un disait que sa voix était la plus touchante d'Italie, l'autre que personne ne jouait la tragédie comme elle, l'autre qu'elle dansait comme une nymphe, et qu'elle dessinait avec autant de grace que d'invention; tous disaient qu'on n'avait jamais écrit ni improvisé d'aussi beaux vers, et que, dans la conversation habituelle, elle avait tour à tour une grace et une éloquence qui charmaient tous les esprits.   (p. 50)

---

[4] Ovid, *Fasti*, trans. Anne and Peter Wiseman (Oxford: Oxford University Press, 2013), 3.

142   CORINNE AT THE CAPITOL

(Oswald wandered the streets of Rome, while waiting for Corinne to arrive. Every minute someone was naming her or talking about some new quality of hers, which pointed to the combination of all the talents that capture the imagination. One said that her voice was the most moving in all of Italy. Another said that nobody performed tragedy like her, another that she danced like a nymph and drew with as much grace as originality. They all said that nobody had ever written or improvised such beautiful verses and that, in everyday conversation, she had by turns a grace and eloquence that charmed the minds of all.)

And yet, despite the abundance of these exceptional gifts, Mme de Staël introduces an element of unease, by emphasizing how generic Corinne appears in this public forum:

Tous l'exaltaient jusques aux cieux; mais ils lui donnaient des louanges qui ne le caractérisaient pas plus qu'une autre femme d'un génie supérieur. C'était une agréable réunion d'images et d'allusions à la mythologie, qu'on aurait pu, depuis Sapho jusqu'à nos jours, adresser de siècle en siècle à toutes les femmes que leurs talents littéraires ont illustrées.   (p. 54)[5]

(Everyone praised her to the heavens; but they gave her praises that didn't distinguish her from any other woman with superior gifts. It was a pleasing constellation of images and allusions to mythology that could have been addressed to all women made notable through literary talent from Sappho to our own day.)

---

[5] Stacie Allan sees this episode as looking back to a different Ovidian episode—the myth of Pygmalion, as recounted in *Metamorphoses* 10: 'Staël equally shows awareness of the consequences of women's national allegorization in terms of individual happiness by comparing Corinne to a statue, which recalls the Pygmalion myth. As Corinne processes through the crowds towards a ceremony that bestows upon her a status of national significance, she is compared to a Greek statue: "ses bras étaient d'une éclatante beauté; sa taille grande, mais un peu forte, à la manière des statues grecques, caractérisaient énergiquement la jeunesse et le bonheur"... Staël draws attention to the sculpted nature of Corinne's body, evoking Pygmalion's careful carving of his statue and the solid contours of masculine neo-classical artistic expression, the style used in Revolutionary allegories. Staël's mention of 'bonheur' [happiness] here raises the question of whether she will be happy in the role that men have carved out for her.' Stacie Allan, *Writing the Self, Writing the Nation: Romantic Selfhood in the Works of Germaine de Staël and Claire de Duras* (Oxford: Peter Lang, 2019), 129–30.

See also Chloe Chard: 'When Corinne herself, the half-Italian heroine, makes her first appearance, as she is about to be crowned on the Capitol in recognition of her talents as an *improvvisatrice*, her beauty is described as resembling that of ancient sculptures...Corinne is dressed in the costume of Domenichino's *Sibyl*, and later proclaims further affiliations with one of the Sibyls through her choice of a spot very close to the Temple of the Sibyl at Tivoli for her *maison de campagne*.' Chloe Chard, 'The Road to Ruin: Memory, Ghosts, Moonlight and Weeds', in Catharine Edwards, ed., *Roman Presences: Receptions of Rome in European Culture 1789–1945* (Cambridge: Cambridge University Press, 1999), 125–39 (pp. 129–30).

Corinne is consecrated by this festival that celebrated her literary achievements, but it is significant that de Staël takes the opportunity to emphasize that she is simply one in a long procession of literary women, in a tradition that extends back as far as Sappho, and that (by extension) might include de Staël herself. In celebrating Corinne as a woman of letters, de Staël is very much working within a French Ovidian tradition, whose *salon* culture, and rich history of translation, fostered female engagement with classical literature far more than was the case for Anglophone women writers of the same period.[6] The freedom to explore and respond to literary works enjoyed by Corinne on the continent stands in stark contrast to the etiquette for young ladies in England to which her stepmother wanted to confine her and which required concealing intelligence and artistic endeavour: 'elle m'avait répondu qu'une femme était faite pour soigner le ménage de son mari et la santé de ses enfants; que toutes les autres prétentions ne faisaient que du mal, et que le meilleur conseil qu'elle avait à me donner, c'était de les cacher si je les avais' (p. 365) (she had answered me by saying that a woman was made to look after her husband's household and the health of her children: that no good came from any other aspirations and that the best advice she could give me was to hide any that I might have).[7]

However, as well as establishing her literary pedigree, the name that Corinne selects for herself also aligns her to the Corinna of Ovid's *Amores*, whose identity also is subject to generic blurring and hazy origins, as Alison Sharrock points out in a passage where references to Ovid's 'catalogue' of women parallel the 'réunion d'images et d'allusions à la mythologie' (conjunction of images and allusions to mythology) that pour forth from the Romans celebrating Corinne:

The biggest game with telling and not telling concerns the identity of Corinna. Is she 'real'? People have been asking this since Ovid's own day, according to the poet himself (*Ars* 3.538)—but of course he could be bluffing. He places Corinna in a catalogue with other elegiac women, as an example of

---

[6] On salonnières, see the essays by Emma Herdman, Jessica DeVos, Helena Taylor, Océane Puche, and Séverine Clément-Tarantino in particular in this volume (Chapters 2, 3, 4, 5, and 6), especially Taylor's observations regarding the cultural authority afforded to women writers in France: 'Throughout the *Femmes illustres* this feminine rhetorical space is also explicitly one of authority and influence.' See also Helena Taylor, *The Lives of Ovid in Seventeenth-Century French Culture* (Oxford: Oxford University Press, 2017).

[7] Corinne does emphasize, however, that the freedom she enjoys in Rome is due in part to her literary and artistic gifts: 'J'ai par mon âge et mes talents, à Rome, la liberté d'une femme mariée' (p. 207). (Through my age and talents I have at Rome the freedom of a married woman.)

144   CORINNE AT THE CAPITOL

how poetry can give fame (so love the poet for the sake of his poetry...). But what use is fame based on a pseudonym? And fame which, Ovid hints, derives from a mistaken reading of the *Amores*. Important work has been done to show how the beloved of elegy may be seen as a manifestation of the poetry itself, rather than as a real woman.[8]

Corinne may have forged her own poetic identity, as opposed to being a *scripta puella*,[9] yet she too is doomed to discover the emptiness of 'fame based on a pseudonym', when all that she has achieved falls to dust in her devastation at her doomed love affair with Oswald, Lord Nelvil. The strong Virgilian allusions indicate that she is re-enacting Dido's tragedy, but the story of Dido and Aeneas also, of course, constitutes one of Ovid's *Heroides*. Just as we might look back to the Virgilian episode of Aeneas gazing at the sight of future Rome through Ovid's *Fasti*, so the rich palimpsest of literary allusion allows us to see Corinne lamenting not only in Virgilian tones, but also in the guise of one of Ovid's abandoned women. (And, of course, when Ovid issued advice in the *Ars amatoria* for women wishing to present themselves as cultured, he archly suggested that they might like to cite from his *Heroides*.)[10]

A story of doomed love heightens its poignancy, of course, if it can look back to auspicious beginnings. Oswald's discovery of Corinne is synonymous with his discovery of Italy and their love affair starts in the city of Rome, the city of love, as the anagram of Roma and Amor reminds us. Corinne serves as

---

[8] Sharrock Alison, 'Ovid and the Discourses of Love: The Amatory Works', in Philip Hardie, ed., *Cambridge Companion to Ovid* (Cambridge: Cambridge University Press, 2002), 150–62 (p. 151). See also Béatrice Didier, *Béatrice Didier présente 'Corinne ou l'Italie' de Madame de Staël* (Paris: Gallimard, 1999), 62: 'Et d'abord, comment dès les premiers mots, l'image de Corinne, liée à la peinture, est susceptible de devenir mythique: de grands mythes donnent à ce personnage une dimension qui excède celle d'une simple femme italienne. Pour n'en citer que trois, outre celle de la Sibylle, celle de la nymphe des eaux, d'Ondine, liée à son origine même: la nymphe de La Motte-Fouquet; enfin le mythe de Sapho, poétesse mal aimée: Corinne, nom d'une autre poétesse grecque, y fait par lui-même référence, tout en écartant l'équivoque de l'homosexualité auquel le nom de Sapho est lié dans la conscience collective. Cette dimension mythique qui semblerait faire échapper le personnage au temps, a, en réalité, dans la mesure où le lecteur connaît ces mythes, une fonction proleptique, et, en annonçant un futur, trace déjà un destin. Le schall lui-même annonce la danse du schall de Corinne. Le portrait est donc travaillé par tout un futur du texte, et par tout un passé de la culture.' (And first of all how Corinne's image, connected to painting, as soon as she starts speaking is liable to become mythical; prominent myths bestow upon this character a dimension that goes beyond that of a simple Italian woman. To cite just three examples, as well as that of the Sibyl there is the water nymph, of Ondine who is connected to her very origins; La Motte Fouquet's nymph, and finally the myth of Sappho, a poetess ill used in love. Corinne, the name of another Greek poetess, alludes to this through the name itself, and as it does so discards any ambivalence about homosexuality which is attendant upon the name of Sappho in the public consciousness. This mythical dimension which appears to release the character from temporal constraints in fact, in as much as the reader is familiar with the myths, serves a proleptic function and, while announcing a future, is already marking out a destiny. The shawl itself presages Corinne's shawl. And so the portrait is shaped by an entire future of the text and by an entire past of the culture).

[9] I am using the term coined by Maria Wyke.   [10] *Ars amatoria* 3.333–46.

a guide to Oswald and the city she reveals to him is haunted by Ovidian echoes. Her own 'salon' contains replicas of mythological figures who have stepped from the pages of the *Metamorphoses*: 'Le salon était décoré par les copies, en plâtre, des meilleures statues de l'Italie, la Niobé, le Laocoon, la Vénus de Médicis, le Gladiateur mourant' (p. 72) (The salon was decorated by plaster copies of the finest statues in Italy—Niobe, Laocoon, the Medici Venus, the Dying Gladiator), and as they walk through the city she highlights the artistic works inspired by his poetry: 'Corinne fit remarquer à Lord Nelvil, lorsqu'ils furent hors de l'église, que sur ses portes étaient représentés en bas-relief les métamorphoses d'Ovide' (p. 106) (Corinne pointed out to Lord Nelvil, when they were out of the church, that on its doors Ovid's metamorphoses appeared in bas-relief). On their travels through Rome they appear to be travelling back in time, to the point where 'Ovide et Virgile pourraient se promener dans ce beau lieu, et se croire encore au siècle d'Auguste' (p. 142) (Ovid and Augustus could walk in this beautiful place and believe that they were still living in Augustan times). Rome and its myriad pasts were vividly present to the two of them: 'On ne peut faire un pas dans Rome sans rapprocher le présent du passé, et les différents passés entre eux' (p. 121) (You can't take one step in Rome without bringing the present closer to the past, and bringing different pasts closer together).[11] But this presence of multiple pasts weighs down the narrative with a sense of doom, since they serve as a reminder of the fleeting nature of happiness and the temporal boundaries circumscribing even the most successful of empires.[12]

Part of Corinne's tragedy is that her erudition, her love of ancient literature, fails to protect her from playing the role of one of Ovid's doomed heroines, whose laments fill the letters of the *Heroides*. Like the Ariadne of *Heroides* 10[13]

---

[11] The multiplicity of Rome's pasts existing simultaneously in the present is explored not only by Martindale in his Introduction to the *Cambridge Companion to Virgil* (p. 5), but also James Zetzel's 'Rome and its Traditions' in the same volume (pp. 188–203), where he observes that 'In the *Aeneid*, moreover, early Italy has more than one history, more than one truth'. (p. 190)

[12] See also 'On eût dit qu'en cet endroit la musique exprimait la vanité des splendeurs de ce monde. On croyait voir dans les airs la grande ombre d'Adrien, étonné de ne plus trouver sur la terre d'autres traces de sa puissance qu'un tombeau' (p. 408) (It was as if in this place music expressed the vanity of this world's splendours. You could almost believe that you could see in the airs the mighty shade of Hadrian, astonished to find that there were no longer any traces of his power on this earth except a tomb).

[13] 'venimus huc ambo; cur non discedimus ambo? / perfide, pars nostri, lectule, maior ubi est? / quid faciam? quo sola ferar? vacat insula cultu', *Heroides* 10.57–9 ('We came to thee both together; why do we not depart the same? Ah, faithless bed—the greater part of my being, oh, where is he? What am I to do? Whither shall I take myself—I am alone, and the isle untilled'). Translation from Ovid, *Heroides and Amores*, trans. Grant Showerman (Cambridge, MA, and London: Loeb, 1986). All translations of the *Heroides* are from this edition.

146   CORINNE AT THE CAPITOL

or the Medea of *Heroides* 12,[14] her misery is compounded by the pain of recalling a time when she was happy and unaware of how fragile such happiness was: "'Je m'examine quelquefois comme un étranger pourrait le faire, et j'ai pitié de moi. J'étais spirituelle, vraie, bonne, généreuse, sensible; pourquoi tout cela tourne-t-il si fort à mal?'" (p. 521) (Sometimes I examine myself as a stranger might and I am sorry for myself. I was witty, true, generous, and full of feeling: why should all that turn so sour?). And because she finds herself unable to give up all hope of uniting with Oswald, she is trapped in an intolerable limbo of despair tempered by increasingly unrealistic hope. Like Ovid's heroines she endures the pain of 'deferral and agonizing doubts' which Efrossini Spentzou defines as 'amongst the fundamental elements of the epistles of the *Heroides*'.[15] Furthermore, she rivals these literary forebears in terms of her erudition and scholarship, since they too, as Spentzou's study richly shows, forge their identities from the earlier literary works from which they were born.[16] De Staël's lament for her heroine establishes Corinne as one in a long procession of wronged literary heroines, which leads us back to Ovid's women, who themselves are haunted by their own literary ghosts: 'Combien elle est malheureuse la femme délicate et sensible qui commet une grande imprudence, qui la commet pour un objet dont elle se croit moins aimée, et n'ayant qu'elle-même pour soutien de ce qu'elle fait' (p. 477) (How wretched is the delicate, sensitive woman who commits a great folly, who commits it for an object by whom she feels less loved and who has only herself to support her in what she does). Corinne's role as abandoned heroine is complemented, towards the end of the book, by Oswald going off to war and metamorphosing in this way into an Ovidian *miles*: 'Oswald, pendant ce temps, se distingua dans la guerre par des actions d'une bravoure éclatante; il exposa mille fois sa vie, non seulement par l'enthousiasme de l'honneur, mais par goût pour le péril' (p. 540) (During this time Oswald distinguished himself at war through deeds of dazzling bravery. He risked his life a thousand times, not only through an enthusiasm for honour but also out of a taste for danger). As Corinne performs in the role of an Ovidian heroine, it is striking

---

[14] 'cur mihi plus aequo flavi placuere capilli, / et décor et linguae gratia ficta tuae', *Heroides* 12.11–12 ('Why did I too greatly delight in those golden locks of yours, in your comely ways, and in the false graces of your tongue?').

[15] Efrossini Spentzou, *Readers and Writers in Ovid's* Heroides (Oxford: Oxford University Press, 2003), 127. On this question, see also the chapters in this volume by Séverine Clément-Tarantino, Thea S. Thorsen, and Florence Klein (Chapters 6, 7, and 11).

[16] Ibid., 28–9: 'In this sense, the heroines' struggle for control over their own destinies is really these feminine literary figures' effort to (re)write their stories, against the will of classical authorities. . . . the heroines become at the same time protagonists and critics, readers and writers, lovers and interpreters.'

that she recalls the happier days at the Capitol, ensuring not only that the happiness of those earlier episodes is darkened by her subsequent abandonment and despair, but also that the Capitol remains a site in which past, present, and future co-exist: '"Ah! ce n'était pas ainsi," pensait Corinne, "ce n'était pas ainsi que je me rendais au Capitole la première fois que je l'ai rencontré"' (p. 489) ('Ah, it was not like that,' thought Corinne, 'it wasn't like that I went to the Capitol the first time that I met him'). In the depths of despair it is still Ovid to whom her artistic and literary leanings lead. As she wanders through galleries it is noticeable that most of the artefacts failed to penetrate her benumbed wretchedness, and yet the statue of Niobe still managed to evoke a response: 'Corinne parcourait tous ces objets, et se sentait avec douleur distraite et indifférente. La statue de Niobe réveilla son intérêt: elle fut frappée de ce calme, de cette dignité à travers la plus profonde douleur' (p. 518) (Corinne glanced over all these objects and was pained to recognize how distracted and indifferent they left her. The statue of Niobe piqued her interest: she was struck by the calm and dignity manifested through the deepest of sorrows).

Her identification with Niobe establishes yet another connection with Ovid, who repeatedly compared his plight as an exile to the suffering endured by this bereaved mother.[17] It is not solely through a shared mythological ancestor, however, that Corinne resembles the exiled poet. It is in Rome that she is most herself, that she comes to life as one of the most notable and gifted women of her age; when she leaves Rome to accompany or to look for Oswald elsewhere, her light dims and she becomes a stranger to herself. This dislocation in her sense of identity echoes Ovid's grief at leaving the city he so loved and his feeling that he could never quite be himself away from the centre of the universe, the centre of poetry and literary pursuit. Like Ovid she has the feeling of leaving something more than bricks and mortar; she is leaving a city that has become animate and that wrenches from her a lament every bit as heartfelt as those that she utters in her guise as Ovidian heroine: 'Cette ville possède un charme pour ainsi dire individuel. On l'aime comme un être animé; ses édifices, ses ruines, sont des amis auxquels on dit adieu' (p. 410). (This city has a charm that is peculiar to itself, so to speak. It is loved as if it were a living being—its buildings and ruins are friends to whom one bids farewell). And indeed, when Corinne does leave Rome, this is exactly what she does: 'Adieu, terre des souvenirs, s'écria-t-elle, adieu' (ibid.) (Farewell, land of

---

[17] Niobe appears in *Tristia* 5.1, *Tristia* 5.12, and *Epistulae ex Ponto* 1.2. It is in this last that Ovid claims that his suffering outweighs hers.

148   CORINNE AT THE CAPITOL

memories, she cried—farewell). It is significant that she qualifies Rome as a
'land of memories', as she revisits not only her doomed love affair with
Oswald, but also the host of memories sheltered within the city, including of
Ovid's verses.

On Corinne's last night before leaving Rome to go in search of Oswald, she
beholds the city by moonlight in a passage that evokes Ovid's painful memories of his own last night, expressed in *Tristia* 1.3:[18]

> Cependant, à la veille de quitter Rome, elle éprouvait un grand sentiment de
> mélancolie. Cette fois elle craignait et désirait que ce fût pour toujours. La
> nuit qui précédait le jour fixé pour son départ, comme elle ne pouvait dormir,
> elle entendit passer sous ses fenêtres une troupe de Romains et de Romaines,
> qui se promenaient au clair de la lune en chantant.   (p. 407)

> (And yet on the day before she left Rome she was plunged into a deep
> melancholy. This time she feared and wished that it might be forever. On the
> night before the day appointed for her departure, since she couldn't sleep,
> she could hear a troop of Roman men and women passing beneath her
> window, who were singing as they walked in the moonlight.)

The episode lures her imagination into revisiting the sites of the city she is
leaving and, significantly, she conjures them up by moonlight. When Mme de
Staël observes of this episode that 'Ce n'est pas connaître l'impression du
Colisée que de ne l'avoir vu que de jour: il y a dans le soleil d'Italie un éclat qui
donne à tout un air de fête; mais la lune est l'astre des ruines' (p. 408) (If you've
only seen the Colosseum by day, you don't really have a proper impression of
it; the Italian sunshine dazzles so that everything appears festive—but the
moon is the star of ruins). These ruins evoke the Romes of times past
including, of course, the Augustan Rome of Ovid, but they also mirror the
personal devastation both of Ovid and of Corinne herself. Moreover Corinne
finds herself enmeshed in a web of memories that mirror the synchronicity of
memory at the Capitol, the site where we first meet her and which is so sacred

---

[18] See lines 27–34: 'iamque quiescebant voces hominumque canumque, / Lunaque nocturnos alta
regabat equos. / hanc ego suspiciens et ad hanc Capitolia cernens, / quae frustra iuncta fuere Lari, /
numina vicinis habitantia sedibus, inquam, / "iamque oculis numquam temple videnda meis, / dique
relinquendi, quos urbs habet alta Quirini, / este salutati tempus in omne mihi"' ('by now all was still, no
voices, no barking watchdogs, / just the Moon on her course aloft in the night sky. Gazing at her, and
the Capitol—clear now by moonlight, close (but what use?) to my home, / I cried / All you powers who
dwell in that neighbourhood citadel, / you temples, never more to be viewed / by me, you high gods of
Rome, whom I must now abandon, accept my salutation for all time'). Ovid, *The Poems of Exile*
Translated by Peter Green (London: Penguin, 1994).

in Augustan Rome, from Virgil onwards. Here, as then, imagined future ruin shadows and darkens the present, filling the text with foreboding: 'Elle s'imagina ces colonnes à présent debout, à demi couchées sur la terre, ce portique brisée, cette voûte découverte; mais alors même l'obélisque des Egyptiens devait encore régner sur les ruines nouvelles; ce peuple a travaillé pour l'éternité terrestre' (p. 409) (She imagined that these columns, standing upright at present, half lying on the ground, that portico broken, that vault opened up; but then even the obelisk of the Egyptians would still have to be reigning over the new ruins; this nation worked for eternity on earth).[19]

This ruin imagery not only presages her destruction as a result of her love for Oswald, but it also looks back to the Capitol imagery with which I began this chapter, and ensures that, in retrospect, we can see that the confident, accomplished woman of the start of the book is already haunted by the devastated shell which she becomes. The ruins of the future that haunt the Capitol are not confined to architectural structures in the world of Mme de Staël.

I have already mentioned how this accomplished version of Corinne, rejoicing in her enjoyment of literature and able to converse about art and architecture, belongs very much within the French tradition of female *salonnières*. But the intertextual echoes that shape the figure of Corinne belong not only to the past, in the form of the *Aeneid* or the *Heroides*, but also to the future, since Corinne is the literary ancestor of the love interest—Cécile—in Michel Butor's 1957 novel *La Modification*, one of the most extended meditations on the power of Rome in any language, but also a powerful examination of the network of links and relationships binding the cities of Paris and Rome. As in *Corinne*, the Rome of *La Modification* is inextricably linked with the figure of the woman with whom the protagonist, Léon Delmont, believes himself to be falling in love. In both works the Roman women Corinne and Cécile are threats, who risk seducing their beloveds and luring them away from their perceived path of duty and family bonds. Butor's Cécile is not only the literary daughter of Corinne, but is also likened via a network of allusions and intertexts to the patron saint of Rome, Cecilia, whose origins are famously unknown; this establishes a further connection to Corinne who goes to great

---

[19] Duncan Kennedy also alludes to Book 8 when commenting on Corinne's farewell to Rome from St Peter's: 'Corinne momentarily takes on the role of narrator [...] she projects a 'future' which an implicit character, an observer of the ruined St Peter's, will inhabit as the 'present', and from which he or she will view Corinne's time as the distant 'past'. Duncan Kennedy 'A sense of place: Rome, history and empire revisited' in Catharine Edwards, ed., *Roman Presences: Receptions of Rome in European Culture 1789–1945* (Cambridge: Cambridge University Press, 1999), 19–34 (24).

150 CORINNE AT THE CAPITOL

lengths to obscure her family history.[20] It is significant that, on the tours around Rome, both women take their lovers to see the tomb of Cecilia Metella. Chard observes that 'Germaine de Staël...invests the Tomb of Cecilia Metella with a power to disrupt the lives of those who view it—or, at least, a power to reinforce processes of disruption that are already at work.'[21] Finally, both women kindle romantic feelings within their beloveds, while taking them on tours around the city of Rome and unveiling the city to foreign eyes. Rome is, indeed, the city of love in both stories, but the tragedy for both Corinne and Cécile is that love dims once Rome is no longer a backdrop to their story, and ultimately without Rome their love stories cannot survive.

Chard also highlights the fact that visiting Cecilia's tomb prompts Corinne to align herself to the hapless females of Roman elegy, though in this instance Corinne thinks of Propertius: 'The allusion to Propertius' elegy, in which a woman speaks from beyond the grave, emphasises the spectral nature of memory: its ability to haul the past into a lurking, shadowy visibility.'[22] As Corinne performs a script written in the Augustan period for the elegiac woman, she not only becomes an incarnation of a Propertian or Ovidian heroine, she not only deepens the pain of Ovidian exile by adding to it her own experiences, but she ensures the visibility of Ovid at the dawn of the nineteenth century. In doing so she writes herself into the French feminine Ovidian tradition, while also penning a meditation on Rome that informs subsequent examinations of the vibrant and multi-faceted relationship between Rome and France.

---

[20] 'Je ne dis à personne mon véritable nom, comme je l'avais promis à ma belle-mère; je pris seulement celui de Corinne, que l'histoire d'une femme grecque, amie de Pindare, et poëte, m'avait fait aimer' (p. 386) (I didn't tell anyone my real name in accordance with the promise I'd made to my stepmother. I simply took the name of Corinne, which the story of a Greek woman who had been friends with Pindar and a poetess, had brought me to love).

[21] Chard, 'The Road to Ruin', 129.

[22] Ibid., 130. Chard also looks back to the Capitol appearance of Corinne and analyses how the future sections of the novel are already anticipated in this early scene: 'Earlier in the narrative, a more general reference to ghostly repositories of memory anticipates this resurgence of the past in the deserted Campagna. During her improvisation on the Capitol, the heroine catches sight of Lord Nelvil, in mourning for his father, and speaks of the painfulness of personal memories; she then immediately presents Rome as a city that offers unusual opportunities to spectral beings' (p. 130).

9

Playful *Metamorphoses*

George Sand's Ovidian Affinities

James Illingworth

George Sand wears her fondness for myth on her sleeve. In her autobiography, *Histoire de ma vie* (1854–5), she fondly recalls childhood readings of her *Abrégé de mythologie grecque*, which she describes as an early awakening of her creative spirit:

> Les nymphes, les zéphyrs, l'écho, toutes ces personnifications des riants mystères de la nature tournaient mon cerveau vers la poésie, et je n'étais pas encore assez esprit fort pour ne pas espérer parfois de surprendre les napées et les dryades dans les bois et dans les prairies.[1]

> (The nymphs, the zephyrs, the echo, all these personifications of nature's pleasant mysteries were turning my head towards poetry, and I was not yet a sufficiently free thinker not to hope to occasionally surprise the Napaeae and dryads in the woods and meadows.)

This creativity provoked by myth remains with Sand throughout her long career. Indeed, such is the prevalence of myth in Sand's œuvre that Isabelle Naginski has dubbed her a mythographer. For Naginski, Sand actively creates and recreates myths fit for her epoch; she emphasizes Sand's texts from the decade between 1836 and 1846 as especially rich in mythic influence, noting that the myths Sand produced were inspired by models found 'dans l'Antiquité, l'ésotérisme, le Celtisme, les sociétés secrètes, et les hérésies médiévales. Leur problématique est à longue portée et touche aux problèmes fondamentaux de l'humanité: d'où venons-nous? Où allons-nous? Avec quels articles de foi, quels espoirs allons-nous voyager?' (in Antiquity, esotericism,

---

[1] George Sand, *Œuvres autobiographiques*, ed. Georges Lubin, 2 vols (Paris: Gallimard, 1971), i, 618. All references are to this edition. Subsequent references will be given parenthetically in the text as *OA*. Unless otherwise stated, all translations are my own.

James Illingworth, *Playful* Metamorphoses: *George Sand's Ovidian Affinities* In: *Ovid in French: Reception by Women from the Renaissance to the Present*. Edited by: Helena Taylor and Fiona Cox, Oxford University Press. © Oxford University Press 2023. DOI: 10.1093/oso/9780192895387.003.0009

152 GEORGE SAND'S OVIDIAN AFFINITIES

Celticism, secret societies, medieval heresies. Their questioning is wide ranging and touches on humanity's fundamental problems: where do we come from? Where are we going? With which articles of faith, which hopes will we travel?).[2] Naginski is certainly right to note the eclecticism of Sand's mythopoeic inspiration, drawing as it does from a diverse range of sources, but Naginski's study mentions Ovid only once, in passing, comparing the Golden Age Sand describes in *Le Poème de Myrza* to that same era described by Plato, Horace, Virgil, Ovid, and Apuleius.[3] This chapter will focus on Sand's engagement with Ovidian myths, and those of the *Metamorphoses* in particular, which has previously been understated.

The overlooking of Ovid's presence in Sand's texts is perhaps unsurprising. Sand herself penned numerous meditations on art and on her own artistic practice, a practice we can trace through her voluminous correspondence, prefaces, essays, and journalistic writings.[4] Yet in her writings on art, Ovid goes unmentioned. His presence, however, is everywhere. Scholars have acknowledged the influence of Orpheus, Cyane, and Pygmalion in various novels, and Sand even published her own *Narcisse* in 1858.[5] Anne McCall sees Sand's *Narcisse* as a closer relative of Rousseau's play of the same name than of Ovid's tale, since she identifies similar explorations of 'the terrifying perspective of paternal power, the ridiculous excesses brought upon by vain and frivolous self-absorption, and the value of moderate self-reflection'.[6] Annabelle Rea, meanwhile, sees a greater resemblance between Sand's and Ovid's versions, suggesting that Sand encourages us to recognize this intertextual reference through her use of the word 'métamorphose' at key moments in the development of the three protagonists: Albany, Juliette, and the

---

[2] Isabelle Hoog Naginski, *George Sand mythographe* (Clermont-Ferrand: Presses Universitaires Blaise Pascal, 2007), 12.

[3] Ibid., 96.

[4] Christine Planté, ed., *George Sand critique 1833–1876* (Tusson: Du Lérot, 2006).

[5] Naginski describes *Consuelo* as a 'reservoir of myths', drawing on Orpheus and Cyane: Isabelle Hoog Naginski, *George Sand: Writing for her Life* (New Brunswick, NJ: Rutgers University Press, 1991), 205. Orpheus' presence has further been discussed in Pierre Laforgue, 'Structure et fonction du mythe d'Orphée dans "Consuelo" de George Sand', *Revue d'histoire littéraire de la France*, 84/1 (1984), 53–66, and Linda Lewis, *Germaine de Staël, George Sand, and the Victorian Woman Artist* (Columbia: University of Missouri Press, 2003), 49. Margaret Waller claims that *Lélia* is Sand's way of 'rewriting the Pygmalion/Galatea script' (Margaret Waller, *The Male Malady: Fictions of Impotence in the French Romantic Novel* (New Brunswick, NJ: Rutgers University Press, 1993), 147), and the relationship between *Lélia* and Pygmalion is further discussed in Nigel Harkness, '"Ce marbre qui me monte jusqu'aux genoux": pétrification, mimésis et le mythe de Pygmalion dans *Lélia* (1833 et 1839)', in Brigitte Diaz and Isabelle Hoog Naginski, eds, *George Sand: pratiques et imaginaires de l'écriture* (Caen: Presses Universitaires de Caen, 2006), 161–71.

[6] Anne McCall, 'Land Use and Property Values: The Commercial Development of Space in George Sand's *Narcisse*', *George Sand Studies*, 20 (2001), 83–101 (p. 98).

eponymous Narcisse.[7] While Sand's Narcisse is able to marry Juliette d'Estorade at the end of the novel, this only takes place on her deathbed, and Juliette, like Echo, 'n'avait pas vécu. Elle avait glissé comme un souffle de grâce' (had not lived. She had floated like a breath of grace).[8] Whatever Sand's inspiration for this text, her use of Ovidian myths and themes conforms to the idea of a 'nineteenth-century disintegration of Ovid' proposed by Norman Vance. That is to say that Ovid and his poems became separated in cultural consciousness, with Ovid functioning as little more than a 'convenient if barely acknowledged source of decorative and sometimes disturbing myths'.[9] The case of Sand seems to bear this out: although she neglects to mention Ovid by name, his work, and particularly *Metamorphoses*, serves as a significant inter-text for her own brand of mythmaking. And Sand was certainly familiar with Ovid; translations of the *Metamorphoses* and the *Amores* figure in the cata-logue of Sand's library at Nohant,[10] and Sand quoted from the *Metamorphoses* in passing in a letter to her daughter, Solange, in 1851.[11]

Reading Sand under the sign of Ovid is not a means of tracing an anxiety of influence, to borrow Harold Bloom's term, but rather to bring to light the playfulness of Sand's writing by focusing on her (knowingly) playful use of metamorphosis. Playful is not a word often associated with Sand. Ovid, meanwhile, is frequently described as such. For David Raeburn, Ovid tells the story of Orpheus and Eurydice 'in his own playful way',[12] and for Lee Frantantuono Ovid is 'a playful poet'.[13] The playfulness of the transformations in Ovid's *Metamorphoses* manifests itself in multiple ways. They display what Marina Warner has described as a 'perverse comedy'.[14] But, as Warner further states, they are also political: 'Tales of metamorphoses express the conflicts

---

[7] Annabelle Rea, '*Narcisse* ou la réécriture d'un mythe', in Simone Bernard-Griffiths and Marie-Cécile Levet, eds, *Fleurs et jardins dans l'œuvre de George Sand* (Clermont-Ferrand: Presses universitaires Blaise Pascal, 2006), 231–44 (p. 240).

[8] George Sand, *Narcisse*, ed. Amélie Calderone (Paris: Honoré Champion, 2019), 153.

[9] Norman Vance, 'Ovid and the Nineteenth Century', in Charles Martindale, ed., *Ovid Renewed: Ovidian Influences on Literature and Art from the Middle Ages to the Twentieth Century* (Cambridge: Cambridge University Press, 1988), 215–32 (p. 216).

[10] *Catalogue de la bibliothèque de Mme George Sand et de M. Maurice Sand* (Paris: Librairie des Amateurs, 1890), 48, 58.

[11] 'C'est le chaos, où tous les éléments de la création existaient bien, mais qui n'étaient, comme dit Ovide, que *rudis indigestaque moles*' (It is chaos, where all the elements of creation existed, but were, as Ovid says, no more than *rudis indigestaque moles*). George Sand, *Correspondance*, ed. Georges Lubin, 25 vols (Paris: Garnier, 1964–91), x, 430.

[12] David Raeburn, 'Book 10', in Ovid, *Metamorphoses*, trans. David Raeburn (London: Penguin, 2004), 380–1 (p. 380).

[13] Lee Frantuono, 'Introduction', in Ovid, *Metamorphoses X*, ed. Lee Frantantuono (London: Bloomsbury, 2014), 1–17 (p. 10).

[14] Marina Warner, *Fantastic Metamorphoses, Other Worlds* (Oxford: Oxford University Press, 2002; repr. 2007), 9.

154   GEORGE SAND'S OVIDIAN AFFINITIES

and uncertainties, and in doing so, they embody the transformational power of storytelling itself, revealing stories as activators of change.'[15] Sand's use of metamorphosis is similarly simultaneously playful and political. It can appear light-hearted, even comedic, but it is also a political act. As we will see, the metamorphoses of Sand's texts throw into sharp relief questions of gender, class, and even aesthetics.

To make the case for Sand's playful metamorphoses, I will turn first to *Histoire de ma vie*, the autobiography she published in *La Presse* in 138 instalments between 1854 and 1855, and which narrates the story of her coming to writing. This reading will spotlight a specific aspect of the text: the creation of Corambé, a peculiar metamorphic entity Sand invented in her youth and which is integral to her emergence as a writer. I will then consider one of her fictions, a fairy tale published in 1850, to demonstrate how the transformational principles of Corambé underpin her fiction. My reading of this fairy tale will draw on Julia Kristeva's theorization of the *chora*, a space within the unconscious that retains a link to the maternal. It is this space, Kristeva argues, that grants poetic language its disruptive potential.[16] Sand's metamorphic beings, I suggest, can be read through the notion of the *chora*, as playful figures endowed with access to both masculine and feminine spaces, and therefore capable of challenging conventions and generating change.

Sand's Metamorphic Muse

Instances of metamorphosis in Ovid's texts, Warner tells us, frequently take place in moments of crisis.[17] The emergence of Corambé in Sand's autobiography also takes place at such a moment. On the one hand, Sand's writing of her autobiography, begun in 1847, was interrupted by the 1848 revolution. But on the other, according to the internal chronology of *Histoire de ma vie*, Corambé emerged sometime around 1816, when Sand's half-brother Hippolyte had gone to Saint-Omer to join a regiment of hussars, leaving the twelve-year-old Sand alone at Nohant with her grandmother and her tutor, Deschartres. This marked the beginning of what Sand describes as 'les deux plus longues, les deux plus rêveuses, les deux plus mélancoliques

---

[15] Warner, *Fantastic Metamorphoses*, 210.

[16] Julia Kristeva, *Revolution in Poetic Language*, trans. Margaret Waller (New York: Columbia University Press, 1984), 25. On Kristeva's own reception of Ovid, see Kathleen Hamel's chapter in this volume (Chapter 12).

[17] Warner, *Fantastic Metamorphoses*, 16.

années qu'il y eût encore dans ma vie' (*OA*, i, 798) (the two longest, the two most dream-filled, the two most melancholy years that I had thus far experienced). In her loneliness she began writing 'descriptions', and sent one to her mother, whose derisive reaction caused Sand to stop writing altogether. It is at this point that Corambé comes to Sand in a dream.

Corambé is a complex entity. Sand gives a list of the mythic and pagan goddesses whose qualities combine to produce Corambé, and the list is strikingly Ovidian: Pallas, Iris, Hebe, Flora, the nymphs, Diana, and the Muses (*OA*, i, 813). She places a particular emphasis on the figures linked with creativity, varyingly as either manifestation or source of poetic inspiration, affirming the inextricable connection between Corambé and writing. Naginski points to Corambé as a manifestation of Sand's heresy, her syncretic relationship to myth and religion which she reconfigures according to her own belief system.[18] Martine Reid and Janet Hiddleston, meanwhile, link Corambé to Sand's writing practices, with Reid citing Corambé as the origin of Sand's creative talents, and Hiddleston suggesting that Corambé and writing both fulfil the same need.[19] But I would go further, inserting Corambé and its influence into the entire creative enterprise, placing it at the heart of Sand's poetic system. As Sand herself tells us: 'il devint le titre de mon roman et le dieu de ma religion' (*OA*, i, 812) (it became the title of my novel and the god of my religion).

Despite its decidedly feminine lineage, Corambé defies gender categorization. It occasionally appears dressed 'en femme' (as a woman), but Sand tells us that 'il n'avait pas de sexe et revêtait toute sorte d'aspects différents' (*OA*, i, 813) (it did not have a sex and adopted all kinds of different aspects). This is the extent of the physical description Sand gives us of her deity. Corambé therefore represents metamorphosis incarnate, if that is not an oxymoron. Critics have frequently sought to ascribe meaning to this mysterious figure, usually as an expression of a fundamental androgyne. Kathryn Crecelius, for instance, suggests that Corambé is a manifestation of a kind of Electra complex, a projection through which Sand displaces her mother in an 'imagined union ... with her father',[20] while Maryline Lukacher interprets the 'androgynous' Corambé as a 'desperate attempt at reconciling the masculine and

---

[18] Naginski, *George Sand mythographe*, 30.

[19] Martine Reid, *Signer Sand: l'œuvre et le nom* (Paris: Belin, 2003), 76; Janet Hiddleston, *George Sand and Autobiography* (Oxford: Legenda, 1999), 48.

[20] Kathryn J. Crecelius, *Family Romances: George Sand's Early Novels* (Bloomington: Indiana University Press, 1987), 14.

156   GEORGE SAND'S OVIDIAN AFFINITIES

the feminine'.[21] However, my reading suggests that Corambé is, rather, *beyond* sex, impossible to describe because it exists outside the discourses that entrench gender difference. In this I follow Nigel Harkness's assertion that in her works 'what Sand is voicing is not a fundamental androgyny, but an understanding of "sexe" as both biological and cultural'.[22] It is in this light that we should understand Corambé, as an early manifestation of Sand's interrogation of the culturally coded rules that underpin gender identity. The metamorphic Corambé is therefore deeply imbricated in Sand's gender politics, a politics that is expressed throughout her literary enterprise.

Sand leaves us in no doubt that Corambé's emergence goes hand-in-hand with her emergence as a writer. Corambé in effect functions as a guide for the young Aurore Dupin, accompanying her as she discovers her writerly powers. Corambé first appeared to Sand when she was twelve years old and just beginning to flex her creative muscles. It is only at the age of twenty-seven that Corambé ceases to be available to her imagination, and the watershed moment that marks her outgrowing of her muse is the completion of her manuscript for *Indiana*, her first full-length novel written alone, and the text that inaugurated the pseudonym that would define her life from that moment on: G. Sand. As Sand writes, once *Indiana* was completed, 'mon pauvre *Corambé* s'envola pour toujours, dès que j'eus commencé à me sentir dans cette veine de persévérance sur un sujet donné' (*OA*, ii, 165) (my poor *Corambé* flew away forever, as soon as I had started to feel this vein of perseverance on a given subject). For Reid, the enigmatically named Corambé serves as a form of mirror stage that marks an initial 'pseudonymic gesture' that would find its full expression as Sand adopts her new name.[23] However, although Corambé as an image is lost to her imagination the moment Sand fully assumes her role as writer, its influence is reinforced:

> Quand je fus dans l'âge où l'on rit de sa propre naïveté, je remis Corambé à sa véritable place: c'est-à-dire que je le réintégrai, dans mon imagination, parmi les songes; mais il en occupa toujours le centre, et toutes les fictions qui continuèrent à se former autour de lui émanèrent toujours de cette fiction principale (*OA*, ii, 166).

---

[21] Maryline Lukacher, *Maternal Fictions: Stendhal, Sand, Rachilde, Bataille* (Durham, NC: Duke University Press, 1994), 67.

[22] Nigel Harkness, *Men of their Words: The Poetics of Masculinity in George Sand's Fiction* (Oxford: Legenda, 2007), 7.

[23] Reid, *Signer Sand*, 81–6.

(When I reached the age where one laughs at one's own naivety, I returned Corambé to its true place: that is to say I reintegrated it into my imagination, among the dreams; but it still occupied the centre, and all the fictions that continued to form around it always emanated from this principal fiction.)

Sand here actively encourages us to read her texts under the influence of Corambé, and each of her texts might thus be framed as the latest metamorphosis of this originary myth. This suggestion is seemingly confirmed when Sand discusses the criticism of her 1833 novel *Lélia*. The criticisms levelled against Sand's text frequently addressed its form, or rather its formlessness, its resistance to categorization. When the *Revue de Paris* announced the publication of the text in 1833, it asked, 'Est-ce un roman? N'est-ce pas plutôt un poème? Est-ce ce qu'on appelle aussi un roman psychologique?' (Is it a novel? Is it not rather a poem? Is it not what we also call a psychological novel?).[24] The *Journal général de la littérature française* recognized a similar dilemma: 'Cette publication n'est pas un roman proprement dit' (This publication is not strictly speaking a novel).[25] When Sand reflects on the reception of this text in her autobiography, it seems therefore fitting that she concludes that *Lélia* was 'trop de l'école de *Corambé*' (*OA*, ii, 165) (too much of the school of *Corambé*).

In addition to structuring Sand's development as a writer and guiding her through the turbulent years of her adolescence, Corambé also structures her childhood play. During one winter at home in Nohant, Sand describes a game she would play with her friends that would involve a mechanism for catching birds: 'À travers tous ces jeux, le roman de Corambé continuait à se dérouler dans ma tête' (*OA*, i, 839) (Through all these games, Corambé's novel continued to unfold in my mind). More than this, though, Corambé is inherently play*ful*. In its form, Sand's 'fantôme' destabilizes gender norms. In its non-conformity to expected social norms, its sexlessness, its metamorphic nature, it is a being radically removed from the dominant codes that Sand's poetics work against. More than just a childhood fantasy, it is a 'rêve permanent', but one that is 'aussi décousu, aussi incohérent que les rêves du sommeil' (*OA*, i, 839) (as disjointed, as incoherent as the dreams of sleep). Indeed, we might consider Corambé as the privileged signifier of the Sandian universe, thereby revealing metamorphosis to be a fundamental principle of Sand's poetics.

---

[24] *Revue de Paris*, 53 (1833), 143.   [25] *Journal général de la littérature française*, 36 (1833), 117.

Gribouille's Playful Metamorphoses

Since Sand encourages us to read her texts under the sign of Corambé, we will now turn to one of these texts to explore how the metamorphically playful principles of her muse manifest themselves in her fiction. *Histoire de ma vie*, the work that introduces us to Corambé, was written at the same time as another text, one much less well-known, and destined for a very different audience. In 1843 Sand's editor, Pierre-Jules Hetzel, launched the project *Le Nouveau Magasin des enfants*, which sought to provide children with a new kind of informative and liberal literature. Contributions to the publication's various instalments came from such authors as Charles Nodier, Alfred de Musset, and Alexandre Dumas, with illustrations by Bertall and Paul Gavarni, and later Sand's son, Maurice. Sand's own contribution to the project reflected her belief that there was no form of literature in nineteenth-century France that really met the needs of children. This much she states in *Histoire de ma vie*, when she complains that 'il n'existe point de littérature à l'usage des petits enfants. Tous les jolis vers qu'on a faits en leur honneur sont maniérés et farcis de mots qui ne sont point de leur vocabulaire' (*OA*, i, 531) (no literature of use to children exists. All the pretty verses we create in their honour are affected and stuffed with words that are not part of their vocabulary). Perhaps unsurprisingly given the role Corambé played in her childhood, she proposes that children's literature must embrace the fantastic, which she believes to be necessary for the development of a child's personality. Hetzel's project therefore appealed to Sand as a means of remedying a lack, in addition to its timing following the disappointment of the 1848 revolution. As Sand wrote in a letter to Hetzel in March 1850: 'Oui, je voudrais vous faire un *Gribouille*...J'ai adoré les petits enfants, j'aurais su leur parler. Je les adore toujours, mais leur vue me serre le cœur à présent' (Yes, I would like to create a *Gribouille* for you. I have loved the little children, I would have known how to speak to them. I love them still, but their present countenance breaks my heart).[26] Just as Sand did in her own childhood when she created the mythic Corambé, she turns to fairy tale in order to provide some kind of artistic relief to a social problem. Dominique Laporte has also acknowledged a connection between these two quasi-mythic figures of Sand's invention. Laporte sees them as emblems of Sand's *engagement*, providing a means of avoiding censorship

---

[26] Sand, *Correspondance*, ix, 498.

by using myth to express her political disappointments.[27] While agreeing that Sand's disillusionment in the wake of 1848 is clearly legible in both texts, and that both figures are certainly politically charged, I argue that their connections go further: they both lay bare the metamorphic mechanisms of Sand's representational system. Indeed, Sand's tale is itself a form of transformation, drawn as it is directly from a proverb—that of the foolish Gribouille who throws himself into water because he is afraid of the rain. Sand's text playfully subverts this proverb, but through its plot it also recalls Ovidian stories of metamorphosis. Pascale Auraix-Jonchière describes *Histoire du véritable Gribouille* as an 'intertextual voyage', but Ovid is not one of the intertexts she cites.[28] My reading proposes that Ovid's *Metamorphoses* function as a model for Sand's Gribouille. In particular, I suggest that we can read in Sand's tale a reworking of the story of Narcissus and Echo.

The metamorphic and playful potential of Gribouille is evident from the text's dedication. Sand dedicated her tale to Valentine, the daughter of her childhood friend, Laure Fleury, writing that 'en gribouillant ce Gribouille, j'ai songé à toi. Je ne te l'offre pas pour modèle, puisque, en fait de bon cœur et de bon esprit, c'est toi qui m'en as servi' (As I scribbled this Gribouille, I thought of you. I do not offer it to you as a model, since, by virtue of your good heart and good soul, it is you that served as the model).[29] There is a double significance to this dedication for an understanding of Sand's approach to the text itself. Not only does it reveal Sand's belief in the remedial potential of art, but it also playfully draws attention to the symbolic potential of the sign that Sand's text explores. The act of 'gribouillant' is, by nature, unfixed, indicating an acute level of symbolic power. This symbolic potential links Gribouille to Corambé, redoubled by Gribouille's apparently masculine nature but feminized name.

The world Gribouille inhabits is clearly inspired by nineteenth-century France; it is one consumed by bourgeois capitalism. Gribouille's parents and siblings are avaricious, miserly, cruel, and while ruled in name by a king, the society Sand depicts is in fact controlled by the tyrannical M. Bourdon, who has slowly accrued vast amounts of wealth and power. Thus the text provides,

---

[27] Dominique Laporte, 'Deux figures emblématiques de l'engagement sandien: Corambé et Gribouille (*Histoire du véritable Gribouille*, 1850)', in Simone Bernard-Griffiths and José-Luis Diaz, eds, *Lire 'Histoire de ma vie' de George Sand* (Clermont-Ferrand: Presses universitaires Blaise Pascal, 2006), 327–33.

[28] Pascale Auraix-Jonchière, *George Sand et la fabrique des contes* (Paris: Classiques Garnier, 2017), 222.

[29] George Sand, *Histoire du véritable Gribouille* (Paris: Blanchard, 1851), 7. All references are to this edition, and will subsequently be given parenthetically in the text as *HG*.

160   GEORGE SAND'S OVIDIAN AFFINITIES

for Dominique Laporte, a thinly veiled political allegory, bemoaning the rise of capitalism since the start of the Second Empire.[30] In what is a common trope of nineteenth-century literature, this wealth fails to bring fulfilment, and beneath a veneer of gold and ornate, decorative objects the people of the society Sand creates in her text are deeply unhappy. At a hedonistic ball filled with drink and gambling held at Bourdon's palace Gribouille notes that 'tout ce monde agité paraissait triste ou en colère' (*HG*, 30) (all these agitated people seemed sad or angry). However, Bourdon himself is absent from the ball. When Gribouille asks him why, Bourdon replies: 'J'ai donné une fête pour montrer que je suis riche, mais je me dispense d'en faire les honneurs' (*HG*, 32) (I have thrown a party to show that I am rich, but I spare myself from honouring the attendees). Within this hedonistic world that Sand constructs as a reflection of the nineteenth century, Bourdon and Gribouille stand out: Bourdon because he understands the nature of symbolic capital and therefore possesses power, Gribouille because he questions the nature of this power. When Bourdon offers to teach him how to use this power, which Bourdon equates with intelligence, Gribouille responds: 'Si, pour avoir de l'esprit, il faut que je devienne méchant, ne m'en donnez point. J'aime mieux rester bête et conserver ma bonté' (*HG*, 18) (If, to have wisdom, I must become wicked, do not give me any. I would rather remain foolish and preserve my goodness). The knowledge Bourdon offers, the knowledge that Gribouille rejects, is equated in this world to a kind of science. But just as language is put to use by the dominant order to maintain systems of power, this science represents for Bourdon the possibility of manipulating others and bending them to his will. As he advises Gribouille, 'il faut apprendre les sciences, mon petit ami. Sachez que je suis un habile homme et que je puis vous enseigner la magie et la nécromancie' (*HG*, 34) (you must learn the sciences, my little friend. Know that I am a skilful man and that I can teach you magic and necromancy). Bourdon does eventually convince the naive Gribouille to expose himself to his 'science'. Under Bourdon's supervision, Gribouille eats an acorn from an oak tree by a stream, and it is revealed that this acorn has soporific properties. We might therefore see in this scene a version of the river Lethe in the *Metamorphoses* which flows through the caves of Hypnos and induces sleep. It is here that Gribouille is transported to a dream world filled with anthropo-morphized insects, where Bourdon has metamorphosed to show his true form: a giant bee. In this domain, Gribouille witnesses insects killing and devouring each other, and once he awakens Bourdon offers him a choice between 'voleur

---

[30] Laporte, 'Deux figures emblématiques', 332.

ou volé, meurtier ou meurtri, tyran ou esclave' (thief or victim, murderer or murdered, tyrant or slave), and reveals the fundamental principle of his 'science': 'Le plus sûr, selon moi, est de laisser travailler les autres, et de prendre, prendre, prendre! Mon garçon, par force ou par adresse, c'est le seul moyen d'être toujours heureux' (*HG*, 60–1) (The most certain, in my opinion, is to leave work to others, and take, take, take! My boy, by strength or by skill, it is the only way to always be happy).

Bourdon's capitalist colonial model is, however, opposed to another kind of science. In the faerie universe of the text, different spatio-temporal realms exist that each have their own guiding principles. While Gribouille's realm resembles the nineteenth century, the others are the domain of the fantastic, inhabited by beings capable of fantastic metamorphoses and prolonging life. In her analysis of *Lucrezia Floriani* and *Le Château des désertes*, Pascale Auraix-Jonchière argues that space in these Sandian texts is transformed by mythic references, through the creation of a space beyond traditional spaces imbued with mythic potential, writing that 'l'écriture romanesque apparaît alors comme le laboratoire expérimental de ce qui procède tout à la fois d'une appropriation et d'une transmutation de l'espace' (the writing of fiction thus appears as the experimental laboratory of what proceeds at the same time from an appropriation and a transmutation of space).[31] A similar process is at work in *Histoire du véritable Gribouille*, though it is not real spaces being transformed into mythic ones, but the beings within them that metamorphose. For those endowed with the knowledge to control signs in this text, this also entails the ability to change their own totemic status, to transform into something other. After Gribouille's parents send him to Bourdon in the hope of gaining greater wealth through the interest Bourdon pays in him, Gribouille returns with gold. However, the moment his avaricious parents take the gold from him, it melts in their hands and turns to honey. The name of Gribouille's father, Bredouille, thus becomes much more than an onomastic signifier. Metamorphosis is the guiding principle of this text, in which signs are especially fluid, destabilizing the distinction between sign and signified.

Given the fluidity of signs in this text, it is perhaps no surprise that in moving between these different realms, Gribouille moves through some form of liquid. As he returns from Bourdon's realm of death and destruction, he falls into another form of fluid, a river of blood that recalls the Styx, and to

---

[31] Pascale Auraix-Jonchière, 'Mythopoétique de l'espace sandien: *Lucrezia Floriani* et *Le Château des désertes*', in Brigitte Diaz and Isabelle Hoog Naginski, eds, *George Sand: Pratiques et imaginaires de l'écriture* (Caen: Presses universitaires de Caen, 2006), 255–64 (p. 263).

162   GEORGE SAND'S OVIDIAN AFFINITIES

escape Bourdon and gain access to the realm of the 'reine des prés' (queen of
the meadows), he jumps into a stream and is carried away by the current. It is
during this moment of crisis that Gribouille undergoes his first metamorphosis. When he awakens in this other, utopian land, he finds that he too has
transformed and, like countless Ovidian characters, has become a branch of a
tree. If the realm from which Bourdon springs is one of greed, destruction, and
death, this new realm represents a communion with nature:

> On ne vivait, dans ce pays-là, que de fruits, de graines et du suc des fleurs;
> mais on les apprêtait si merveilleusement, leurs mélanges étaient si bien
> diversifiés, qu'on ne savait lequel de ces plats exquis préférer aux autres. Tout
> le monde préparait, servait et mangeait le repas. On ne choisissait point les
> convives: qu'ils fussent jeunes ou vieux, gais ou sérieux, ils étaient tous
> parfaitement agréables.   (*HG*, 81)

> (In this country, they lived only on fruit, seeds, and the sap of flowers; but
> these items were so magnificently prepared, the combinations so wonderfully
> diverse, that it was hard to know which of these exquisite dishes to prefer.
> Everyone prepared, served, and ate the meal. Guests were not chosen;
> whether they were young or old, lighthearted or serious, they were all
> perfectly agreeable.)

In this world all are equal, live peacefully, and possess a heightened sense of
respect for nature. In her analysis of vision in Sand's novels, Manon Mathias
argues that Sand embraces natural sciences, not as a means of controlling the
world, but of celebrating its diversity, writing that Sand's 'knowledge of
geology and entomology leads not to control and domination over nature
but to aesthetic and metaphysical wonderment. Sand rejects the scientific eye
as a means of mastering and fixing the real and celebrates instead the dyna-
mism and mystery of the natural world.'[32] Here, too, while Bourdon retains his
'science' for himself in order to accrue power, the queen shares her knowledge
with all: 'Tout le monde, dit la reine, tout le monde est aussi savant que moi,
puisque j'ai donné à tous mes enfants ma sagesse et ma science' (*HG*, 77–8)
(Everyone, said the queen, everyone is as knowledgeable as me, since I have
given all my children my wisdom and my science). Her 'science', we later
learn, is the 'science d'aimer et d'être aimé' (*HG*, 103) (science of loving and
being loved). In *Histoire du véritable Gribouille* the real is anything but fixed,

---

[32] Manon Mathias, *Vision in the Novels of George Sand* (Oxford: Oxford University Press, 2016), 5.

and notions of fluidity and vitality pervade concepts of the natural world. But these concepts are coupled with another central trope of Sand's œuvre: the redemptive possibilities of art. In a further recollection of the Corambé ideal, while associated with nature, this utopia is also an artistic haven: 'Partout on pouvait rejoindre des groupes qui faisaient de la musique ou qui célébraient la beauté de la nature et le bonheur de s'aimer' (*HG*, 82) (Everywhere you could join groups who were playing music and celebrating the beauty of nature and the joy of love). Where this utopia diverges is through its explicit association with the feminine. Whereas Corambé denotes a genderless vision of the ideal, this utopia is a patently maternal space, constructed in direct opposition to the paternal space of Bourdon. The queen speaks with a 'ton maternal' (*HG*, 73) (maternal tone) , refers to herself as Gribouille's 'marraine'(*HG*, 75) (godmother), and the inhabitants of this realm are described as 'cette race heureuse et charmante dont elle était la mère' (*HG*, 83) (this happy and charming race of which she was the mother). The geography of Sand's faerie landscape seemingly recalls the ideal city of the utopian Saint-Simonian movement, at the centre of which a colossal temple was envisaged in the form of a woman.[33] Sand's vision, however, as the Corambé myth exemplifies, is far from promoting the feminine *over* the masculine in a reversal of social order. Instead, she yearns for equality for *both* sexes. Thus it is to Gribouille that the queen turns in order to establish this utopian ideal of balance and harmony.

Just as the names of Bourdon and Bredouille prove overly deterministic, it is at this juncture that the significance of Gribouille's name comes to the fore. Denoting an indeterminate scribble, Gribouille's name is emblematic of his exceptional position within the logic of the world the text creates is exceptional. As yet uncorrupted by either the forces of capitalism or utopianism, he is in many ways a kind of empty vessel, and it is for this reason that both Bourdon and the queen take such an interest in him. In *La Révolution du langage poétique* Julia Kristeva posits poetic language as a mechanism for engendering radical change and turns to the symbolists of the late nineteenth century as the agents of such change. Kristeva challenges Lacan's assertion that after the mirror stage the pre-Oedipal child breaks with the mother and moves into the Symbolic, governed by the law of the Father. Instead, Kristeva proposes the notion of the *chora* as the part of the unconscious that retains

---

[33] 'My temple is a woman!' declared Charles Duveyrier, who imagined that this giant structure in the form of a woman would form the centre of Saint-Simonian life. Charles Duveyrier, 'La Ville nouvelle, ou le Paris des saints-simoniens', in *Paris ou le livre des cent-et-un*, 12 vols (Paris: Ladvocat, 1832), viii, 315–44 (p. 339).

164   GEORGE SAND'S OVIDIAN AFFINITIES

a link to the maternal space.[34] While etymologically the term designated in Greek a space beyond the *polis*, beyond the realm beholden to dominant codes, Kristeva attributes her understanding of the term to Plato's *Timaeus*, where it refers to 'an essentially mobile and extremely provisional articulation constituted by movements and their ephemeral stases'.[35] The repressed psychic energy held within the *chora* is, she argues, what disrupts and contests the authority of patriarchal discourse, and it this energy that imbues poetic language with its potential for symbolic violence.

Gribouille might be considered as performing the same symbolic functions as this *chora*. In this reading, the land of Bourdon can be viewed as the Symbolic realm, while the maternal land of the 'reine des prés' can be read as the Semiotic. It is, after all, in the land of the Semiotic that Gribouille's real *Bildung* takes place, and, as Kristeva writes, it is the mother's body that 'mediates the symbolic law organizing social relations and becomes the ordering principle of the semiotic *chora*, which is on the path of destruction, aggressivity, and death'.[36] After spending a hundred years in the queen's land, Gribouille is sent back to the world he left with a mission to spread the utopian ideology she had instilled in him. Despite the time he has spent away, however, he has not aged, remaining in his youthful state. When he returns, only Bourdon, like the eternal Law of the Father, remains of what he left behind. Recognizing the threat Gribouille poses, Bourdon has him captured and imprisoned, in a further attempt to reassert control over the signifying order, 'afin de le garder comme un talisman contre le malheur' (in order to keep him as a talisman against danger) (*HG*, 106). In his despair, Gribouille begins to sing the songs he had learnt in the land of the fairies. Lizards, salamanders, rats, and spiders, all imprisoned alongside him, gather at his side and echo his 'chant de mort' in their own language. They reveal that they are in fact men, who had clung to notions of respect and justice after Gribouille's initial departure a century earlier, and Bourdon had consequently punished them with their 'hideuses métamorphoses' (*HG*, 113) (hideous metamorphoses), one of three uses of the term in the text. The queen's voice, carried by Gribouille, has stirred in them the possibility of liberation: 'Nous avons entendu les mots de la fée et nous voyons que l'heure de notre délivrance est venue' (*HG*, 113) (We have heard the words of the fairy and we see that the hour of our deliverance has come). We might therefore see in Gribouille's tale a reworking of Ovid's Narcissus and Echo. As Gayatri Spivak reminds us, while Ovid's tale is one of 'mortiferous self-knowledge',

---

[34] Kristeva, *Revolution in Poetic Language*, 25.   [35] Ibid., 23.   [36] Ibid., 27.

this punishment is gendered.[37] Narcissus is able to find some form of self-consolidation in death, but the body of Echo, as the reverberation of the words of others, 'has no identity proper to itself. It is obliged to be imperfectly and interceptively responsive to another's desire, if only for the self-separation of speech.'[38] In Ovid's telling, Echo is subsidiary. In Sand's tale, however, the female voice is given intention. Gribouille bridges the aporia between the narcissistic Bourdon and the altruistic queen, and through his own imitation of her words her message starts a revolution. As Gribouille and his fellow prisoners sing, the queen arrives with an army of winged creatures and the oppressed citizens of Bourdon's kingdom revolt.

As the forces of Bourdon and the queen face each other, Bourdon brings forth his prisoner and promises to burn him alive should the queen continue her advance. Refusing to be used as a tool to support the masculine order, Gribouille sets himself ablaze. According to Freud's myth of the primordial murder, the father of the ruling primal horde is killed by his sons who wish to possess his wives, but their guilt then leads them to renounce their claim to these women, thus inaugurating social order in the name of the Father.[39] Kristeva argues that sacrifice, as a re-enactment of this original murder, is both an act of violence and an act that seeks to control acts of violence, thereby effecting control over the Symbolic. Read in this light, Gribouille's self-sacrifice represents a means of altering the symbolic order at work in the text. Indeed, it is here that Sand reveals her rewriting of the original Gribouille proverb. Bourdon attempts to mock Gribouille's sacrifice, as his followers call out 'Ce Gribouille-là est aussi fin que l'ancien, qui se jeta dans l'eau par crainte de la pluie, puisqu'il se jette dans le feu par crainte d'être brûlé' (*HG*, 119–20) (This Gribouille is as stupid as the old one, who jumped into the water for fear of the rain, since he throws himself into the fire for fear of being burned). For all their 'science', they have failed to understand the symbolic potential of Gribouille's self-sacrifice. Bourdon and his supporters are roundly defeated, and the queen's utopian ideology is brought to the 'real' world. Thus, the text confirms Kristeva's assertion that 'because the subject is always *both* semiotic *and* symbolic, no signifying system he produces can be either "exclusively" semiotic or "exclusively" symbolic, and is instead necessarily marked by an indebtedness to both'.[40] Through the *chora*, through Gribouille, a revolution occurs that brings harmony between the two halves of the psyche,

---

[37] Gayatri Chakravorty Spivak, 'Echo', *New Literary History*, 24 (1993), 17–43 (p. 22).
[38] Ibid., 27.
[39] Sigmund Freud, *Totem and Taboo*, trans. Abraham A. Brill (New York: Cosimo, 2009), 183.
[40] Kristeva, *Revolution in Poetic Language*, 24.

166   GEORGE SAND'S OVIDIAN AFFINITIES

between the paternal and the maternal, between Narcissus and Echo, between the real and the ideal. Indeed, just as Kristeva writes that discourse both rejects and depends upon the *chora*, Gribouille never truly departs the world.[41]

In yet another instance of metamorphosis that recalls Ovid's tale, when the queen returns to the pyre on which Gribouille died she finds no body, just a mountain of ash, upon which a flower has bloomed. The queen carries his floral form to the faerie realm and plants it beside a stream (in one final echo of Narcissus), where he is able to alternate between flower and sylph. Spivak's reading of the Narcissus myth interprets this flower as a sign of 'the *a-letheia* (truth as unforgetting) of the limits of self-knowledge'.[42] In this new form Sand playfully brings together Narcissus and Echo, as Gribouille is not just any flower, but a forget-me-not, and on the anniversary of his death the country's inhabitants would bring bouquets of forget-me-nots and sing the song Gribouille had taught them. While Echo's voice goes on blindly repeating, Gribouille's song allows his altruistic message to be continuously heard.

Conclusion: George Sand's Metamorphoses

In this chapter I have sought to delineate George Sand's Ovidian affinities. Although Ovid's influence on Sand's works may be somewhat oblique, with Ovid's name seldom appearing under her pen, this analysis has demonstrated firstly that the two writers shared interest in metamorphosis and secondly that they share a certain playfulness. And metamorphosis is a fundamental part of Sand's poetic project. Literary history has, at least since her passing, considered Sand an idealist, with her work categorized against the realist mode of her male contemporaries. Representing as it does a utopian aspiration towards a better world, metamorphosis is of course at the heart of idealism. Corambé and its avatar Gribouille certainly seem to embody such a metamorphic idealist yearning. Yet, as I have sought to suggest in my analysis of the role of Gribouille, there is more to Sand's texts than a simple utopian dream. I would agree with Naomi Schor's proposition that 'Sandian idealism is a politics at least as much as an aesthetics'.[43] Both Corambé and Gribouille carry

---

[41] As Kristeva writes: 'Our discourse—all discourse—moves with and against the *chora* in the sense that it simultaneously depends upon and refuses it.' Ibid., 26.

[42] Spivak, 'Echo', 25.

[43] Naomi Schor, *George Sand and Idealism* (New York: Columbia University Press, 1993), 14.

a significant political charge. But in Schor's conception, idealism is 'the only alternative representational mode available to those who do not enjoy the privileges of subjecthood in the real'.[44] Idealism has therefore been considered as an aesthetic mode in competition with the more materialist realism. Sand's writing, so the story goes, rejects the materialism of her (male) contemporaries, gesturing towards a more transcendent poetic model. This categorization has been subjected to scrutiny in recent criticism, and I follow Martine Reid's suggestion that such a binary does not reflect the more complex reality of the literary field of nineteenth-century France.[45] Indeed, Sand herself tells us as much, citing a conversation with Balzac in which he states to her that he, too, idealizes, albeit 'en sens inverse' (*OA*, ii, 162) (in the opposite direction): Sand exaggerates beauty, while he exaggerates ugliness. Attending to Sand's use of metamorphosis reveals that we should be sceptical of any such attempt to categorize her work using such binary schema. Corambé, the emblem of Sand's writerly creativity, and Gribouille, seem instead to represent in-between spaces. Metamorphoses in Sand's texts, above all, serve as playful rejections of binary modes of thinking. Sand's metamorphoses are, therefore, thoroughly modern.

This chapter has considered only two of Sand's texts, and transformation is of course an underpinning principle of fairy tale. But the presence of metamorphosis can be seen across her œuvre: in the spectacular transformations of Laura in the crystalline world of *Laura, voyage dans le cristal*; in the questioning of gender identity of Gabriel/le, a biological girl raised as a boy to facilitate an inheritance scam; in the peculiar entomological transformations of the ball-goers of *Le Secrétaire intime*; or in the many uncanny doubles that permeate Sand's fictional universe.[46] Metamorphosis is therefore central to Sand's creative enterprise, and while it is often political, it is always playful. But then, what else should we expect from the writer Michael Garval has qualified as 'polymorph'?[47] She is, to quote Théobald Walsh, 'par excellence, l'être

---

[44] Ibid., 54.

[45] Martine Reid, 'Post-scriptum: Naomi Schor trente ans après', in Damien Zanone, ed., *George Sand et l'idéal. Une recherche en écriture* (Paris: Honoré Champion, 2017), 449–57.

[46] On Sand's extensive use of doubles, see Marilyn Yalom, 'Dédoublement in the Fiction of George Sand', in Natalie Datlof and others, eds, *The George Sand Papers: 1978* (New York: AMS Press, 1982), 21–31; Sylvie Richards, 'A Psychoanalytic Study of the Double in the Novels of George Sand', in Armand E. Singer, Mary W. Singer, and Janice S. Spleth, eds, *West Virginia George Sand Conference Papers* (Morgantown: West Virginia University Press, 1981), 45–53; and Françoise Ghillebaert, *Disguise in George Sand's Novels* (New York: Peter Lang, 2009), 21–60.

[47] Michael Garval, '*A Dream of Stone*': Fame, Vision, and Monumentality in Nineteenth-Century French Literary Culture* (Newark: University of Delaware Press, 2004), 130.

168 GEORGE SAND'S OVIDIAN AFFINITIES

multiple, ondoyant et divers, que nous saluons du nom de poète' (par excellence, the multiple, changeable, and diverse being that we salute with the name of poet).[48] Duncan Kennedy notes that in the modern reception of Ovid, '*Metamorphoses* holds pride of place.'[49] There are perhaps few writers who embody this theme as fully as George Sand.

[48] Théobald Walsh, *George Sand* (Paris: Hivert, 1837), 172. Coincidentally, the second part of Walsh's work takes as its epigraph a line from Ovid's *Metamorphoses*.

[49] Duncan F. Kennedy, 'Recent Receptions of Ovid', in Philip Hardie, ed., *The Cambridge Companion to Ovid* (Cambridge: Cambridge University Press, 2002), 320–35 (p. 320).

10

Cahun

An Ovidian Tiresias for Modern Times

Catherine Burke

Allusion is itself a way of looking before and after, a retrospect that opens up a new prospect.[1]

Charles Fontaine describes Ovid as 'un singulier poëte en invencion, grace et facilité' (a poet unique for his invention, grace, and ease), while asserting that the *Heroides* 'ont tousiours esté, au iugement de tous savans, estimées de tres grand artifice' (scholars have always praised it for its great skill and artifice).[2] The same could be used to recommend Claude Cahun and her 1925 text, *Héroïnes*, a series of monologues in which Cahun challenges and subverts the traditional narrative of fifteen female figures from cultural history.[3] Beginning with the first woman, Eve, and ending with 'Celui qui n'est pas un héros' (The one who is not a hero), the series includes Penelope, Sappho and Salmacis among others. I have written extensively elsewhere about the importance of the Homeric source for Cahun's *Héroïnes* and indeed about the deeply Homeric presence in the life and work of Claude Cahun.[4] As for Ovid, 'the contiguity of Ovid to Homer ... is a vast and little-explored territory; it is likely, and entirely understandable, that the structures of learning so long in place have obscured a vital element in the literary history

---

[1] Christopher Ricks, *Allusion to the Poets* (Oxford: Oxford University Press, 2002), 86. Cited in Barbara Boyd, *Ovid's Homer: Authority, Repetition, Reception* (Oxford: Oxford University Press, 2017), 11.

[2] Charles Fontaine, cited in Paul White, 'Ovid's "Heroides" in Early Modern French Translation: Saint-Gelais, Fontaine, Du Bellay', *Translation and Literature*, 13/2 (2004), 165–80 (p. 166). English translation is my own. For further discussion of Fontaine's sixteenth-century translation, see the chapter by Jessica DeVos in this volume (Chapter 3).

[3] Claude Cahun, *Héroïnes*, ed. François Leperlier (Paris: Mille et une nuits, 2006). First published in 1925. Claude Cahun, *Heroines*, trans. Norman MacAfee, in Shelley Rice, ed., *Inverted Odysseys: Claude Cahun, Maya Deren, Cindy Sherman* (Cambridge, MA: Massachusetts Institute of Technology Press, 1999), 43–110. All subsequent references will be to these editions and are given after quotations in the text.

[4] Catherine Burke, 'Voices from the Outside: Homeric Exiles in Twentieth-Century French Writing', thesis submitted for doctoral degree award, University College Cork, 2021.

Catherine Burke, *Cahun: An Ovidian Tiresias for Modern Times* In: *Ovid in French: Reception by Women from the Renaissance to the Present*. Edited by: Helena Taylor and Fiona Cox, Oxford University Press. © Oxford University Press 2023. DOI: 10.1093/oso/9780192895387.003.0010

170 CAHUN: AN OVIDIAN TIRESIAS FOR MODERN TIMES

that produces Ovid.'[5] That is not to say that Cahun was not influenced by Ovid or did not have a role to play in his conception in France. Rather it speaks instead to the many classical influences in her work and how her relationship with Ovid was one inevitably inflected by Homer, both through Ovid's own undeniable interaction with the Greek master and her own personal artistic exchange with her Greek forefather.[6] In this chapter, I turn to the Ovidian in Cahun's story and in particular the Ovidian intertext, the *Heroides*, and its role in the creation of Cahun's rescripted monologues.[7] I will focus on two epistles from the *Heroides*—that of Penelope and Sappho—which bookend Ovid's text and which are revisited by Cahun in *Héroïnes*.[8] Drawing out the comparisons and divergences between these representations will serve as a foundation to explore how Ovidian themes are central to Cahun's work and her very act of reception.[9] This reading will map Cahun's *Héroïnes* onto techniques that are found in her self-portrait, the next stage in tracing Cahun's Ovidian legacy. Here I will examine how key themes such as inversion and pluralistic identity come sharply to the fore. This image could function as the visual avatar of Cahun's *Héroïnes*. Each story is an aberration, where the object and its image fail to coalesce in a perfect reproduction. Each woman reflects and refracts her perceived image. Von Oehsen states: '"Héroïnes" provided Cahun with an opportunity to experiment with perception and public restriction, as well as the reception and projection of *appearance*' [my emphasis].[10] This leads neatly to the final section and Cahun's engagement with Ovid's *Metamorphoses*.[11]

---

[5] Boyd, *Ovid's Homer*, 4.

[6] Throughout this chapter I use the pronouns 'her' and 'she' to refer to Cahun, as is the custom in Cahun criticism; in today's world Cahun may well have opted for the pronouns 'their' and 'they'.

[7] Ovid, *Heroides*, Loeb Classical Library, https://www-loebclassics-com.ucc.idm.oclc.org/view/ovid-heroides/1914/pb_LCL041.11.xml. All subsequent references (and translations) will be to this edition.

[8] On other reworkings of Ovid's Sappho, see Thea S. Thorsen on Constance de Salm's eighteenth-century opera version and Florence Klein on Marguerite Yourcenar's Sappho in her 1936 novel, *Feux* (Chapters 7 and 11 and respectively in this volume).

[9] 'Si monumentum requiris circumspice. Ovid is everywhere.' Thus, Charles Martindale opens his 1988 book *Ovid Renewed: Ovidian Influences on Literature and Art from the Middle Ages to the Twentieth Century*, ed. Charles Martindale (Cambridge: Cambridge University Press, 1988), 1. With these words, Martindale captures the wide appeal of Ovid and the wealth of cultural and critical output that he has generated throughout the centuries. Martindale's words resonate into the twenty-first century where writers and critics continue to engage with this most fascinating of classical writers. See, for example, Tessa Roynon and Daniel Orrells, eds, 'Ovid and Identity in the Twenty-First Century', *International Journal of the Classical Tradition*, 26/4 (December 2019) [special issue], Ali Smith's *Girl Meets Boy* (Edinburgh: Canongate, 2007), and Jeffrey Eugenides *Middlesex* (Toronto: Random House of Canada, 2002).

[10] Kristine Von Oehsen, 'The Lives of Claude Cahun and Marcel Moore', in Louise Downie, ed., *Don't Kiss Me: The Art of Claude Cahun and Marcel Moore* (London: Tate Publishing, 2006; New York: Aperture, 2006), 10–23 (p. 14).

[11] Ovid, *The Metamorphoses*, trans. and with an introduction by Mary M. Innes (Harmondsworth, Middlesex: Penguin Books, 1955).

It is an engagement that is anchored through the figure of Tiresias, the mythical seer whose renown derives as much from his sexuality as from his prophecies and whose tale is recounted by Ovid in Book 3 of the *Metamorphoses*.[12] But Cahun's Tiresian qualities are not restricted to his status as the first transgender figure. Tiresias is famed for his prophecies, a renown stemming from the accuracy and veracity of his prophecy about Narcissus, recounted in Book 3. Cahun's self-portrait as Harlequin visualizes Ovid's Narcissus and the theme of reality versus fiction/appearance that they both explore textually in *Héroïnes* and *Heroides* respectively. Through Tiresias, the disparate elements of Cahun's artistic concerns merge, revealing the imprint of Ovid's legacy on this most metaphoric of individuals.

The Enigmatic Claude Cahun

Born Lucy Schwob in 1894, Cahun entered a literary dynasty of prominent Jewish men. It was an intellectual and artistic coterie where Cahun could explore and develop her creative proclivities. But such a familial and patrilineal legacy also played a part in her desire and search for independence and autonomy, a distantiation emphatically signalled and effected by her adoption of the pseudonym Claude Cahun. This nominal ambiguity undoubtedly contributed to Cahun's historical obscurity but her connection with surrealism as well as her own aversion towards categorization in any form were primary factors in her neglect. Harris observes:

> Although the oblivion into which Cahun's reputation fell for fifty years is partly due to a lack of attention by historians and critics to so-called minor figures, Cahun had an extremely ambivalent relation to success, and a good part of her disappearance was self-willed.[13]

Thrust into the spotlight by François Leperlier, Cahun was quickly claimed by the feminist and postmodern debates, which viewed her photographic output as anticipating and reflecting their respective concerns—around gender,

---

[12] Tiresias enjoys a rich cultural legacy, for example, in *The Theban Plays* by Sophocles; Euripides' *Bacchae*; Dante, *La Commedia* (*c*.1308): *Inferno*, Canto 20; Tennyson, *Tiresias and Other Poems* (1885); T. S. Eliot's *The Waste Land* (1922). A dense network of allusions is summoned up when this mythological figure is evoked. Cahun's Tiresian identity is imbued with heightened poignancy due to these literary echoes.

[13] Steven Harris, 'Coup d'œil', *Oxford Art Journal*, 24/1 (2001), 91–111 (p. 102 n. 48).

172 CAHUN: AN OVIDIAN TIRESIAS FOR MODERN TIMES

identity, social norms, and subjectivity, to name a few.[14] This newfound fame proved the inverse of her contemporary unpublicized renown, with her pictures now taking centre stage over her literary works. Fast forward, and Cahun's writings swing back into focus, with critics such as Lauren Elkin advocating for a renewed appreciation of her literary œuvre.[15] The inaccessibility of her works (only two have been translated into English) is undoubtedly a factor in the prominence of her visual art over her literary work.[16] But the work itself is also a contributing factor as it textualizes the indecipherability of her visual art. The same blurring of boundaries, the same pastiche of genres, the same flouting of convention is evident in her writings, and at the additional remove of language for Anglophone readers. Heralded as the precursor to artists such as Cindy Sherman, her work continues to be framed by such connections. But she was not simply a writer or a visual artist. She was an actor, a political activist, a collaborator. As Lucy Lippard astutely observes: 'The zeitgeist [sic] provides the context for the work. If Claude Cahun had been rediscovered in the 1970s instead of the 1990s, we would perceive her work differently.'[17] Feminism, modernism, postmodernism, ethnicity, surrealism—each offers an elliptical reading that reduces the remit and devalues the impact of her work. Whether Cahun's affinity for alterity was the product of a life experienced on the outside or a natural inclination fostered and cultivated by that life, Cahun was the very embodiment of the other.[18] Forgotten among the women excised from the story of surrealism, itself described as the 'radical other of Modernism' by Benjamin, Cahun was an outsider on the margins of the margins, with layer upon layer of

[14] François Leperlier published a biography and a volume of collected works: Leperlier, *Claude Cahun, l'écart et la métamorphose* (Paris: Jean-Michel Place, 1992), and Claude Cahun, *Écrits*, ed. Leperlier (Paris: Jean-Michel Place, 2002).

[15] Lauren Elkin, 'Reading Claude Cahun', *The Quarterly Conversation*, 13 (2008).

[16] Cahun, *Heroines*, 43–110. Cahun, *Disavowals: or Cancelled Confessions*, trans. Susan de Muth (Cambridge, MA: Massachusetts Institute of Technology Press, 2008).

[17] Lucy Lippard, 'Scattering Selves', in Shelley Rice, ed., *Inverted Odysseys: Claude Cahun, Maya Deren, Cindy Sherman* (Cambridge, MA: Massachusetts Institute of Technology Press, 1999), 27–42 (p. 36).

[18] In this discussion, I will be using the term 'other' as a synonym of 'outsider', describing something different and distinct from the norm, not in its capacity as 'Other', the capitalized subject of an entire field of study, where the 'Other' is largely perceived as inherently lesser and dangerous, darkly and threateningly different in relation to the Self, and frequently identified as a woman or the Orient. I do this fully cognizant of the impossibility of definitively demarcating the signification of both, so entwined are they. For more, see, for example, Jacques Lacan, 'Subversion du sujet et dialectique du désir dans l'inconscient freudien' in *Ecrits* (Paris: Éditions du Seuil, 1966); Nancy Bauer, *Simone de Beauvoir, Philosophy, and Feminism* (New York: Columbia University Press, 2001); Jean-Paul Sartre, *L'Être et le néant: Essai d'ontologie phénoménologique* (Paris: Gallimard, 1943); Christopher Bush, 'The Other of the Other?: Cultural Studies, Theory, and the Location of the Modernist Signifier', *Comparative Literature Studies*, 42/2 (2005), 162–80.

otherness—racial, sexual, cultural, political, gender, aesthetic—casting her as an exile.[19]

As an exile, Cahun shares an obvious link to the Roman poet, Ovid, himself exiled for his lascivious writings during the reign of Emperor Augustus. But the links to Ovid are more nuanced than that of exile and outsider. Ovid and Cahun share many similarities. Both underwent a significant recuperation in the second half of the twentieth century. Both choose to rewrite the stories of mythological and historical women in their works: Ovid in his *Heroides* and Cahun in the *Héroïnes*. Both exhibit a predilection for inversion and transformation, indicated by the titles of their work. Many would immediately think of Ovid's *Metamorphoses* in this context, but his preference for change and shape shifting can be seen in *Heroides*, where he assumes the voice of famous figures, many of whom are female, and reinvigorates their stories. In Cahun's case, the link to inversion and change might seem more obscure. Written in 1925, most of the *Héroïnes* monologues were published in either *Mercure de France* or *Le Journal littéraire*.[20] As one of the two of Cahun's writings to be translated into English, *Heroines* was the first and remains the only English translation of the text, published in 1999 as part of a work significantly entitled *Inverted Odysseys: Claude Cahun, Maya Deren, Cindy Sherman*.[21] The title of this collection proves prescient. While clearly evoking Homer, the use of 'inverted' draws to mind Ovid and his narrative of inversions, the *Metamorphoses*, indicative of a sustained and intricate classical connection perhaps unconsciously signalled by its authors and yet discernible throughout Cahun's œuvre, both literary and visual.

Penelope and the Art of Narration

For Ovid, the themes of transformation, perception, and reinvention are intricately connected with storytelling. This is very much evident in his epistle from Penelope, with which he opens the *Heroides*. The epistle begins as one

---

[19] Natalya Lusty, *Surrealism, Feminism and Psychoanalysis* (London: Ashgate Publishing, 2007), 10.

[20] 'Ève la trop crédule', 'Dalila, femme entre les femmes', 'La Sadique Judith', 'Hélène la rebelle', 'Sapho l'incomprise', 'Marguerite, sœur incestueuse', and 'Salomé la sceptique' were published in *Le Mercure de France*, 639 (1 February 1925). 'Sophie La Symboliste' and 'La Belle' were published in *Le Journal littéraire*, 45 (28 February 1925). The remaining six—'L'Allumeuse (Pénélope irrésolue)', 'Marie', 'Cendrillon, l'enfant humble et hautaine', 'L'Épouse essentielle ou la Princesse inconnue', 'Salmacis la suffragette, and 'Celui qui n'est pas un héros' were published posthumously.

[21] While missing the title page and some other pages, this is the most complete version of *Héroïnes*, derived from the collection held by the Jersey Heritage Trust. While most of the monologues were published in 1925, as we see from n. 20, Penelope was among the six rejected.

174 CAHUN: AN OVIDIAN TIRESIAS FOR MODERN TIMES

would expect, with Penelope expressing longing and worry for her long-absent husband. But the tone of the letter becomes more powerful and energized as it develops, with Penelope growing increasingly suspicious and indeed angry over Odysseus' protracted absence. What Ovid draws attention to, and which Cahun later exploits, is the dependence on storytelling. Penelope relies on related narrative for news of Odysseus: 'For the whole story was told your son, whom I sent to seek you; ancient Nestor told him, and he told me' (*Heroides* 1.37–8).[22] She draws attention to the layers of narration and the subjectivity of storytelling: 'We sent to Sparta, too; Sparta also could tell us nothing true' (*Heroides* 1.65).[23] Penelope bemoans her 'powerless' state (*Heroides* 1.97),[24] yet her very act of voicing, indeed narrating, her own version of events undercuts that powerlessness and affirms her strength. Cahun follows suit in her reworking of Penelope, with the theme of narration and the subjectivity of representation to the forefront. These are themes that dominate her artistic œuvre, giving it a rather Ovidian shape.

Cahun's *Héroïnes* is a fitting starting point for an unravelling of this relationship with Ovid, containing as it does the monologues dedicated to Penelope and Sappho. I will begin by looking at Penelope, the fourth mono-logue in the series, entitled 'L'Allumeuse (Pénélope l'irrésolue)' ('The Tease (Penelope the Irresolute)'). Like Ovid's version, Cahun's is voiced by Penelope herself, the ensuing monologue telling the well-known story but with a dramatic new twist. The reader is forcefully alerted to this departure by the opening identification of Penelope as 'l'allumeuse' (the tease), a stark replace-ment of her traditional epithets. Far from mourning the loss of her husband, Penelope is revelling in the freedom and control that his absence brings. The pressure to choose a suitor is indeed causing her great distress, but this because she has to choose simply *one*: 'Mais accepter un homme, et surtout renvoyer les autres—c'est une responsabilité terrible!' (p. 22) ('But to accept one man, and especially to send the others away—it's a terrible responsibility!') (p. 56). In a series of reversals, she does not resent the suitors' invasion of the household but happily welcomes and encourages their advances. This is in direct contrast to Ovid's Penelope who bemoans her lot and refuses to commit to any man but Odysseus, though she does level blame at his feet: 'Why tell you of Pisander, and of Polybus, and of Medon the cruel, and of the grasping hands of Eurymachus and Antinous, and of others, all of whom through shameful

---

[22] 'Omnia namque tuo senior te quaerere misso / rettulerat nato Nestor, at ille mihi', *Heroides* 1.37–8.

[23] 'Misimus et Sparten; Sparte quoque nescia veri', *Heroides* 1.65.

[24] 'Sine viribus uxor', *Heroides* 1.97.

absence you yourself are feeding fat with store that was won at cost of your blood?' (*Heroides* 1.91–4).[25]

For Penelope must have one lover, while a man can have many, a double standard bitterly alluded to when Cahun's Penelope speaks of Odysseus' protracted stay with the goddess Calypso: 'Ulysse revient trop tard! (Il paraît qu'il s'est un peu trop endormi auprès de Calypso...)' (p. 24) ('Ulysses has returned too late! (it seems he was a bit lulled beside Calypso...)') (p. 57). Framing the statement as an aside, in parenthesis, serves to underscore the injustice, mirroring the irrelevance with which his infidelity has been treated in the account and subsequent dissemination of his story. It is this that frustrates Penelope—it is not their story but his, and she has no control over her role or rather her perceived role within it. Penelope is eager to correct the (mis)representation of her—she is not the sorrowful wife, pining for her husband's return: 'Le goût des embruns lui fera voir *les pleurs que je n'ai point versés*' (p. 22) ('The feel of the sea spray will make him see *the tears I have not shed*') (p. 56), with the italics underscoring the sense of bitterness at her portrayal in cultural history. She points to the fallacious nature of the story thus conceived: 'où sont décrites, où sont imaginés, les pérégrinations et la mort du malheureux Ulysse' (p. 24) ('which describes, which imagines the wanderings and death of the unhappy Ulysses') (p. 57). It is a misperception that she is more than willing to rectify.

Upon hearing the poet Phemius sing, Penelope decides to tell her own story: 'Mais retournant au festin j'entends le chanteur Phemios, et je suis prise par sa voix. Je *tisserai* le poème héroïque, celui qu'il compose avec un tel génie' [my emphasis] (p. 24) ('But, returning to the feast, I hear the singer Phemios, and I am swept away by his voice. I will *weave* the heroic poem that he composes with such genius') (p. 57). Significantly, Cahun uses the word '*tisserai*' or weave, drawing on Penelope's established weaving abilities to suggest a comparable skill at narration.[26] And if the two are analogous, then it also presumes a similar level of narrative trickery and competence. She is finally ready to commit her story to cultural memory. Her labour of love, '*la toile immense et délicate*' (p. 24) ('*The immense and delicate cloth*') (p. 57), is almost complete, and her secret union is imminent. But Odysseus returns and Penelope's marriage, the consummation of her narrative voice, is denied. From here,

[25] 'Quid tibi Pisandrum Polybumque Medontaque dirum / Eurymachique avidas Antinoique manus / atque alios referam, quos omnis turpiter absens / ipse tuo partis sanguine rebus alis?', *Heroides* 1.91–4.

[26] Of course, the connection between weaving and narrating is well established, with the Latin word 'textum' translated as variations of 'fabric', 'cloth', 'that which is woven'. See for example James Olney, *Memory and Narrative: The Weave of Life-Writing* (Chicago: University of Chicago Press, 1998).

176 CAHUN: AN OVIDIAN TIRESIAS FOR MODERN TIMES

the monologue rapidly assumes a grimmer tone. Odysseus is a murderer, a cheat. But he is also controlling, with far-reaching consequences. Penelope indicts Odysseus as orchestrator of a lie, a lie driven by a self-serving desire to preserve his glory. This lie is a story that seemingly exalts his wife and accentuates his masculinity while covering a harrowing truth of marital rape and enforced complicity: 'Rusé renard! Il exaltera sa très chaste épouse, et la violera lâchement par-derrière—et la fera crier entre les murs épais' (pp. 24–5) ('Sly fox! He'll exalt his most chaste wife, and like a coward violate her from behind—and make her shriek between the thick walls') (p. 57). The reference to 'les murs épais' ('the thick walls') intensifies the imagery, for Penelope's voice cannot be heard and her ordeal remains hidden. Penelope infers that oppression and violation through literary and cultural history, the propagation of a patriarchal narrative, is much more insidious and difficult to overthrow: 'Quoi! je me tairais pour ne pas ternir sa gloire mal acquise? Ah! si je pouvais la souiller aussi facilement que sa couche!' (p. 24) ('What! Did I say anything to tarnish his ill-gotten glory? Ah! if I can sully it as easily as his bed!') (p. 57). She threatens to vitiate his legacy, to defile his glory as he has defiled hers for centuries. She follows her angry outburst with a reference to the ancient tradition of burning laurel: 'Brûler leurs lauriers, les brûler encore verts—plaisir de femme!' (p. 24) ('To burn the laurels, to burn them when still green, is a pleasure unique to woman!') (p. 57). The laurel is synonymous with the nymph Daphne, who was turned into a laurel bush in her attempt to preserve her virginity and flee the amorous Apollo, as recounted by Ovid in *Metamorphoses* Book 1. It is at the site of this metamorphosis that the Delphic oracle is located and it is here that the priestess burnt laurel leaves and barley in preparation for her oracular utterances.[27] In this allusion, then, Cahun conveys the complexity of the female position: female vulnerability at the hands of patriarchal control, the lauded feminine ideal of the chaste female, and the female muse or vessel of inspiration and mystical powers. The monologue ends with a pithy and sobering admission: 'Choisir, subir: mots flatteurs, mots menteurs.—C'est la même chose' (p. 25) ('To choose, to submit: words as flatterers, words as liars.—They are the same') (p. 57). Penelope's sense of entrapment is palpable. Choice and subjugation are synonymous for her, with the connection between language and the inimical propagation of a patriarchal narrative clearly culpable.

---

[27] I am grateful to Dick Collins, Alex Davis, and Jesse Weiner for their thoughts on this. For more, see Michael Scott, *Delphi: A History of the Center of the Ancient World* (Princeton: Princeton University Press, 2014), and *Pausanias's Description of Greece*, trans. and with a commentary by J. G. Frazer (London: Macmillan, 1898).

But despite this bleak conclusion, Cahun's sketch offers hope, portraying a female who is not a passive witness to her fate. Cahun's subversive reprisal of a familiar tale highlights the role of *narration* in the narrative and significantly its reception. By telling the same story but from a different perspective, Cahun corrodes the almost adamantine conventional representation. The telling impacts on the perception of events, with the skilled narrator blurring the boundaries between fact and fiction, disguising truth under layers of facade. Cahun intricately brings together these themes in the figure of the poet Phemius and Penelope's decision to weave a story like his. Weaving represents the potential of female creativity, and Penelope's decision to choose the poet as her lover is indicative of the future role that lies ahead, where she will be the author of her own story: 'Je tiendrai: le chanteur sera mon amant' (p. 24) ('I will keep my promise: the singer will be my lover') (p. 57). Whether she is faithful or a tease within that story is almost inconsequential. No longer to be the paradigm of an externally imposed female ideal designed to divide and oppress, that is the desired objective.

But what of Ovid's Penelope? While fitting with the conventional portrayal of Penelope as faithful and lovesick, it nevertheless creates *lacunae* or space for an alternative story. After all, telling her story from her perspective is an act of power and defiance as mentioned earlier. Through her words, Penelope gives voice to her grievances and her suspicions, ensuring that Odysseus does not escape untarnished in her account. In addition, her Odysseus remains the absent addressee of her words, with attention firmly rooted on her story. Both Ovid and Cahun are interested in the power of storytelling as a means of altering expectations, perceptions, and reception. In the words of Derek Gladwin: 'Everyone is a storyteller. Recognising our ability to rewrite our personal narratives allows for creative spaces of personal and social transformation.'[28] Ovid and Cahun were proponents of the transformative power of narration.

Sappho and the Art of Destruction

The second epistle to link Ovid and Cahun is that of the poet Sappho.[29] While both Ovid and Cahun write as the poet Sappho in their respective works, they

---

[28] Derek Gladwin, *Rewriting Our Stories: Education, Empowerment and Well-being* (Cork: Atrium, 2021), 10.
[29] On other reworkings of Ovid's Sappho, see Thea S. Thorsen in this volume on Constance de Salm's eighteenth-century opera (Chapter 7) and Florence Klein on Marguerite Yourcenar's Sappho in her 1936 novel, *Feux* (Chapter 11).

178   CAHUN: AN OVIDIAN TIRESIAS FOR MODERN TIMES

do so with radically different outcomes. The story of the poet Sappho is recounted by Ovid in his fifteenth and final letter. In this long epistle Ovid emulates the lyric poet with his own deeply lyrical version of Sappho's tale of abandonment and rejection. Here, Sappho's difference, her sexuality, is recast as she mourns the loss of her lover, Phaon, in an epistle that foregrounds this heterosexual rejection: 'Unworthy one, the love that belonged to many maids you alone possess' (*Heroides* 15.20).[30] Throughout the letter Sappho recounts the effect of Phaon's departure, citing him as her reason to live and, significantly, as the source of her artistic talents. Without him, she cannot create: 'My genius had its powers from him; with him they were swept away' (*Heroides* 15.206).[31]

In the hands of Cahun, Sappho assumes a very different tone and tale. The title indicates the direction and intention of Cahun, 'Sapho, l'incomprise' [Sappho the Misunderstood]. This Sappho has long been misrepresented by society, Ovid included, and Cahun is keen to rewrite the history of this famed poet, ensuring that the reader is shocked out of passive compliance in the misrepresentation. In the opening quotation, attributed to Sappho herself, Cahun makes her divergence from Ovid clear. This is not a lovelorn ode: 'Vous n'êtes rien pour moi. Je ne ressens pas de ma colère, et j'ai l'esprit serein' (p. 33) ('*You are nothing to me. I do not feel the effects of my anger, and I am serene of spirit*') [italics in the translation] (p. 63). In fact, Phaon does not get a mention until page 36 and it is clear that Sappho is far from the jilted lover. Instead she is a strong woman who is eager to escape her renown as a sought-after lesbian and whose overriding desire is to create: 'Créer, c'est mon bonheur' (p. 34) ('To create is my joy') (p. 64). In a reversal of traditional gender stereotypes, Phaon is cast as the vulnerable ingénu and Sappho as the authoritative and outspoken lover, with italics to reinforce the incontestability of her remarks: 'J'ai beau faire et beau dire: *Avec moi, mon cher, on ne se fait jamais remarquer*. Il s'intimide; il a peur; il quitte le pays' (p. 36) ('I do and say whatever I like: *With me, my dear, one never points such things out*. He is intimidated; he is afraid; he leaves the country') (p. 65).

Like Penelope before her, Sappho is attuned to the subjectivity of representation: 'Je sais, on m'attribue une fille' (p. 35) ('I know: They attribute to me a daughter') (p. 64).[32] It is a subjectivity deriving from patriarchal dominance, in open disregard of the female or her truth: 'Je fis semblant de la mettre au monde pour éviter d'être répudiée (beaucoup d'Athéniennes agissent ainsi)'

---

[30] 'Inprobe, multarum quod fuit, unus habes', *Heroides* 15.20.

[31] 'Ingenio vires ille dat, ille rapit', *Heroides* 15.206.

[32] 'And as if there were lack of things to weary me endlessly, a little daughter fills the measure of my cares' ('Et tamquam desint, quae me sine fine fatigent, / accumulat curas filia parva meas'), *Heroides* 15.69–70.

(p. 35) ('I pretended to bring her into the world to avoid being divorced (many Athenians did the same))' (p. 64). Sappho desires and obtains her own exile, longing for the chance to give birth to her own creation. But her hopes are dashed, and in the end, she stages her own death in the ultimate act of self-empowerment: 'Pas si bête! Ce n'était qu'un mannequin de son que Cleis, caché, poussa dans la mer violette. (On s'y trompe bien au cinéma)' (p. 37) ('I'm no fool! It was only a mannequin of hers that Cleis, hidden, pushed into the violet sea. (They do the same thing in the movies.))' (p. 65). Free from the controlling hands of society, she can act as she wishes. Only now, destruction has replaced creation as her artistic outlet: 'Quand on renonce à créer, il ne reste plus qu'à détruire: car aucun vivant ne peut se tenir debout—immobile—sur la roue du destin' (p. 37) ('When one renounces creation, only destruction remains: For no one living can stand upright—unmoving—on the wheel of fate') (p. 65).

Cahun's Sappho seems much removed from that of Ovid. She turns her confinement at the hands of patriarchal representation into an opportunity for self-empowerment where she discovers new avenues for her creativity. Again, Cahun has exploited the spaces in Ovid's portrayal. For Ovid's Sappho does recognize her own artistic prowess and is proud of her poetic skills: 'If I am slight of stature, yet I have a name fills every land; the measure of my name is my real height' (*Heroides* 15.33–4).[33] The letter, while mourning the loss of her lover and thus her artistic muse, nevertheless showcases her poetic craft. It is the longest of the epistles and closes Ovid's narrative of female voices. And while the tradition of Sappho committing suicide is anchored by Ovid, the letter does not end with Sappho falling to her death but rather with a hyperbolic flourish: 'But if your pleasure be to fly afar from Pelasgian Sappho . . . ah, at least let a cruel letter tell me this in my misery, that I may seek my fate in the Leucadian wave!' (*Heroides* 15.217–20).[34] Ovid is a nebulous source of mythology that casts him as a protean literary forefather.[35]

Self-Portraiture or the Act of Inversion

The theme of inversion is central to Cahun's body of work, creatively explored in her literary work and also in her photographs. Through it, she challenges first the reader and then the viewer. By shifting the perspective in the narrative,

[33] 'Sim brevis, at nomen, quod terras inpleat omnes,est mihi', *Heroides* 15.33–4.
[34] 'Sive iuvat longe fugisse Pelasgida Sappho . . . / hoc saltem miserae crudelis epistula dicat, / ut mihi Leucadiae fata petantur aquae!', *Heroides* 15.217–20.
[35] See the chapter in this volume by James Illingworth for similar Ovidian echoes in George Sand's work (Chapter 9).

180   CAHUN: AN OVIDIAN TIRESIAS FOR MODERN TIMES

Cahun forces the reader to view the central female in a new light and thus to reconsider the veracity or rather cultural dominance of the traditional narrative. Similarly, in her photographs, Cahun challenges the viewer's preconceptions—regarding art, its function, the subject, the photographer. She disrupts the conventional relationship between the visual and the viewer. The symbol and vector of this theme of inversion is the mirror, a signpost embedded in her œuvre. As both object and motif, the mirror links her textual and visual output, featuring prominently in many of her portraits as well as in the title of her incomplete memoir *Confidences au miroir*. The centrality and significance of the mirror in Cahun's work is evidenced by Sarah Pucill, a British artist who has authored two films inspired by Claude Cahun: *Magic Mirror* (2013), based on *Aveux non avenus*, and *Confessions to the Mirror* (2016), based on *Confidences au miroir*. Cindy Sherman, so often identified as Cahun's twentieth-century counterpart or offspring, articulates the complexity of the mirror: 'As soon as I stop looking in the mirror that's when I feel like myself again.'[36] For Cahun, too, the mirror is where one becomes (an)other. It is not a site of affirmation but of possibility, of play, of dissemblance. Outside of the mirror, one can reassemble oneself. Is the reassembled self the 'true' self or merely the one that is presented to society? Is the mirrored self, with its endless reservoir of possibilities, the 'true' self, an accurate representation of our multitudinous identity? The medium of photography, in potent union with the mirror, facilitates Cahun's multifaceted assault, allowing a questioning and inversion of many preconceptions about gender, identity, and art.

This is vividly exemplified in her 1928 self-portrait (Fig. 1).[37] For me, this photograph is key to an understanding of Cahun as it neatly encapsulates the disparate, complex, interwoven strands of her artistic tapestry. In the centre of the photograph Cahun stands before a mirror. She is in side profile, dressed in a checked jacket and gazing out at the camera. Her reflection, the image in the mirror, is gazing backwards, away from the camera in the opposite direction. Kline remarks that Cahun, the non-reflected version, 'registers the presence of the viewer and does not flinch from eye contact.'[38] Cahun is looking at the viewer from within the image, and it is a defiant look. As with *Héroïnes*

---

[36] Thom Thompson, 'A Conversation with Cindy Sherman', in *Cindy Sherman* (Stony Brook, NY: State University of New York Art Gallery, 1983), n.p. [exh. catalogue]. Cited in Lippard, 'Scattering Selves', 38.

[37] Louise Downie, ed., *Don't Kiss Me: The Art of Claude Cahun and Marcel Moore* (London: Tate Publishing, 2006; New York: Aperture, 2006), 120 [DKM catalogue].

[38] Katy Kline, 'In or Out of the Picture: Claude Cahun and Cindy Sherman', in Whitney Chadwick, ed., *Mirror Images: The Women, Surrealism and Self-Representation* (Cambridge, MA: Massachusetts Institute of Technology Press, 1998), 66–81 (p. 69).

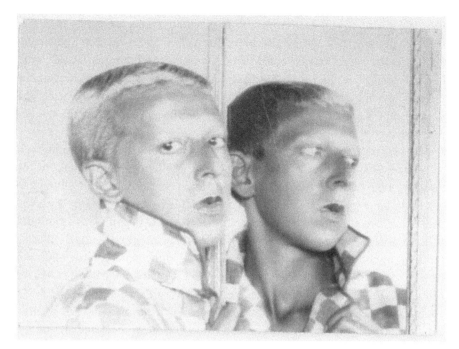

Fig. 1 Self Portrait in the Mirror, Claude Cahun, 1928. 179mm × 237mm; JHT/1995/00030/g negative.
Courtesy of the Jersey Heritage Collections

three years earlier, Cahun now wrong-foots the viewer, turning the tables on the traditional viewer/viewed relationship and its associated power dynamic. The object of the photograph now controls the gaze and it is the viewer who is uncomfortable, forced out of the conventional role and into that of object.[39] That the outward challenging gaze belongs to a woman heightens the disruption of the traditional visual discourse. Typically, in visual media, the female is subjected to the voyeuristic omnipotent male gaze.[40] As a conduit for male desire, her sexuality and identity are formative in the construction of those of the male observer. More than a simple reversal of the trend, Cahun subverts and adopts the controlling patriarchal male gaze without assuming its autocratic pretensions. She carries her subversion further by refusing to comply with the social constructs of stereotypical gender roles. With close cropped hair and a

---

[39] It is a position that Cahun shares with the viewer due to the imbrication of object with subject in the creation of such self-portraits.
[40] For more on this, see Laura Mulvey, *Visual and Other Pleasures* (Basingstoke, Hampshire: Palgrave Macmillan, 1989).

182   CAHUN: AN OVIDIAN TIRESIAS FOR MODERN TIMES

long jacket that covers her frame, Cahun is neither characteristically male nor female, adopting an androgynous appearance that would become a recurrent feature in her work. Having constructed the photographic frame herself, with her partner Marcel Moore as the likely collaborative eye behind the camera, Cahun has not only autonomized the female object, but in replacing the voyeuristic male gaze with that of a female, she challenges the viewer's hetero-normative preconceptions.[41]

The self, reflected in the mirror, adds to the complexity of the photograph as the viewer's attention is divided between the relentless eye contact of the non-reflected Cahun as well as the far-off gaze of the reflected Cahun. The conventional expectation of the mirror, providing a 'mirror' image, is under-cut as the two Cahuns do not match.[42] In this way, the mirror's dominant cultural image as an emblem of female narcissism is challenged. Widely reflected in cultural iconography, it is an image indoctrinated into childhood development as epitomized by the Snow White fairy tale mantra 'Mirror Mirror on the wall, who is the fairest of them all?'. Thynne observes: 'In countless nineteenth-century representations of a woman at her toilette, the subject gazes at herself in a mirror while her body is on display for the viewer.'[43] The female is cast as narcissistic while at the same time having that self-absorption manipulated by the controlling and voyeuristic gaze of the onlooker. Speaking of Cahun's portrait, Latimer writes: '[Cahun] maintains both a literal and symbolic distance from her proper reflection.'[44] Cahun's photograph rejects and subverts this traditional imagery of the mirror as a site of female vanity and self-obsession but also as a site of female subjugation where the mirror conveys the interiority of the female world and the way in which she is both 'seen' and meant to be seen by society, and in essence the patriarchal gaze. Cahun exploits the complexity of the mirror to highlight female creativity while simultaneously recasting a symbol of repression, van-ity, and interiority as one of expression and autonomy. She turns the mirror

---

[41] There is a complementary and 'mirror' image of Moore that underlines the subversive homo-sexuality of the composition, where even the gaze of the reflected Cahun is directed at a female object of affection (Downie, *Don't Kiss Me*, 155). For more on this, see Jennifer Shaw, *Reading Claude Cahun's Disavowals* (Farnham: Ashgate Publishing, 2013), 98–9.

[42] That this photograph was enlarged suggests its significance in Cahun's work. The enlargement, focusing on the head and shoulders, intensifies Cahun's steady gaze while highlighting the centrality and importance of the mirror (Downie, *Don't Kiss Me*, 121).

[43] Lizzie Thynne, 'Surely You Are Not Claiming to Be More Homosexual than I?': Claude Cahun and Oscar Wilde' in Joseph Bristow, ed., *Oscar Wilde and Modern Culture: The Making of a Legend* (Ohio: Ohio University Press, 2008), 180–208 (p. 191).

[44] Tirza True Latimer, 'Looking Like a Lesbian: Portraiture and Sexual Identity in 1920s Paris', in Whitney Chadwick and Tirza True Latimer, eds, *The Modern Woman Revisited: Paris between the Wars* (New Brunswick: Rutgers University Press, 2003), 127–44 (p. 135).

outwards, to reflect a world profoundly shaped by its pernicious social constructs. In Cahun's hands, the mirror becomes an ontological marker of uncertainty rather than certainty.

In her dual role as observer and observed, Cahun undercuts the conventions of portrait representation. Cahun is neither the epitome of femininity nor the subjected victim. She is defiant and present on the one hand, aloof and absent on the other. Shaw notes:

> What is most striking about this photograph is its disjunctiveness, the contrast between the self reflected in the mirror, captured second-hand by the camera—physically exposed, unaware, seemingly lost in contemplation— and the self captured directly by the camera—self-possessed, meeting the camera's gaze head on.[45]

I would argue here however that the self in the mirror is not exposed, as this suggests a vulnerability. Instead I propose that the self in the mirror is indifferent to the viewer's gaze, unperturbed by it in a seemingly passive act that matches the active defiance of the Cahun who challenges the gaze head on. Both undermine the traditional use of the mirror—one through direct eye contact and the other through simple yet effective indifference.

However, many have interpreted this destabilization of self and representation as a symptom of an inner personal conflict. In her 2005 article, Andersen challenges the heavily biographical and gendered bias of such criticism.[46] She quotes Dickran Tashijan, one of the contributors to Chadwick's 1998 volume on women and surrealism: 'The transgressions of androgyny were deeply felt in the multiple representations of self that became self-portraiture, as though she [Cahun] needed continual reassurance of her chosen identity.'[47] Andersen takes issue with the patronizing downgrading of Cahun's work to self-portraiture and the gender connotations implicit in that label: 'A great deal of criticism tends to suggest that women artists that work primarily in self-representation are narcissists; their work is often misconstrued as evidence of their solipsism.'[48]

---

[45] Jennifer Shaw, 'Narcissus and the Magic Mirror', in Downie, *Don't Kiss Me*, 35.

[46] Corinne Andersen, '"Que me veux-tu? / What do you want of me?": Claude Cahun's *Autoportraits* and the Process of Gender Identification', *Women in French Studies*, 13 (2005), 37–50.

[47] Dickran Tashijan, 'Vous Pour Moi?: Marcel Duchamp and Transgender Coupling', in Whitney Chadwick, ed., *Mirror Images: The Women, Surrealism and Self-*Representation (Cambridge, MA: Massachusetts Insitute of Technology Press, 1998), 36–65 (p. 40). Cited in Andersen, 'Que me veux-tu? / What do you want of me?, 38.

[48] Andersen, 'Que me veux-tu? / What do you want of me?, 38. Self-portraiture was associated with narcissism, which in turn was linked with femininity. See Tirza True Latimer, 'Narcissus and Narcissus:

184 CAHUN: AN OVIDIAN TIRESIAS FOR MODERN TIMES

This critical appraisal of Cahun's work as confessional self-portraiture is emblematic of a wider tendency to view the work of female artists as autobiographical and therapeutically personal. This is an outlook that limits the subversive potential and indeed inherent complexity of the work. Why is it assumed of a female artist that her work is biographical, that a discussion of identity correlates to an inevitable gender crisis on a deeply personal level? Cahun's work documents or journals her private emotional insecurities no more than can be said of any artist. This need for 'continual reassurance', this seeking of approval, is not conveyed in her œuvre. Often she is defiant, frustrated, and, at times, vulnerable. But never pitied or pitiable. Perhaps this 'identity crisis' is a more accurate portrayal of humanity, where a stable definitive fixed identity is neither realistic nor desirable. And perhaps this is why there is such imperative to assign the gender fluidity to an internal crisis, as an identity without limits is an unsettling and chaotic concept.

Tiresias, Narcissus, and the Mirror

It seems that Cahun's sexuality is the more palatable and compelling component of her legacy. In this, Cahun resembles Tiresias. In the same way as Tiresias espouses mutable identity, Cahun does not exhibit a stable identity. Not one to separate life and art, Cahun embodied her artistic themes, where her ambiguous appearance, indeterminate gender, and sexual preferences cast her as other or, in the sexiological discourse of the later nineteenth century, a 'sexual invert' or 'third sex'.[49] In his transition from male to female and back to male, Tiresias is the personification of the performative and fluid gender that Cahun espoused and repeatedly exhibits throughout her work. Imitating typically masculine and feminine mannerisms, interspersed with androgynous and asexual poses, Cahun is a Tiresias for the modern age. It seems however that Cahun has been subject to the categorization she so vehemently opposed and strived so hard to overturn. Much of Cahun's work, especially the images, has garnered a critical appraisal strongly rooted in conventional categories,

---

Claude Cahun and Marcel Moore', in *Women Together/Women Apart: Portraits of Lesbian Paris* (New Brunswick: Rutgers University Press, 2005), 68–104. Cahun subverts this traditional label for the genre. Firstly, her portraiture is not self-portraiture in the strict sense. Secondly, equating narcissism with femininity was glaringly ironic as it is the mythical male Narcissus who falls in love with his reflection. In her reimagining of the Narcissus myth, the association of self-portraiture and narcissism is inverted and becomes one of agency and empowerment rather than denigration and negativity.

[49] For more on this, see Laura 'Lou' Bailey and Lizzie Thynne, 'Beyond Representation: Claude Cahun's Monstrous Mischief-Making', *History of Photography*, 29/2 (2005), 135–48.

particularly from the point of view of gender, with many studying her images in relation to the sexiological and psychoanalytical discourse and debates of the time.[50] Quotes from Cahun are arbitrarily rolled out as feminist currency, deprived of their full agency and impact. Certainly, Cahun's work invites a feminist reading, but it does not prioritize it and in fact rails against such Cycloptic restrictive readings that subsume the individual within the collective. Indeed, the best advocate for a non-gendered response to Cahun's work is Cahun herself. In her writings and photographs, Cahun invites and demands an inclusive approach, where her destabilization of gender binaries is *one* of the many themes explored—themes such as the fact/fiction dichotomy, the nature of artistic creation, the 'otherness' of self, and fluidity of identity. The notion of gender as one facet among many encapsulates her and her work, where gender is a recurrent thread rather than the completed tapestry. In so doing, she underscores the importance of affording the individual voice, and in particular the individual female voice, its full range of expression.

Shaw writes:

Cahun's and Moore's work stood apart from the general trend of feminism during this period (1920s). For rather than demanding autonomy or rights for women, *Aveux non avenus* deconstructed the category of woman at the same time as it proposed new sources of artistic creativity.[51]

Even in the feminist movement of the 1920s, Cahun was an outsider, engaged in an approach that diverged from the mainstream. Shaw goes on to say:

Phrasing the issues in terms of the myth of Narcissus, we might identify the figure of the 'new' or 'modern' woman as a rejection of the role of Echo—the female supplement to Narcissus whose only purpose was to echo the words of the male poet—in favour of imagining a female Narcissus: a woman whose belief in her own self-cultivation might result in significant cultural production, even works of art.[52]

---

[50] Robert Pilgrim summarizes the many approaches to Cahun—politics, gender, psychoanalysis, and ethnicity. Pilgrim argues that Cahun's identity as one of the few female surrealist artists, coupled with her bold and subversive approach, made 'her adoption by feminist art historians something of an inevitability' (p. 16). He also stresses, as Lippard and Chadwick before him, the importance of timing to the way in which she was received—rediscovered in the 1980s era of feminism. But Pilgrim goes on to argue for a strongly Jewish reading of Cahun, somewhat undermining his argument and falling into the same restricted perspective of criticism. Robert Pilgrim, *Que me veux-tu?: Claude Cahun's Photomontages* (Croyde, Devon: Majaro Publications, 2012).

[51] Shaw, 'Narcissus and the Magic Mirror', 37.   [52] Ibid., 37.

186   CAHUN: AN OVIDIAN TIRESIAS FOR MODERN TIMES

The choice of the myth of Narcissus is significant. While for Shaw this myth is central to an understanding of Cahun's text *Aveux non avenus* and symbolism, here it assumes additional importance given Cahun's identification as Tiresias.[53] Narcissus is one of those about whom Tiresias delivers a prophecy. In her role as Tiresias, Cahun too prophesies the fate of Narcissus. In a radical reimagining, Narcissus like Tiresias undergoes a transition and emerges as a female with her own agency and legitimacy. Cahun has foreseen a fate where women are a creative force with an independent voice rather than one of passive mimicry. One could argue that this prophecy has been and continues to be fulfilled by the wave of female artists continuing to exercise their creative powers in the field of classical reception. It is important to note that, for Cahun, this fate is one in which female creativity is finally visible and acknowledged rather than newly conceived. Given her views on gender binaries and categorization, the transitory figures of Tiresias and Narcissus, I think it is safe to argue that for Cahun this is a fate inclusive of artists of all gender identities, where ultimately it is the *individual* who emerges with an autonomous creative voice of multiple selves. This resonates with Ovid whose *Metamorphoses* is replete with shape-shifting figures of the artist.[54] Helen Morales, in her work *Antigone Rising: the Subversive Power of the Ancient Myths*, highlights the genderfluidity of classical mythology, drawing on Ovid's depiction of Caenus, Hermaphroditus, Iphis and Ianthe, and Tiresias to support her argument for transmythology and the espousal, or rather the possibility, of the fluidity of gender identity.[55] Morales believes that Ovid facilitates transmythological interpretations by writers such as Ali Smith, who take the narrative and metamorphose it to accommodate a new voice or voices. 'Ovid's very fluid, as writers go, much more than most. He knows, more than most, that imagination doesn't have a gender . . . He honours all sorts of story.'[56] Cahun had exposed this aspect of Ovid in the early twentieth century, already reshaping and refashioning his work to respond to her cultural moment. Removing layers of patriarchal interpretation, Cahun exposed the alternative multifarious voices, the potential fluidity of gender and identity.

Coda: Cahun—An Ovidian Tiresias

In his prophecy to Odysseus, Tiresias augurs further hardship and future journeys (*Odyssey* 11.120–37). Cahun too foreshadows what is to come.

---

[53] Ibid., 33–45.   [54] I am grateful to Helena Taylor for this observation.
[55] Helen Morales, *Antigone Rising: the Subversive Power of the Ancient Myths* (London: Wildfire, 2020).
[56] Ali Smith, *Girl Meets Boy* (Edinburgh: Canongate, 2007). Cited in Morales, *Antigone Rising*, 140.

Since her revival, she has been cast as the antecedent to a wave of contemporary artists, appearing in exhibitions alongside artists such as Tacita Dean, Maya Deren, Cindy Sherman, and Gillian Wearing. While between fifty and seventy years separates these artists, these contemporaneous exhibitions reveal the enduring relevance of Cahun's work,[57] anticipatory of later subversive and innovative techniques, a visionary presence acknowledged by Wearing: 'We were born in different times, we have different concerns, and we come from different backgrounds. She didn't know me, yet I know her.'[58] Cahun was a forerunner for these artists, her 'prophecies' continuing, with her work prescient of the twenty-first-century explosion of gender and identity exploration, where self-portraiture is experienced and experimented with through social media rather than photography. One would imagine that Cahun would be queen of the 'selfie'—an 'art form' that removes the ambiguity of the photograph (photographer or self-timer), affording Cahun unlimited potential to push the boundaries of creativity, art, and culturally established norms.[59] While some prioritize and advocate her photography for this very appeal, citing her writing as dated,[60] I think that Cahun's writing, and in particular *Héroïnes*, speaks more than ever to an ostensibly liberal world flooded with images and declarations, a world that often reaffirms old values and commodifies people under the guise of spurious autonomy. Cahun tackles and deconstructs conventions of sex, gender, class, and race at a time of social and political upheaval where art and politics merged in fraught response. The parallels are clear. Cahun signifies a modern-day Ovidian Tiresias, whose work encapsulates the female voices of the past and prefigures those of the future. Under her pivotal Tiresian gaze, Cahun advocates for the voice of the creative *individual*, freeing both herself and others from the binary restrictions of gender categorization.

---

[57] Her resurgence shows no signs of abating, with the publication of Jennifer Shaw's *Exist Otherwise: The Life and Works of Claude Cahun* (London: Reaktion Books, 2017), the first English critical biography devoted to Cahun.

[58] Adrian Searle, 'A Ghost in Kiss Curls: How Gillian Wearing and Claude Cahun Share a Mask', *Guardian*, 8 January 2017. And subsequent review of the exhibition in March 2017, https://www.theguardian.com/artanddesign/2017/mar/08/gillian-wearing-and-claude-cahun-behind-the-mask-another-mask-review-national-portrait-gallery [accessed 3 October 2020].

[59] The 'selfie' would also evoke the myth of Narcissus as it centres on the self and is often perceived as an act of vanity and self-promotion. Cahun would certainly have seen the artistic potential of the 'selfie'.

[60] Gen Doy, *Claude Cahun: A Sensual Politics of Photography* (London: I. B. Tauris, 2007), 3.

11

Marguerite Yourcenar's 'Feminism' and the Ambivalence of Ovidian Models in *Feux*

Florence Klein

Feux, an early work by Marguerite Yourcenar, is a unique collection. It alternates brief first-person diary entries with short stories that present an erudite and unconventional rewriting of heroines from mythology and Greco-Roman literature, with a particular focus on their love affairs. The first story reworks the tale of Phaedra's passionate love; in the second we see Achilles dressed as a young girl on the island of Skyros; and later we witness the monologue of Clytemnestra, who murdered Agamemnon out of love, pleading her case before the judges...We could also cite, among others, the tale of Lena, a courtesan who took part in Harmodius' and Aristogeiton's assassination plot in 525 BC, or the story of Mary Magdalen as depicted by the Golden Legend, in which she is the abandoned fiancée of John the Evangelist, who leaves her to follow Jesus. The series of nine texts ends with the character of Sappho, depicting her transition from loving girls to loving Phaon, and ending with her suicide. The classical tradition is thus revisited from the point of view of women in love who are driven by erotic desire, or, in the case of male characters (Achilles, Patroclus, Phaedo), with a particular emphasis on blurring the boundaries between the sexes and (apparently) emphasizing gender ambiguity.[1] As a collection of stories about (mainly) mythological women that focuses on sentiment, *Feux* can be read as a response to Ovid's *Heroides*, which also rewrite a heroic literary tradition from a female perspective, stressing erotic passion in works which align pathos with a form of playful erudition, allusiveness, dramatic irony, and anachronisms. Although Yourcenar does not

---

[1] For a detailed summary of the shifts between sexual and sentimental roles in *Feux*, see C. Biondi, 'Neuf mythes pour une passion', *Bulletin de la Société Internationale d'Études Yourcenariennes*, 5 (1989), 27–33.

Florence Klein, *Marguerite Yourcenar's 'Feminism' and the Ambivalence of Ovidian Models in* Feux In: *Ovid in French: Reception by Women from the Renaissance to the Present*. Edited by: Helena Taylor and Fiona Cox, Oxford University Press. © Oxford University Press 2023. DOI: 10.1093/oso/9780192895387.003.0011

evoke this model herself and the connections are not necessarily self-evident, in this chapter I will suggest that reading them in tandem offers new perspectives on each.

We know that Yourcenar was familiar with the *Heroides*. For example, she compares Ariadne's pleas from *Heroides* 10 to Catullus 64 in the preface to *Qui n'a pas son Minotaure ?* [To Each his Minotaur].[2] In her presentation of Sappho's poems that she translated in *La Couronne et la lyre* [The Crown and the Lyre], she underlines the importance of *Heroides* 15, 'Sappho to Phaon' (and 'the great popularity' Ovid enjoyed 'over eighteen centuries'), in the image of the Greek poetess created by this tradition.[3] (In fact, even though the Ovidian model is never evoked in relation to *Feux*, it should be noted that both works finish with the figure of Sappho, who is implicitly presented as a double of the author.[4]) I will therefore endeavour first of all to suggest that *Feux* was inspired by the Ovidian epistolary volume, even if the author herself never explicitly claimed this source.[5]

---

[2] Marguerite Yourcenar, 'Aspects d'une légende et histoire d'une pièce', preface to *Qui n'a pas son Minotaure ?*, in *Théâtre II* (Paris: Gallimard, 1971), 163–231 (p. 172).

[3] 'Il faut descendre jusqu'aux *Héroïnes* d'Ovide, écrites au temps d'Auguste, pour trouver l'histoire de Sappho et de Phaon sous la forme pathétique qu'elle a gardée à peu près jusqu'à nous dans la littérature, les beaux-arts et les librettos d'opéra.... C'est à l'immense vogue du poète latin pendant dix-huit siècles qu'on doit l'image de la belle désespérée, armée d'une lyre et flottant au fil de l'eau, qui a fini par aborder dans les vers de Baudelaire' (We must go back to Ovid's *Heroides*, written in the time of Augustus, to find the story of Sappho and Phaon in the moving form in which it has been passed down through literature, the arts, and opera librettos.... It is the Latin poet's great popularity over eighteen centuries that we have to thank for the image of the desperate, beautiful woman, armed with a lyre and floating along the waterside, later taken up in Baudelaire's verse). M. Yourcenar, *La Couronne et la lyre. Poèmes traduits du grec par Marguerite Yourcenar* (Paris: Gallimard, 1984), 72–3. Unless otherwise stated, translations from French are by Eleanor Hodgson.

[4] On the subject of Ovid depicting (and playing with) Sappho as a poet, see F. Bessone, 'Saffo, la lirica, l'elegia: su Ovidio, *Heroides* 15', *Materiali e discussioni per l'analisi dei testi classici* (2003), 51, 209–44; V. Rimell, *Ovid's Lovers: Desire, Difference, and the Poetic Imagination* (Cambridge: Cambridge University Press, 2006), 123–55. In *La Couronne et la lyre* [The Crown and the Lyre] (1984), Yourcenar noted that 'Pour les Anciens comme pour nous, toutefois, Sapho demeure avant tout l'interprète de ses propres émois amoureux' (p. 75) (For the Ancients and for us, Sappho remains above all the interpreter of her own amorous turmoil). In *Feux*, it is at the start of the mythological tale of 'Sappho, or Suicide' that first-person narration (perhaps autobiographical) is used, a voice reserved until this point for the fragments of diary entry texts interspersed between each short story: 'Je viens de voir au fond des miroirs d'une loge une femme qui s'appelle Sappho' (*Feux*, p. 1157) ('I have just seen, reflected in the mirrors of a theatre box, a woman called Sappho') (*Fires*, p. 115). This is perhaps an indication that Sappho is, to a certain extent, a reflection of the author. See R. Poignault, 'Dans le miroir de Sappho. De l'impossibilité d'être femme', *Bulletin de la Société Internationale d'Études Yourcenariennes*, 11 (1993), 21–40 (p. 22). For other discussions of responses to Sappho in this volume, see the chapter by Thea S. Thorsen, analysing the eighteenth-century opera, *Sapho*, by Constance de Salm (Chapter 7), and by Catherine Burke, analysing the 1926 Sappho of Claude Cahun's *Héroïnes* (Chapter 10).

[5] I explored this hypothesis in my master's dissertation 'Lecture comparée des *Héroïdes* d'Ovide et de *Feux* de Marguerite Yourcenar', submitted at the Université Paris-Sorbonne in June 2000. The source of inspiration for this study was A. Michel, 'Des *Héroïdes* modernes: *Feux* de Marguerite Yourcenar', in R. Chevallier, ed., *Colloque Présence d'Ovide* (Paris: Les Belles Lettres, 1982), 455–60. It is also of note that this relationship is mentioned in passing in Jacques Cormier, 'La Survie littéraire

190 MARGUERITE YOURCENAR'S 'FEMINISM'

Moreover, both Ovid's *Heroides* and Yourcenar's *Feux* are grounded in a similar approach, which, in the majority of cases, involves manipulating a traditional mythological tale in order to focus on a feminine point of view. Both works are distinctly shaped by a gendered perspective and a constant awareness of the opposition between masculine and feminine (even when this awareness gives rise to games of gender-reversal).[6] Because Ovid's works tend to give space to a female voice and to offer sensitive representations of women's subjectivity, the poet has been seen as sympathetic to them.[7] But the idea that he writes in support of women has been largely questioned by feminist studies, and obviously Ovidian scholarship has not reached a unanimous verdict on the issue of the poet's 'proto-feminism.'[8] For example, how far the poet colludes with the objectification of women (and their roles as sexualized and powerless victims) in his texts remains a very delicate issue. With this question in mind, Alison Sharrock applies to interpretations of the representation of women in Ovid's work the distinction between 'optimistic' and 'pessimistic' readings—a terminology well known in Virgilian scholarship: to sum up, while the pessimistic reader considers that the poet (compromised by the misogynist society in which he belongs) is responsible for women's reification in his work, the optimistic one, seeing the poet as sympathetic to women, believes that he only *delineates* this reification in order to expose it, rather than *enact* it.[9]

Concerning the *Heroides* in particular, critics are also divided in their opinions of whether a such work, which lets women speak so they can tell of the torments of love, made Ovid a defender of women ahead of his time, and the question of whose voice we hear when reading 'the heroines' letters' has animated the scholarship for a long time.[10] While Ovid seems to give the

---

d'Ovide', *Cahiers de l'AIEF*, 58 (2006), 270: 'L'influence de ces mêmes *Héroïdes* se retrouve aussi dans *Feux* de Marguerite Yourcenar' (The influences of the *Heroides* are also found in *Fires* by Marguerite Yourcenar).

[6] For example, we find the dominant motif of cross-dressing in *Heroides* 9, with the exchange of virile and feminine attributes between Hercules and Omphale, and *Feux*'s 'Achilles, or the Lie' rewrites the future warrior's hiding place while he is disguised as a young girl on the island of Skyros.

[7] See, for example, L. P. Wilkinson, *Ovid Recalled* (Cambridge: Cambridge University Press, 1955), 86: '[Ovid] had also a tender side to his nature which gave him an interest in the weaker sex and a certain insight into what their feeling might be.'

[8] For a critical survey, see A. Sharrock, 'Gender and Sexuality', in Philip Hardie, ed., *The Cambridge Companion to Ovid* (Cambridge: Cambridge University Press, 2002), 95–107.

[9] A. Sharrock, 'Gender and Transformation: Reading, Women, and Gender in Ovid's *Metamorphoses*', in A. Sharrock, D. Möller, and M. Malm, eds, *Metamorphic Readings: Transformation, Language, and Gender in the Interpretation of Ovid's Metamorphoses* (Oxford: Oxford University Press, 2020), 33–53. In this article, Sharrock's discussion of the terminology *resisting vs releasing reading* with regards to an interpretation of the representation of women in Ovid's work is also very useful.

[10] The *Heroides* are particularly pertinent when exploring questions such as that formulated by S. Felman: what does it mean for a male author to be *speaking 'as' a woman*? (S. Felman, 'Women and Madness: The Critical Fallacy', *Diactrics*, 5 (1975), 2–10 (p. 3)). The two opposing schools of

mythological heroines a voice, and with it the opportunity to give their own account of the legends to which they belong, this opportunity does not appear to be as empowering as it could be: as Sara Lindheim puts it, 'the Ovidian women, while potentially in possession of the power to create and to cast themselves in roles central to their stories, instead enter into a conversation with the prior telling(s), managing, through epistolary conventions, to rewrite to their own disadvantage even texts in which they play secondary roles.'[11] As we will see, the *Heroides*' unique literary device also means that these women are imprisoned in a sort of helpless pathos, reducing them to the expression of a passionate and often lamenting love in which these speakers are, in reality, trapped. My point here will not be to settle the question whether this confinement is exposed or enacted by Ovid, but to suggest that reading *Feux* in parallel can throw some light on this important feature of the *Heroides*.

Indeed, it would seem that for Yourcenar such a foregrounding of the feminine point of view, and an interpretation of the world focused solely on erotic sentiment, could not be qualified as feminist—far from it. The author who claimed not to be a feminist, refusing divisive categories,[12] instead, provocatively, declared herself to be a misogynist as she deplored the narrowness of women's worlds. In a letter to Helen Howe Allen criticizing May Sarton's *Plant Dreaming Deep*, she writes:

> À tout vous dire, un livre comme celui de May Sarton me révèle à moi-même ma foncière misogynie, laquelle, bien entendu, ne tient pas contre quelques exceptions aimables ou admirables. *Pourquoi les femmes s'enferment-elles si souvent dans leur petit monde étroit, prétentieux, pauvre?* (Je pense à la phrase que je fais employer à Hadrien: 'Je retrouvais *le cercle étroit des femmes*, leur dur sens pratique, et leur ciel gris dès que l'amour n'y joue plus...')[my emphasis].[13]
>
> (To be completely frank, a book such as May Sarton's makes me see my fundamental misogyny which, of course, does not hold up against likeable or

---

thought—considering that the *Heroides* allow us to read feminine voices that disturb the conventional, masculine tradition of heroic myths, or, in contrast, reading the epistles as the masculine author engaging in an act of ventriloquism, speaking through his characters—are discussed respectively in two monographs from the same year: E. Spentzou, *Readers and Writers in Ovid's 'Heroides'* (Oxford: Oxford University Press, 2003) and S. Lindheim, *Mail and Female: Epistolary Narrative and Desire in Ovid's 'Heroides'* (Madison, WI: University of Wisconsin Press, 2003).

[11] Lindheim, *Mail and Female*, 8–9.

[12] Maurice Delcroix, ed., 'Entretien avec Claude Servan-Schreiber', in *Marguerite Yourcenar, Portrait d'une voix, Vingt-trois entretiens (1952–1987)* (Paris: Gallimard, 2002), 284.

[13] Marguerite Yourcenar, '*Lettre à Helen Howe Allen* (février 1968)', in Michèle Sarde and Joseph Brami, eds, *Lettres à ses amis et à quelques autres* (Paris: Gallimard, 1995), 275–7 (p. 276).

admirable exceptions. *Why do women so often trap themselves in such a small, narrow, pretentious, and poor world?* (I think of the line I had Hadrian say: 'I encountered *the narrow domain of women*, their stern sense of practicality, and their grey horizons once love is no longer on their side...').)

Similarly, in her interviews with Patrick de Rosbo, who questions her about the fact that none of the main characters in her great novels is a woman,[14] she answers by stating that she had asked herself the same question, and wondered why, for example, she had not decided to focus on Plotina instead of Hadrian:

> Pourquoi ne pas faire d'elle le personnage central d'un livre? Tout simplement parce que la vie des femmes, à cette époque et à toutes les autres, a été *trop limitée* dans ses manifestations.
>
> Si nous prenions Plotine comme héroïne et comme narratrice, il fallait laisser tomber l'expérience directe de la guerre, l'expérience directe des coulisses et de la cuisine de la politique, et bien d'autres que je n'énumérerai pas. Ses vertus mêmes ont sans doute été un obstacle à son expérience. *Nous nous trouverions malgré tout avec elle dans ce domaine féminin restreint et fermé, d'une manière ou d'une autre, où la plupart des femmes ont vécu.*
>
> Je ne sais si nous pourrions trouver, où que ce soit, un personnage féminin historique égalant, je ne dis pas en grandeur (c'est une autre affaire), mais en envergure, un personnage masculin du même temps [my emphasis].[15]
>
> (Why not make her the central character of the book? Quite simply because the life of women, in both this era and in all others, is *too limited* in what it can express.
>
> If we took Plotina as the heroine and narrator, we must leave aside all direct experience of war, of what happens in the wings and on the sidelines of politics, and many other experiences that I shall not list. Her qualities would also doubtlessly hinder her experience. *In spite of everything, we would find ourselves with her in a restricted and closed feminine space, in one way or another, where most women have lived.*
>
> I do not know if we could find, wherever it may be, a female historical character equal not in grandeur (that is another matter), but in stature to a male character of the same period.)

---

[14] P. de Rosbo, 'Entretiens radiophoniques avec Marguerite Yourcenar', *Mercure de France* (1972), 87.
[15] Ibid., 88.

Later on, once again commenting on the quotation regarding the 'narrow domain of women' from the *Memoirs of Hadrian* cited above, she adds:

> Pour des raisons en partie naturelles et biologiques, en partie sûrement sociales, la femme accepte trop souvent l'image artificielle que la société où elle vit lui renvoie d'elle-même, consent, comme à plaisir, à *s'enfermer étroitement* dans des intérêts souvent facticement féminins, au lieu d'être en tout, et magnifiquement, un être humain femme. [my emphasis][16]

> (For partly natural and biological reasons, and no doubt partly social, all too often women accept the artificial image that the society in which they live projects onto them, and consent, almost willingly, to be *narrowly confined* within matters that are often falsely feminine, rather than being above all, and magnificently, a female human being.)

Contrary to her declarations, we could perhaps interpret this condemnation of the (self)-imprisonment of women within a narrow-minded and singular universe as indicating a feminist standpoint. In this chapter I shall show how Yourcenar in *Feux* thematically explores these very limits as well as the motif of imprisonment in a solely feminine world in a way that resonates with Ovid's work.

First, I shall establish the formal and thematic similarities between the two texts to support the argument for reading them in parallel: in particular, I will suggest that Yourcenar's specific use of anachronisms regarding epistolarity could perhaps be interpreted as a particular reference to Ovid's work. I will also show how the playful games with literary tradition in both works paradoxically intensify the pathos with which the mythological heroines are represented, imprisoned within a predestined (/already written) future and feminine roles they cannot escape. I will then explore how *Feux* resonates with the *Heroides* in thematizing the limits within which the passionate women are trapped. Finally, I shall focus in particular on two stories from *Feux*—Achilles, or the Lie', and 'Sappho, or Suicide'—which on the surface appear to complicate these limits by highlighting indeterminacy around gender and sexual orientation; by examining their hero(ine)'s attempt to escape a restrictive universe, I will explore how this yearning to leave the confined space of the feminine condition is strengthened by the memory of another Ovidian work: the *Metamorphoses*. This work provides a representation of a fluid world

---

[16] Ibid, 96.

194   MARGUERITE YOURCENAR'S 'FEMINISM'

which transcends fixed categories, but which in Yourcenar's texts instead serves to fix gender identities and reinforce the opposing fates of the two sexes.

Anachronisms and Playful Manipulation of Classical Myths

In Ovid's *Heroides* and in Yourcenar's *Feux*, the female perspective on the literary tradition, from which the heroines (or feminized heroes) are drawn, is accompanied by a form of rewriting that shrinks the original myth. The most unique, grandiose, or even supernatural elements are often reimagined from a more quotidian point of view, creating a type of universalism of feminine passion. We find one such example in *Heroides* 1. Penelope weaves a shroud during her husband's absence, but this action has no link to the *Odyssey*'s famous plot, as it is simply an activity to avoid boredom while she awaits his return. In fact, she writes that if Ulysses had not gone to Troy, she would not have had cause to complain of her solitude, 'nec mihi quaerenti spatiosam fallere noctem / Iassaret viduas pendula tela manus' ('nor would the hanging web be wearying now my widowed hands as I seek to beguile the hours of spacious night') (*Heroides* 1.9–10).[17] In a similar manner in *Feux*, Thetis' divine schemes to save Achilles from death are compared to a rural tradition: 'Comme les paysannes mettent des robes de filles à leurs garçons malades pour dépister la Fièvre, elle l'avait revêtu de ses tuniques de déesse qui dérouteraient la Mort' (*Feux*, p. 1091)[18] ('Like peasant women putting their sick boys in women's dresses to dodge Fever, she had dressed him in her goddess tunics to mislead Death') (*Fires*, p. 14).[19] Furthermore, the murder of Iphigenia that the oracle ordered the king of kings to commit is evoked by Clytemnestra in such a way that the epic hero becomes an ordinary, middle-class man: 'Je l'ai laissé sacrifier l'avenir de nos enfants à ses ambitions d'homme: je n'ai même pas

[17] Ovid, *Heroides. Amores*, trans. Grant Showerman, rev. G. P. Goold (Cambridge, MA: Harvard University Press, 2014). Hereafter, all text references to *Heroides* will be from this edition. Certainly, to the mind of a reader who knows the Homeric version of the tale, the verb 'fallere' evokes the ruse through which Penelope attempts to dupe her suitors. Yet here, through a deceptive effect, the term takes the complement 'spatiosam noctem'. In this way, Penelope becomes another abandoned woman who tries to kill time during her husband's absence, just like Cynthia, who declares 'purpureo *fallebam* stamine noctum' (For now I was beguiling sleep by spinning crimson thread) (Propertius, *Elegies* 1.3.41). [my emphasis]

[18] Marguerite Yourcenar, *Feux*, *Œuvres romanesques* (*Alexis ou le Traité du Vain combat; Le Coup de grâce; Denier du rêve; Mémoires d'Hadrien; L'œuvre au noir; Anna, soror; Un homme obscur—Une belle matinée; Feux; Nouvelles orientales;* supplément: *La nouvelle Eurydice*) (Paris: Gallimard, 1982). Hereafter, all in-text page references to *Feux* are from this edition.

[19] Marguerite Yourcenar, *Fires*, trans. Dori Katz, in collaboration with the author (Chicago: University of Chicago Press, 1981). Hereafter, all in-text page references to *Fires* are from this edition.

pleuré quand ma fille en est morte' (*Feux*, p. 1148) ('I let the future of our children be sacrificed to his own personal ambitions: I didn't even cry when my daughter died of them') (*Fires*, pp. 102–3).

In both works this simplification, or generalization, reduces the mythical prophetesses' gifts of clairvoyance to nothing more than premonitions, a sort of feminine intuition common to all women unhappy in love. In Oenone's letter to Paris, Ovid deliberately deprives the nymph of the prophetic powers with which she is endowed in the mythological tradition.[20] This modification is emphasized by the importance accorded to Cassandra, and by the similarities between the two women, who have both endured and suffered the consequences of Apollo's advances. Stripped of her gift of prophecy, Ovid's Oenone does not understand Cassandra's prediction. However, she appears nevertheless to experience the physical effects of clairvoyance. Speaking of the goddesses' judgement, she observes that 'attoniti micuere sinus, gelidusque cucurrit, / ut mihi narrasti, dure, per ossa tremor' ('My bosom leaped with amaze as you told me of it, and a chill tremor rushed through my hard bones') (*Heroides* 5.37–8). Similarly, the sight of Helen provokes what seems like a prophetic trance: 'tunc vero rupique sinus et pectora planxi / et secui madidas ungue rigente genas, / implevique sacram querulis ululatibus Iden' ('Then indeed did I rend my bosom and beat my breast, and with the hard nail furrowed my streaming cheeks, and filled holy Ida with wailing cries of lamentation') (*Heroides* 5.71–3). Yet, to use the Ciceronian distinction, the prophetic furor is no more than *praesagitio*, as the prophecy is reduced to a slightly belated premonition or a feeling of imminent misfortune.[21]

This downplaying seems to be extended and even commented on by Yourcenar in 'Clytemnestra, or Crime', when Cassandra is demoted from the role of prophetess in the *Heroides* to that of a simple palm reader who entertains the guests at the banquet:

> Il paraît qu'elle avait le don de deviner l'avenir: pour nous distraire, elle nous lut dans la main. Alors elle pâlit et ses dents claquèrent. Moi aussi, messieurs les juges, je savais l'avenir. Toutes les femmes le savent, elles s'attendent toujours à ce que tout finisse mal.   (*Feux*, pp. 1151–2)

---

[20] Oenone is presented as a prophetess by Parthenius of Nicaea, in stories 3 and 34 of the *Erotica Pathemata*. She predicts that Paris will leave her, will fall in love with a foreign woman, will bring war to Ilion, and will be injured in combat. These injuries are also announced by Conon and Apollodore. See J.-C. Jolivet, *Allusion et fiction épistolaire dans les* Héroïdes. *Recherches sur l'intertextualité ovidienne* (Rome: Collection de l'École Française de Rome, 2001), p. 13 onwards for literary and iconographic sources.

[21] Cicero, *De Divinatione* 1.65–6.

196   MARGUERITE YOURCENAR'S 'FEMINISM'

(It appeared that she had the gift of telling the future: to amuse us, she read our palms. Thereupon she paled and her teeth chattered. I also, gentlemen of the jury, knew the future. All women know it; they always expect things to end badly.)   (*Fires*, p. 109)

In the same way that Ovid strips Oenone of clairvoyance, Cassandra's powers of prophecy, which Aeschylus was able to exploit with virtuosity when Agamemnon's murder occurs off-stage, are reduced here to a form of bad premonition, of intuition, that the speaker notes is common to 'all women'.

Anachronisms are a second way in which myths are generalized and toned down in both Ovid's *Heroides* and Yourcenar's collection. Ovid has often been reproached for making his heroines speak like the women of Augustan Rome.[22] In a gesture of one-upmanship, in *Feux*, references to the modern day are also unashamedly omnipresent. Achilles leaves the 'collège des Centaures' (*Feux*, p. 1092) ('Centaurs' College') (*Fires*, p. 14), just as Hippolyte is forced 'dès le collège, dès les vacances du jour de l'an d'éviter les pièges tendus par sa belle-mère' (*Feux*, p. 1085) ('since school, since the New Year's Day bank holiday, to skip over obstacles an inimical step-mother has raised') (*Fires*, p. 6). Thetis sees in Jupiter's eyes 'le film des combats où succomberait Achille' (*Feux*, p. 1091) ('the film of battles Achilles would die in' (*Fires*, p. 13), and Mary Magdalene references 'les journaux du soir pour qui la Passion servait de fait divers' (*Feux*, p. 1129)' ('the evening papers that had treated the Passion as just another news item' (*Fires*, p. 74). When Phaedra arrives in Athens as Theseus' wife, 'elle laisse s'enfoncer à l'ouest dans un brouillard de fable les abattoirs géants de son espèce d'Amérique crétoise. Elle débarque, imprégnée de l'odeur du ranch et des poisons d'Haïti, sans se douter qu'elle porte avec soi la lèpre contractée sous un torride tropique du Cœur' (*Feux*, p. 1085) ('She lets the gigantic slaughterhouses of her American Crete sink in the West behind her, in a fog of fables. She lands, permeated with the odor of the ranch and of fish from Haiti, unsuspectingly carrying the leprosy contracted in a

---

[22] 'Il transforme volontairement ces héroïnes en femmes de son temps' (He willingly transforms these heroines into women of his time). A. F. Sabot, *Ovide, poète de l'amour dans ses œuvres de jeunesse: Amores, Heroides, Ars amatoria, Remedia amoris, De Medicamine faciei femineae* (Paris: Ophrys 1976), 47; 'Le plaisant est qu'elles parlent sur le ton qu'employaient les contemporaines d'Ovide quand elles écrivaient à leurs amis et amies' (The amusing thing is that they all talk in the tone used by Ovid's contemporaries when writing to their friends and lovers). P. Veyne, *L'élégie érotique romaine. L'amour, la poésie et l'Occident* (Paris: Seuil, 1983), 142; 'On y a souvent souligné le contraste entre la parfaite modernité des sentiments exprimés et l'antiquité légendaire des personnages et des situations' (The contrast has often been highlighted between the perfect modernity of the emotions expressed and the ancient legendary status of the characters and events). Hubert Zehnacker and Jean-Claude Fredouille, *Littérature latine* (Paris: Presses Universitaires de France, 1993), 196.

torrid-heart Tropic' (*Fires*, p. 5). At the end, she dies, and 'poussée par la cohue de ses ancêtres, elle glisse le long de ces corridors de métro, pleins d'une odeur de bête, où les rames fendent l'eau grasse du Styx, où les rails luisants ne proposent que le suicide ou le départ' (*Feux*, p. 1087) ('pushed by the throng of her ancestors, she slides along these subway corridors filled with animal smells; here oars split the oily waters of the Styx, here shiny rails suggest either suicide or departure' (*Fires*, p. 8).[23]

The legends are also sometimes, even if partially, transposed into another epoch. In 'Patroclus, or Destiny', the Trojan war features a 'contingent de soldats' (*Feux*, p. 1101) ('contingent of soldiers') (*Fires*, p. 27), '[l']invention des tanks' (*Feux*, p. 1101) ('the invention of tanks') (*Fires*, p. 27), and a 'décor kaki, feldgrau, bleu horizon' (*Feux*, p. 1103) ('khaki, field-gray, horizon-blue setting' (*Fires*, p. 31), which all evoke the First World War in a Europe in which Penthesilea is likened to a 'Slave' ('Slavic woman') and the combat 'un ballet russe' (*Feux*, p. 1104) ('Russian ballet') (*Fires*, p. 32). As for Sappho, transformed into a circus artist, Yourcenar notes in the preface to *Feux* that she belongs to the 'monde international du plaisir de l'entre-deux-guerres' ('the international inter-war world of pleasure'),[24] where 'le directeur, le joueur de trombone, l'agent de publicité l'ont dégoûtée des moustaches cirées, des cigares, des liqueurs, des cravates rayées, des portefeuilles de cuir' (*Feux*, p. 1158) ('the director, the trombone player, the publicity agent, all made her sick of waxed mustaches, cigars, liqueurs, striped ties, leather wallets' (*Fires*, p. 117). However, Sappho is not only transposed from one era to another, she also travels across these epochs. The same woman, older of course, 'est acrobate comme aux temps antiques elle était poétesse' (*Feux*, p. 1157) ('is an acrobat, just as in ancient times she was a poetess' (*Fires*, p.116), just as Penthesilea 'changeait de formes avec les siècles, de teintes selon les projecteurs' (*Feux*, p. 1104) ('changed forms with each ensuing century, changed tint depending on the spotlights' (*Fires*, p. 32). Yourcenar thus explicitly highlights the essentially anachronistic dimension of her rewriting of ancient myths as if, perhaps, to exonerate Ovid from accusations of irreverence towards the classical tradition that he allegedly 'over-modernized' through his playful rewriting in the *Heroides*.

Whilst this last point can evidently not be confirmed without Yourcenar's explicit acknowledgment, it is nevertheless tempting to return to it in relation

---

[23] In the French, there is an anachronistic pun on the word 'rames' which evokes the trainlines of the metro.

[24] M. Yourcenar, preface [dated 2 November 1967], *Feux* (3rd edn; Paris: Plon, 1968), 1076.

198   MARGUERITE YOURCENAR'S 'FEMINISM'

to a particular motif for which Ovid was also criticized for much of the nineteenth and twentieth centuries: the choice of the epistolary form for his mythological heroines' passionate monologues. For example, in 1898, in his introduction to Arthur Palmer's commentary,[25] Louis Claude Purser, seeing in the 'epistolary setting' 'little more than a mere form which gives an apparent reason for these soliloquies being committed to writing at all', claims that it is 'shallow wit to object to Ariadne's letter to Theseus because there was no regular postal service between Naxos and Athens'.[26] This kind of objection to the epistolary form can be found summarized thus in a French guide to Latin literature:

> La vraisemblance, dès lors, importe peu. Car il ne faut surtout pas poser la question de savoir comment Pénélope a bien pu écrire à Ulysse, puisqu'elle ignore où il se trouve, et qu'il l'ignore souvent lui-même! Il ne faut pas se demander davantage si une lettre d'Ariane à Thésée, ou de Didon à Énée, avait la moindre chance de parvenir à son destinataire, ni non plus si l'écriture à des fins épistolaires était déjà pratiquée en ces temps lointains.[27]

> (From then on, plausibility matters little. We certainly must not question how Penelope could possibly have written to Ulysses, since she didn't know where he was, and he too was often none the wiser! We must also refrain from asking ourselves whether a letter from Ariadne to Theseus, or from Dido to Aeneus, had even the slightest chance of reaching its recipient, or whether letter writing even existed in such ancient times.)

Feux is just as full of deliberately anachronistic references to letter writing as the *Heroides*, perhaps with the intention of provoking similar criticism, or even to provocatively respond to it. Set in the sixth century BC, in 'Lena, or the Secret' the face of Hipparchus appears on 'timbres-poste' (*Feux*, p. 1116) ('stamps') (*Fires*, p. 52). The Greeks go in search of Achilles on Skyros after being 'avertis par une lettre anonyme' (*Feux*, p. 1093) ('warned by an anonymous letter' (*Fires*, p. 16). Clytemnestra, who receives 'des lettres aux jours d'anniversaires' ('letters on birthdays') notes that her life was spent 'à épier

---

[25] Arthur Palmer, *P. Ovidi Nasonis Heroides* (Oxford, Clarendon Press, 1898).

[26] Ibid., xi. See also 'the choice of the epistolary form for what are really tragic soliloquies was not entirely happy', in Lancelot-Patrick Wilkinson, *Ovid Recalled* (Cambridge: Cambridge University Press, 1955), 86. For a brief summary on the scholarship and brilliant thoughts on the Ovidian poet making sense of epistolary form in the *Heroides*, see Duncan F. Kennedy, 'Epistolarity: the *Heroides*', in Philip Hardie, ed., *The Cambridge Companion to Ovid* (Cambridge: Cambridge University Press, 2002), 217–32.

[27] Zehnacker and Fredouille, *Littérature latine*, 195.

sur la route le pas boiteux du facteur' (*Feux*, p. 1149) ('watching the road for the limping footsteps of the mailman' (*Fires*, p. 104). In the vain hope of fuelling her husband's jealousy, she adds 'au courrier qu'on lui remettrait à bord une lettre anonyme' (*Feux*, p. 1150) ('to the mail that would reach him on board an anonymous letter' (*Fires*, p. 107), telling him of her affair with Aegisthus, the 'enveloppe déchirée' (*Feux*, p. 1151) ('torn envelope') (*Fires*, p. 109) of which later sticks out of Agamemnon's pockets during the meal. Still besotted with her ex-lover, Sappho's beloved Attys 'va chercher à la poste restante des lettres qu'elle déchire après les avoir lues' (*Feux*, p. 1160) ('gets letters at a post-office box and she tears them up after reading them') (*Fires*, p. 121). Later, when Sappho has forgotten the absconded young girl and instead favours Phaon, she 'déchire devant lui une lettre par laquelle Attys lui annonce son retour, et dont elle n'a même pas pris la peine de déchiffrer l'adresse' (*Feux*, p. 1163) ('tears up, in front of him, a letter in which Attys announces that she is coming back; she doesn't even bother to make out the return address') (*Fires*, p. 125). Could these deliberate anachronisms, which make modern postal services a feature of the classical past, be read as a way of alluding to the *Heroides* and their unlikely transformation of mythological heroines into letter writers?

Recalling Literary Tradition: From Scholarly Games to the Pathos of Feminine Powerlessness

Both *Feux* and the *Heroides* are closely linked with their intertextual models. Several scholars have shown how Ovid's readers' common knowledge of epic and tragic texts allowed him to set the letters at precise moments within these works, sometimes in a meaningful and virtuosic manner.[28] *Feux* also plays with this technique of linking its narratives to a particular play. For example, regarding Phaedra's suicide and her inevitable reunion with Hippolytus in hell, we are told that 'elle ne l'a pas revu depuis la grande scène du troisième acte' (*Feux*, p. 1087) ('she has not seen him since the fatal scene of Act Three') (*Fires*, p. 8), referring to Racine's *Phèdre*. As for the Aeschylean model, it is so present in 'Clytemnestra, or Crime' that the dramatic form appears to be

---

[28] For example, D. Kennedy, 'The Epistolary Mode and the First of Ovid's *Heroides*', *Classical Quarterly*, 34 (1984), 413–22, A. Barchiesi, 'Future Reflexive: Two Modes of Allusion and Ovid's *Heroides*', *Harvard Studies in Classical Philology*, 95 (1993), 333–65; Jolivet, *Allusion et fiction épistolaire*. On this question, see also the chapters by Séverine Clément-Tarantino and Thea S. Thorsen in this volume (Chapters 6 and 7).

200   MARGUERITE YOURCENAR'S 'FEMINISM'

inextricably linked to the narrative, presented as Clytemnestra's plea before the judges: 'J'ai devant moi d'innombrables orbites d'yeux, des lignes circulaires de mains posées sur les genoux, de pieds nus posés sur la pierre...vous êtes venus pour que la scène du meurtre se répète sous vos yeux un peu plus rapidement que dans la réalité' (*Feux*, p. 1147) ('I stand before countless eyes, circles of hands folded on knees, bare feet placed on stone...You came here so that the playing out of the murder could be repeated before your eyes a little faster than in reality' (*Fires*, p. 101).

For both Ovid and Yourcenar, this precise use of works from the literary tradition is also accompanied by scholarly games based on erudite and playful allusions to mythographic or exegetical debates. Once again, Jean-Christophe Jolivet has drawn attention to this approach in the *Heroides*, such as in Laodamia's letter to Protesilaus, in which the young woman foresees her husband's gruesome end:

> Hectora, quisquis is est, si sum tibi cara, caveto;
>   Signatum memori pectore nomen habe.
> Hunc ubi vitaris, alios vitare memento
>   Et multos illic Hectoras esse puta
>
> (Heroides 13.65–8)

(Of Hector, whoe'er he be, if you have thought for me, beware; keep his name stamped in ever mindful heart! When you have shunned him, remember to shun others; think that many Hectors are there.)

And a little further:

> Parcite, Dardanidae, de tot, precor, hostibus uni,
>   Ne meus ex illo corpore sanguis eat.
>
> (Heroides 13.79–80)

(O ye sons of Dardanus, spare, I pray, from so many foes at least one, lest my blood flow from that body!)

Laodamia's prayer echoes one of the 'Homeric problems' commented on by Alexandrian philologues: specifically, that the *Iliad* does not name the murderer of Protesilaus.[29] Eustathius of Thessalonica's commentary mentions

---

[29] *Iliad* 2.701: τὸν δ'ἔκτανε Δάρδανος ἀνὴρ (he was slain by a Dardanian warrior). For discussion of other responses to Laodamia, see Helena Taylor's chapter in this volume (Chapter 4).

the controversy surrounding this matter.[30] The most generally accepted hypothesis is that Hector was the murderer; however, this is often contested by the argument that, had this been the case, the poet would likely have given his name. Notable names among the other suggested combatants are Aeneas, King of the Dardanians, or a man named 'Dardanos', homonym of the Dardanian people. Laodamia (and thus the *doctus poeta*) alludes to these philologic and mythologic debates by underlining a sense of uncertainty ('quisquis is est'), and through her choice of noun with which to refer to Hector as she asks all 'sons of Dardanus' to spare her husband. She even seems to distance herself from the literary debates by suggesting that numerous Trojans could transform themselves into multiple Hectors ('illis multos Hectoras esse'), as if to ridicule the exegetical speculation regarding the murderer's identity.[31]

The same type of allusions to mythographic debates can be found in *Feux*. For example, the description at the start of 'Patroclus, or Destiny' of Helen 'peign[ant] sa bouche de vampire d'un fard qui faisait penser à du sang' (*Feux*, p. 1101) ('painting her vampire mouth with lipstick that made one think of blood' (*Fires*, p. 27) is a way of evoking versions of the Trojan war that contradict the *Iliad* concerning the abduction of Helen, referring to the εἴδωλον (phantom) that Stesichorus first claimed had accompanied Paris to Troy while the real Helen remained faithful to Menelaus. In 'Phaedra, or Despair', Yourcenar brings in another intertext: Racine's *Phèdre* (1677). When Yourcenar writes that the heroine 'forge de toutes pièces l'inexistante Aricie' (*Feux*, p. 1086) ('his non-existent Aricia is wrought from scratch [by the heroine)] (*Fires*, p. 6)], we can clearly see the author making a comment on Racine's version of the play in which he introduced the character of Aricie, through the implications that she was too lifeless and merely there to prevent Hippolytus from coming across as homosexual in his refusal of women,[32] while also entering the debate regarding the legitimacy of the French playwright's addition to Euripides' *Hippolytus*. This legitimacy was not contested because of the character of Aricie herself, but rather because of the love that she inspires in Hippolyte, who is thereafter no longer 'ce jeune homme vierge, ce jeune homme-fleur' ('the young virgin man, the young tender flower'), as described by Yourcenar in 'La dernière Olympique' [The Last Olympian].[33]

---

[30] Eustathius, *Commentarii ad Homeri Iliadem pertinentes*, 325, 55 ff.

[31] Jolivet, *Allusion et fiction épistolaire*, 71–5.

[32] R. Poignault, *L'Antiquité dans l'œuvre de Marguerite Yourcenar. Littérature, mythe et histoire*, 2 vols (Bruxelles : Latomus, 1995), p. 25.

[33] 'La dernière Olympique', *En pèlerin et en étranger*, in Marguerite Yourcenar, *Essais et mémoires* (Paris: Gallimard, Bibliothèque de la Pléiade, 1991), 430.

202   MARGUERITE YOURCENAR'S 'FEMINISM'

Thus, by writing that Phaedra 'isole de lui cette pureté détestable pour pouvoir la haïr sous la forme d'une fade vierge' (*Feux*, p. 1086) ('to be able to hate it under the guise of an insipid virgin, [she] removes his detestable purity' (*Fires*, p. 6)], the author comments on and denounces the change made to the character of Hippolyte in Racine's play. In addition, another game of erudite glossing and/or playful correction of the literary models upon which Yourcenar's stories are built can be found in 'Clytemnestra, or Crime'. Before telling her version of Agamemnon's murder to her judges, Clytemnestra defiantly proclaims, 'Vous savez mon histoire, il n'est pas un de vous qui ne l'ait répétée vingt fois à la fin des longs repas' (*Feux*, p. 1147) ('You know my story; there isn't one among you who didn't repeat it twenty times at the end of long meals' (*Fires*, p. 101), as if with an emboldened awareness of her status as a literary figure. Moreover, she does not shy away from correcting Aeschylus' text: 'On a parlé de flots rouges: en réalité, il a très peu saigné' (*Feux*, p. 1152) ('There has been talk of red floods: in truth, he bled very little' (*Fires*, p. 111), contradicting her own account in the ancient play.[34]

   These deliberate scholarly games, with their manipulation of famous literary models, serve as a nod to the reader familiar with the intertextual references, and perhaps even aware of the subsequent exegetic debates that they sparked. Such games could appear to diminish the pathos evoked by the unhappy passions expressed by these female voices; however, I suggest that they in fact intensify this effect. The inclusion of layers of accounts by female protagonists within well-known texts highlights the powerlessness of these women who are unable to change their fate, since it has already been written. When Dido asks Aeneas for a little time in *Heroides* 7 ('tempora parua peto', 178), this echoes the *tempus inane* that she tries to obtain in the *Aeneid*: 'tempus inane peto, requiem spatiumque furori / dum mea me victam doceat fortuna dolere' ('for empty time I ask, for peace and reprieve for my frenzy, till fortune teach my vanquished soul to grieve') (*Aeneid* 4.433–4).[35] However, in the structure of the *Heroides*, this 'empty time', or this 'time for nothing', takes on a performative quality by expanding itself to the temporal dimensions surrounding the writing of the letter. In fact, at the very start of the letter the queen justifies writing it, stating that, having already lost everything (her reputation and her modesty), 'the losing of words is a matter slight indeed' ('perdere verba leve est', *Heroides* 7.6). Programmatically, the letter is defined

---

[34] Aeschylus, *Agamemnon*, vv. 1389–90: 'he coughed up a sharp spurt of blood and hit me with a black shower of gory dew.'

[35] Virgil, *Eclogues, Georgics, Aeneid I–VI*, trans. H. Rushton Fairclough, rev. G. P. Goold (Cambridge, MA : Harvard University Press, 1999).

as 'lost' words written in empty time that cannot change the course of the story or, to be precise, the myth, such as it has been shaped by the previous literary works onto which the Ovidian epistles are fictitiously superimposed. For example, although Laodamia warns her husband to be cautious, the *Iliad* tells us that he is already dead as she writes the letter, rendering her words pointless as they confront the pre-existing myth.[36] As noted by Jacques Gaillard, in the letters overshadowed by intertexts that envelop and define them, 'la *narratio* se module en regrets et la *peroratio* se teinte de désespoir (faussement) prémonitoire' (the *narratio* becomes a lament, and the *peroratio* is coloured by a (falsely) prophetic despair).[37]

This process is fundamentally the same in *Feux*, even when third person narration is used. Thus, Phaedra 'assiste avec dégoût à ce qu'elle finira par devenir' (*Feux*, p. 1085) ('witnesses with disgust what she will end up being' (*Fires*, p. 5). As for Thetis, she has seen in Jupiter's eyes 'le film des combats où succomberait Achille' (*Feux*, p. 1091) ('the film of battles Achilles would die in' (*Fires*, p. 13), and as such, the hero's disguise as a young girl will not change this fate. When Misandra gives the hero 'ramassant ses jupes' ('gathering his skirts') a mirror:

> sa pâleur de marbre, ses cheveux ondoyant comme la crinière d'un casque, son fard mêlé de pleurs collant à ses joues comme le sang d'un blessé rassemblaient au contraire dans ce cadre étroit tous les futurs aspects d'Achille, comme si ce mince morceau de glace avait emprisonné l'avenir.
>
> (*Feux*, p. 1095)

> (this marble pallor, this hair waving like the mane on a helmet, this makeup mixed with tears that stuck to his cheeks like blood from a wound—all this, on the contrary, gathered in the narrow frame every forthcoming aspect of Achilles, as though this small piece of glass had captured the future.)
>
> (*Fires*, p. 20)

This future is also 'captured', since the story of Achilles has already been written in past works, as watched in the previously mentioned anachronistic 'film' that Thetis sees in Jupiter's eyes. Additionally, when Misandra contemplates

---

[36] If, on the contrary, the hypotext confirms the letter writers' words and prayers, these are no less useless. As H. Fränkel writes regarding the letters from Penelope et Briseis, their interventions were unnecessary: 'because the course of the events is independently moving in the desired direction... The epistles... are unavailing, and the reader, familiar as he is with the stories, is expected to recognize their futility'. H. Fränkel, *Ovid: A Poet between Two Worlds* (Berkeley: University of California Press, 1969), 37.

[37] J. Gaillard, 'L'imaginaire ludique ovidien dans les *Héroïdes*', in J. Thomas, ed., *Les Imaginaires des Latins. Actes du Colloque international de Perpignan (12-13-14 novembre 1991)* (Perpignan: Presses Universitaires de Perpignan, 1992), 101–12 (p. 105).

for a moment 'si elle ne prendrait pas sur ses propres épaules le poids du sort d'Achille, de Troie en flamme et de Patrocle vengé' (*Feux*, p. 1095) ('taking on her own shoulders the weight of Achille's destiny, of burning Troy, of Patroclus avenged') (*Fires*, p. 21), her awareness of the future seems to be linked to her status as a reader of an ancient work that may have been (too) literally translated. This is shown by the use of the noun phrase 'Patrocle vengé' ('Patroclus avenged') (based on the model of 'Sicilia amissa'), where the phrase 'la vengeance de Patrocle' ('Patroclus' vengeance') may have been more commonly used.

Therefore, in both *Feux* and the *Heroides* the placement of the narrative within the chronological framework of a well-known work renders the present time frame 'empty time', in the sense that events which occur within it cannot alter the predefined future of its characters. The futility of this exaggerated present time frame is characterized by a tension between the intensity of emotions experienced by the characters, and the reader's knowledge of the reality presented by the literary tradition in which these figures are caught. Their passionate love, as hyperbolic and unique as it may be, fills the present time frame of the narrative without affecting their future. Thus, the Ovidian letter writers and the mythological characters in *Feux* could perhaps be said to echo the author's thoughts: 'J'ai beau changer: mon sort ne change pas. Toute figure peut être inscrite à l'intérieur d'un cercle' (*Feux*, p. 1098) ('No matter how I change, my luck does not change. Any figure can be drawn within a circle' (*Fires*, p. 24). To me, this image of the circle, imprisoning its enclosed characters within a predestined mythological future they can comment on but not alter (just like philologues and exegetes engaging in a virtuosic game of glossing the literary tradition that shaped them), aligns in particular with Yourcenar's condemnation of the 'narrow domain of women'—*cercle* (circle) in French—and their narrow-minded and restricted world. We must therefore see how this structural power-lessness of the amorous heroines—who are enclosed in both the *Heroides* and *Feux* within narratives that are effectively 'empty time' with regards to their heroic or tragic hypotexts that cannot be changed—finds its thematic counterpart in the strict division between masculine and feminine universes, and the aware-ness of a boundary between these spheres that cannot be crossed.

Feminine World/Masculine World: Limits and Imprisonment

Above all, both works are marked by a strong division between each gender's interests and activities, which generally takes the form of an opposition between the values of the heroic world and the erotic world. In the *Heroides*, this amounts to a generic clash of epic and elegy, particularly when the letter writer is the lover or wife of a Homeric or Virgilian hero (Penelope in *Heroides* 1, Briseis in *Heroides* 3, Dido in *Heroides* 7, or Laodamia in *Heroides* 13). The opposition between feminine and masculine, being featured in terms of genre, is often shown by the respective motives of erotic seduction and of war, such as when Laodamia summarizes the gap that separates her, against her will, from her husband who has gone to fight in Troy:

> Ipsa comas pectar, galea caput ille premetur;
> Ipsa novas vestes, dura vir arma feret?
>
> > *(Heroides* 13.39–40)
>
> (Am I to dress my hair, while his head is weighed down by the helm? Am I to wear new apparel while my lord wears hard and heavy arms?)

Laodamia then goes on to project an erotic pattern onto the Trojan war, in a type of 'infection' of the epic by the elegy. In this way, she wishes to characterize Protesilaus as a lover more than as a warrior, transforming the epic values of military heroism into a militia Veneris. Yet it must be noted that this projection of elegiac values onto the epic world appears to be erroneous (Protesilaus dies in battle all the same) and in fact only serves to create tragic irony in the Ovidian epistle. As Jean-Christophe Jolivet writes: 'Au-delà d'une critique implicite des cruelles réalités épiques, la lettre de Laodamie, comme celle de Briséis, constitue une tentative pour concilier, dans un monde littéraire idéal, élégie et épopée. Cette tentative se heurte à la volonté de Zeus et se termine en tragédie' (Beyond an implicit criticism of the cruel reality of the epic sphere, Laodamia's letter, like that of Briseis, is an attempt to unite the elegiac and the epic in an ideal literary world. This attempt collides with the will of Zeus, and ends in tragedy).[38]

In *Feux*, the same 'infection' transforms the appearance of virile warrior-like traits into qualities of feminine seduction. On the island of Skyros, 'Les casques maniés par les six mains fardées rappelaient ceux dont se servent les coiffeurs; les ceinturons amollis se changeaient en ceinture' (*Feux*, p. 1093) ('the helmets handled by the six manicured hands recalled hoods of hair dryers; pliant

---

[38] Jolivet, *Allusion et fiction épistolaire*, 93. On Briséis, see J.-C. Jolivet, 'La dispute d'Ovide et des Alexandrins ou Briséis γραμματικωτάτη: trois problèmes homériques et une *quaestio ovidiana* dans la troisième *Héroïde*', in J. Fabre-Serris and A. Deremetz, eds, *Élégie et épopée dans la poésie ovidienne (Héroïdes et Amours). En hommage à Simone Viarre* (Villeneuve d'Ascq: Université Charles de Gaulle Lille 3, 1999), 15–39.

206 MARGUERITE YOURCENAR'S 'FEMINISM'

sword belts were transformed into sashes') (*Fires*, p. 17), and in the following story 'Le sang collait, comme du fard, aux joues méconnaissables des cadavres' (*Feux*, p. 1101) ('blood stuck like rouge on the unrecognizable cheeks of corpses') (*Fires*, p. 27) on the Trojan battlefield. Although this mixing of genres/gender, and indeed the cross-dressing of Achilles, seems at first to be an exception to the strict division between the erotic, feminine world, and the warlike, masculine world, I will suggest that it is nothing of the sort, and that 'Achilles, or the Lie' in fact further confirms this divide.

In both *Feux* and the *Heroides* the opposition between genres articulated by gendered categories makes women's breasts the symbol of the feminine universe, in contrast to heroic grandeur. In *Heroides* 3 Briseis (mistakenly) interprets Achilles' refusal to fight as an elegiac attitude, and defines his behaviour thus: 'Tibi plectra mouentur, / te tenet in tepido mollis amica sinu' ('you are wielding the plectrum, and a tender mistress holds you in her warm embrace!') (*Heroides* 3.113–14). As we have already seen, when Laodamia infects the epic universe with elegiac qualities, she describes the warrior's return to her mistress, who 'Exuet haec reduci clipeum galeamque resoluet / excipietque suo corpora lassa sinu' ('will strip him of his shield, unloose his helm, and receive to her embrace his wearied frame') (*Heroides* 13.147–8). Similarly, this opposition between heroism and love appears to be taken up by Mary Magdalene in *Feux*: 'Dès que Jean comprendrait que Dieu n'était qu'un homme, il n'aurait plus de raison de ne pas lui préférer mes seins' (*Feux*, p. 1127) ('As soon as John would understand that God is only a man, all reason not to prefer my breasts to Him would vanish' (*Fires*, p. 70).

Above all, breasts symbolize the imprisonment of women within an unchangeable gender identity. Sappho, an apparently hybrid being, knows deep down that 'sa gorge contient un cœur trop pesant et trop gros pour loger ailleurs qu'au fond d'une poitrine élargie par des seins' (*Feux*, p. 1158) ('her chest holds a heart too heavy and too big to be lodged elsewhere than in a broad bosom') (*Fires*, p. 116). At the end of 'Achilles, or the Lie', Misandra is tempted by the heroic universe that lies beyond Skyros:

> Un instant, la plus dure de ces deux femmes divines se pencha sur le monde, hésitant si elle ne prendrait pas sur ses propres épaules le poids du sort d'Achille, de Troie en flamme et de Patrocle vengé, puisqu'aussi bien le plus perspicace des dieux ou des bouchers n'aurait pu distinguer ce cœur d'homme de son cœur. Prisonnière de ses seins, Misandre écarta les deux battants qui gémirent à sa place, poussa du coude Achille vers tout ce qu'elle ne serait pas. La porte se referma sur l'ensevelie vivante. (*Feux*, p. 1095)

(For a moment, the hardest of these two divine women leaned over the world, contemplating taking on her own shoulders the weight of Achilles' destiny, of burning Troy, of Patroclus avenged, since the most discerning of gods or butchers could not have distinguished this man's heart from her own. Prisoner of her breasts, Misandra opened the double doors that seemed to groan for her own destiny, and with her elbow she shoved Achilles out toward everything she would never be. The doors closed on this woman buried alive.)   (*Fires*, pp. 20–1)

This woman, a 'prisoner of her breasts', is condemned to remain on Skyros and to renounce the outside world, with its heroic adventures and militaristic exploits.

The doors that close 'on this woman buried alive' lead us to consider another structural motif of both the *Heroides* and *Feux*: that of the threshold that delineates and separates the masculine and feminine spheres, thus illustrating the confinement of women in the narrow and limited world that Yourcenar deplored. In *Heroides* 6 the clash between the epic world of the Argonauts' adventures and the elegiac world in which the besotted and betrayed Hypsipyle awaits Jason's return is triggered by the intermediary of a messenger who arrives at her threshold: 'tactum vix bene limen erat' ('scarce had he crossed the threshold') (*Heroides* 6.24). The threshold that separates these worlds takes on an explicit stylistic dimension in Laodamia's letter. Taking a verse from Tibullus—'offensum in porta signa dedisse pedem' (stumbling at the gate, it had warned me of disaster!)[39]—to evoke the bad omen surrounding her husband's departure for battle, Laodamia modifies it slightly to make the image of the threshold explicit: 'pes tuus offenso limine signa dedit' ('your foot, stumbling upon the threshold, gave ill sign') (*Heroides* 8.88). The 'limen' is the very threshold that separates the erotic world of Laodamia's recent union with the Homeric warrior who deserts her, and the epic world of the Trojan war. Consequently, the 'foot' ('pes') which comes up against this threshold in a metapoetic manner can be interpreted as a poetic foot (in a wordplay often practised within elegies, and particularly by Ovid).[40] The threshold crossed by Protesilaus is thus a generic threshold that separates elegiac and epic poetry, distinguishable in their metre by an additional foot. As for Laodamia, can it be suggested that she is to blame for the bad omen she interprets? After all, in projecting onto the epic world of the *Iliad* an erotic world that she wishes at all costs to associate with Protesilaus, her use of an elegiac metre (the *Heroides* is written in elegiac couplets) collides with the

[39] Tibullus, *Elegies* 1.3.20.   [40] See, for example, Ovid, *Amores* 3.1.

208 MARGUERITE YOURCENAR'S 'FEMINISM'

threshold that separates the genres, clashing with, and returning her to, her epic fate.

The image of a threshold between masculine and feminine worlds is also found in *Feux*. Clytemnestra, who in Yourcenar's collection becomes a devoted wife abandoned by her husband, awaits his return from Troy. Aware that she has aged during Agamemnon's ten-year absence, and knowing that her beloved will no longer want her, she laments:

> À la place de sa jeune femme, le roi trouverait sur le seuil une espère de cuisinière obèse; il la féliciterait du bon état des basses-cours et des caves: je ne pouvais plus m'attendre qu'à quelques froids baisers. Si j'en avais eu le cœur, je me serais tuée avant l'heure de son retour, pour ne pas lire sur son visage la déception de me retrouver fanée. Mais je voulais au moins le revoir avant de mourir.   (*Feux*, p. 1050)

> (Instead of his young wife, the king would find a fat cook on the threshold; he would congratulate her on the good condition of the chicken coops and the cellars; all I could expect was a few cold kisses. If I had the heart for it, I would have killed myself before the hour of his return, to avoid reading on his face his disappointment in finding me so faded. But I wanted at least to see him again before dying.)   (*Fires*, pp. 106–7)

Later, Clytemnestra welcomes Agamemnon back from the war: 'j'attendais sur le seuil de la porte des Lionnes' (*Feux*, p. 1051) ('I was waiting before the threshold of the Lioness Gate') (*Fires*, p. 107). When Mary Magdalene watches John follow God rather than stay with her (aligning with the narrative model of abandoning the erotic world for a heroic mission), the mistaken interpretation of the abandoned fiancée's tears again gives rise to the motif of the threshold: 'une servante aux aguets de l'autre côté du seuil prenait peut-être mes sanglots pour des hoquets d'amour' (*Feux*, p. 1125) ('a servant on the lookout on the other side of the threshold mistook my sobs perhaps for gasps of love' (*Fires*, p. 66). And, of course, on Skyros this threshold completely separates the epic world of the Greek warriors (who have come to find Achilles and take him to fight) from the feminine world in which the young man is hiding in his cross-dressed disguise. When these worlds collide, 'les portes grandes ouvertes firent entrer la nuit, les rois, le vent, le ciel plein de signes' (*Feux*, p. 1093) ('The huge open door brought in the night, the kings, the wind, the sky full of signs' (*Fires*, p. 16), and when this door closes, 'les rois déconcertés se retrouvèrent de l'autre côté du seuil' (*Feux*, p. 1094) ('disconcerted, the kings found themselves on the other side of the threshold' (*Fires*, p. 18). It is this threshold that Achilles will finally cross, pushed by Misandra, while the young woman, 'prisoner of her breasts', that is, trapped by a restrictive feminine identity, looks on as the open doors to the heroic outside world close on her.

The shoreline, used in the *Heroides* to define the island landscapes in which the abandoned heroines are trapped, is another variant of the threshold motif. In Ovid's work, this boundary symbolizes the impossibility for the heroines of crossing this generic and physical frontier. This is evident from the case of Ariadne, who, abandoned on the island of Naxos, cries:

> Specto siquid nisi litora cernam;
> Quod videant oculi, nil nisi litus habent.
>
> (*Heroides* 10.17–18)

(I bend my gaze to see if aught but shore lies there. So far as my eyes can see, naught do they find but shore.)

Later, having climbed onto a promontory, she can only watch as the sails of Theseus' ship disappear into the distance (vv. 29–30). Other heroines are kept prisoner by the coastline that separates them from the man that they love after he has escaped to sea, such as Phyllis, who writes 'Maesta tamen scopulos fluctuosaque litora calco' ('Heavy in soul, none the less do I tread the rocks and the thicket-covered strand') (*Heroides* 2.121). She then goes down to the shore, right up to where the waves meet the sand, but clearly can go no further, and faints (*Heroides* 2.127–30). In 'Achilles, or the Lie' it is also on an island that Thetis attempts to hide her son from the masculine world in which his fate will be decided: 'elle avait cherché dans toutes les mers du monde une île, un roc, un lit assez étanche pour flotter sur l'avenir' (*Feux*, p. 1091) ('she sought in all the seas of the world an island, a rock, a bed so water-tight that it could float toward the future') (*Fires*, p. 13); elle 'avait rompu les câbles sous-marins qui transmettaient dans l'île l'ébranlement des batailles' (*Feux*, p. 1091) ('had broken the underground cables that transmitted the battle's commotion to the Island') (*Fires*, pp. 13–14). As to Sappho, she is 'née dans une île' (*Feux*, p. 1158) ('born on an island') (*Fires*, p. 117) and later replaces this prison with another, as the sky into which she dives in her acrobatic circus routines becomes an 'espace abstrait limité de tous côtés par la barre des trapèzes' (*Feux*, p. 1158) ('abstract space bordered on all sides by trapeze bars') (*Fires*, p. 117).

It is with these two examples that I would like to conclude, by comparing the fates of Sappho and Achilles. On the surface, both figures seem to blur

210 MARGUERITE YOURCENAR'S 'FEMINISM'

gender categories: Achilles cross-dresses and his mother wishes to imprison him on Skyros behind a threshold that would separate him forever from the Trojan war; Sappho is presented as a hybrid being who is 'fatigué de n'être qu'à demi-femme' (*Feux*, p. 1164) ('tired of being only half woman') (*Fires*, p. 128). As we will see, the two texts also appear to borrow from the *Metamorphoses* models of fluidity: but just as this poem of flux in fact displays, quite surprisingly, remarkable stability in gender, in the stories of Sappho and of Achilles the division between the narrow world of women and the masculine universe is further entrenched.

Attempting to Escape the 'Narrow Domain of Women': The Rigidity of Gender Division

Let us start with Achilles' stay on Skyros, where he is disguised as a young woman. To all appearances, this could be taken as a counterexample of strict gender divisions that lead to the imprisonment of women in the restrictive and limited world that Yourcenar so criticized. There, the cross-dressing young man experiences this imprisonment first-hand: 'l'abri féminin où l'enfermait sa mère devenait pour cet embusqué une sublime aventure' (*Feux*, p. 1092) ('The feminine shelter his mother had locked him into became for this dodger a sublime adventure') (*Fires*, p. 14); 'il croyait échapper au fond de cette prison de femmes aux sollicitations de ses victimes futures' (*Feux*, pp. 1092–3) ('he thought that in this women's prison he could escape the solicitations of his victims-to-be') (*Fires*, p. 16). The intrusion of a man dressed as a woman within this feminine universe blurs both points of reference and identities, and suggests that the most influential Ovidian model used here might not be the *Heroides*, but rather the *Metamorphoses*. 'Transfuge du camp des mâles, Achille venait risquer ici la chance unique d'être autre chose que soi' (*Feux*, p. 1093) ('Like a turncoat coming from the male camp, Achilles could take the unique chance here to be someone other than himself) (*Fires*, pp. 14–15): in other words, he is tempted by a type of metamorphosis. And, in fact, we think of the *Metamorphoses* when reading this passage:

> Gainé de soie, voilé de gazes, empêtré de colliers d'or, Achille s'était faufilé par son ordre dans la tour des jeunes filles; il venait de sortir du collège des Centaures: fatigué de forêts, il rêvait de chevelures; las de gorges sauvages, il rêvait à des seins. (*Feux*, p. 1092)

(Sheathed in silk, veiled in gauze, entangled in gold necklaces, Achilles, following her orders, had sneaked into the maiden's tower; he had just come out of the Centaurs' College: weary of woods, he dreamed of flowing hair; tired of hard chests, he dreamed of breasts.)   (*Fires*, p. 14)

The transformation of the outside word (forests and wild 'gorges', or 'chests') into signals of femininity (hair and breasts) evokes the Ovidian epic, which depicts multiple transformations from the human world to the natural landscape and back again. The *Metamorphoses* also teaches readers to perceive the striking similarity between women's hair and the foliage of the trees into which they are transformed (with an emblematic example in the metamorphosis of Daphne in Book 1). In contrast, the second transformation of which Achilles dreams, which turns wild 'gorges' into women's breasts, is based on wordplay around the word 'gorge' (meaning both 'gorge' and 'chest' or 'breast'). In a different way, this also alludes to Ovid's use of linguistic ambivalence to suggest metamorphosis.

The fluidity and transformation that characterize the *Metamorphoses* seem to dominate on the island of Skyros: 'La robe noire de Misandre ne se distinguait plus de la robe rouge de Déidamie; la robe blanche d'Achille était verte sous la lune' (*Feux*, p. 1091) ('You could no longer tell Misandra's black gown from Deidamia's red one; Achilles' white gown was green in the moonlight' (*Fires*, p. 13). This blurring appears to also affect gender attributes: 'le jour n'était plus le jour, mais le masque blond posé sur les ténèbres; les seins de femmes devenaient des cuirasses sur des gorges de soldat' (*Feux*, p. 1090) ('Daylight was no longer day but a blond mask placed on darkness; women's breasts became chest plates on young soldiers' (*Fires*, p. 13). However, as we have seen, these women's breasts will be used at the end of the story to reinforce Misandra's feminine identity and her fate to remain trapped on the island from which Achilles can escape. Indeed, if we think first and foremost of the *Metamorphoses* to understand this apparent blurring of the boundaries between identities, in reality it is not so much a case of completed metamorphosis here, but rather of dressing-up and 'disguise'. This is highlighted when the Greek soldiers arrive on the island in the hopes of exposing Achilles, mixing war weapons with the accoutrements of feminine seduction:

Les marins de l'escorte déclouaient des caisses, déballaient, mêlées aux miroirs, aux bijoux, aux nécessaires d'émail, les armes qu'Achille sans doute allait se hâter de brandir. Mais les casques maniés par les six mains fardées rappelaient ceux dont se servent les coiffeurs; les ceinturons amollis

212   MARGUERITE YOURCENAR'S 'FEMINISM'

se changeaient en ceintures; dans les bras de Déidamie, un bouclier rond avait l'air d'un berceau. Comme si le déguisement était un mauvais sort auquel rien n'échappait dans l'île, l'or devenait du vermeil, les marins des travestis, et les deux rois des colporteurs.   (*Feux*, p. 1093)

(The sailors of the escort unpacked the boxes and took out the jewellery, the enamel toilet kits, and the weapons Achilles would undoubtedly hurry to brandish. But the helmets handled by the six manicured hands recalled hoods of hair dryers; pliant sword belts were transformed into sashes; in Deidamia's arms a shield looked like a cradle. Disguises, like an inescapable bad spell on the Island, were everywhere; gold became silvergilt, sailors transvestites, and the two kings door-to-door salesmen.   (*Fires*, p. 17)

Achilles' status as Deidamia's lover demonstrates that he is a cross-dressing heterosexual who identifies as a man, described as 'le dur contraire d'une fille' (*Feux*, p. 1092) ('the hard opposite of a girl' (*Fires*, p. 15), despite 'son déguisement de jeune fille' (*Feux*, p. 1094) ('his girlish disguise' (*Fires*, p. 18).

Among the emissaries sent to bring the boy back to the masculine and heroic world, Patroclus, armed and powerful, stirs the desire of Deidamia, and Achilles strangles the young woman 'de ses mains de fille envieuse du succès d'une compagne' (*Feux*, p. 1094) ('like a girl spiteful of the success of her friend' (*Fires*, p. 18). Through this fateful gesture he seems once and for all to have denied himself the possibility of leaving the island and gaining access to the heroic world:

Les portes se refermant avec un bruit de milliers de soupirs étouffèrent les derniers hoquets de Déidamie: les rois déconcertés se retrouvèrent de l'autre côté du seuil. La chambre des dames s'emplit d'une obscurité suffocante, interne, qui n'avait rien à voir avec la nuit.... Il se leva, tâtant les murs où ne s'ouvrait plus aucune issue, honteux de n'avoir pas reconnu dans les rois les secrets émissaires de son propre courage, sûr d'avoir laissé fuir sa seule chance d'être un dieu. Les astres, la vengeance de Misandre, l'indignation du père de Déidamie s'uniraient pour le maintenir enfermé dans ce palais sans façade sur la gloire: ses mille pas autour de ce cadavre composeraient désormais l'immobilité d'Achille.   (*Feux*, p. 1094)

(doors closing with a musical sound muffled Deidamia's last gasps: disconcerted, the kings found themselves on the other side of the threshold. The women's quarters were filled with a suffocating obscurity unrelated to night.... He rose, groped along the smooth walls, ashamed not to have recognized in the kings the secret emissaries of his own courage, certain to have let slip his only chance to be a god. The stars, Misandra's revenge, Deidamia's father's indignation, all would unite now to keep him locked up in this palace with no frontage on fame: now his comings and goings around this corpse would be like standing still.)   (*Fires*, pp. 18–19)

Achilles runs the risk of being 'locked up' in a strictly feminine world, limited and restricted, 'with no frontage on fame', until Misandra leads him to an exit and allows him to escape to the outside world:

Une porte enfin s'ouvrit sur les falaises, les digues, les escaliers du phare: l'air salé comme le sang et les larmes jaillit à la face de l'étrange couple étourdi par cette marée de fraîcheur [...]. Prisonnière de ses seins, Misandre écarta les deux battants qui gémirent à sa place, poussa du coude Achille vers tout ce qu'elle ne serait pas. La porte se referma sur l'ensevelie vivante: lâché comme un aigle, Achille courut le long des rampes, dégringola des marches, dévala des remparts, sauta des précipices, roula comme une grenade, fila comme une flèche, vola comme une Victoire.   (*Feux*, p. 1095)

(At last a door opened on the cliffs, the seawall, the lighthouse stairs, air, salty as blood and tears, rushed to the faces of this strange couple startled by the invigorating coolness [...]. Prisoner of her breasts, Misandra opened the double doors that seemed to groan for her own destiny, and with her elbow she shoved Achilles out toward everything she would never be. The doors closed on this woman buried alive. Released like an eagle, Achilles ran along the ramps, tumbled down the steps, rushed down the ramparts, leapt over precipices, gilded like an arrow, flew like a Victory.)   (*Fires*, pp. 20–1)

The end of the story thus confirms the extreme contrast between the fortunes of Misandra, a 'prisoner of her breasts' destined to be 'buried alive' on the island, and Achilles, who can finally pursue his heroic destiny in the real world. In spite of Achilles' cross-dressing, the text reaffirms the fundamental permanence of gendered identities. Marguerite Yourcenar thus appears to be here at one with Ovid in the *Metamorphoses*, whose tendency to fix gender identities within an ever-changing world (as paradoxical as it may seem) alongside a predictable preference for male gender has been recently explored by Alison Sharrock.[41] Looking at the stability or

---

[41] Sharrock, 'Gender and Transformation'.

214 MARGUERITE YOURCENAR'S 'FEMINISM'

otherwise of gender categories in Ovid's poem of transformations, Sharrock observes that it remains remarkably stable: most metamorphosed characters maintain their original gender, except of course when the metamorphosis is precisely in the matter of gender (that is, in the few stories of sex changes). She also notes that the poem predominantly victimizes the women during the process of metamorphosis, whereas 'powerful' transformations (like apotheoses) are predominantly male. As to the stories of sex changes, they all display a privileging for male gender (for example, while Hermaphroditus is distressed by his transformation, and Tiresias prefers to be a man, Caenis' and Iphis' lives have been greatly improved by their metamorphosis into men). One may suggest that Sharrock's observations on the *Metamorphoses* resonate with the very end of Achilles' story. Whereas on the island of Skyros, a 'women's prison', no real change is possible, it is only when the hero escapes from this 'restricted and closed feminine space' that the text hints at the possibility of a real metamorphosis.

> Une chaîne tendue par le ressac amarrait au môle la barque déjà toute trépidante de machines et de départ: Achille s'engagea sur ce câble des Parques, les bras grands ouvertes, soutenu par les ailes de ses écharpes flottantes, protégé comme par un blanc nuage par les mouettes de sa mère marine. Un bond hissa sur l'arrière du vaisseau de haut bord cette fille échevelée en qui naissait un dieu. (*Feux*, p. 1096)
>
> (Ready for departure, a boat bristling with war machines was moored to the breakwater, its chain stretched tight by the undertow. As though protected by a white cloud of sea gulls coming from his marine Mother, Achilles started walking on this fated cable, arms spread out, held up by the wings of his floating scarfs. With one leap, this disheveled girl in whom a god was emerging landed in the back of the boat.) (*Fires*, pp. 21–2)

In contrast to the temporary disguises portrayed earlier, the completed metamorphoses in this narrative are found first in Achilles taking flight on the 'wings' of a bird, and then in the epiphany that sees a god emerge within the boy in the girl's disguise. With Sharrock's analysis in mind, we note that Achilles' sex change is more positively connoted when it is from (disguised) female to male, but also that it is only in the man's world that powerful metamorphoses (first a bird, then a god) are granted to him.

To finish, I want to read Sappho's story, which concludes Yourcenar's collection, in conjunction with Achilles' escape from the 'narrow domain of women'. From the start, she is clearly presented as a hybrid being:

> Créature aimantée, trop ailée pour le sol, trop charnelle pour le ciel, ses pieds frottés de cire ont rompu le pacte qui nous joint à la terre...De loin, nue, pailletée d'astres, elle a l'air d'un athlète qui refuserait d'être ange pour ne pas enlever tout prix à ses sauts périlleux; de près, drapée de longs peignoirs qui lui restituent ses ailes, on lui trouve l'air d'être déguisée en femme.
>
> *(Feux*, pp. 1157–8)
>
> (She's a magnetic creature, too winged for the ground, too corporal for the sky, whose wax-rubbed feet have broken the pact that binds us to the earth...Naked, spangled with stars, from afar she looks like an athlete who won't admit being an angel lest his perilous leaps be underrated; from close up, draped in long robes that give her back her wings, she looks like a female impersonator.) (*Fires*, p. 116)

The passage echoes Achilles' 'metamorphosis' into a bird or a divine being (here, an angel). Yet, whereas the young man was really 'a female impersonator', this is only what Sappho *looks like*. In fact, as quoted earlier, she 'knows that her chest holds a heart too heavy and too big to be lodged elsewhere than in a broad bosom' (*Fires*, p. 116), which assimilates her to Misandra, who was prisoner of her breasts, rather than to the disguised boy. But, just like him, Sappho is 'suffocating' in the restrictive world of women: in the company of the young girls she loves and protects, she is forced to

> se trouver de plain-pied avec leur vie toute rapiécée de chiffons qui ne sont même pas des langes, de sorte que cette tendresse finit par prendre l'aspect d'un congé du samedi, d'un jour de permission passé par le gabier en compagnie des filles. Étouffant dans ces chambres qui ne sont qu'une alcôve, elle ouvre sur le vide la porte du désespoir, avec le geste d'un homme obligé par l'amour à vivre chez les poupées. (*Feux*, p. 1158)
>
> (come...to their level, to share their ragged, patchy lives, so that affection ends up like a Saturday pass, a twenty-four hour leave a sailor spends with easy women. Suffocating in these rooms no bigger than alcoves, she opens the door to the void with the hopeless gesture of a man forced, by love, to live among dolls.) (*Fires*, pp. 117–18)

216 MARGUERITE YOURCENAR'S 'FEMINISM'

And just like Achilles, she will try to escape through a final flight, and the desired metamorphosis into a bird:

> Elle se hisse d'un coup de rein sur le seul point d'appui auquel consente son amour du suicide: la barre du trapèze balancée en plein vide change en oiseau cet être fatigué de n'être qu'à demi femme; elle flotte, *alcyon de son propre gouffre*, suspendue par un pied sous les yeux du public qui ne croit pas au malheur. (*Feux*, p. 1164) [my emphasis]

> (With one pull, she brings herself to the last support her will to die will allow: the trapeze bar swinging in mid-air transforms this creature, tired of being only half woman, into a bird; she glides, sea gull of her own abyss, hanging by one foot, under the gaze of a public which does not believe in tragedy.) (*Fires*, p. 128)

We can see here the influence of the *Metamorphoses* as a model for a more fluid world, and a possible escape: like Achilles, Sappho could transform herself into a bird, and Yourcenar's specific choice of bird ('alcyon') signals an allusion to the character of Alcyone in Book 11 of the *Metamorphoses*.[42] Such an allusion is all the more interesting given that the Ovidian Alcyone can be linked in more ways than one to the abandoned lovers of the *Heroides*—for example, she tries to prevent her husband Ceyx from leaving when he prepares to depart on a dangerous quest;[43] later, after a dream informs her of her beloved's death, she roams the shores, filling the air with her sorrowful lament.[44] In particular, Alcyone reminds us of Phyllis' letter in *Heroides* 2.[45] Unable to cross the waves that separate her from her absconded lover, Phyllis imagines a suicide that would allow her to be with him once more:

> Est sinus, adductos modice falcatus in arcus;
> Ultima praerupta cornua mole rigent.
> Hinc mihi suppositas inmittere corpus in undas
> Mens fuit; et, quoniam fallere pergis, erit.
> Ad tua me fluctus proiectam litora portent,
> Occurramque oculis intumulata tuis!
>
> (*Heroides* 2.131–6)

---

[42] Readers should note that the published translation of *Feux* renders 'alcyon' as 'sea gull', rather than retaining the term 'alcyon' or 'halcyon' (the mythological sea bird), and thus losing an explicit allusion to the character of Alcyone in the *Metamorphoses*.

[43] *Metamorphoses* 11.416–43.   [44] *Metamorphoses* 11.674–713.

[45] For another discussion of the reception of *Heroides* 2, see the chapter in this volume by Jessica DeVos (Chapter 3).

(There is a bay, whose bow-like lines are gently curved to sickle shape; its outmost horns rise rigid and in rock-bound mass. To throw myself hence into the waves beneath has been my mind; and, since you still pursue your faithless course, so shall it be. Let the waves bear me away, and cast me up on your shores, and let me meet your eyes untombed!)

In the *Metamorphoses*, after having wandered on the sand and discovered Ceyx's body, brought back to her by the waters (mirroring Phyllis' fantasy), Alcyone drags herself up to a height to throw herself into the water, echoing the abandoned letter writer. However, in contrast to Phyllis, Alcyone's suicide attempt ends with her metamorphosis into an alcyon:

> adiacet undis
> facta manu moles, quae primas aequoris undas
> frangit et incursus quae praedelassat aquarum.
> Insilit huc, mirumque fuit potuisse: uolabat
> percutiensque leuem modo natis aera pennis
> stringebat summas ales miserabilis undas.
>
> (*Metamorphoses* 11.728–33)

(Near by the water was a mole built which broke the first onslaught of the waters, and took the force of the rushing waves. Thither she ran and leaped into the sea; 'twas a wonder that she could; she flew and, fluttering through the yielding air on sudden wings, she skimmed the surface of the water, a wretched bird.)

Sappho's leap into the void, which 'transforms her into a bird' and makes her 'sea gull [alcyon] of her own abyss', draws on the Ovidian model of Alcyone as a way of going beyond the fate of the trapped women in the *Heroides* who are imprisoned within the confines of their feminine world. In it we see an attempted metamorphosis, and within this an attempt to break away from the restricted world of the *Heroides* and to surpass what I suggest is *Feux*'s intertextual model.

But Sappho's escape and final flight are destined to fail (and with them, this desire to surpass the model of the *Heroides*):

> ceux qui manquent leur vie courent aussi le risque de rater leur suicide. Sa chute oblique se heurte à une lampe pareille à une grosse méduse bleue. Étourdie, mais intacte, le choc rejette l'inutile suicidée vers les filets où se prennent et se déprennent des écumes de lumière; les mailles ploient sans

218   MARGUERITE YOURCENAR'S 'FEMINISM'

céder sous le poids de cette statue repêchée des profondeurs du ciel. Et bientôt
les manœuvres n'auront plus qu'à haler sur le sable ce corps de marbre pâle,
ruisselant de sueur comme une noyée d'eau de mer.   (*Feux*, p. 1165)

(those failing at life run the risk of missing their suicide. Her oblique fall is
broken by a lamp shining like a blue jellyfish. Stunned but safe, she is thrown
by the impact toward the netting that pulls and repulses the foamy light; the
meshes give but do not yield under the weight of this statue fished out from
the bottom of the sky. And soon roustabouts will only have to haul onto the
sand this marble pale body streaming with sweat like a drowning woman
pulled from the sea.)   (*Fires*, p. 129)

Unlike Alcyone (and Achilles), the avian metamorphosis does not work; or
rather, it is replaced by a different type of metamorphosis, itself inspired by the
Ovidian poem. Sappho's flight fails, and it is in the form of a 'statue' that she
appears at the end of the story. If the 'marble pale body streaming with sweat'
evokes the statues in the *Metamorphoses* that retain a single human attribute
(such as the weeping marble into which Niobe is transformed),[46] this other
metamorphosis is obviously a disempowering one, and one that calls for
empathy for the victim of the transformation, a feature that is predominantly
female, according to Sharrock's analysis. It also confirms the fact that Sappho
is unable to escape feminine imprisonment, here symbolized by the stitches of
the net in which the castaway is caught.

Thus, despite an apparent blurring of gender roles, and a shared desire to
allow their hero(in)es to escape from 'the narrow domain of women' in both
texts, the stories dedicated to Achilles and Sappho further entrench in their
own way the rigidity of gender identities and the imprisonment of women in
the limited feminine world that Yourcenar criticized.

One might not agree with the author herself when she affirms, not without
provocation, that this explicit denunciation makes her a misogynist: on the
contrary, deploring the narrowness of the domain within which women are
trapped seems to be rather a feminist gesture. By echoing and underlining
the pathos of the Ovidian heroines' confinement in a strictly feminine universe
and their inclusion within the layers of well-known hypotexts, *Feux* sheds light
on the *Heroides* as a supposedly proto-feminist poem. Moreover, while the
two stories of Sappho and Achilles explore the need of their characters to
move beyond binary categories and have recourse to the fluid world of the

[46] Ovid, *Metamorphoses* 6.312: 'lacrimis etiam nunc marmora manant' (even now, tears trickle from
the marble).

Metamorphoses as another Ovidian model, they end up displaying a similar (paradoxical) stability in gender, the impossibility for women to escape their female condition, and the privilege of male gender, as Achilles is granted an empowering metamorphosis that is denied to Sappho. Yourcenar's notion of feminism, even as she pronounces its very failure, might contribute in its own way to the debate between 'optimist' and 'pessimist' readers of Ovid's treatment of women in the *Heroides*.

Translated by Eleanor Hodgson

12

Kristeva's Ovidian World

'Un monde en mutation'

Kathleen Hamel

Ovid's *Metamorphoses* is a significant and recurring presence in Julia Kristeva's writing. That the doyenne of intertextuality should have an affinity with the author of the *Metamorphoses*, itself an intertextual masterpiece, is very appropriate. In her 1991 fantastical detective novel, *Le Vieil Homme et les loups*, the *Metamorphoses* provides the backdrop for an autofictional retelling of the traumatic events associated with the death of her father, Stoyan, and her own experience of migration. The poem's prominence attests to its significance in the armoury of tales and stories bequeathed to her by Stoyan whom she describes as 'passionné de littérature' (passionate about literature).[1]

Kristeva's Ovidian inflections go further than a predilection for intertextuality: they can be observed in her self-identification as an exile. Between the shifting qualities of the *Metamorphoses* and the tense uncertainty of an exile's situation, Ovid's biography and poetry have much to offer as a totem for the displaced and dislocated.[2] In an autobiographical essay, Kristeva writes:

> C'est en Roumanie, à Constance, que le vieil Ovide, exilé de Rome, a mis la dernière main à ses *Métamorphoses*, à l'aube de notre ère. Il y voyait les hommes et les dieux se transformer en bêtes féroces et lubriques, pas vraiment doués pour l'intégrité politique. Observateur subtil de l'instabilité des êtres et des frontières, Ovide a créé des personnages en proie au transformisme sans frein que nous vivons en ce début du 3e millénaire. Il révèle la fureur d'un monde qui ne connaît plus de lois.[3]

---

[1] Julia Kristeva, *Je me voyage: Mémoires: Entretiens avec Samuel Dock* (Paris: Fayard, 2016), 20. All translations from this and other French sources are my own.

[2] See Jennifer Ingleheart, ed., *Two Thousand Years of Solitude: Exile after Ovid* (Oxford: Oxford University Press, 2011).

[3] Julia Kristeva, 'A l'Est, l'Europe en souffrance', first published in *Libération* (19 November 2009), repr. on the Julia Kristeva website, http://www.kristeva.fr/a-l-est.html.

Kathleen Hamel, *Kristeva's Ovidian World: 'Un monde en mutation'* In: *Ovid in French: Reception by Women from the Renaissance to the Present.* Edited by: Helena Taylor and Fiona Cox, Oxford University Press.
© Oxford University Press 2023. DOI: 10.1093/oso/9780192895387.003.0012

(It was in Constanţa, Romania, at the dawn of the present age, where, ageing Ovid, banished from Rome, put the finishing touches to his *Metamorphoses*. There he saw men and gods, lacking in moral integrity, transform into ferocious and licentious beasts. Exposing the fury of a lawless world, Ovid, the discerning witness to the instability of beings and boundaries, created characters beset by an unbridled transformation similar to that which we are experiencing at the beginning of the third millennium.)

Living in France, of Eastern European origins, Kristeva has an exile mentality that is deeply rooted. It dates back to her Bulgarian childhood, where, owing to Stoyan's adherence to his orthodox faith, she and her family were marginalized. And since, according to her *mémoires*, her family did not conform 'to the communist ideals', Kristeva was denied entry to the *lycée anglais*.[4] Her parents' influence on her *formation* is palpable: for them, 'reading was crucial.'[5] Stoyan's ambition was to 'sortir ses filles de l'intestin de l'enfer' (extricate his daughters from the bowels of hell) of communist Bulgaria; he regarded the acquisition of languages as the passport to realizing this objective.[6] In *Le Vieil Homme*, Kristeva's alter ego, Stéphanie Delacour, ruefully comments how her father: 'En me faisant don des langues, ... me séparait, en fait, de son tombeau' (p. 242) (by gifting me languages effectively cut me off from his tomb). This determination to escape the restrictions of Eastern Europe was underscored when, having received a scholarship to study in France, Kristeva hastened her departure on Christmas Eve, with only five dollars in her pocket, leaving Bulgaria 'en catimini' (secretly).[7] Despite her acceptance in France, Kristeva has never felt that she fully belonged. In her *mémoires* she describes herself as 'L'étrangère que je demeure' (the outsider which I remain).[8] Exile is a persistent theme in her first three novels, *Les Samouraïs* (1990), *Le Vieil Homme* (1991), and *Possessions* (1996). *Le Vieil Homme* is set in a fictional Santa Barbara which has resonances of Tomis, Ovid's place of exile; it is a place where 'il y avait de moins en moins

---

[4] Kristeva, *Je me voyage*, 34. This is replicated in *Le Vieil Homme* when Delacour recalls her own exclusion from the *lycée anglaise*. Kristeva, *Le Vieil Homme* (Paris: Fayard, 1991), 222–3. All references will be to this edition and will be in text.

[5] Kristeva, *Je me voyage*, 20.

[6] Ibid., 19. An aspiration echoed by the Vieil Homme: 'la meilleure chose que j'aie fait dans ma vie est de sortir mes filles de l'enfer' (my life's greatest achievement may have been freeing my daughters from hell) (p. 48) and 'J'ai arraché mes filles à l'enfer. C'est même tout ce que j'aurai fait d'intéressant dans cette vie' (p. 243) (Snatching my daughters from hell, is in itself, the most interesting thing that I have done in this life).

[7] Kristeva, *Je me voyage*, 54.   [8] Ibid., 51.

222   KRISTEVA'S OVIDIAN WORLD

à manger. Les loups emportaient tout' (p. 59) (there was less and less to eat; the wolves were taking everything).[9]

Fiction is key to Kristeva's examination of her life. She describes the modern novel as resulting from of 'a 'working-out' of self', a kind of continuous 'lay analysis' and she calls on Ovid explicitly to articulate how

> novelistic writing is an immense and very powerful means of guiding us more deeply into our crises and farthest away from them at the same time—a kind of repeat descent and reemergence such as Orpheus could not achieve, a sort of Orphic experience, but that of a conquering Orpheus, a possible Orpheus, an Orpheus triumphant.[10]

She invites the reader to participate in her journey: 'un parcours qui comprend l'exil, l'étrangeté, la maternité, le désir de comprendre, et aussi de se déprendre du comprendre' (comprising otherness, motherhood, a desire to understand and also freedom from understanding).[11] Kristeva's novels are a ongoing act of self-examination which provide no definite or set answers: 'je me vis comme en voyage: mon élément serait l'eau vive et mon but, poursuivre ce flux, frayer la route. J'écris des romans pour rendre cet éprouvé palpable, transmissable' (I saw myself as being on a journey; my element was running water; I aimed to follow the current and forge a path. I write fiction to encapsulate and convey this experience).[12] The peripatetic themes of her fiction are echoed in the title of her *mémoires, Je me voyage*.

This approach might explain why her first novel, *Les Samouraïs*, was not well received: Goldhammer described it as 'plotless and shapeless', accusing Kristeva of inventing a new genre 'narcissist realism, in which bulldozer-heroines fall in love with their own reflections'.[13] She counters the criticism by arguing that that there has been 'a lot of superficial reading',[14] noting that *Les Samouraïs* 'was read by the press in a certain fashion, a certain light and on

---

[9] In the *Tristia* and *Epistolae ex Ponto*, Ovid uses the analogy of sheep threatened by wolves to describe the threats to Tomis from outside forces (*Tristia* 4.9 and *Epistulae Ex Ponto* 1.2.17).

[10] Julia Kristeva and Margaret Waller, 'Intertextuality and Literary Interpretations' in Ross Mitchell Guberman, ed., *Julia Kristeva Interviews* (Columbia: Columbia University Press, 1996), 188–203 (p. 194).

[11] Josyane Savigneau, 'Quand les Samouraïs répondent aux Mandarins', *Le Monde* (March 1990).

[12] Kristeva, *Je me voyage*, 51.

[13] Arthur Goldhammer, review of J. Kristeva, *Les Samouraïs*, in *French Politics and Society*, 8/4 (1990), 102–7.

[14] Julia Kristeva and Vassilike Kolocotroni, 'Avant-Garde Practice', in Ross Mitchell Guberman, ed., *Julia Kristeva Interviews* (New York: Columbia University Press, 1996), 211–25 (p. 220). First published in *Textual Practice*, 5 (1991), 157–70.

the surface, but [that she hopes] people go further in their own reading'.[15] Her
desire for readers to 'go further' renders the detective genre appropriate in her
quest for self-understanding; readers are invited to join in deciphering the
clues pointing to Kristeva's presence in the text. Such clues not only comprise
multiple intertextual references, but also the physical and biographical characteristics of her various alter egos which are 'des pans vécus ou redoutés de sa
propre biographie' (p. 98) (the real or frightening flashes of her own biography). This is underscored when *Le Vieil Homme*'s narrator refers to sharing
'les éclats de son moi' (p. 98) (shards of her persona) among the protagonists.
Like the *nouveaux romans* she came to France to study, Kristeva's novels are
challenging in their referentiality and ambiguity.

Le Vieil Homme, like her first novel, also received a mixed reception;[16]
Theodore Ziolkowski comments that 'Kristeva . . . is presumably a better psy-
choanalyst and theoretician than a writer of fiction',[17] while Jean-Michel
Rabaté labelled it a 'terrible flop'.[18] Conversely, Greaney takes issue with
Rabaté's 'peremptory classification' of Kristeva as 'a good theorist but a bad
novelist',[19] because it 'rests on the kind of suspiciously convenient oppositions
between theoretical and fictional discourse that Kristeva herself has called into
question'.[20] Greaney notes how Kristeva revels in boundary blurring, making
'a virtue of her texts' generic undecidability'.[21]

Kristeva is explicit about the autobiographical dimension of *Le Vieil*
Homme, situating it 'au point de rencontre d'un choc individuel qui est celui
de deuil (la mort de mon père . . .) et d'un trouble collectif, . . . du désarroi
général d'une société' (at the juncture of personal shock, that of mourning the
death of my father . . . and the collective misery of a society in general chaos).[22]
Stoyan died shortly before the fall of the Berlin wall. In his interviews with
Kristeva Samuel Dock says that *Le Vieil Homme* 'est le fruit du deuil, difficile,
de [son] père, victime des expérimentations médicales qu'on pratiquait à
l'hôpital en Bulgarie' (arose from her anguish following the death of her father,
a victim of medical experimentation carried out in the Bulgarian hospital).[23]

---

[15] Ibid.

[16] See also Anny Brooksbank Jones, 'Kristeva and her Old Man', *Textual Practice*, 7 (1993) 1–12,
which examines a number of critical responses including those of Braudeau and Henri-Lévy.

[17] Theodore Ziolkowski, *Ovid and the Moderns* (Ithaca: Cornell University Press, 2005), 143.

[18] Michael Greaney, 'Violence and the Sacred in the Fiction of Julia Kristeva', *Theology and*
Sexuality, 14 (2008), 293–304 (p. 294), citing Jean-Michel Rabaté, *The Future of Literary Theory*
(Oxford: Blackwell, 2002), 91.

[19] Greaney, 'Violence and the Sacred', 294.   [20] Ibid., 294–5.   [21] Ibid., 295.

[22] Julia Kristeva and Bernard Sichère, 'Roman noir et temps présent', *L'infini*, 37 (1992), 75–86
(pp. 75–6).

[23] Kristeva, *Je me voyage*, 273.

224 KRISTEVA'S OVIDIAN WORLD

Le Vieil Homme also draws on other genres: fiction, philosophy, and detective fiction. At the outset, the eponymous Vieil Homme fears that Santa Barbara is facing an invasion of wolves who contaminate and transform its inhabitants. He sees their traces everywhere: 'elles s'emparaient des villages et des villes, elles s'infiltraient sous la peau des gens, le monde entier devenait de plus en plus canin, féroce et barbare' (p. 14) (seizing towns and villages, they infiltrated people's skins, the whole world was becoming more and more canine, ferocious and savage). His concerns are heightened when his beloved student, Alba, marries the 'impitoyable et coupant' (p. 60) (ruthless and cutting) Vespasien who has already been contaminated by the invading hordes. As time goes on, Alba and Vespasien's relationship deteriorates and the potential for a crime to be committed arises. And so, it seems, a murder does take place, but who is the victim? Does Vespasien murder Alba or is it, vice versa, she who tries to poison him? Could it be the Vieil Homme who dies an agonizing death in hospital? Not to mention a mysterious body found in a lake, the identity of which is never established, but which bears an uncanny likeness to Alba. Determined to solve the mystery, Stéphanie, the Vieil Homme's former student, a reporter turned detective, takes over the narrative. She begins to conflate her father's (ergo Kristeva's father) life-story and death with that of the Vieil Homme. Ultimately, Stéphanie departs Santa Barbara determined to tell of the metamorphoses that she has witnessed, but crucially without resolving the mystery. Of one thing she is certain, however: the principal cause of the Vieil Homme's death was 'l'effacement de la frontière entre le bien et le mal' (p. 267) (the obliteration of the boundary separating good from evil).

The Vieil Homme's identity is never made clear; no one knows his real name: 'Mais on l'appelait plus couramment le Professeur, Septicius Clarus, *alias* Scholasticus, *alias* le Professeur, *alias* le Vieil Homme' (p. 15) (But we usually referred to him as the Professor, Septicius Claus, *alias* Scholasticus, *alias* the Vieil Homme). As for the Vieil Homme himself, he has his own ideas: 'Il s'est reconnu plus facilement dans l'exil d'Ovide et dans les chants morbides de Tibulle' (p. 212) (He readily identified himself with Ovid's exile and Tibullus' morbid songs). In this fluid novel, where characters are not strictly delineated, Kristeva allows the characters of Stéphanie's father and the Vieil Homme, 'son double' (p. 236), to merge: 'Je reçois un télégramme. Un décès. Le nom, illisible. Quelque chose me dit que c'est papa. Je distingue à peine les initiales diluées sous un flocon, on dirait un S, un C. Le Professeur' (p. 232) (I receive a telegram. A death. The name is illegible. Something tells me that it is Papa. With difficulty I decipher the initials which are dissolving in the snow, there seems to be an S, a C. The Professor). This fusion of identities which includes Stoyan also occurs in an episode re-enacting an encounter that occurred when Kristeva accompanied Mitterrand to Bulgaria: an old man waves at her as she stands alongside the president. When questioned about the old man's identity, her answer is vague: 'Évidemment...Septicius Clarus...La face cachée de Santa Barbara...Mon père...Un amour d'homme' (p. 254) (Clearly...Septicius Clarus...The hidden face of Santa Barbara...My father...A lovely man).

By blurring the identities of Stoyan, the Vieil Homme, and Stéphanie's father, Kristeva directs attention to the novel's autobiographical focus. She remarks on how '[l]e thème du deuil est...central et le Professeur est d'abord un père' (the theme of mourning is central...and the Professor is first and foremost a father).[24] The heartless treatment of Stoyan prior to his death coupled with references to experimentation on the elderly, and the subsequent inhumane disposal of his body, clearly continue to be traumatic in *Le Vieil Homme*: 'ceux de Santa Barbara l'ont brulé...Pourtant, je ne pardonnerai jamais aux loups de lui avoir refusé le droit au sol....Lui ils l'ont mis en cendres' (pp. 247–8) (He was incinerated by those in Santa Barbara. I will never forgive those wolves who, reducing him to ashes, denied him his right to burial).

Stoyan's cremation is particularly distressing as it violated his religious convictions.[25] Kristeva's distress is exacerbated by the irony that had he remained alive for another few months, until after the fall of the Berlin wall, she could have arranged proper treatment for him, perhaps preventing his death; but at the very least, ensuring his proper burial.

> Pendant presque deux ans, ce fut un état de deuil douloureux, et un genre littéraire s'est imposé à moi et m'a permis de panser la plaie: le 'polar métaphysique' *Le Viel Homme et les loups* (Fayard, 1991). Dans ce livre noir, un vieil homme—mon père—voit les hommes se transformer en loups. J'avais repris inconsciemment *Les métamorphoses* d'Ovide (écrites au premier siècle de notre ère, au bord de la Mer Noire, dans l'actuelle Roumanie, autre pays de loups...), les dessins d'un Goya noir, et surtout une pensée de Freud que je partage totalement: le pacte social est fondé sur un meurtre

---

[24] Kristeva, 'A l'Est, l'Europe en souffrance'.
[25] Kristeva revisits this in 'Comme un polar métaphysique', first published as 'Julia Kristeva: Automne 1989, l'assassinat de mon père', *Regards*, 66 (2009). An edited and corrected version can be found on the Julia Kristeva website: http://www.kristeva.fr/comme-un-polar-metaphysique.html.

226 KRISTEVA'S OVIDIAN WORLD

commis en commun. Les régimes totalitaires sont un exemple paroxystique de cette criminalité sous-jacente à toute société, quand elle oublie l'homme, et la femme, au singulier.[26]

(For almost two years, I was in a painful state of mourning. To ease my distress a literary genre came to mind and I was impelled to write the metaphysical detective novel, *Le Vieil Homme et les loups* (Fayard, 1991). In this bleak story an old man, my father—sees men transforming into wolves. Subconsciously I was revisiting Ovid's *Metamorphoses* (written in the first century CE, in present-day Romania near the Black Sea, another country of wolves), Goya's black paintings, and, above all, Freud's conviction (with which I fully agree) that the social pact is founded on communal murder. Totalitarian regimes, where the individual men and women are forgotten, provide a brutal example of this criminality which underlies every society.)

Exposing 'a self in shock, in motion, in crisis',[27] she says: 'Je n'ai pas pu, au moment du deuil, en parler autrement que sous la forme d'un roman' (In my grief, fiction was the only way by which I could express myself on this matter).[28] Thus, *Le Vieil Homme* represents a 'working through' of her trauma where 'Kristeva seems to be both on the couch and at its side'.[29]

Uncertainty (of location, of identity) permeates this novel: it is not even certain if a crime has been committed. This is matched by the uncertainty regarding the novel's form: is it philosophy, fiction, autobiography, or a detective novel? Greaney reads this genre-defying uncertainty through the prism of 'metamorphosis', describing it as 'an ambiguously Ovidian text' and arguing:

[M]etamorphosis is clearly a structural principle of the novel, which shape-shifts before our eyes from a Gothic political fable into a highbrow whodunnit into a quasi-autobiographical meditation on loss and bereavement. One could argue perhaps that the novel is trying to redeem at the level of form what it deplores at the level of content, were it not for the fact that the form/content opposition is subject to the very fluctuations that apply to every

---

[26] Kristeva, 'Comme un polar métaphysique'.

[27] Vassilli Kolocotroni, 'A Little Inner Mythology: Kristeva as Novelist', *New Formations*, 21 (1993), 146–57 (p. 157).

[28] Julia Kristeva, 'Un père est battu à mort', *The Dead Father*, international symposium (2006), Columbia University, as reproduced on the Julia Kristeva website: http://www.kristeva.fr/pere.html.

[29] Kolocotroni, 'A Little Inner Mythology', 152.

other boundary in the text.... For all its horror at a reality that melts and transforms before our eyes, [*Le Vieil Homme*] undergoes a whole series of fluid, protean literary transformations.[30]

Anticipating her view of literature as a type of psychoanalysis providing 'a tremendous opportunity for the sublimation of our crises and malaises',[31] *Le Vieil Homme*, Kristeva says, is 'ancré dans une douleur que l'allégorie vise à signifier sans la fixer, mais en l'irradiant, en la faisant vibrer, onirique, selon les ressources personnelles de chaque lecteur, dans le temps et espaces de ses épreuves personnelles, de ses choix' (anchored in suffering which the allegory aims to signify without giving it definition, instead diffusing it so that, dream-like, it resonates with each reader's personal experiences within the times and spaces of their personal ordeals and choices).[32] To this end, as I will now examine, Ovid and particularly his *Metamorphoses* are powerful presences in *Le Vieil Homme*, facilitating the articulation of her profound grief and disillusionment.

Le Vieil Homme and Ovid's Metamorphoses

From the outset, the *Metamorphoses* is a major presence in *Le Vieil Homme*. Signalling Kristeva's intentions, the novel's epigraph cites the first lines of Ovid's prologue: 'J'ai formé le dessein de conter les métamorphoses des êtres en formes nouvelles' (I intend to tell of the metamorphoses of beings into new forms).[33] *Le Vieil Homme* has been the subject of much analysis and its Ovidian elements have been remarked upon by a number of critics. Martha Reineke describes how Ovid and Tibullus 'function as touchstones' emphasizing the 'incidents of lethal violence that dominate the novel's narrative', associating the presence of the wolves, typified by Ovid's Lycaon, with René Girard's writings on scapegoating.[34] She underscores a major theme of the novel, the perennial importance of ancient culture as a source of preserving Western civilization by observing how the Vieil Homme's perceptions have been honed by his reading of Ovid, enabling him to identify the threats faced

---

[30] Greaney, 'Violence and the Sacred', 304.   [31] Guberman, *Julia Kristeva Interviews*, 194.

[32] Kristeva and Sichère, 'Roman noir et temps présent', 75–6.

[33] With minor alterations Kristeva uses Joseph Chamonard's translation: Ovide, *Les Métamorphoses* (Paris: Flammarion, 1996).

[34] Martha Reineke, 'Not a Country for Old Men: Scapegoats and Sacrifice in Santa Varvara', in Begnino Trigo, ed., *Kristeva's Fiction* (New York: SUNY, 2013), 57–78 (p. 59).

228 KRISTEVA'S OVIDIAN WORLD

by Santa Barbara. Carol Bové refers to Ovid in her examination of the Italian presence in Kristeva's novels. She touches on the musicality of the *Metamorphoses* as a means of expressing humiliation and abjection, recognizing Ovid's role in our understanding of the internal conflict between good and evil as experienced by the narrator and the Vieil Homme.[35] Bianca Rus's 2018 analysis of *Le Vieil Homme* draws on the work of Hannah Arendt, aligning 'feminine thought to political revolt'.[36] She shows how the Vieil Homme's citations of the ancient poet represent his 'continuous efforts to revive the Roman culture... [which] constitute[s] his only form of revolt against the communist regime'.[37]

My focus is derived from a close reading of the text in conjunction with Ovid's *Metamorphoses* and an exploration of how Kristeva uses Ovid's poem to present a virtuoso display of intertextual practice. While demonstrating the breadth and depth of Kristeva's personal engagement with the *Metamorphoses*, I will show how she considers the *Metamorphoses* to be a vital cornerstone of Western civilization, a bulwark against the threat of banalization, brutality, and indifference. Ziolkowski writes:

> Although he never appears, Ovid is the dominating presence in this philosophic novel on the power of evil to corrupt: as author of the *Metamorphoses*, a poem that symbolizes the transformations reshaping the modern world; and as the exiled author, whose destiny prefigures that of the mysterious Old Man, who indeed might even be Ovid reincarnate in this world of transformation.[38]

Furthermore, through its recitation and repetition, *Le Vieil Homme* ensures the continuity of the *Metamorphoses*, thereby transferring the baton of Ovidian transmission to the narrator, Stéphanie (and by inference Kristeva herself), who becomes an 'Ovide de nos métamorphoses' (p. 268) (Ovid of our metamorphoses).

On an initial reading, the novel may appear to be an untidy agglomeration of genres and Latin texts, vaunting its author's erudition, with a particular emphasis, as noted, on Ovid's *Metamorphoses*. Kristeva's use of the *Metamorphoses* is in line with her pioneering work on intertextuality, showing

---

[35] Carol Mastrangelo Bové, 'Revolution Has Italian Roots: Kristeva's Fiction and Theory', in Begnino Trigo, ed., *Kristeva's Fiction* (New York: SUNY, 2013), 45–55 (p. 54).

[36] Bianca Rus, 'Thought as Revolt in *The Old Man and the Wolves*', *Hypatia*, 34 (2019), 20–38 (p. 22).

[37] Rus, 'Thought as Revolt', 22.   [38] Ziolkowski, *Ovid and the Moderns*, 143.

'how a text always communicates with another text or other texts, in a polyphony of different voices that meet in the act of reading, which engender other, and new, interpretations of the text'.[39] Like Ovid in the *Metamorphoses*, Kristeva draws attention to her presence in the text. Not only is she present in the guise of her alter ego, Stéphanie, but she also reminds the reader of her role in developing intertextual theory through the novel's in-depth engagement with the *Metamorphoses*, showcasing a variety of intertextual practices, including direct quotations in Latin, quotations translated into French, paraphrase and parody, allusions to myths, and ultimately depictions of transformations which, although not forming part of the *Metamorphoses*, would sit comfortably within the poem.

Her use of Latin has several effects. Firstly, it serves as a paean to Western culture, including French literature, so beloved by Stoyan who was 'de ces gens cultivés qui pouvaient s'exprimer en latin' (one of those learned people who could converse in Latin).[40] A shared love of Latin connects him to the Vieil Homme, a 'Professor of Latin'. He is named Septicius Clarus after Hadrian's prefect, who was described by Pliny as 'the most plain, sincere, candid and trustworthy man' he ever knew (Pliny, *Epistulae* 2.9),[41] indicating that the Vieil Homme/Stéphanie (and therefore also Stoyan) share these virtues in direct contrast to those contaminated by the wolves, exemplified by Vespasien, who 'symbolisent la barbarie, la criminalité de chacun' (symbolize everyone's barbarity and criminality).[42]

Secondly, Kristeva uses Latin and its poetry to warn of the dangers confronting the French language and culture and by extension Western civilization, replicating the impact of the Iron Curtain which had resulted in the total isolation and separation experienced by Eastern European intellectuals.[43] Kristeva is especially concerned about the creeping loss of culture and cultural difference which has taken place since the collapse of communism, resulting in the foundation stones of Western civilization in Europe no longer being fully respected and preserved.[44] To expand the novel's remit to include the West,

[39] Birgitte Huitfeldt Mittun, 'Crossing the Borders: An Interview with Julia Kristeva', *Hypatia*, 21 (2006), 164–77 (p. 165).

[40] Kristeva and Sichère, 'Roman noir et temps présent', 80.

[41] Pliny, *Letters*, trans. William Melmoth, rev. W. M. L. Hutchinson (London: Heinemann, 1915), 118–19. Pliny dedicated the first volume (at least) of his letters to Septicius Clarus; in addition, Suetonius dedicated *De Vitae Caesarum* to Septicius Clarus.

[42] Kristeva and Sichère, 'Roman noir et temps présent', 76.

[43] Ieme van der Poel, 'Linda Lè et Julia Kristeva: citoyennes de la langue française', in Bruno Blanckeman, Alena Mura-Brunel, and Marc Dambre, eds, *Le Roman Français au tournant du XXIe siècle* (Paris: Presses Sorbonne Nouvelle, 2004), 241–8 (p. 246).

[44] See Rus, 'Thought as Revolt', 21–4, on Kristeva and Arendt for the significance of the foundations of Roman civilization.

230 KRISTEVA'S OVIDIAN WORLD

the Vieil Homme, unlike Stoyan, dies after the fall of the Berlin wall.[45] Kristeva's use of Latin is intended to show the threat facing the French language (itself a representation of Western culture), she says that there is 'une déperdition de la langue comme il y a une déperdition générale de la culture' (an erosion of language just like there is a general disintegration of culture).[46] For Kristeva, Latin is 'la mémoire paternelle' (paternal memory) of French.[47] Stéphanie remarks: 'Tout le monde a une langue maternelle. La mienne me vient de papa. De ses chants, des poésies qu'il me récitait et que j'apprenais vite par cœur' (p. 241) (Everyone has a maternal language. Mine came from Papa. From the songs and poems he recited to me and which I quickly learned by heart). Stoyan provided her with the repository of myths, the basis for constructing her own *Metamorphoses*.

Lamenting the decline in the study of Classics, the Vieil Homme asks where have Ovid, Tibullus, and even Suetonius gone? Vespasien's ironic response is that they have 'disappeared' (p. 90), connoting the 'disappeared', victims of totalitarian regimes. '[C]omparing the decay that surrounds the magnificent writing of the Roman poets with his own society's slide into hypocrisy and compromise',[48] the Vieil Homme mourns: 'On a perdu le lien...le sens du lien.... [L]e lien qui inspirait l'élégie de Tibulle ou les contes d'Ovide était passionnément un lien sacré, je veux dire *respectueux*' (pp. 138–9) (We have lost the connection...the sense of connection...The intensely sacred, dare I say *reverential* even, connection which inspired Tibullus' elegies or Ovid's myths). She repeats these words in her *mémoires*, underlining Stoyan's love of the Latin poets, and emphasizing his respect for and fears for the classical tradition.[49]

Towards the end of the novel Kristeva calls attention to the significance of the quotation used in the epigraph to embed Ovidian metamorphoses into the fictional process. She repeats the lines in the original Latin, and then recites Ovid's prologue in full in French, replacing the words *êtres* and *formes* with *corps* ascribing substance to the transformations.

'*In noua fert animus mutatas dicere formas corpora.*' J'ai formé le dessein de conter les métamorphoses des corps en des corps nouveaux. Ô dieux (car ces transformations furent, elles aussi, votre œuvre) favorisez mon entreprise et guidez le déroulement ininterrompu de mon poème depuis l'origine même du monde jusqu'à ce temps qui est le mien.   (p. 267)

---

[45] Kristeva and Sichère, 'Roman noir et temps présent', 80.   [46] Ibid., 80–1.   [47] Ibid., 80.
[48] Anna Smith, *Julia Kristeva: Readings of Exile and Estrangement* (London: Macmillan, 1996), 192.
[49] Kristeva, *Je me voyage*, 48, cites pages 138 and 139 of *Le Vieil Homme*: instead of Stéphanie she refers to Clarus' daughter, further blurring the boundaries between the characters in the text.

('*In noua fert animus mutatas dicere formas corpora.*' I intend to tell of bodies metamorphosed into new bodies. O gods (for these transformations were also your work), encourage my undertaking and guide the unbroken unfolding of my poem from the beginning of time until the present day in which I live.)

The Vieil Homme recites: 'Les vers d'une fin de monde, le monde romain qui fut avant nous, comme nous sommes maintenant avant on ne sait quelle barbarie ou simple métamorphose' (p. 28) (verses belonging to the twilight days of the Roman era which, like the present day, was facing unknown barbarity or simple transformation). He recognized this transition:

> Dans les formes instables qui peuplaient les pages d'Ovide, transfigurant une fille incestueuse en essence parfumée, une femme assassine en chienne, un égotiste en fleur, une sœur amoureuse en fleuve, des dames excitées en arbres, un roi en pivert, une ville en héron, César en astre—mais pas encore un homme en Dieu. Car ces mutations ovidiennes étaient des punitions ou du moins des sanctions.   (p. 31)

> (In the volatile shapes that filled Ovid's pages: an incestuous daughter transformed into a scented essence, a female killer into a dog, a narcissist into a flower, a besotted sister into a river, rabid women into trees, a king into a woodpecker, a town into a heron, Caesar into a star—but not as yet, a man into God. Because these Ovidian mutations were retributions or at least inevitable consequences.)

While Ovid's *Metamorphoses* seeks to impose a form of intelligibility (in the guise of a cleverly constructed poem) on implausible, irrational, and disturbing events, the narrator of *Le Vieil Homme* uses the *Metamorphoses* to extract events from apparent rationality, exposing the irrationality beneath. Kristeva likens Santa Barbara to the end of the Roman Empire, where stories cannot unfold in a simple or straightforward way, and characters cannot embody fixed identities: 'Les décalages dans le récit, le dédoublement ou la dissémination des identités, renvoient à l'évidence de ce que nous sommes en train de vivre, cette culture moderne en pleine métamorphose' (The shifts in narrative, the doubling and proliferation of personalities confirm that we are experiencing modern culture in the midst of metamorphosis).[50]

---

[50] Kristeva and Sichère, 'Roman noir et temps présent', 76.

232   KRISTEVA'S OVIDIAN WORLD

A change from the omniscient third person in the first section to a first-person narrative crystallizes Stéphanie's identity as the narrator for the remainder of the novel. This is matched by a move from 'l'univers onirique et brouillé de la première partie' (the dreamlike universe of the first part) to a detective novel.[51] However, as the novel progresses, rather than achieving clarification, it becomes further embroiled in uncertainty. Dismantling the traditional borders that delineate the individual characters within and beyond the text and addressing the reader, Kristeva writes: 'Le Vieil Homme n'est plus seulement le Vieil Homme, Alba, c'est peut-être vous, et Vespasien?' (p. 100) (The Vieil Homme is no longer only the Vieil Homme, Alba, perhaps it is you, and Vespasien?). By thus implicating the reader, she conveys a universal applicability from which no one is exempt including Stéphanie, whose efforts to bait Vespasien transform her into a 'chien-loup' (p. 127) (wolfdog), a hound traditionally associated with hunting wolves; has she been contaminated?

The threat of the contagion is contextualized as follows:

> Ces loups qui menacent, qui se déchaînent sur leurs victimes rappellent l'invasion des armées rouges, l'installation du totalitarisme—mes lecteurs à l'Est n'ont eu aucun mal à les identifier. Plus sournoisement, les loups sont contagieux, ils contaminent les gens de sorte qu'on ne distingue plus de visages humains—à cet égard, ils symbolisent la barbarie, la criminalité de chacun. Ils signifient enfin l'invasion de la banalité qui efface tout critère de valeur dans le gangstérisme, la corruption, les 'affaires'.[52]

> (Those threatening wolves, unleashing themselves on their victims, recall the invasion of the Red Armies and the establishment of totalitarianism—which my Eastern European readers easily recognized. More insidiously, these wolves are contagious, they contaminate people so that human faces can no longer be identified; in this regard they symbolize everyone's barbarity and criminality. Ultimately they represent the invasion of banality which extinguishes all moral standards amid criminality, corruption, and profiteering.)

Through the medium of the *Metamorphoses*, the novel tracks the transformation of Alba and Vespasien's relationship from love to hatred. 'Alba Ram lapses into inertia, when she marries Vespasien...and settles for a life of deadening hatred that comes from "playing at the ordinary",' writes

---

[51] Ibid., 77.   [52] Ibid., 76.

Anna Smith.[53] While Karl Galinsky remarks that the 'main subject of the [*Metamorphoses*] . . . is love',[54] Vassilike Kolocotroni claims Kristeva's novel is 'about hatred, the sort of hatred that kills people'.[55]

Ovidian transformation is also key to the Vieil Homme's death scene. Dying in hospital, the Vieil Homme sees himself surrounded by wolves, 'Lycaon, Vespasien, Alba, les infirmières, la Collègue du lifting . . .' (pp. 71–2) (Lycaon, Vespasien, Alba, the nurses, the plastic surgeon). Intertwining the myth of Lycaon (the first human transformation in the *Metamorphoses* 1.211–12) with the dying man's nightmarish thoughts, the Ovidian aspects of Vespasien's lupine transformation are expanded to apply to all of Santa Barbara:

> Avec ce qui lui restait de conscience, le Vieil Homme se demandait en quel siècle il était. 'La réputation de ce siècle dépravé était venue à mes oreilles, criait Jupiter, je la souhaitais fausse. Mais cette infâme réputation était elle-même encore en-deçà de la vérité.' Qui ne connaît le monstre Lycaon?
>
> (p. 171)

> (With what little consciousness he had left, the Vieil Homme wondered which century he was in. 'An account of this degenerate age had come to my attention, Jupiter cried, I wanted it to be false. But this vile rumour was well short of the truth.' Who has not heard of monstrous Lycaon?)

Kristeva follows by quoting Jupiter's address to the gods describing Lycaon's transformation (1.232–41), interspersed with Latin verses repeating the portrayal of Lycaon transformed: 'Canities eadem est, eadem uiolentia uultus / Idem oculi lucent, eadem feritatis imago est' ('There is the same grey hair, the same fierce face, the same gleaming eyes, the same picture of beastly savagery') (p. 171 and *Metamorphoses* 1.23–39).[56] She continues in French and switches again to Latin, repeating and underscoring Jupiter's intention to punish the whole world: '*Qua terra patet, fera regnat Erinyes*' ('Where ever the plains of earth extend, wild fury reigns supreme') (p. 171 and *Metamorphoses* 1.241). No one is immune: Alba, the 'témoin vibrant de telles métamorphoses était déjà un témoin contaminé' (p. 77) (Alba, the enthusiastic witness of such metamorphoses was already contaminated); either she will leave Vespasien,

---

[53] Smith, *Julia Kristeva: Readings of Exile and Estrangement*, 192.
[54] Karl Galinsky, *Ovid's Metamorphoses: An Introduction to the Basic Aspects* (Oxford: Blackwell, 1975), 97.
[55] Guberman, *Julia Kristeva Interviews*, 219.
[56] Latin translations are taken from Ovid, *Metamorphoses*, trans. Frank Justus Miller, rev. G. P. Goold, 2 vols (London and Cambridge, MA: Heinemann and Harvard University Press, Loeb Classical Library, 1977 and 1984).

234   KRISTEVA'S OVIDIAN WORLD

'ou elle deviendra comme lui' (p. 92) (or she will become like him). Aside from the Vieil Homme, no one is exempt from contamination, not Alba, not even Stéphanie who, on the final page, admits her indifference: 'Le crime me laisse indemne. J'en suis. Une louve' (p. 269) (The crime leaves me unscathed. I am one of them. A she-wolf).

A letter from Alba exemplifies the transformative power of Kristeva's writing. Amending Ovid's depiction of the Maenads' metamorphosis following their murder of Orpheus (11.67–84), Alba makes it her own using the first person:

> Mes pieds collent au sol, telles des racines; je tente vainement de fuir, immobile, tout m'est impossible. Et quand je cherche où sont mes doigts, où mon pied, mes ongles: inutile de crier—je vois du bois monter autour de mes chevilles. Et si j'essaie d'éprouver de la douleur en me frappant la cuisse du plat de la main, c'est encore du bois que je heurte. Ma poitrine devient de bois, de bois sont mes épaules; on pourrait aussi prendre les bras que j'allonge pour de véritables branches, et l'on ne se tromperait pas en le pensant 'Pectus quoque robora fiunt / Robora sunt umeri; porrectaque bracchia ueros / Esse putes ramos et non fallare putando'.   (p. 145)

> (My feet are rooted to the ground; in vain, I try to flee, paralysed, I am unable to do anything. And when I seek out my fingers, or my foot, my nails—there's no point in screaming, I see wood creeping up around my ankles. And if I strike my thigh with the palm of my hand to feel pain, all I feel is wood. My chest is becoming wood, my shoulders are wood; one would think that my outstretched arms are real branches, and in so thinking one would not be wrong. 'You would think her jointed arms were real branches, and in so thinking you would not be deceived'.)

Her repetition of the last line 'My chest is becoming...' in Latin (11.83–4) enables the reader to witness a metamorphosis on the page, with the change in language highlighted by a change in typescript italicizing the Latin. Alba underscores her association with the Maenads: 'Je n'ai rien d'une bacchante et Vespasien n'est pas un chantre. Mais d'attenter à sa vie me laisse de bois: insensible comme une bûche, rugueuse opaque. Te souviens-tu de ces femmes édoniennes métamorphosées en racines tortueuses' (p. 145) (I'm no more a bacchante than Vespasien a bard. But attacking him would leave me wooden, lacking in feeling like a rough impenetrable log. Remember those Edonien women transformed into gnarly roots). The transformation of the Maenads closely echoes that of the Heliades, Phaeton's sisters, whose grief initiates their painful transformation to poplar trees. While their feet are rooted to the ground, and bark encases their limbs, their tears continue to flow. These tears turn to amber to be worn by the future brides of Rome (2.364–6). When the Vieil Homme lies dying, outside his window he sees 'les peupliers couleur d'ambre' (p. 168) (amber-coloured poplars), mourning his passing.

In a description as visceral as any of Ovid's, Kristeva depicts Alba's over-whelming hatred: 'La haine s'incurve chez les femmes comme un utérus. Elle s'invagine, impensée mais onctueuse, pas nécessairement endolorie ni saisis-sable, parfois sanglante' (p. 75) (Hatred, like a uterus, twists itself inside women. It invaginates, unthought-of yet unctuous, not necessarily painful or graspable, but occasionally bloody). Like the Bacchantes, intent on exacting revenge, Alba becomes a modern Medea thereby transforming Vespasien into a potential victim: '[l]e poison est une invention de cette femme de bois que je suis à présent et qui laisse tomber les gouttes mortelles dans la nourriture' (pp. 143–4) (poison is an invention of this woman of wood that I am right now, who lets the lethal drops fall into the food).

Alba is also aligned with Hecuba. 'Plus elle se desséchait dans sa détestation entravée, plus Alba prenait l'apparence d'une nèfle' (pp. 75–6) (The more desiccated she became in her paralysing detestation, the more Alba took on the appearance of a *nèfle*). The *nèfle* is a Kristevan addition, referring to a medlar fruit which needs to rot or decay before it can be eaten, a particularly apt description for Alba's degenerating state of mind. 'La nèfle devient facilement Hécube' (p. 77) (The *nèfle* easily becomes Hecuba). Hecuba's traumatic sufferings after the fall of Troy (13.429–575) culminate on her discovery that her only remaining son has been murdered by Polymester, his guardian and protector. Kristeva quotes Ovid's description of Hecuba's reaction to Polymester's betrayal (13.567–64):

> Elle le regarde d'un air farouche tandis qu'il parle et se parjure, et la colère monte et déborde en elle. La colère lui donne des forces. Elle enfonce ses doigts dans les yeux du perfide, arrache les globes de leurs cavités, y plonge les mains et, souillée du sang du criminel, elle creuse, non pas l'œil dont il ne reste plus du trace, mais la place de l'œil. (p. 78)

> (Savagely watching him as he speaks and perjures himself, her anger surges within her and overflows. Strengthened by rage, she sinks her fingers into the eyes of the treacherous man, gouging the globes from their cavities, ramming her hands in, and befouled by the criminal's blood, she digs not into the eye which has completely disappeared but into the hole where the eye once was.)

236   KRISTEVA'S OVIDIAN WORLD

Following this harrowing passage, Kristeva switches to Latin for the climax of the Ovidian citation, Hecuba's metamorphosis from Trojan queen to a raging dog (13.567–75). As with Lycaon and the Maenads above, the shift to Latin takes place at the point of transformation enabling the reader to witness a metamorphosis on the page. Like many of Ovid's victims Hecuba can no longer speak, her voice is transformed to a howl. The use of Latin emphasizes Hecuba's new-found difficulty in communicating which, but for Kristeva's translation, is only accessible to those familiar with Latin.

Kristeva merges the citation with Alba's reflections reminding the reader of the myth's modern context, and underlining the universality of the theme of victim turned avenger. The metamorphosis from victim to attacker is a typically Ovidian manoeuvre of the kind depicted by Amy Richlin.[57] Delacour muses:

> D'ailleurs, pourquoi ne pas être à la fois victime et assassin? Le mari comme la femme jouant les deux rôles à la fois: la plaie et le couteau, le soufflet et la joue, [...] Si Alba mourait, si Vespasien se tuait, il y aurait autant de raisons pour que l'assassin de l'un soit de l'autre (Vespasien assassin d'Alba, Alba assassin de Vespasien) qu'il y aurait de motifs que le même assassin soit victime (Vespasien victime d'Alba, Alba victime de Vespasien.   (pp. 150–1)

> (Incidentally why shouldn't one be victim and assassin at the same time? Husband and wife playing both roles at once: the wound and the knife, the slap and the cheek...If Alba died, if Vespasien killed himself there would be as many reasons to suspect that the murderer of one was the other (Vespasien, Alba's killer, Alba, Vespasien's killer) as reasons why the murderer her/himself was a victim. Vespasien, Alba's victim and Alba Vespasien's victim.)

This hypothesis is reiterated towards the end of the novel, when Stéphanie speculates that perhaps a double crime had occurred: 'le meurtre simultané et réciproque de la victime et du bourreau, interchangeables?' (p. 269) (the simultaneous and reciprocal murder of the victim and the assassin, inter-changeable). Ovid encapsulates this reciprocity in Medusa, who is both assassin and victim at once. In *Visions Capitales: Arts et rituels de la décapitation* (published following the 1998 exhibition Kristeva helped curate in the Louvre),

---

[57] Amy Richlin, *Arguments with Silence: Writing the History of Roman Women* (Ann Arbor, MI: University of Michigan Press, 2014), 143.

Kristeva comments: 'le regard de Méduse tue, mais c'est le *reflet*—figure du dédoublement, de la représentation qui finit par tuer Méduse' (Medusa's glance kills, but it is the *reflection*—the representation of her reflected face which succeeds in killing Medusa).[58] Medusa, punished for being raped, is Ovid's most famous embodiment of the blurring of the boundaries between victim and victimizer. Adopting a different slant, Reineke sees a Medusan element in the *Collègue du lifting* (plastic surgeon) who accompanies Vespasien and Alba to the Vieil Homme's funeral as infecting those in attendance with her 'monstrous presence'.[59]

Apart from dissolving the distinctions between victims and aggressors Kristeva extends her fondness for collapsing boundaries to Santa Barbara, allowing this dystopian city to invade familiar places—'Santa Barbara est partout' (p. 268) (Santa Barbara is everywhere)—and by referring to diverse locations such as Italy, Spain, and California and familiar landmarks such as the Beaubourg.[60] This is a reminder of Jupiter's assertion that the threat of contagion is universal. Kristeva reiterates that 'Santa Barbara est partout et la France n'y échappe pas' (Santa Barbara is everywhere, and France is not exempt).[61] Elsewhere she states: 'Je n'ai pas voulu excepter l'Occident, les malaises de nos propres sociétés' (I did not want to exclude the West and the troubles affecting our own societies);[62] and 'cette banalisation qui est l'un des traits de la sauvagerie moderne' (this banalisation which is one of the characteristics of modern savagery).[63] Santa Barbara is 'la cité du ressentiment, aux antipodes de la pensée' (the city of resentment, the opposite of reflection),[64] where

> la politique est... réduite à un câblage technocratique, qu'une personnalité politique peut se dire en toute sincérité 'responsable mais non coupable'—ce qui veut dire que toute dimension subjective et morale est résorbée, éliminée, par la marche inexorable d'une bureaucratie d'ailleurs de plus et plus anonyme et autoresponsable. Il n'y a plus de crime à Santa Barbara: puisque le bien et le mal n'existent pas et que la bureaucratie totale, autre version du totalitarisme, a banalisé l'humain, elle l'a animalisé: lisez *Le Vieil Homme et les loups*, nous sommes à Santa Barbara.[65]

---

[58] Julia Kristeva, *Visions Capitales: Arts et rituels de la décapitation* (Paris: Fayard, 2013), 32.
[59] Trigo, *Kristeva's Fiction*, 66–7.   [60] Kristeva and Sichère, 'Roman noir et temps présent', 76.
[61] Kristeva, 'Un rêve à Byzance', interview reproduced on the Julia Kristeva website: http://www.kristeva.fr/meurtreabyzance.html.
[62] Kristeva and Sichère, 'Roman noir et temps présent', 76.   [63] Ibid., 86.   [64] Ibid.
[65] Ibid., 85.

238 KRISTEVA'S OVIDIAN WORLD

(Politics is reduced to a technocratic cabal, that a politician can claim in all sincerity to be 'responsible but without blame'—that is to say the inexorable advance of bureaucracy has diminished and eliminated every subjective and moral aspect, becoming increasingly anonymous, answerable only to itself. There is no longer any crime in Santa Barbara: since good and evil don't exist, and its total bureaucracy (another version of totalitarianism) has trivialized humanity, has animalized it: read *Le Vieil Home et les loups*, we are in Santa Barbara.)

It is a banal world of violence and indifference, where the difference between *victimes* and *assassins* is indiscernible. By situating the Vieil Homme's death after the fall of the Berlin wall Kristeva extends the novel's temporal ambit, increasing its universal relevance.

The Vieil Homme's death results from his disillusionment following the collapse of the wall and from facing '[le] désarroi général d'une société, la nôtre tout d'abord' (the universal disarray of society in general, predominantly ours)[66] and his recognition of the universality of the banality and violence that he rejects. Stéphanie remarks:

[L]e Vieil Homme est mort du jour où il a découvert que les loups ne se comptaient pas uniquement parmi les envahisseurs, les ennemis, les 'autres'; mais que les plus proches, son Alba elle-même (ne parlons pas pour l'instant de moi) partageaient les tares sauvages. Il a craqué quand il s'est aperçu avec désarroi que le 'mur de Berlin' n'existait plus entre les loups et les siens. Cette interpénétration des deux mondes que sa conscience, forcément morale, tenait pour inconciliables, m'apparaît logiquement comme la vraie cause de sa fin.   (p. 260)

(The Vieil Homme died on the day when he realized that the wolves were not only to be found among the invaders, the enemies, the 'others'; but when those closest to him, his beloved Alba herself (we won't mention me for the moment) shared the savage traits. He gave up when he realized with dismay, that the 'Berlin wall' no longer separated the wolves from his loved ones. I think that the real cause of his death was the intermingling of the two worlds, which, given his moral standpoint, he had believed to be irreconcilable.)

---

[66] Ibid., 75.

It remains for Stéphanie to keep vigilant, becoming a witness whose writing must aim to protect the world from this banalization, indifference, and effacement of boundaries. 'Il suffit alors que quelqu'un demeure conscient depuis l'enfer pour que les autres recouvrent leur forme' (p. 182) (It is enough for someone to remain aware from hell so that others may regain their form).

Following his cremation, the Vieil Homme is reduced to nothingness, 'néant'; his memorial reads *Nada*. Despite this, the defiant narrator vows to take his words allowing him to live on through her:

> Le feu l'a ravagé, aboli, renvoyé au néant, mais il n'était plus là. Il n'a jamais été là, il a été dans mes yeux et mes oreilles, dans mes mots. Il n'a atteint la plénitude de sa passion qu'après sa mort—pour moi. Il était de passage, une adresse qu'il m'a transmise. Les loups peuvent garder les cendres, j'emporte ses paroles et ses hantises, ses chants et ses maux, il s'est transféré en moi. Une métamorphose qui aurait peut-être amusé l'obstiné lecteur d'Ovide. Le néant a glissé en moi...Je suis ce néant.   (p. 249)

> (Once ravaged by flames, destroyed, and returned to oblivion he was no longer there. He was never there, for he was in my eyes and ears and in my words. I believe that his passion was only fulfilled after his death. He was passing through, with a message for me. The wolves can keep his ashes, but I have his words and fears, his songs and pains, he has transferred himself to me. It is a metamorphosis that would perhaps have amused Ovid's tenacious reader. His nothingness has slipped into me...I have become that nothingness.)

His words endure, in the person of the narrator, an embodiment of the apotheosis at the end of the *Metamorphoses*. Emphasizing the poem's continued existence through *Le Vieil Homme*, the following passage paraphrases Ovid's famous epilogue 'quod nec Iovis ira nec ignis nec poterit ferrum nec edax abolere vetustas' ('which neither the wrath of Jove, nor fire, nor sword, nor the gnawing tooth of time shall ever be able to undo') (15.871–2):

> Il n'est pas mort, il ne peut pas mourir, pas plus que ne meurent les mots. Essayez: vous pouvez clore les bouches, brûler les livres, couper les pages au ciseau, faire ce que vous voulez. Vous verrez que le sens perdure pourvu quelqu'un l'ait entendu ne serait-ce qu'une fois.   (p. 192)

240 KRISTEVA'S OVIDIAN WORLD

(He isn't dead, he couldn't die, no more than words can die. You can try: you can silence mouths, burn the books, cut the pages with scissors, do whatever you like. But you will see that the meaning will endure provided it has been heard even if only once.)

Conclusion

For Kristeva, the role of the writer is fundamental to the survival of culture and society. With *Le Vieil Homme*, she demonstrates the importance of writing in revealing often uncomfortable and unpalatable truths not only about individual behaviour but also about the world in which we live. Ovid too is frequently seen as a critic of society, mocking the gods (most notably Jupiter) in his *Metamorphoses*. Kristeva regards writing as an anarchistic act: 'le rôle de l'*écrivain*...n'est-il pas de circonscrire cet espace politique pour le réinventer sans cesse, le contourner même? (Isn't it the *writer*'s role to constrain the political sphere in order to continuously renew and even subvert it?).[67] Kristeva continues to be haunted by her father's death: 'mon père fut incinéré, contrairement à sa foi et à ses dernières volontés' (my father was cremated, against his faith and his wishes).[68] The potency of the word 'incinéré' recalls Europe's bleak and cruel history offering a horrendous reminder of what happens when banality, indifference, and cruelty become normalized, so that the wolves finally vanquish.

Underscoring her role in the development of intertextuality in this intensely personal novel, Kristeva, like Ovid, uses old forms to tell something new. Interweaving the words of Ovid and Tibullus into her text, she demonstrates how, by recognizing the weft of antecedent writings with which texts are constructed, meanings and implications are amplified and enriched. *Le Vieil Homme* provides a masterclass on the way in which intertextual theory is put into practice.

Accepting Kristeva's invitation to delve into the text rather than reading it on a superficial level, the reader is not only rewarded with a social critique which is even more relevant today, but also provided with a link to Ovid's treasure trove, the *Metamorphoses*, a timeless reminder of the unstable and tenuous nature of our existence. Inheriting the Vieil Homme's mission of ensuring the continuation of Ovid's *Metamorphoses*, Stéphanie leaves Santa Barbara 'à la recherche des autres métamorphoses' (p. 260) (seeking

---

[67] Ibid., 86.   [68] Kristeva, *Je me voyage*, 274.

out other metamorphoses). In the final chapter, following her departure, Stéphanie repeats the epigraph quoting Ovid's introductory words to the *Metamorphoses*, but now in the original Latin, thereby bookending the text with Ovid's famous quote, 'In nova fert animus mutatas dicere formas corpore' (p. 267) (I intend to tell of the metamorphoses of beings into new forms). The switch to Latin suggests that a transformation has already taken place, and that she has now become an Ovid of our times. By adopting Ovid's mantle, Kristeva provides optimism in her demonstration of the staying power and continuing relevance of Ovid's poetry, fulfilling his promise, 'Vivam'.

13

'Il faut raconter mon long parcours'

Migration and Ovidian Presences

Fiona Cox

Marie Cosnay movingly ends her contribution to this volume, her meditation on Ovid's relevance to the contemporary world, with an evocation of the plight of today's refugees, attempting to make their way to a Europe that grudgingly welcomes only a tiny proportion of those who hope for better lives. This is not the first time that Cosnay has filtered her perception of contemporary crises through her readings and understanding of ancient literature. Her novel, *Des métamorphoses* (2012),[1] draws heavily from her readings of Ovid, as indicated by its title, but is set in the contemporary world, and explores the experiences of migrants. In an interview Cosnay observes of the main character:

> Kemal is there at the start of the story to represent the possibility of a double-natured character. He's all the characters. He becomes a woman, or rather the perspective of the narrator turns him into a woman. When he's no longer there, the narrator sleeps. When she wakes up a young woman, Lise, is there. Lise is also my way of personifying migrants. She has a sea-crossing behind her (as well as a mother who bade her farewell from her deathbed.) Lise is Kemal to some extent. So Lise and Kemal are the two sides of the migrant...[2]

Of her earlier polemic entitled *Comment on expulse—Responsabilités en miettes*,[3] Cosnay observed: 'L'exil, la frontière, l'étranger, le droit: autant de thèmes que traite, depuis son antiquité, notre civilisation. J'avais besoin que la politique contemporaine du droit (ou non-droit) des étrangers dialogue avec

---

[1] Marie Cosnay, *Des métamorphoses* (Devesset: Cheyne, 2012). The novel should not be confused with Cosnay's translation of the *Metamorphoses*, entitled *Les Métamorphoses*, which was published in 2017.

[2] Marie Cosnay, interview with Fiona Cox, *Practitioners' Voices in Classical Reception Studies*, 4 (2013) [special issue: *Contemporary Women Writers*].

[3] Marie Cosnay, *Comment on expulse—responsabilités en miettes* (Bellecombe-en-Bauges: Éditions du croquant, 2011).

Fiona Cox, *'Il faut raconter mon long parcours': Migration and Ovidian Presences* In: *Ovid in French: Reception by Women from the Renaissance to the Present.* Edited by: Helena Taylor and Fiona Cox, Oxford University Press.
© Oxford University Press 2023. DOI: 10.1093/oso/9780192895387.003.0013

les grandes figures mythiques, les textes fondateurs, de Platon à Ovide qui en dirent jadis quelque chose'[4] (Exile, borders, foreigners, rights—these are all themes with which our civilization has been wrestling from antiquity onwards. I needed today's politics of the right (or non-right) with regard to foreigners to speak with the major mythical figures, our foundation texts, from Plato to Ovid who had things to say about this once upon a time).

In a chapter entitled 'Juin 2009' Cosnay muses upon the House of Fame, depicted at the start of *Metamorphoses* 12. The imagery of a place at the centre of the world, belonging to no country, roaring like the ocean with stories that needed to be told, evoked, to her mind, the plight of the contemporary migrant. She observes that 'La rumeur est sans pays, elle est au beau milieu du monde, elle n'obéit à la loi constituée d'aucun pays, elle n'est pas close dans un espace, les portes de sa maison sont ouvertes et elle vibre à l'infini. Les histoires qu'elle produit, reproduit, transforme et métamorphose font autant de bruit que la mer ou l'orage. Elles sont aussi fortes et aussi vraies que les bruits premiers du monde' (Rumour has no country—she lives slap bang in the middle of the world. She doesn't obey the laws set up in any country; she's not confined to one space; the doors of her house stand open and her repercussions are infinite. The stories that she produces, reproduces, trans-forms, and metamorphoses generate as much noise as the sea or storm. They are as strong and as true as the first sounds of the world).[5] Cosnay, who has worked for many years with, and on behalf of, refugees, has heard many of the stories from the House of Fame that shelters the narratives of migrants. She speaks of the urgency with which people voice their narratives, needing them to be heard, and of the life stories that can lead people ultimately into psychiatric units, which are, of course, another incarnation of the House of Fame:

Les personnes en quête de subsistence, déplacées de pays en pays et malmenées devant les lois constituées des anciens États nations composant l'Europe, disent, quand on les rencontre: *il faut raconter*, raconter mon long parcours.

Je pense à M. Jean, de la République démocratique du Congo. Il voulait, sur son lit de l'hôpital psychiatrique de Mousseroles, qu'on le prenne en photo. Il a parlé longuement, racontant ses trajets de RDC à Paris, de Paris à Nantes.

---

[4] Blurb on back cover of Cosnay, *Comment on expulse*. Unless otherwise stated, all translations are my own.
[5] Cosnay, *Comment on expulse*, 60.

244 MIGRATION AND OVIDIAN PRESENCES

De Nantes, d'où il fut expulsé à la suite d'un arrêté préfectoral de reconduite à la frontière. Retour en RDC. Il a raconté l'assassinat de sa femme et de ses enfants et son rôle double auprès des gouvernements du Congo et de RDC. Il disait être un 'agent double'. Danger de mort pour lui s'il retournait en RDC. Il a raconté son retour en Europe par bateau, jusqu'en Espagne. Le bateau. Il a longuement insisté sur le moment où il monte sur le bateau, s'y cache. La soif sur le bateau, il buvait par jour l'équivalent d'un petit bouchon de bouteille d'eau minérale. Son parcours du sud de l'Espagne au Pays Basque, où il fut arrêté de nouveau, puis l'hôpital psychiatrique.[6]

(People who are seeking a means of living, who are displaced from country after country and abused at the mercy of laws set up by the former nation states that constitute Europe, say when they meet you: '*I need to tell you*, to tell you about my long journey.'

I'm thinking of M. Jean from the Democratic Republic of Congo. He wanted his photo taken as he lay back on his bed in the psychiatric hospital in Mousseroles. He spoke at length, telling us about his trips from DRC to Paris, and from Paris to Nantes. He spoke of going from Nantes after he was expelled from there and taken back to the border after he was arrested by local authorities. He returned to the DRC. He told us about the assassination of his wife and children and of the dual role he played for the governments of the Congo and of the Democratic Republic of Congo. He said he was a 'double agent'. If he returned to the DRC he risked death. He told us about his return to Europe, as far as Spain, by boat. The boat. He lingered for a long time on the moment of getting onto the boat and hiding there. He spoke of the thirst on the boat—each day he would drink the equivalent of a small lid from a mineral water bottle. He spoke of his journey from the south of Spain to the Basque country, where he was arrested once again, and then the psychiatric unit.)

The stories that need to be told of contemporary migrations, the most recent narratives from Cosnay's version of the House of Fame, frequently deploy metamorphosis as a theme that evokes the feeling of not quite belonging, of existing between two worlds, while belonging to neither. Deborah B. Gaensbauer highlights this link through the title 'Migration and Metamorphosis in Marie NDiaye's *Trois femmes puissantes*' of her study of

---

[6] Ibid., 62–3.

NDiaye's 2009 novel.[7] While NDiaye does not allude explicitly to Ovid, her focus on metamorphosis combined with several classical allusions make her novel an interesting case study for the phenomenon of migration narratives merging with tales of metamorphosis.[8] The first of the three powerful women of the title is Norah, who is of half-French half-Senegalese descent, and whose Senegalese father left her, her sister, and her mother when he returned to Senegal with his infant son. The story echoes circumstances of NDiaye's own experiences, since her father, too, left his family in France, taking only her brother with him when he returned to Senegal. The novel tells of how the adult Norah, now a lawyer, is summoned by her father to Senegal to defend her brother, who has been imprisoned for a murder (which, it transpires, was committed by their father). The second woman is Fanta, a Senegalese teacher, who has followed her husband back to France, but who must watch him spiral into self-destruction, threatening the security of his wife and child as he does so. The third woman, Khady Demba, was a maid who worked for Norah's father; when she was widowed she moved in with her husband's family, who eventually sent her to make her way from Senegal to Europe with the instruction that she was to look for a distant relative, Fanta (the teacher mentioned above), and when settled, to send money back to them. Khady is betrayed by her lover, who steals all her money, and she fails to survive the perilous journey. The end of all three life narratives is marked by a section entitled 'contrepoint', which presents the three women as birds.[9]

---

[7] Deborah B. Gaensbauer, 'Migration and Metamorphosis in Marie Ndiaye's *Trois Femmes Puissantes*', *Studies in 20th & 21st Century Literature*, 38/1 (2014), Article 5.

[8] A suggestive comparison might be made with Marie Darrieussecq's *Truismes* (1997), which is widely accepted as an Ovidian narrative, yet which contains no explicit allusion to Ovid. See, for example, Edith Hall, 'Subjects, Selves, Survivors', *Helios*, 34/2 (2007), 125–59; and Theodore Ziolkowski, *Ovid and the Moderns* (Ithaca: Cornell University Press, 2005). Indeed, Darrieussecq has stated that she was not thinking of Ovid at all when writing the book (Marie Darrieussecq, interview with Fiona Cox, *Practitioners' Voices in Classical Reception Studies*, 4 (2013) [special issue: *Contemporary Women Writers*], https://www.open.ac.uk/arts/research/pvcrs/2013).

[9] Shirley Jordan observes of the bird imagery in this novel that 'Thematically birds seem consistent with this novel's emphasis on journeying between Africa and France and with the depiction of migration in the final story, where people traffickers converge terrifyingly with crows and would-be migrants huddle like a desperate, grounded flock.' Shirley Jordan, *Marie Ndiaye: Inhospitable Fictions* (Oxford: Legenda, 2016), 48. Interestingly Jordan also argues persuasively that NDiaye's novel *La Naufragée* looks back to Homer: 'Most notably, although it has escaped critical notice, Ndiaye's core intertext is undoubtedly the founding book of Western hospitality, Homer's *Odyssey*. The legend's structuring around a sequence of hospitality scenes and its focus on different kinds and degrees of (in) hospitality shown to the traveller Odysseus and his men seem to offer the very model to which Ndiaye repeatedly returns. Further, her persistent underscoring of the vulnerability of travellers and of their reliance on the hospitality of strangers in an increasingly diasporic world is intriguingly underpinned by the scenario in ancient Greece where *xenia* ('guest-friendship') was essential for similar reasons.' Ibid., 12.

246   MIGRATION AND OVIDIAN PRESENCES

The blending of metamorphosis and the depiction of the difficulties facing all three women who must make choices about their Senegalese heritage and their lives in France points to an important and developing period within classical reception studies, as Lorna Hardwick pointed out in 2007: 'There is much research still to be done on the role of classics in modern cultural shifts.... the intersection between classical and post-colonial is part of that wider picture.'[10] When classical reception is used to explore the dynamics between colonizing and colonized nations, one of the dominant legacies is shame. Shame infuses the experiences of NDiaye's protagonists, but they are experiencing on an individual level the wider complexities in the relationship between France and Senegal. Barbara Goff's words in an essay reflecting upon the classical adaptations of the Nigerian playwright Femi Osofisan depict a comparable tension and point to an equally fraught history that has led to these classical receptions that probe post-colonial friction:

> African adaptations raise questions about what it means to claim a 'Western' tradition in the wake of colonialism. Such adaptations also struggle with the fact that the very presence of Greek and Roman Classics within African culture, however fruitful for creative endeavour, testifies to the disruption of African history by decades of colonial exploitation.[11]

Shame is not confined to responses to the classical worlds by writers exploring the post-colonial legacy within Africa: we shall see that the French writer of Vietnamese descent, Linda Lê, has penned works that are flooded with shame.

Gaensbauer observes of the metamorphoses within *Trois femmes puissantes* that 'Avian imagery features prominently throughout the novel'.[12] While this is most apparent in the 'contrepoint' sections, which are lyrical and tend towards a feeling of peace and harmony, there are multiple other instances of bird metamorphosis throughout the novel, many of which are sinister and threatening. Gaensbauer describes Norah's first encounter with her father, when she arrives in Senegal. She has been imagining a reunion with the fiercely well-presented man she remembered from her childhood, but 'She is met instead by an unkempt figure whom, in an association to past experiences of

---

[10] Lorna Hardwick, 'Introduction', in Lorna Hardwick and Carol Gillespie, eds, *Classics in Post-Colonial Worlds* (Oxford: Oxford University Press, 2007), 1–11 (p. 11).

[11] Barbara Goff, 'Antigone's Boat: The Colonial and the Postcolonial in *Tegonni: An African Antigone* by Femi Osofisan', in Lorna Hardwick and Carol Gillespie, eds, *Classics in Post-Colonial Worlds* (Oxford: Oxford University Press, 2007), 40–53 (p. 40).

[12] Gaensbauer, 'Metamorphosis and Migration'.

the paternal bigotry that has deformed familial relations, she likens to an enfeebled bird of prey.'[13]

Indeed, at the end of Norah's story, when it has transpired that her father murdered his young wife on discovering that she and his son had fallen in love (in a horrible distortion of the myth of Phaedra, Hippolytus, and Theseus), the 'contrepoint' depicts her father as a bird and shows us Norah through his eyes:

> Mais il n'en éprouvait pas d'irritation: sa fille Norah était là, près de lui, perchée parmi les branches défleuries dans l'odeur sure des petites feuilles, elle était là sombre dans sa robe vert tilleul, à distance prudente de la phosphorescence de son père, et pourquoi serait-elle venue se nicher dans le flamboyant si ce n'était pour établir une concorde définitive?   (p. 98)[14]

> (No, he was not cross: his daughter Norah was there, close by, perched among the branches that now were bereft of flowers, surrounded by the bitter smell of the tiny leaves; she was there in the dark, in her lime-green dress, at a safe distance from her father's phosphorescence. Why would she come and alight on the flame tree if it was not to make peace, once and for all?)   (p. 76)[15]

The bird-of-prey imagery resurfaces in the second story, which is told from the viewpoint of Fanta's husband, Rudy, an academic who lost his job after fighting with a student, and who ekes out a humiliating and paltry living as a failing kitchen salesman. As his life spirals further and further out of control, he is pursued more and more aggressively by a buzzard that swoops onto his succession of failures with increasing hostility. The buzzard recalls the sinister figures of the Harpies from *Aeneid* 3, a reading that is encouraged by the evocation of Cerberus in the form of the dogs whom Fanta wants to attack:

> Un coup de sifflet lancé par leur maître invisible avait arrêté les chiens tout net, cependant que Rudy lentement reculait, son bras tendu devant Fanta comme s'il avait voulu la dissuader de sauter à la gorge des trois monstres.
>
> (p. 108)[16]

---

[13] Ibid.

[14] Marie NDiaye, *Trois femmes puissantes* (Paris: Folio, 2009). All references are to this edition and will appear hereafter as references in the text.

[15] Marie NDiaye, *Three Strong Women*, trans. John Fletcher (London: Maclehose Press, 2012), 76. All translations of this work will be from this edition, with references given in the text.

[16] Gaensbauer draws attention to the potent fusion of mythological allusions within the novel: 'Contextualised as a contemporary feminist fusion of Western and African myths and mythological figures, Fanta's ostensible metamorphosis symbolizes the potential for an empowering transformation.'

248 MIGRATION AND OVIDIAN PRESENCES

(Their invisible master had whistled to the dogs and stopped them in their tracks. Rudy meanwhile was slowly backing away, holding his arm out in front of Fanta as if he had wanted to dissuade her from leaping at the three monsters' throats.) (p. 87)

Eventually Rudy realizes that the buzzard pursuing him with such malevolent determination is the spirit of his discontented wife, who has been uprooted from her native land and forced to follow him across the sea to an alien land, where she bears witness to his successive failures. Like a furious Harpy she screams at him: 'La buse eut un frémissement de tout son poitrail, cependant elle sembla affermir encore la position de ses serres et, sans quitter de son regard froidement accusateur le visage de Rudy, elle poussa un cri qui parut à celui-ci d'un chat furieux' (p. 192)[17] ('The buzzard's whole breast shuddered. It seemed to be tightening its grip on the windscreen-wipers and, still looking coldly and accusingly at Rudy, it gave out a screech like an angry cat') (p. 158).

However, in the 'contrepoint' to Fanta's section she is seen through the eyes of her neighbour, Pulamire, an elderly woman whom Rudy telephones to ask her to go and check on his wife. Under the gaze of this different set of eyes, freed from the burden of anger and resentment, Fanta metamorphoses into a different bird, one that is slender and gracious enough to undergo a further metamorphosis into a lovely, young flourishing branch, an indication of her potential if she could free herself from being dragged down by her husband:

puis elle porta son regard vers la fenêtre du salon face au fauteuil et vit de l'autre côté de la haie le long cou et la petite tête délicate de sa voisine qui paraissait surgir du laurier comme une branche miraculeuse, un improbable surgeon pourvu d'yeux grands ouverts sur le jardin de Pulmaire. (p. 258)

(then looked towards the living-room window opposite her armchair and saw on the other side of the hedge her neighbour's long neck and small

---

[17] See also 'Cependant un battement d'ailes au-dessus de lui, doux frôlement de plumes et d'air chaud dans le silence, il leva les yeux. Comme à un signal convenu, la buse fondit sur lui' (p. 231) ('Hearing a wing beat, the gentle flutter of feathers in the warm, still air above his head, he looked up. As if on cue the buzzard dived towards him') (p. 190); and 'Allait-il maintenant jamais, se demanda-t-il, allait-il pouvoir sortir de sa voiture sans que l'oiseau vindicatif s'acharnait à vouloir lui faire payer ses vieux torts?' (p. 236) 'Was he ever now, he wondered, was he ever now going to be able to get out of his car without that vindictive bird pursuing him relentlessly over his old misdeeds?' (p. 195)). Gaensbauer observes of this metamorphosis that 'The pursuit by the powerful raptor he assigns to Fanta suggests a guilty projection on Rudy's part that assigns to the unhappy Fanta the vengeful role of the Greek Furies, guardians against ethical crimes and protectors of strangers.'

delicate head which seemed to emerge from the bay-tree like a miraculous branch, an unlikely sucker looking at Madame Pulmaire's garden with big wide eyes). (p. 213)

It is notable that NDiaye specifies that the tree is a laurel tree, since this is one of the most mythologically resonant trees from the ancient world. Furthermore, the evocation of perpetually open eyes glances at the myth of Argus and Juno's insertion of eyes onto the peacock's feathers from Ovid, *Metamorphoses* 2.

Classical imagery underpins the narrative of the third section—the story of Khady Demba. The imagery of a perilous journey to an unknown and sinister land charges Khady's fears about the journey imposed upon her by her dead husband's family: 'elle, Khady qui ne gagnait pas dans la famille de son mari ce qu'elle coûtait en nourriture et dont on se débarrassait par ce moyen, mais, oh, les billets coincés dans l'élastique de sa culotte serviraient-ils à payer son passage vers ce lieu certainement funeste, terrible?' (p. 284) ('she, Kady, who had not earned enough in the family to pay for her food and who was being got rid of in this way, but, oh, were the banknotes tucked in the elastic of her knickers intended to pay for her passage to that undoubtedly baleful, terrible place?') (p. 237). The obols, the coins traditionally used to pay for the passage to the underworld, are here transformed into the pittance that Khady must use to pay for her journey from Africa to France. A ghostly evocation of Charon's overcrowded bark, bearing the souls of the countless dead to the underworld, haunts NDiaye's depiction of the boat in which Khady Demba risks her life: 'Le fond de la barque était rempli d'eau. Elle agrippa son paquet, s'accroupit contre l'un des côtés du bateau. Une odeur incertaine, putride montait du bois. Elle resta ainsi hébétée, stupéfaite, tandis que grimpait encore dans la barque un tel nombre de personnes qu'elle craignit d'être étouffée, écrasée' (p. 296) ('The bottom was filled with water. Gripping her bundle, she crouched on one of the sides. A doubtful putrid smell rose from the wood. There she remained, stunned and dazed. Such a large number of people were still climbing into the boat that she was afraid of being squashed or suffocated') (p. 247).

The sheer length of this journey undergone by so many thousands of migrants creates an infinity of odysseys whose desired end, the security of a new start in Europe, remains tauntingly out of reach:

Ce qu'il convenait de garder toujours présent à l'esprit: le voyage pouvait durer des mois, des années, ainis que cela s'était passé pour un voisin de Lamine qui n'avait gagné l'Europe (ce que c'était exactement que cela,

250   MIGRATION AND OVIDIAN PRESENCES

l'Europe, et où cela se trouvait, elle remettait à plus tard de l'apprendre) qu'au bout de cinq ans après son départ de la maison.   (p. 304)

(What had to be kept continually in mind was this: the journey could take months, even years, as it had for a neighbour of Lamine's who had only reached Europe (what 'Europe' was exactly, where it was situated, she put off until later to find out) five whole years after leaving home.)   (p. 253)

Europe assumes the dimensions of a mythical world, a destination that seems unattainable, and this status of mythical land reminds us that in Ovid's *Metamorphoses* 2 the continent of Europe comes into being precisely through the figure of Europa crossing the sea perilously on the back of Jupiter, in his guise of a bull.

Khady Demba's journey is not over once she has crossed the sea. Rather, she is forced to finance the rest of her passage through prostitution, especially after she is betrayed by her lover, who steals all her money. She herself becomes a point of destination for thousands of men, seeking comfort and contact on their journeys far from home: 'comme la plupart des hommes qui venaient la voir, qui erraient là depuis des années, ayant perdu le compte exact, venus de pays divers où leur famille devait les croire morts car ils n'osaient, honteux de leur situation, donner de leurs nouvelles, et dont le regard flottant, apathique, passait sur toute chose sans paraître rien voir' (p. 325) ('like most of the men who visited her, who had come from several different countries and who had been wandering around the place for years, their eyes flitting apathetically but seeming to take nothing in. They had lost count of how long they had been there, and people back home must have thought them dead because, feeling ashamed of their situation, they had failed to keep in touch with their families') (p. 270). NDiaye portrays Khady Demba as a carnal Sibyl, sought by men who are too jaded to be looking for guidance or for wisdom, but who are seeking to satisfy their bodily desires through her services. Khady Demba, herself, achieves a state of dissociation which is strong enough for her to feel 'lente, paisible, hors d'atteinte à l'abri de son inaltérable humanité' (p. 330) ('gentle and calm, beyond reach, shielded by her unshakeable humanity') (p. 274).

On the last night of her life, however, when she participates in a mass exodus that entails attempting to scale a wall with homemade ladders, she metamorphoses from this heavy, bovine existence to a state of being that is far more ephemeral and fragile. Where once her clients failed to see her, because of their own dulled and wearied outlook, now she is imperceptible because she has become so slight and substanceless. She resembles Ovid's Echo in her lightness, the insubstantiality of her being: 'Ils s'ébranlèrent à la nuit, des dizaines et des dizaines d'hommes et de femmes parmi lesquels Khady se sentait particulièrement tenue, presque impalpable, un souffle' (p. 331) ('They set off at night, dozens and dozens of men and women amongst whom Khady felt particularly diaphanous, almost impalpable, a mere puff of wind') (p. 275).

With an Ovidian flourish NDiaye rescues Khady through metamorphosis. As she falls from her ladder in a doomed attempt to scale the wall, the lightness of her being saves her. Just as her head smashes against the ground she sees a delicate, long-winged bird, and realizes that this is her new being. Her avoidance of death through transformation in the heavens also glances at Ovid's famous declaration of his own immortality at the end of the *Metamorphoses*, when he asserts that he will live for all eternity amid the stars. And yet, as readers, we are painfully aware of the inhuman brutality of her final moments, which take place in the harsh, unforgiving light of the projectors:

> tombant en arrière avec douceur et pensant alors que le propre de Khady Demba, moins qu'un souffle, à peine un movement de l'air, était certainement de ne pas toucher terre, de flotter éternelle, inestimable, trop volatile pour s'écraser jamais, dans la clarté aveuglante et glaciale des projecteurs.
>
> C'est moi, Khady Demba, songeait-elle encore à l'instant où son crâne heurta le sol et où, les yeux grands ouverts, elle voyait planer lentement par-dessus le grillage un oiseau aux longues ailes grises—c'est moi, Khady Demba, songeat-elle dans l'éblouissement de cette révélation, sachant qu'elle était cet oiseau et que l'oiseau le savait.   (pp. 332–3)
>
> (falling slowly backwards, and thinking then that the essence of Khady Demba—less than a breath, scarcely a puff of air—would surely never touch the ground, would float eternal, inestimable, too evanescent ever to be made to crash in the cold, blinding glare of the floodlights.
>
> She was still thinking 'It's me, Khady Demba' the moment her skull hit the ground. With staring eyes she saw a bird with long grey wings hovering above the fence. 'It's me, Khady Demba', she thought, dazed by the revelation, knowing that she was the bird, and that the bird knew it too.)   (p. 276)

Once more, the focus in the 'contrepoint' to this section is on harmony and reconciliation. Khady Demba is not alone in recognizing herself as a bird. Her former lover, the one who betrayed her, remembers her, and talks to her, and, when he does so, observes the flight of a bird beyond the horizon. The image is freighted with memories of separated lovers within the *Metamorphoses*, but is

252 MIGRATION AND OVIDIAN PRESENCES

perhaps especially reminiscent of the beautiful but doomed tale of Ceyx and Alcyone, especially since Ovid emphasizes how Ceyx voices the name of his lost lover and talks to her, until the moment of his own death:

> Et quand, à certaines heures ensoleillées, il levait son visage, l'offrait à la chaleur, il n'était pas rare qu'un demi-jour tombât soudain inexplicable, et alors il parlait à la fille et doucement lui racontait ce qu'il advenait de lui, il lui rendait grâce, un oiseau disparaissait au loin.   (p. 333)
>
> (And when, on bright days, he raised his eyes and let the sun warm his face, it was not unusual for the sky to cloud over suddenly for no obvious reason, and then he would talk to the girl and tell her softly what had become of him. He would then give thanks to her. A bird flew away: far, far away.)   (p. 277)

The ache of exile, the anguish of losing one's native land and never reaching the longed-for destination, or never quite managing to feel at home, charges NDiaye's treatment of metamorphosis with a particular poignancy. In the first story, when Norah chides her father for his ruthless treatment of his servants, he turns to her with genuine surprise and explains that he doesn't have to treat them as equals, because 'Nous n'avons pas le même pays' (p. 21) ('We don't live in the same country') (p. 12). It is an observation that expands from this singular context to show how Ovid's presence is extending into the franco-phone world. Though NDiaye is herself French, and has always lived in France, she belongs to a family that was fractured when her father returned to his native Senegal taking her brother with him. Her preoccupation with the crossings and journeys linking France and Senegal is richly evidenced in this book. Ovid's significance within this literature of migration is not limited to the importance of transformations and metamorphosis; the fact that he himself ended up in exile, in a country that spoke a different language and where he was desperately homesick, creates an immediate and obvious reson-ance for writers exploring the themes of dislocation and exile.[18]

The loss of one's native country, language, and family members is funda-mental to the work of the writer Linda Lê. Lê arrived in France in 1977 at the age of fourteen with her sisters, mother, and grandmother, her father having stayed in Vietnam. Her books explore in detail the themes of loss, of non-belonging, and of the urge to find different ways of feeling at home and of establishing an identity. Alexandra Kurmann observes that 'For Linda Lê, a

---

[18] For another exploration of this aspect of Ovid's reception, see the chapter by Kathleen Hamel in this volume (Chapter 12).

forced migrant with a personal history of cultural and linguistic loss, "être le fils de personne, d'aucune patrie, c'est pour [elle] la seule attitude possible" [being the child of no one, having no homeland, for [her] is the only possible attitude] to take as a writer.'[19] Lê's strategy to compensate for her feelings of alienation is to establish a home in literature, particularly Western literature. She has written four books of essays on writers to whom she feels a particular bond, one of which is devoted to writers who have explored or experienced exile. Lê articulates the impact of emigration upon her through her response to other writers:

'On n'habite pas un pays, on habite une langue. Une patrie, c'est cela et rien d'autre': cette célèbre phrase de Cioran pourrait tenir lieu de profession de foi à bien des apatrides qui ont subi la terrible mais exaltante épreuve de l'exil et, pour certains, ont changé de langue, se mettant dans la position d'un renégat poursuivi par ses origines, mais à ce point subjugué par son idiome d'emprunt qu'il vit un perpétuel cauchemar, partagé entre le besoin de renier sa langue, de rompre avec ses ancêtres, avec ses souvenirs peut-être avec lui-même, et la recherche incessante d'un port d'attache, si illusoire soit-il.[20]

('You don't inhabit a country, you inhabit a language. A fatherland is that and nothing else': Cioran's famous statement could stand as a profession of faith for many who lack a country, who have undergone the dreadful, yet exalting, experience of exile and who, in some cases, have changed their language, putting themselves into the position of a renegade haunted by their origins but so subjugated by the language they have borrowed that they live an unending nightmare, torn between the need to deny their language, to cut ties with their ancestors, with their memories and perhaps with their own selves and the incessant search for a homeport, however illusory this might be.)

It is unsurprising, then, that Ovidian allusions should pervade Lê's 1997 novel, entitled *Les Trois Parques*.[21] Although the classical resonances are foregrounded through the reference to the Parcae, whose story appears on several

---

[19] Alexandra Kurmann, *Intertextual Weaving in the Work of Linda Lê: Imagining the Ideal Reader* (Washington, DC: Lexington Books, 2016), 7. Kurmann goes on to observe: 'Correspondingly, Lê denies her Vietnamese origins while maintaining an ambivalent relationship with the French language. As if to compensate, her repeated intertextual engagement with a predominantly European cohort of writers points towards the substitutive construction of an imaginary home in literature.' *Intertextual Weaving* (7).

[20] Linda Lê, *Par ailleurs (exils)* (Paris: Bourgois, 2014), 93.

[21] Linda Lê, *Les Trois Parques* (Paris: Bourgois, 1997). All references will be to this edition and subsequently given in the text.

254 MIGRATION AND OVIDIAN PRESENCES

occasions in the *Metamorphoses*,[22] critical attention has focused rather more on the references to King Lear, whose presence is signalled more frequently and more overtly throughout the book. The novel tells of three young women, the narrator and her two cousins, who are preparing for a visit to France of the cousins' father, who stayed behind in Vietnam, when all of them emigrated to France, and whom they have not seen for twenty years.[23] Lê explores the clash between the comfortable lifestyle led by the young women in France (much is made of the elder sister's brand new kitchen provided by her wealthy husband) and the much simpler, rural existence of 'le roi Lear' who had stayed at home in Vietnam. The book closes before the visit takes place, as the three women receive word from Saigon of the old man's death.

This is not the only time that Lê has explicitly drawn upon classical literature to explore her relationship with Vietnam. In 2010 her novel *Cronos*, a retelling of *Antigone*, was published to great acclaim. It is interesting that Lê figures herself as a classical figure even in the writing of it, as Kurmann observes: 'When speaking of her novel, *Cronos*, Lê commented that she "tissé" (wove) the text together "avec une patience de Pénélope".'[24]

Les Trois Parques is a challenging book to read. This is, in part, because Lê delights in wordplay and neologisms, evoking within her readers the discomfort of struggling to follow the language, of feeling alien, of having to step into the shoes, even if only briefly, of the exile. The abundance of intertextual references which intersect and overlay the past on the narrative present contribute to the oneiric quality of the narrative: the three women inhabit a space that is neither French nor Vietnamese, neither present nor past, neither fantasy nor quite real. It is significant that the most sustained and overt intertext in the book is *King Lear*, since this demonstrates Lê's interest in engaging with the cornerstones of Western culture. In *Les Trois Parques* the thorny relationship between different generations is made more complicated by the fact that 'le roi Lear' was left behind on a different continent, and by the fact of his daughters achieving a prosperity that can be scarcely imaginable to him. The callousness of Goneril and Regan is sustained through the two sisters carefully meting out the days of the old man's visit, and through their intention to show him a glimpse of a finer life before sending him back to end his days in comparative poverty back in Vietnam:

---

[22] For example, Book 2, Book 5, Book 8, and Book 15.

[23] There is a parallel here with Kristeva's father who was left in her native Bulgaria. See her treatment of this in *Le Vieil Homme et les loups* and Hamel's discussion of this in this volume (Chapter 12).

[24] Kurmann, *Intertextual Weaving*, 25. Kurmann demonstrates persuasively that the myth of Antigone pervades much of Lê's œuvre.

Il ne restait, pour assurer cette réputation de piété, qu'à procurer au vieillard délaissé un dernier plaisir, lui permettre de quitter son trou, de franchir les mers, de venir applaudir à l'étalage et à l'ordonnance des vertus domestiques—la petite famille, la cuisine rutilante et la chambre d'enfant— que le vieillard pourrait inaugurer, et investir pour trois semaines, un mois, pas plus. Le temps de lui faire le tour de propriétaire, de le laisser humer le bonheur, palper l'opulence, avant de le renvoyer sous les tropiques, dans la petite maison bleue, où il pourrait attendre la mort en se remémorant son escale au paradis.   (p. 14)

(All that remained, to seal her pious reputation, was to procure the neglected old man one last joy, make him leave his squalor, cross the oceans, and come applaud this display and disposition of domestic virtues—the little family, the gleaming kitchen, and he child's nursery, which the old man could inaugurate and inhabit for three weeks, maybe a month, but no longer. Just long enough to let him tour the domain, fill his lungs with contentment, and finger some opulence—before they shipped him back to the tropics and his small blue house, where he could relive his ascent to Heaven while waiting for death.)   (p. 6)[25]

Though it is the Shakespearean intertext which dominates, the fact that he will be sent back once more across the seas to Vietnam having been prepared for death allows the two sisters and their cousin to perform the role of the Parcae, whose function is to allot, measure, and cut the threads of life for mortals. And as the two sisters perform the role of the Parcae and of Goneril and Regan at the same time, so their younger cousin also manages to be both one of the Parcae and a Cassandra figure, who can perceive impending disaster, when the stump of her arm begins to tingle:[26]

me fiant aux fourmillements de mon moignon, qui avait commencé à me démanger dès que mes cousins avaient parlé de procurer un dernier plaisir à l'oublié. Mon moignon m'a toujours prévenue des catastrophes.   (p. 9)[27]

[25] Linda Lê, *The Three Fates*, trans. Mark Polizzoti (Cambridge, MA: New Directions, 2010). All translations of this text will from this edition, with references given in the text.

[26] See Sabine Loucif, 'Le Fantastique dans *Les Trois Parques* de Linda Lê', in Margaret-Anne Hutton, ed., *Redefining the Real: The Fantastic in Contemporary French and Francophone Women's Writing* (Oxford, Bern, Berlin: Peter Lang, 2009), 115–27. Loucif identifies the eldest sister with Clotho, the youngest with Atropos, and the narrator with Lachesis (pp. 117–18).

[27] See also 'Les fourmillements incendiaient le bout de mon poignet gauche, à mesure que les projets de mes cousines prenaient forme autour de la grande table rutilante' (p. 11) ('A tingling sensation swarmed over my left wrist, intensifying as my cousins' plans gelled around the large gleaming table') (p. 4).

256 MIGRATION AND OVIDIAN PRESENCES

(I trusted the itch in my stump, which had started up the minute my cousins mentioned granting the forgotten old man his one last joy. My stump can always foretell disaster)   (p. 3)

Her intimations of catastrophe are explained, in part, by the fact of the old man dying even before he is able to leave Vietnam, but they perhaps also point to the fact that all is not well in the older sister's household, however well-appointed and opulent it might be. The elder sister is pregnant, particularly vulnerable, and unsettled by and resentful of her young cousin's qualms, believing that these are the cause, rather than the intimation of, trouble:

> tandis que la Manchote se caressait le menton du bout de son moignon, en promenant sur la compagnie un œil inspiré, à l'affût de l'incartade annoncée, qui frapperait, comme la foudre, la maison du bonheur.   (p. 19)

> (while Southpaw rubbed her chin with the end of her stump, gazing over those present with an alert eye, watching for the imminent bolt of lightning to strike the abode of happiness.)   (p. 10)

Lê evokes a thunderbolt, a classically Jovian form of punishment (perhaps for those who fail in their filial duties), but it becomes increasingly clear that this is not a harmonious household, and that the young cousin ('la Manchote') causes resentment because of the likelihood of her exposing the tensions and difficulties. In her role of awkward presence, liable to voice uncomfortable truths, she joins the ranks of other difficult and shunned women from antiquity—the Sibyl, Cassandra, and Antigone:

> Un orage en prime, et la sibylle manchote serait au septième ciel, d'où elle espérait bien contempler le spectacle des ruines annoncées. Elle jouait les pures, les Antigone, les Cassandre, toute la ménagerie virginale. Dans le genre, c'était plutôt l'immaculée catacombe.   (p. 35)

> (One more storm and the single-handed sibyl would be in seventh heaven, from where she hoped to witness the promised ruination. She played at being pure, an Antigone, a Cassandra, the whole virginal menagerie—though in that regard, she was more like an immaculate catacomb.)   (p. 21)

Part of the trouble rumbling in the household revolved around the elder sister's husband, Théo, who initially appeared in the guise of a god through his good looks and wealth: 'Toute la littérature du monde pour une cuisse de jeune fille, avait encore dit Théo, qui tenait toujours en réserve une formule de derrière les fagots. À l'époque il était un dieu pour la mignonne, dont le cœur palpitait, espérait des miracles qui transfigureraient ses jours monotones' (p. 21) ('All the literature in the world for a young girl's thigh, Theo had also said, always keeping in reserve an expression he could pull from his sleeve. At the time he was a god for the pretty young doll, whose heart went pitter-pat, anticipating all the miracles that would transfigure her monotonous days') (p. 11). There is an irony in the fact of the sisters enduring long and leaden days, when their intention is to rescue briefly 'le roi Lear' from his own monotonous existence, by displaying their Western lifestyle and wealth. The eldest sister, Théo's wife, is now wise to his wiles and the more he scatters evidence of his wealth in the form of gold dust, the more her legs prickle, an imagery that recalls her cousin's ability to tell the future through the pins and needles in her stump: 'Le divin Théo parlait avec abondance et chacune de ses paroles faisait monter les fourmis dans les jambes de la mignonne, qui piaffait, l'œil ébloui par la poudre d'or que répandait Théo, le vendeur d'orviétan, le jongleur de rêves' (p. 22) ('The divine Theo spoke volubly and each of his words sent ants crawling up the pretty young doll's legs; she pranced, her eye dazzled by the gold dust wafting about Theo the snake-oil salesman, the juggler of dreams') (p. 11). The unhappy relationship between the married couple unfolds in a horrible distortion of the Pygmalion myth—'la mignonne' rejects Théo's advances by assuming a marmoreal presence:

> La mignonne, Théo le répétait à qui voulait l'entendre, mesurait ses ardeurs, ne se laissait jamais aller au râle, son corps d'anguille se dérobait sous l'assaut, sa vulve se rétractait, ses seins pointus répugnaient à être pétris, ses belles gambettes se protégeaient des caresses avec le dédain d'une statue antique que rebuteraient les attouchements du profane.   (p. 23)

> (The doll, as Theo liked to repeat to all and sundry, when parcelling out her ardors, rarely let go a rattle. Her eel-like body writhed out of his grasp, her vulva slammed shut, her pointed breasts recoiled at his kneading, her gorgeous gams protected themselves from caresses with the disdain of ancient idols repulsed by profane gropings.)   (p. 12)

As the book progresses it becomes increasingly clear that the three women are not only victims, but are also capable of exerting their own pervasive influences. Lê employs a great deal of sibylline imagery, not least in situating the sibyls on phone lines, where people phone in to hear

258 MIGRATION AND OVIDIAN PRESENCES

their fates.[28] The conversations are meticulously monitored for length so that they can be appropriately charged: 'Ce qu'en sa conscience l'extralucide du bigophone se refusait à faire, s'étant imposé comme règle (tournez, compteurs!) de ne dire que l'aveugle vérité' (p. 178) ('something that in all good conscience the phoneline clairvoyant could not do, as she strictly adhered to the rule (run, meters, run!) of speaking only the blind truth') (p. 122). In this section of the book the phrase 'tournez, compteurs' ('run, meters run') is repeated in a kind of refrain, reminding us of the cost of the minutes ticking away—and also evoking the refrain of Catullus 64, where the Parcae also make an appearance, and where the spindles measure the time that is inexorably slipping away.[29]

They are not only descendants of Lear's daughters, not only the three Fates, not only part of a band of Sibyls,[30] but they are also the avatars of the weird sisters from Macbeth. Lê endows them with malign capabilities, blaming them for the descent into madness of 'le roi Lear': 'Plus rien n'arrêtait les fantasques dans leurs caprices. Et, sous couvert de piété, elles avaient détraqué la cervelle du roi Lear' (p. 190) ('Now nothing held the princesses in check. And, under cover of filial piety, they had unbalanced King Lear's mind') (p. 130). While the guilt of unfilial behaviour and of betraying their father creates an obvious link with Lear, as we have seen, the sense of being monstrous, unnatural beings also gestures towards Macbeth. Cooking becomes an activity that segues from preparing a meal to engaging in witchcraft in a passage that recalls the weird sisters chanting over their cauldron: 'Lady Chacal noyait une à une les crevettes roses dans une farine mélangée à des ingrédients de son cru, puis elle les jetait dans l'huile bouillante, comme on jette des chatons dans une rivière, et elle racontait des histoires de sorcière' (p. 231) ('One by one, Lady Jackal plunged the pink shrimps into the mixture of flour and her special blend of spices, then tossed them into boiling oil the way one tosses kittens in a river, while spinning tales about witches whose hands flew off in the night and went looking for souls') (p. 159). The state-of-the-art kitchen, the marker of Western prosperity and success, is filled with the ghost stories, sorcery, and

---

[28] The fusion of classical imagery with the telephone goes back as far as Proust, whose narrator, famously, performed the role of Orpheus, when he tried to converse with his grandmother on the telephone and felt that she was fading away irrevocably from him.

[29] Catullus, 64.254: 'currite dicentes subtegmina, currite fusi' ('Fly, guiding threads, fly spindle') [trans. A. S. Kline].

[30] 'D'ailleurs, le gang des sibylles du bigophone, dans leur solicitude sororale, organisait régulièrement des séminaires, conciles d'amour pour la sauvegarde de toutes les insatisfaites de corps et d'esprits' (p. 179) ('Moreover the clutch of phone-line sibyls, in their sisterly solicitude, regularly organized seminars, councils of love to safeguard all the unsatisfied, in body and mind') (p. 123).

imprecations of the past texts, which have shaped the personalities and lived experiences of the three women.

Inevitably, the power that the three women exert is limited. As the text nears its end Lê reminds us more and more frequently that 'les trois Parques' are unable to stave off the hour of death. In the sparkling new kitchen, where they are attempting to finalize preparations for the old man's visit, we are told that 'Elles comprenaient la langue des fantômes et les fourmillements des catastrophes, mais il n'était plus en leur pouvoir d'en accélerer le mouvement ni d'en détourner le cours' (p. 238) ('They understood the language of ghosts and the tingling in their stumps warned them of disaster, but it was no longer in their power to hasten its movement or divert its course') (p. 164). They are enclosed in a world that seems outside of time, yet which is as subject to the laws of time as any other human existence. The imagery of the Fates becomes more and more insistent, as Lê cleverly generates within her readers the sense of time running out, of a human life drawing to a close. There is a tension between the unstoppable course of Fate, and the stillness within the kitchen as the young women hover on the brink of the inevitable news of 'le roi Lear's death. The phrase (*Les ciseaux du destin ont coupé la corde de sa tente. Et le marchand d'espoir l'a vendu pour une chanson*) (p. 239) ('*The shears of Fate have cut the tent-ropes of his life, And the broker of Hope has sold him for nothing*') (p. 164) is closely followed by an arresting tableau of the three Fates frozen as the moment of death is about to be announced:

> Mais les cariatides restaient immobiles, l'une devant sa boîte bien rangée, l'autre devant son livre fermé, la troisième devant le vide, sourdes aux cris du cor qui réclamaient une oreille et au crissement de pneus sur le gravier qui annonçait le retour du méditatif.   (p. 239)
>
> (But the caryatids remained unmoved, one before her well-ordered box, the other before her closed book, the third before the void, deaf to the clapper clamouring for an audience and to the crunch of tires on gravel that signaled the meditator's return.)   (p. 165)

The well-ordered box is suggestive of the threads and scissors that are traditionally the accoutrements of the Parcae, while the closed book is more suggestive of the Sibyl. However, the emptiness facing the third Fate offers a new dimension, a recognition of the rootlessness and dislocation that can follow in the wake of a death. In Lê's text the old man is dispatched quite as brutally as any victim in the *Metamorphoses*: '*Trois roulements de tambour et voilà la garce de destinée remplie. Un coup d'épée et la putain de vie s'en est allée'* (p. 241) ('*Three beats of the drum and so the bitch of fate was served. A stroke of the sword and so the whore of life was gone*') (p. 166).

Such brutality is, however, gentled by the presence of other intertexts that surface towards the end of the book. One of these is Hugo's most famous poem of loss, 'Demain dès l'aube', in which he writes of his annual pilgrimage to his beloved daughter's grave. Lê's repeated refrain 'Je ne puis demeurer loin de toi plus longtemps' ('I can remain far from you no longer'), which is the fourth line of the poem, both adds to the intertextual richness of the novel, but also evokes a terrible longing, a yearning to be with somebody whom you are fated never to see again. In an epilogue to the novel Lê writes of how she succumbed to a serious mental collapse, immediately after finishing the book, thanking those who helped her through this, but also remembering 'l'absent, dont le murmure sut dominer cette "voix épouvantable qu'on appelle ordinairement le silence"' (p. 249) ('he who is absent, whose murmur overcame "the dreadful voice that men often call silence"') (p. 171). Lê's personal experiences reverse 'Demain dès l'aube', which in this book speaks poignantly of the daughters who will never again see their father, who will have to bear the guilt of leaving him behind in the country that they have also forsaken. Subha Xavier observes of this guilt that 'Lê not only reminds us that survival is laden with guilt, tainted by the death of all those who perished along the way, but that the writerly and readerly function of this narrative genre is equally complicit in the deaths that line its literary success.'[31] It is striking that Xavier is writing about Lê in an essay devoted explicitly to the stories of those who have been forced to travel by sea because of displacement. Though she does not refer explicitly to Cosnay, her predictions about future narratives map neatly onto Cosnay's accounts from the refugees whom she meets through her work: 'In years to come, more stories will undoubtedly emerge in French from the refugees of Calais and Dunkirk, the migrant Roma camps in France and Europe, the multitude of asylum seekers at Canadian borders, and the many survivors of lethal boat journeys across the Mediterranean each day. Vietnamese and Haitian boat literature challenges our imaginary around forced migration in the age of the Anthropocene and prepares the literary shorelines for what is yet adrift.'[32]

---

[31] Subha Xavier, 'Wretched of Sea: Boat Narratives and Stories of Displacement,' in Anna Louise Milne and Russell Williams, eds, *Contemporary Fiction in French* (Cambridge: Cambridge University Press, 2021), 184–98 (p. 189).

[32] Ibid., 198.

FIONA COX 261

When Lê left Vietnam, she not only left her native land, but she also left her father and, eventually, her native tongue. Xavier explores the weight of guilt she carries for being able to leave, for being able to establish her literary career elsewhere: 'Lê [...] suggests that any retelling of the 'boat people' experience in literary form results in a type of anthropophagy, feeding on human life for its existence. [...] Lê not only reminds us that survival is laden with guilt, tainted by the death of all those who perished along the way, but that the writerly function of this narrative genre is equally complicit in the deaths that line its literary success.'[33]

As we saw in the case of Marie NDiaye, the intersection between the classical world and individuals wrestling with post-colonial legacies is filled with shame. Within *Les Trois Parques* Lê explores the power of language to underscore both a sense of exile and the complex blend of love and antagonism towards the past, and the representatives of that past.[34] Beyond the mythological scaffolding of the Parcae, the Sibyls, and Pygmalion, Lê's affinity with Ovid charges this book with a particular significance, because she knew that Ovid understood what it was like to end up in exile, speaking a foreign tongue. In her volume of essays on exile, *Par ailleurs (exils)*, she observes of Ovid: 'Mais le plus navrant à ses yeux, c'était qu'en quelques années il avait désappris sa langue' (But the most annoying factor in his eyes was that over the course of a few years he had begun to forget his language).[35] And, of course, beyond the shared emotional complexity of forging a new identity in a different language, Ovid was able to express the trauma and grief of exile. Lê argues that, in his articulation of his sorrow, he was able to speak on behalf of all migrants, all those forced to leave their native lands:

Loin de se laisser aller aux gémissements Ovide à Tomes donnait à ses chants une dimension universelle en évoquant en des termes élégiaques la douleur de l'exilé....Il mourut sans avoir revu Rome, léguant à ses successeurs des pages où il mettait son cœur à nu et ne réclamait qu'un peu de compréhension: c'était aussi à la place de tous les égarés, séparés de leur patrie, qu'il avait pris la plume.[36]

---

[33] Ibid., 189. Xavier is discussing Lê's short story 'Vinh L'. Cosnay also explores the theme of cannibalism in Chapter 14 of this volume.

[34] For example: 'Au moment où l'on s'y attendait le moins, une salve d'imprécations contre le roi Lear, hurlées dans un vietnamien strident, venait déchirer la mélopée des Ave, dits en français d'une voix traînante' (p. 68) ('And, just when you least expected it, a hail of imprecations against King Lear, tore through the threnody of Aves that she murmured in languid French') (p. 44).

[35] Lê, *Par ailleurs (exils)*, 19–20.   [36] Ibid., 20.

262 MIGRATION AND OVIDIAN PRESENCES

(Far from giving in to laments, Ovid in Tomis bestowed a universal dimension upon his poems by evoking in elegiac tones the sorrow of the exile ... He
died without seeing Rome again, bequeathing to his successors pages where
he laid bare his heart and demanded only a little understanding. It was also
on behalf of all lost souls, who have become separated from their native
country, that he had picked up his pen.)

Lê offers an unusually positive account of Ovid's response to exile, here, as
many scholars have commented on his tendency to exaggerate his woes and
hardships, yet this is hardly the point. As Ovid's experiences of exile deepened
his understanding of alienation, dislocation, and loss, emotions that he had
already explored in the *Metamorphoses* particularly, his became a voice whose
Nachleben would have a particular resonance for writers exploring the lives of
those coming from outside dominant Western cultures.

Epilogue

The Soul That Is Chewed Up

Marie Cosnay

I have a question. My question didn't come to me at the time when I was translating Ovid's *Metamorphoses,* but later on when we were living through the extraordinary experience of lockdown in the spring of 2020. The experience of lockdown immured us within a present tense where there was no hope and no looking ahead and no images; and perhaps it was this exceptional experience of being trapped within a horizonless present that prompted the question that I'll ask.

In truth, however we lived through that period (rather more easily if we had a house, some home comforts, and a propensity for being alone), we sensed that what came afterwards—always assuming that the virus would disappear or would become manageable—would be indelibly marked by the danger of being exposed to other people that had been represented that spring.

There were no images for that present about which I'm speaking; we were confined to one place. We knew the fate of those who cannot move. When we went out, it was only for round trips of no more than 100 kilometres.

This present about which I'm speaking was full of pasts (epidemics that arose in the Middle Ages, in antiquity—the plague at Aegina that Ovid tells us about in Book 7 of the *Metamorphoses*); it was also replete with a future to which many references were made, but which people preferred to think of as a possibility. A future collapse in which we'd see epidemic after epidemic, glaciers melting, the loss of fauna, the upheaval of our living conditions hung over us; avoiding this came with conditions. We would outline these conditions for our survival.

A present that was enclosed within one room, and then to a 100-kilometre round trip, sent us back to everything—to a past and a future filled with legends and fantasies. Back to everything—except to the present. For the present doesn't exist unless you can allow it mentally to grow in time with a step back and a step forward. The present didn't exist.

Marie Cosnay, *Epilogue: The Soul That Is Chewed Up* In: *Ovid in French: Reception by Women from the Renaissance to the Present.* Edited by: Helena Taylor and Fiona Cox, Oxford University Press. © Oxford University Press 2023. DOI: 10.1093/oso/9780192895387.003.0014

264 EPILOGUE: THE SOUL THAT IS CHEWED UP

The past: the past of our childhoods was affected. Our parents were the very people of whom it was being said that they could die without being resuscitated because of the shortage of ventilators. Our childhood's sweet nostalgia suddenly switched to a slice of horror. And we were of an age, no matter how steadfast our faith in withstanding any ordeal, to doubt our collective ability to choose for the world that would ensue, conditions that would establish something that was fairer, healthier, and less extreme. So much for the future.

I still haven't asked my question.

The virus raised important questions about humanity and wildness, about humans and animals, the transmissions between them and the circulation from one species to another—and, at one point, it was thought to be connected to eating. What should we eat? What shouldn't we eat? Roots, vegetables, meat, blood, human blood, entrails, pets, animals to whom we are close, dogs, cats, small birds, wild animals, game, wolves, bears, disgusting animals, bats, hogs, coypus. The lines of separation established by religions or an ethical sense are not straightforward. They are even less straightforward in the works of ancient authors.

Lycaon starts off Ovid's great cycle in the *Metamorphoses*. Because of him it is not an epidemic which befalls the human race, but the flood. From the flood two people will be saved, Deucalion and Pyrrha, who take care of the past and the future and, in so doing, renew the human race. Lycaon, a cruel and cunning man, is going to set a trap for Zeus, who is disguised as a man. He pretends to give him good meat to eat and gives him human flesh. He gives a human to a god who is passing for a human.

When I was telling this story to a little girl I said: you can't eat human meat, it's not allowed.

Why?

We can't eat our fellow humans. Lycaon wanted to make Zeus do it and he got punished.

The little girl gazed at me, aghast.

Disbelieving.

After a moment the little girl said: 'But Zeus isn't a man; he can eat what he wants.'

If Zeus, who isn't a man, eats human flesh, in truth he isn't committing a crime of cannibalism. He's not eating his like. He's not hurting his fellow. He's not infringing any kind of taboo. The feast that Lycaon offers Zeus echoes in some ways the feast of Atreus. Atreus made his brother, who did not recognize him, eat the boiled limbs of his children. Horror and woe when the brother realized what had happened. Not only his *fellow*, and the *same*, but his sons and the flesh of his flesh. There is an instance in the *Metamorphoses* (Book 6) of just so cruel a meal, when a father learns that he has eaten from his own bloodline (unforgivable). Since the son played no part in his father's misdeeds, we must believe that he, the son, was worth above all his father's blood. Itys is somewhat overlooked in mythology and yet he had an appalling end. His father, Tereus, both guilty and victim, will be changed into a hoopoe. His mother, both guilty and victim, will be changed into a bat. He, the son, boiled and devoured, will be changed into nothing at all.

In Book 1 the scene is set as a flood, which will mark the end of humanity. That's it. Yet Lycaon was not suggesting a stand-off between man and man. He was suggesting that it should be between man and god. The difference is a very significant one and the small girl (to whom I was telling the story) and I had paused to think about it. There was no transgression of the taboo. On top of this the eaten man was nobody's son, and that made things even worse, as there was nobody to weep for him. Any feelings were being dismissed altogether. Lycaon's cruelty was not being gauged in terms of the status of the prey he'd chosen. There was absolutely no affect.

And yet Zeus is horrified. Worse than that. The deed was certainly hateful, however one might choose to look at it, for, not content with killing and boiling a man, Lycaon is perfectly happy with the idea of a man eating a man since, to his mind, this idea of being a god is just crap. Of course it is, since he wants to prove that there was no god. He traps Zeus within his lie. Zeus wants to present himself as a man? He'll make him into an animal. And there he is, the man who refused to make any distinction between species, transformed by Zeus into a wolf.

So well done, Lycaon, who is the champion of blurring the difference between species. Now he is intimately acquainted with two—man and animal. If he can hear us he is still sniggering. Because to his mind god, human, or animal is one and the same species.

The little girl said, wide-eyed, that 'if Zeus had endured eating a person, while disguised as a man, he would have eaten from another species from his own, at least as far as he is depicted: a species afflicted by weak reasoning and capable of doing worse things.' The gods are too pure and perfect to eat— eating is that business where questions (and miseries) arise. When he was disguised as a man Zeus guessed that he was being given a man to eat. When he realized that the man was behaving, in his view, like a wolf (capable of more heinous crimes, pouncing indiscriminately on his prey, setting disloyal traps) he turned him into a wolf. Zeus wanted and demanded a world view that included clearly delineated species, which were well established and cleanly

266   EPILOGUE: THE SOUL THAT IS CHEWED UP

categorized. Yet he himself was strangely ambiguous, wasn't he? A god and a man at one and the same time. Too perfect to eat and yet ready to join in at a banquet, cheating in the way that only a man (or a wolf) can do. It's all pretty slippery.

There's no question of allowing Zeus to be the only one to duplicate his nature. Lycaon demands the same thing. It's true that he is a man and already something of a wolf (he holds human taboos in contempt, he is prepared to eat a man, or to make another man do so). That's not enough though. He will also be the one who dictates who will eat what—he's the one who hands it out. It's not so much that he aspires to be an animal—he wants to be god. He is certainly among those who are trans-genres, trans-species. Lycaon pays for this rejection of the order of the world, this rejection of the order dictated by Zeus with his metamorphosis, and the world pays for it with a flood. He rejected the order dictated by Zeus and wanted to be as powerful as Zeus, whom nothing prevented from taking on the part of a man. So Lycaon will play the part of both animal and god.

One might read Lycaon's story as a fable that asserts the freedom of species. But it might also be read as a kind of social revenge, of unbridled ambition.

Because, apart from rebellion and an assertion of the free movement of species, nothing really bad happened, as the little girl pointed out: Zeus, the god of gods and guarantor of the division of species, disguised as a man, worth a man, was refusing to partake of roasted man.

The cynical Lycaon had allowed himself to be played: since you believe in difference and in a taxonomy of species, come and have a little piece of man. Just as you might say to a guileless consumer—do you want to try some meat? Eat your dog who's your friend—or some rat, or a bit of panther or some fried cockroaches. Eating the inedible (deemed too closely related, too wild, or too disgusting)—eating the inedible brings about disaster. So said Zeus.

I still haven't asked my question. Up until now I've tried to give an honest account of my train of thought. A virus has just written part of our history. This part of history is both human and animal at one and the same time. And no doubt that played a part in the way I read, or re-read, the story of Lycaon. Perhaps it influenced my reading or re-reading of all of Ovid.

We've seen that it's Zeus who sees. The least that we can say is that that is quickly established—divine reaction is immediate. Zeus' response equates with the order of the world that he pronounces and dictates. Everything is in its place—that one who's a man, that one who's an animal, me a god. Lycaon becomes a wolf.

His clothes changed into bristling hairs, his arms to legs, and he became a wolf. [...] But, though he was a wolf, he retained some traces of his original shape. The greyness of his hair was the same, his face showed the same violence, his eyes gleamed as before, and he presented the same picture of ferocity.[1]

Here, at last, is my question. How is that Ovid—who sings of circulation and freedom, who sings of change, of the opposite of being frozen; how is it that he, who portrays girls as flowers, fountains, trees, and men as animals, stags, crows, bears and birds; how is it that he, who bids in various—almost infinite—ways for the mobility of things; how is it that he presents to us a wolf who was already a wolf? A wolf who was nothing other than a wolf (however much he might seem to be a man and however much he might wish to be a god). Is it a question of fate, of a destiny that nothing can undo? How is it that Ovid opens his long poem about changed forms with a story about an identity returning to itself? I remembered my surprise when, at the end of ten years of working on the translation, I realized that the semantic field of words to do with adherence, of fixing, of attaching, was one of the broadest fields. What can we make of that? Were we, then, only ever mobile, free, and capable of transformation by virtue of the opposite? By virtue of this being ascribed to our condition—our human condition? Are metamorphosis and identity two sides of the same thing? And I think, up till now, that is how I had answered the question (which was not, therefore, a completely new one).

The question was not perhaps completely new, but it had become more precise. There was this character that had had a significant impact on me while I was translating. He didn't know how to listen, he was bad at listening, and he was flayed for his pains. I'm talking about Marsyas. He preferred Pan's celebrations to Apollo's lyre and because of that he was skinned, was cut to the quick. He was left with no skin, nothing to encase him, no form. No beauty. No ears—and the result was that nobody's gaze could settle on him. This story, which is one of the lesser-known ones from the *Metamorphoses*, was one of the ones that affected me the most.

Once Marsyas' flesh had been stripped bare, he became water and flowed. I think that a body reduced to that state of extreme suffering and annihilation seems to suggest that, if Ovid was indeed the poet of evasion and flight, of

---

[1] Ovid, *Metamorphoses* 1.236–9. Ovid, *Metamorphoses*, trans. Mary Innes (Harmondsworth, Middlesex: Penguin, 1955, repr. 1982), 35. Cosnay's translation of the Latin into French reads: 'Ses habits s'effacent en poils, ses bras en jambs. / Il devient loup et garde les traces de son ancienne forme. / Même blancheur, visage de même violence, / même brilliance, même image de cruauté.'

268   EPILOGUE: THE SOUL THAT IS CHEWED UP

forms changed into forms changed into forms only to be changed into forms yet again, it was because he was aware of death which inflicts stasis. If Ovid sang of transformations, he was singing from a place of pain. He was singing, knowing that his songs were in vain, that *driving forward a poem that has no end* is a vain pursuit, that it is impossible to depict the final point.

Today, having endured lockdown and having had a talk with the little girl, I find this question opening up and burrowing into my mind even further.

I was even wondering whether Lycaon wasn't right on one point, if we can set his cruelty aside. We were *from the same species*, making our way towards the same goal for better (whatever that might be) or for worse (and Lycaon put up a spirited defence, when it came to the worse), in the same boat. When it came down to it, it made little difference whether we were sailing from one species to another. The possibility of flight and movement wasn't contained in the journey, but rather in the teaching that Pythagoras finally assumes in his own way at the end of the long poem (perhaps that's what 'for better' means): a soul goes from body to body (it doesn't really matter which ones—the different bodies are worth pretty much the same), but whatever happens, you don't eat anyone. Anyone, at all—do you get it? Nobody. Lycaon was right—he who could be a wolf from the very start, pass himself off as a man every day, confound a god disguised as a man, powerful and free as a god. All that to say that the god of gods, a minor god, a famous hero, an animal or a tree—it's all the same thing.

The question is not about metamorphosis, but about sharing a common destiny. It's about equality between all beings. Furthermore, there's something else to be said when it comes to equality between beings and sharing a common destiny. Something for anyone who has been, will be, or is still being, eaten.

In Lycaon's story, since it's of interest to a small girl and me, there is definitely someone who may have managed to avoid the sacrilege of being devoured, but is nevertheless chopped into pieces, boiled, and roasted. He is the hostage of the Molossi, somebody who lost the war. What we know of him can be summed up in a couple of words—we know that he was a hostage and we know what tribe he belonged to. That's it. We don't know the man who is eaten (his half-dead limbs, still twitching, simmer away in the pot). He has no name. He leaves us indifferent. Nothing becomes of him. He doesn't take on any creative form. Itys, Procne's small son in the story we've already spoken on from Book 6, is also eaten and this time the tale is replete with ambivalence—his mother loves him and kills him. It's as tragic as it gets. The fate of the eaten boy is the same as the hostage of the Molossi—neither of them metamorphoses. Itys isn't changed, even though his criminal parents got that opportunity. Those who are eaten are those of whom nothing remains. Quite frankly, if it hadn't been for our spring spent dealing with the pandemic I don't know if I'd have seen in the *Metamorphoses* quite how much truth there is in this every single time. Those who are eaten, who are masticated by teeth, turn to nothing. They have no more chances, no more strength or name. I'll come back to this point.

Let's go back to the nameless hostage of the Molossi. Even Zeus doesn't give much of a damn. Quite honestly even we, as readers, aren't very moved. Who is going to be eaten (or can be eaten) because of Lycaon? Somebody who doesn't do very much for us. Zeus, who oversees the order of things, is opposed to the consuming of human limbs that are partly boiled and partly roasted. His opposition doesn't spring from any pity or respect for the hostage of the Molossi. He cares as little about the hostage of the Molossi as Lycaon does.

It's clear here that Lycaon's system (which forges the way in opening up the borders between species and races) has a crack in it and this crack is social. The loser of the story is immaterial. The loser of the stories (of the wars and conquests) can be eaten. There's no afterwards for him. No story. And as we'll see shortly he quite possibly has no soul.

One scene in the *Metamorphoses* that lies between the story of Lycaon and the episode with Pythagoras was very important to me. The scene takes place in Book 10 of this epic of altered shapes.

In Book 10 Orpheus, who has failed to save Eurydice, has settled in a place that has been set up for singing. He is going to tell a load of stories and men, gods, trees, rocks, and animals want to listen to these tales of men, gods, trees, and animals. That is because all the things that I've mentioned are animate beings. Ancient animate beings. It's the same difference whether they are ancient or contemporary. Sometimes, as in the case of the cypress, they have a story that will be sung; sometimes they have no story or else it's one that won't be known. When the animated beings or ex-animated beings have a story, it's a love story and, preferably, a story of unhappy love. The rocks, trees, and beasts with unhappy histories in love who have come to listen to Orpheus have set out, have made their way, and here they are. They have spent lives crammed with sadnesses, surprises, dreadful traps, they have loved and lost, they have ossified or liquefied. Having been on the road they constitute the landscape. They constitute the landscape, having been the road. There are no sacred or natural spaces, Ovid tells us (long before others make this same point); every outdoors scene, every landscape is constructed. Nature is as

270 EPILOGUE: THE SOUL THAT IS CHEWED UP

beautiful as art. Ovid makes this point repeatedly—nature is as beautiful as art. As if art came first.

Art comes first. We (humans, trees, rocks, animals) have never ceased to move forward, to make, to compose, to arrange the landscape.

In *Par delà nature et culture* Philippe Descola, speaking of the Australian Aborigines and contesting the myth of *terra nullius*, writes: 'the entirety of the landscape that has been traversed is inhabited as a spacious, familiar dwelling, arranged to the taste of successive generations with such discretion that any touches bestowed upon it by the series of tenants have become almost imperceptible.' There's no sacred wildness pitted against domesticity; there's no pitting animals against humans; it's not a question of 'natural' on one side as opposed to 'touched by art' on the other. There is a world.

There's no question of a happy ending or of a possible escape. There's a flayed man who ends up as a river; a scalded hostage who's lost all shape. There's a stag with whom a god has fallen in love, and the stag becomes a tree. The tree becomes the tree of the dead. Whether you are stag or nothing or tree, whether you are dead or a river—what song should be sung? What song should be sung in this immobile place which is made up of all previous mobilities? A song without end, obviously. Who possesses (and the skin and shape torn from Marsyas and Orpheus' body, which is so soon torn to pieces, illustrate this point) their own impossibility and their own uselessness? Tragedy is sheltered within the epic of forms.

It's a long time ago now that I started to translate the *Metamorphoses*. At the very beginning I didn't have a project. Or I didn't ask myself about the project. That's the absolute truth. But not having a project didn't mean that there wasn't continuity. There was a regularity—I did a few verses every day. Quite honestly I found very quickly that things were going well between Ovid and me and very early on I thought that this was a happy meeting. I would move from story to story, from peak to peak without any difficulty. I could anticipate the syntax and I adopted its rhythms. People said afterwards—or I said afterwards—that my syntax in the novels I was writing that had nothing to do with Ovid was, in some ways, coloured by his Latin. It was the recurring signifiers, the sounds, sentences that constituted episodes or parentheses. Today, now that some time has passed, I dare to believe that perhaps there was something in Ovid's Latin, in that poem by Ovid, that was familiar to me even before I began to translate it. Afterwards I followed his sentences and rhythms. All I did was follow him. I spend my time pursuing Ovid.

Later I translated a bit of Virgil's *Aeneid*, moving from peak to peak, from bank to bank, episode after episode. Virgil's epic, in my French, was a constant source of surprises to me. I didn't at all have the same sense of familiarity as I had felt with Ovid. Don't get me started on Lucretius—the anti-Ovid. It's not that I feel ill-at-ease but I had to adopt a rhythm that was completely foreign to me. Every pebble is next to a pebble and that makes up a carpet (too bad about the pebble metaphor), a surreal, pointillist landscape, a picture which you have to come back to, moving backward and forward, never wearying until you weave together the whole thing very slowly. When it came down to it with all these authors I was simply trying out epic. Virgil's epic followed the ancient models. Lucretius' epic was philosophical. Following them Ovid did a bit of everything and it seemed to me that I could see him doing it with his chiasmuses, games, acceleration, falls, moments of amusement, wordplay, and cruelty—there was always cruelty. It wasn't his own nor was it Lycaon's but it belonged to everything and everyone. It was the cruelty of the human condition from which we've always, from the beginning of time, had to escape. Ovid manipulated the words as Orpheus manipulated his animated listeners.

For a long time I had been translating short extracts for the pupils I was teaching at the time. They were young, between ten and fourteen, and there was a good rapport between them and Ovid as well. I would translate with them, and then after them so that we could get to the end of the story more quickly. I was driven by impatience. Then the opportunity (semi-official) arose to translate the three books which at the time were set texts on the literary baccalaureats—'Books 10, 11, and 12 *From Orpheus to Achilles*.' Here Ovid was reworking not his public, like Orpheus (although he was also inventing a new public for himself at every turn), but the substance of epic. He was, quite simply, retelling the *Iliad*. These three songs were brought out in a free translation on the Musagora website. It was a first for me in terms of putting out my translations to be read. And that must be the moment when we can start to talk about it as a project. The project lasted ten years. I took my time, the time of life, story after story, song after song; I took the time of my life among children—both my own and other people's. The time of lots of metamorphoses. I was teaching in schools; the children were growing up, things were happening—Ovid's things, those things which move all the time, remained. They were there. It's astonishing for metamorphoses to be the stable point in a life which is moving on. That they should be what isn't moving on. At the end of what really did become a project over time, I saw that the *Metamorphoses* were still at work, that they were still asking questions.

272 EPILOGUE: THE SOUL THAT IS CHEWED UP

At the end of his poem Ovid said:

If there be any truth in poets' prophecies, I shall live to all eternity, immortalised by fame.[2]

I now know that he doesn't mean that he'll be known for all eternity. Or at any rate that's not all he means. He means that he will be living. He will, in truth, be living and alive and asking us living questions. After the events of the pandemic, after the wildness, after the virus lurking in our organisms and our spittle, after the presence of this tiny, minuscule thing which forced us to keep away from each other, and to wonder with whom and how we should live and what we must and mustn't eat, Ovid was well and truly alive.

I translated; time passed; the children grew up; little by little I got to the end of this long, living poem and the living questions were still being asked. They were shifting slightly, as adjectives do from verse to verse. The shifts were barely perceptible. Book 15 is the book where there is the apotheosis of Julius Caesar whose soul, borne by Venus up to the stars, carries a train of stars in the wake of the moon; it's the book about metempsychosis; it's the book where Hippolytus, a well-known character (Phaedra's stepson), was the prey of his stepmother's desire and father's gullibility and subsequently became a minor god, a very small god, a nobody that nobody had ever heard of. It's in Book 15, just as at the start of the poem, that there is another issue of eating or of being eaten. And I am going to pause on this as well by way of a conclusion.

We've reached the end and Ovid introduces to us a new character—Pythagoras. He introduces him at the end just as at the beginning of his poem Lucretius introduced another character, Epicurus. Ovid does Lucretius, just as elsewhere he does Virgil—he borrows, transforms, and metamorphoses epics and subject matter. Epicurus and Pythagoras are, then, two men, two Greek men, two philosophers, the first of whom appears in the works of Lucretius and the second of whom appears, a little later, in Ovid's poem, to combat the fear of the gods and to speak about the causes and the nature of the universe. They don't both use the same tools to fight. Both of them are, as Ovid puts it, 'far from the gods and their region of the heavens', but 'close to them in thought'.

---

[2] Ovid, *Metamorphoses* 15.879. Ovid, *Metamorphoses*, trans. Innes, p. 357. Cosnay's translation of the Latin into French reads: 'j'irai connu à travers siècles / et s'il y a quelque chose de vrai dans les oracles d'un poète, je vivrai.'

Pythagoras has two things to say at the point at which he is introduced by the poet, who is shortly going to be drawing to a close. The first is that the soul is immortal—nothing ever ends. The second is that you don't eat animals.

We're looping back here to the questions posed at the start of the poem. What is a man? What is a god? With a nod to Lucretius who spends his time explaining to us that the gods aren't anything, Ovid responds that a man is a philosopher, that is to say someone who is close to the gods. A man who thinks, who is exiled at the threat of tyranny, who observes everything and instructs all of us about what he has observed, about the basic facts of the world. Such a man tells us that souls go from one being to another:

All things change, but nothing dies: the spirit wanders hither and thither, taking possession of what limbs it pleases, passing from beasts into human bodies, or again our human spirit passes into beasts, but never at any time does it perish.[3]

We are a long way from the time when Zeus wanted to categorize the different classes of beings—animals, men, and gods. A man is a god through his capacity to think; a man is an animal; an animal is a man through the breathing that they both have in common. The response is clear. One is the other and the soul is one. There is always a return to exactly the same thing on the understanding that there is recognition of multiplicity. The soul is one— the bodies that house it are multiple. It makes more sense that the wolf should become a wolf. This is the answer of Pythagoras and Ovid to Zeus and Lycaon. The nature of the soul, its immortality and unity, settles the other matter. The other matter that is still in limbo. The matter which preoccupied us at the start of the poem, which preoccupied us during the pandemic, a time when we were contemplating that the wild, which humans may have approached and ingested, might be responsible for a tiny virus that could spread across the entire planet. That matter is—what can we eat?

We mustn't forget that in Ovid nothing changes once it's been in some-body's mouth. Nothing can be done with flesh that has been masticated and chewed up. What happens to the soul of the being that is eaten? There's something here that defies thought. It's for this reason that Pythagoras, Ovid's Pythagoras, urges us so severely not to eat animals. There aren't categories of

---

[3] Ovid, *Metamorphoses* 15.165–8. Ovid, *Metamorphoses*, trans. Innes, p. 339. Cosnay's translation from the Latin into French reads: 'Tout change, rien ne périt; il erre d'ici / à là et de là à ici, il occupe les corps que tu veux, / le soufflé; des bêtes il passe aux hommes/et de nous aux bêtes, en aucun temps il ne meurt.'

274 EPILOGUE: THE SOUL THAT IS CHEWED UP

species, there aren't sub-souls—there is just the one soul that belongs to me and to the wolf, the bat, and the sheep. It's even, to be sure, the soul of the hostage of the Molossi. It's the soul of those who are losing and who have been lost. Barbarism is bloodstained teeth. Killing is one thing, but eating the poor, wounded flesh is quite another. Filling your bloodthirsty belly always entails eating something that is the *same* as you are. It always entails eating something with a soul. And it's forbidden.

> Know and understand that when you put the meat of slaughtered oxen in your mouth, the flesh you eat is that of your own labourers.[4]

And so I think I have my answer for the small girl. You're right—Zeus isn't a man; he wouldn't be committing so terrible a crime if he put in his mouth the human flesh that Lycaon offers him. And yet, yes he would commit a crime, an appalling crime, because there is no division among the species. Pythagoras has replaced Zeus—an animal is a man who is a god (a philosopher), and when you eat an animate being it's the soul that bleeds. It's the soul that is torn to shreds and that bleeds.

Our age knows how to tear the soul to pieces. Through the mouthpiece of Ovid, who never falls silent, Pythagoras says that it's barbarism. Our present age knows how to commit barbarism, but that is another question that we'll leave to one side. As I write the closing lines of this essay one hundred and eighty refugees, prevented by our borders from seeking a better life, wait in Europe until a port opens up for them. But no port comes forward—they are left to die of hunger on board, within reach of the shore, and why not—let them eat each other. The souls that are chewed up call for help in vain.

Translated by Fiona Cox

---

[4] Ovid, *Metamorphoses* 15.141–2. Ovid, *Metamorphoses*, trans. Innes, p. 338. Cosnay's translation into French of these lines reads: 'Quand vous donnerez à vos palais, les membres des bœufs massacres, sachez-le, sentez-le, vous mangez vos paysans.'

Bibliography

Turin, Biblioteca Nazionale Universitaria, MS 8 Peyron Franc

Adam, Jean-Michel, and Ute Heidmann, eds, *Textualité et intertextualité des contes. Perrault, Apulée, La Fontaine, Lhéritier* (Paris: Classiques Garnier, 2010)

Aeschylus, *Oresteia: Agamemnon. Libation-Bearers. Eumenides*, ed. and trans. Alan H. Sommerstein (Cambridge, MA: Harvard University Press, Loeb Classical Library, 2009).

Allan, Stacie, *Writing the Self, Writing the Nation: Romantic Selfhood in the Works of Germaine de Staël and Claire de Duras* (Oxford: Peter Lang, 2019)

Andersen, Corinne, '"Que me veux-tu? / What do you want of me?": Claude Cahun's *Autoportraits* and the Process of Gender Identification', *Women in French Studies*, 13 (2005), 37–50

Aneau, Barthélemy, *Imagination poétique* (Lyons: Macé Bonhomme, 1552)

Aneau, Barthélemy, *Picta Poesis* (Lyons: Macé Bonhomme, 1552)

Auraix-Jonchière, Pascale, and Catherine Volpilhac-Auger, eds, *Isis, Narcisse, Psyché entre lumieères et romanticisme: mythe et écritures, écritures du mythe* (Clemont-Ferrand: Presses Universitaires Blaise-Pascal, 2000)

Auraix-Jonchière, Pascale, 'Mythopoétique de l'espace sandien: Lucrezia Floriani et Le Château des désertes', in Brigitte Diaz and Isabelle Hoog Naginski, eds, *George Sand: Pratiques et imaginaires de l'écriture* (Caen: Presses Universitaires de Caen, 2006), 255–64

Auraix-Jonchière, Pascale, *George Sand et la fabrique des contes* (Paris: Classiques Garnier, 2017)

Bacholle, Michèle, 'For a Fluid Approach to Céline Sciamma's *Portrait of a Lady on Fire*', *French Cultural Studies*, 34/2 (2022), 147–60 https://journals.sagepub.com/doi/full/10.1177/09571558221099637

Bailey, Laura 'Lou', and Lizzie Thynne, 'Beyond Representation: Claude Cahun's Monstrous Mischief-Making', *History of Photography*, 29/2 (2005), 135–48

Ballestra-Puech, Sylvie, *Métamorphose d'Arachné: l'artiste en araignée dans la littérature occidentale* (Geneva: Droz, 2006)

Balzi, Marta, and Gemma Prades, eds, *Ovid in the Vernacular: Translations of the Metamorphoses in the Middle Ages and Renaissance* (Oxford: The Society for the Study of Medieval Languages and Literature, 2021)

Barbier, M. L., 'Notice biographique sur Madame la princess Constance de Salm-Dick [*sic*]', *Biographie Universelle*, 81 (1847), 3–8

Barchiesi, Allesandro, 'Future Reflexive: Two Modes of Allusion and Ovid's *Heroides*', *Harvard Studies in Classical Philology*, 95 (1993), 333–65

Bardon, Henri, 'Sur l'influence d'Ovide en France au XVIIe siècle', *Atti del Convegno Internazionale Ovidiano*, 2 (1959), 69–83

[Barrin, Jean], *Les Epistres et toutes les élégies amoureuses d'Ovide* (Paris: Barbin, 1676)

[Barrin, Jean], *Les Epitres amoureuses d'Ovide traduites en François, nouvelle édition augmentée et embellie de figures* (Cologne: Marteau, 1702)

Bauer, Nancy, *Simone de Beauvoir, Philosophy, and Feminism* (New York: Columbia University Press, 2001)

276 BIBLIOGRAPHY

Beagon, Mary, 'Ordering Wonderland: Ovid's Pythagoras and the Augustan Vision', in Philip Hardie, ed., *Paradox and the Marvellous in Augustan Literature and Culture* (Oxford: Oxford University Press, 2009), 288–309

Beaulieu, Jean-Philippe, '"Moy Traductrice": le façonnement de la figure auctoriale dans le paratexte des traductions de Marie de Gournay', *Renaissance and Reformation*, 35/4 (2012), 119–34

Behn, Aphra, 'Oenone to Paris', in *Ovid's Epistles Translated by Several Hands* (London, 1680)

Belle, Marie-Alice, 'Locating Early Modern Women's Translations: Critical and Historiographical Issues', *Renaissance and Reformation/Renaissance et Réforme*, 35/4 (2012), 5–23 [special issue: *Women's Translations in Early Modern England and France*]

Bellefleur, L.-J., *Les Amours d'Ovide, avec ... les Épistres de Sapho à Phaon et de Canacé à son frère Macarée* (Paris: Petit-Pas, 1621)

Bellegarde, Jean-Baptiste Morvan de, *Les Métamorphoses d'Ovide* (Paris: Emery, 1701)

Benson, Fiona, *Vertigo and Ghost* (London: Cape, 2019)

Berchorius, Petrus, *Metamorphosis ovidiana moraliter explanata* (Paris: Ascensius, 1511)

Bercot, Martine, Michel Collot, and Catriona Seth, eds, *Anthologie de la poésie française XVIIIe siècle, XIXe siècle, XXe siècle* (Paris: Gallimard, 2000)

Berenguier, Nadine, 'Publish or Perish! Constance de Salm's Identity Crisis and Unfulfilled Promise', *Dix-Neuf*, 21/1 (2017), 46–68

Bessone, Federica, 'Saffo, la lirica, l'elegia: su Ovidio, *Heroides* 15', *Materiali e discussioni per l'analisi dei testi classici*, 51 (2003), 209–44

La Bible des poëtes (Paris: 1493–4)

Biondi, Carminella, 'Neuf mythes pour une passion', *Bulletin de la Société Internationale d'Études Yourcenariennes (Mythe et idéologie dans l'œuvre de Marguerite Yourcenar)*, 5 (1989), 27–33

Biot, Brigitte, *Barthélemy Aneau, régent de la Renaissance lyonnaise* (Paris: Champion, 1996)

Blanchard, Pierre, 'De la querelle des femmes—la guerre des satires. Les combats de Constance de Théis', in Laurance Vanoflen, ed., *Femmes et philosophie des Lumières. De l'imaginaire à la vie des idées* (Paris: Garnier, 2020), 305–22

Bolduc, Benoît, *Andromède au rocher: fortune théâtrale en France et en Italie 1587–1712* (Florence: Olschki, 2002)

Bolton, M. Catherine, 'Gendered Spaces in Ovid's *Heroides*', *The Classical World*, 102/3 (2009), 273–90

Boyd, Barbara, *Ovid's Homer: Authority, Repetition, Reception* (Oxford: Oxford University Press, 2017)

[Bressey, Charlotte Antoinette de, marquise de Lezay-Marnésia], *Lettres de Julie à Ovide* (Rome, 1753)

[Bressey, Charlotte Antoinette de, marquise de Lezay-Marnésia], *Lettres de tendresse et d'amour, contenant les Lettres de Julie à Ovide, et d'Ovide à Julie; suivies des Lettres Galantes d'une chanoinesse portugaise; des lettres de Babet et des réponses de son Amant; des Lettres d'Amour d'une Dame philosophe; des lettres de la Présidente de Ferrand au Baron de Breteuil; et celles d'Héloïse et d'Abeilard* (Paris: Collin, 1808)

Brightenback, Kristine, 'The Metamorphoses and Narrative Conjointure in *Deus amanz, Yonec* and *Le laustic*,' *Romanic Review*, 72/1 (1981), 1–12

Brown, Hilary, *Women and Early Modern Cultures of Translation: Beyond the Female Tradition* (Oxford: Oxford University Press, 2022)

BIBLIOGRAPHY 277

Brown, Sarah Annes, 'Women Translators', in Stuart Gillespie and David Hopkins, eds, *The Oxford History of Literary Translation in English* (Oxford: Oxford University Press, 2005), 111–20

Brundin, Abigail, 'Vittoria Colonna in Manuscript', in Abigail Brundin, Tatiana Crivelli, and Maria Serena Sapegno, eds, *A Companion to Vittoria Colonna* (Leiden: Brill, 2016), 39–68

Bruni, Leonardo, *Sulla perfetta traduzione*, ed. Paolo Vitti (Naples: Liguori, 2004)

Burke, Catherine, 'Voices from the Outside: Homeric Exiles in Twentieth-Century French Writing', PhD thesis, University College Cork, 2021

Bush, Christopher, 'The Other of the Other?: Cultural Studies, Theory, and the Location of the Modernist Signifier', *Comparative Literature Studies*, 42/2 (2005), 162–80

Cahun, Claude, *Heroines*, trans. Norman MacAfee, in Shelley Rice, ed., *Inverted Odysseys: Claude Cahun, Maya Deren, Cindy Sherman* (Cambridge, MA: Massachusetts Institute of Technology Press, 1999), 43–110

Cahun, Claude, *Écrits*, ed. François Leperlier (Paris: Jean-Michel Place, 2002)

Cahun, Claude, *Héroïnes*, ed. François Leperlier (Paris: Mille et une nuits, 2006)

Cahun, Claude, *Disavowals: or Cancelled Confessions*, trans. Susan de Muth (Cambridge, MA: Massachusetts Institute of Technology Press, 2008)

Cancik, Hubert, and Helmut Schneider, eds, *Brill's New Pauly: Antiquity* (Leiden: Brill, 2002)

Catalogue de la bibliothèque de Mme George Sand et de M. Maurice Sand (Paris: Librairie des Amateurs, 1890)

Cave, Terence, 'The Transit of Venus: Feeling Your Way Forward', in Neil Kenny, Richard Scholar, and Wes Williams, eds, *Montaigne in Transit: Essays in Honour of Ian Maclean* (Cambridge: Legenda, 2016), 9–18

Cave, Terence, '"Tu facto loquar": Philomela's Afterlives in Rabelais, Ronsard and Shakespeare', in Wes Williams and Neil Kenny, eds, *Retrospectives: Essays in Literature, Poetics and Cultural History by Terence Cave* (London: Legenda, 2009), 76–86

Cerrito, Stefania, and Marie Possamaï-Pérez, eds, *Ovide en France du Moyen Âge à nos jours* (Paris: Classiques Garnier, 2021)

Chadwick, Whitney, ed., *Mirror Images: The Women, Surrealism and Self-Representation* (Cambridge, MA: Massachusetts Institute of Technology Press, 1998)

Chadwick, Whitney, and Tirza True Latimer, eds, *The Modern Woman Revisited: Paris between the Wars* (New Brunswick: Rutgers University Press, 2003)

Chamberlain, Lori, 'Gender and the Metaphorics of Translation', in Lawrence Venuti, ed., *The Translation Studies Reader* (New York and London: Routledge, 2000), 314–42

Chard, Chloe, 'The Road to Ruin: Memory, Ghosts, Moonlight and Weeds', in Catharine Edwards, ed., *Roman Presences: Receptions of Rome in European Culture 1789–1945* (Cambridge: Cambridge University Press, 1999), 125–39

Chatelain, Marie-Claire, 'L'Héroïde chez Mademoiselle de Scudéry', in Delphine Denis et Anne-Elisabeth Spica, eds, *Mlle de Scudéry: une femme de lettres au XVIIe siècle* (Arras: Artois Presses Université, 2002), 41–58

Chatelain, Marie-Claire, *Ovide savant, Ovide galant: Ovide en France dans la seconde moitié du XVII siècle* (Paris: Champion, 2008)

Chatelain, Marie-Claire, 'L'Héroïde comme modèle épistolaire: l'exemple des *Lettres Amoureuses* de Malleville', *Littératures Classiques*, 71 (2010), 129–51

Cherbuliez, Juliette, *The Place of Exile: Leisure Literature and the Limits of Absolutism* (Lewisburg: Bucknell University Press, 2005)

278 BIBLIOGRAPHY

Chénier, André, 'Notice biographique sur la vie et les écrits de Mme la princesse Constance de Salm-Dyck', *Fastes nobiliaires* (Paris: Imprimerie d'Amédée Saintin, 1845), 3–20

Clark, James, Frank Coulson, and Kathryn McKinley, eds, *Ovid in the Middle Ages* (Cambridge: Cambridge University Press, 2011)

Clarke, Danielle, 'Translation', in Laura Lunger Knoppers, ed., *The Cambridge Companion to Early Modern Women's Writing* (Cambridge: Cambridge University Press, 2010), 167–80

Clément-Tarantino, Séverine, 'The *Aeneid* and "Les Belles Lettres"', in Susanna Braund and Zara Martirosova Torlone, eds, *Virgil and his Translators* (Oxford: Oxford University Press, 2018), 209–23

Clément-Tarantino, Séverine, 'Les Cabinets de Bailleul ornés de scènes mythologiques ou le triomphe d'Ovide', in Rémy Poignault and Hélène Vial, eds, *Présences ovidiennes* (Clermont-Ferrand, Collection Caesarodunum LII-LIIIbis, 2020), 485–519

Le Congrès de Cythère (septième édition), et Le Jugement de l'amour sur le Congrès (Pisa and Paris: Maradan 1789)

Conihout, Isabelle de, and Pascal Ract-Madoux, 'Ni Grolier, ni Mahieu: Laubespine', *Bulletin du Bibliophile*, 1 (2004), 63–88

Cooley, M. G. L., and B. W. J. G. Wilson, eds, *The Age of Augustus* (2nd edn; London: London Association of Classical Teachers, 2013)

Cormier, Jacques, 'La Survie littéraire d'Ovide', *Cahiers de l'AIEF*, 58 (2006), 251–75

Corneille, Thomas, *Pièces choisies d'Ovide* (Paris: G. de Luynes, 1670)

Cosnay, Marie, *Comment on expulse—responsabilités en miettes* (Bellecombe-en-Bauges: Éditions du croquant, 2011)

Cosnay, Marie, *Des Métamorphoses* (Chambon-sur-Lignon: Cheyne, 2012)

Cosnay, Marie, Interview with Fiona Cox, *Practitioners' Voices in Classical Reception Studies*, 4 (2013) [special issue: *Contemporary Women Writers*]

Cosnay, Marie, *Les Métamorphoses* (Paris: L'Ogre, 2017)

Cox, Fiona, 'Ovid on the Channel Islands: The Exile of Victor Hugo', in Jennifer Ingleheart, ed., *Exile after Ovid: Two Thousand Years of Solitude* (Oxford : Oxford University Press, 2011), 173–88

Cox, Fiona, 'Women's Education and the Classics', in William Brockliss, J. Gnoza, and E. Archibald, eds, *Learning Greek and Latin from Antiquity to the Present* (Cambridge: Cambridge University Press: 2015), 156–65

Cox, Fiona, *Ovid's Presence in Contemporary Women's Writing: Strange Monsters* (Oxford: Oxford University Press, 2018)

Cox, Fiona, 'An Amazon in the Renaissance: Mlle de Gournay's Translation of Virgil, *Aeneid* 2', in Susanna Braund and Zara Martirosova Torlone, eds, *Virgil and his Translators* (Oxford: Oxford University Press, 2018), 97–106

Cox, Fiona, and Elena Theodorakopoulos, eds, 'Translation, Transgression and Transformation: Contemporary Women Authors and Classical Reception', *Classical Receptions Journal*, 4/2 (2012) [special issue]

Cox, Fiona, and Elena Theodorakopoulos, 'Female Voices: the Democratic Turn in Ali Smith's Classical Reception', in S. J. Harrison and Lorna Hardwick, eds, *A Democratic Turn?: Classics in the Modern World* (Oxford: Oxford University Press, 2014), 263–75

Crecelius, Kathryn J., *Family Romances: George Sand's Early Novels* (Bloomington: Indiana University Press, 1987)

Crenne, Hélisenne de, *Les Quatre Premiers Livres des Eneydes* (1541)

Crenne, Hélisenne de, Les Epistres familieres et invectives, ed. Jerry C. Nash (Paris: Champion, 1996)

BIBLIOGRAPHY   279

Cuers de Cogolin, J., *L'Art d'aimer et le* Remède d'amour, *traduction d'Ovide* (Amsterdam: 1751)

Curran, Leo, 'Rape and Rape Victims in Ovid's Metamorphoses, *Arethusa*, 11 (1978), 213–41

Dangel, Jacqueline, 'Réécriture topique en réception polyphonique: Sapho lyrique revisitée par Ovide élégiaque (Héroïde XV)', *Latomus*, 67 (2008), 114–29

Dante, *La Comedia di Dante Alleghieri* (Foligno: Johann Numeister and Evangelista Angelini da Trevi, 1472)

Darrieussecq, Marie, *Truismes* (Paris: POL, 1996)

Darrieussecq, Marie, *Tristes pontiques* (Paris: POL, 2008)

Da Silva, Jill, 'Ecocriticism and Myth: The Case of Erysichthon,' *Interdisciplinary Studies in Literature and Environment*, 15/2 (2008), 103–16

Deimier, Pierre, *Lettres amoureuses non moins pleines de belles conceptions que de beaux discours* (Paris: Sevestre, 1612)

DeJean, Joan, *Fictions of Sappho: 1546–1937* (Chicago: University of Chicago Press, 1987)

DeJean, Joan, *Ancients against Moderns: Culture Wars and the Making of a Fin de Siècle* (Chicago: University of Chicago Press, 1997)

Delcroix, Maurice, ed., *Marguerite Yourcenar, Portrait d'une voix, Vingt-trois entretiens (1952–1987)* (Paris: Gallimard, 2002)

Delon, Michel, 'Les *Lettres de Julie à Ovide* (1753): de l'implicite à l'amplification', conference given at the Université de Rouen-Normandie, 25 April 2017 (seminar by S. Provini), https://webtv.univ-rouen.fr/videos/les-lettres-de-julie-a-ovide-1753-de-limplicite-a-lamplification-par-michel-delon-professeur-emerite-a-paris-sorbonne_50849/

Demetriou, Tania, and Rowan Tomlinson, eds, *The Culture of Translation in Early Modern England and France, 1500–1660* (Basingstoke: Palgrave Macmillan, 2015)

Denis, Delphine, *Le Parnasse galant: institution d'une catégorie littéraire au XVII siècle* (Paris: Champion, 2001)

Desmond, Marilynn, *Ovid's Art and the Wife of Bath: The Ethics of Erotic Violence* (Ithaca: Cornelle University Press, 2006)

Desmond, Marilynn, 'When Dido Reads Vergil: Gender and Intertextuality in Ovid's *Heroides* 7', *Helios*, 20 (1993), 56–68

Desmond, Marilynn, and Pamela Sheingorn, 'Queering Ovidian Myth: Bestiality and Desire in Christine de Pizan's Epistre Othea', in Glenn Burger and Steven Kruger, eds, *Queering the Middle Ages* (Minneapolis: University of Minnesota Press: 2001), 3–27

Desportes, Philippe, *Diverses amours et autres œuvres meslées*, ed. Victor E. Graham (Geneva: Droz, 1963)

Des Roches, Madeleine, and Catherine des Roches, *Les Œuvres*, ed. Anne R. Larsen (Geneva: Droz, 1993)

Des Roches, Madeleine, and Catherine des Roches, *Les Secondes Œuvres*, ed. Anne R. Larsen (Geneva: Droz, 1998)

Des Roches, Madeleine, and Catherine des Roches, *Les Missives*, ed. Anne R. Larsen (Geneva: Droz, 1999)

DeVos, Jessica, 'Ronsard's Poetic Progeny: Fashioning Madeleine de l'Aubespine's Poetic Persona', *Yale French Studies*, 134 (2018), 126–44

Dickie, Matthew W., 'Ovid, *Metamorphoses* 2.760–64', *The American Journal of Philology*, 96 (1975), 378–90

Didier, Béatrice, *Béatrice Didier présente 'Corinne ou l'Italie' de Madame de Staël* (Paris: Gallimard, 1999)

280   BIBLIOGRAPHY

Diller, George E., *Les Dames des Roches: étude sur la vie littéraire à Poitiers dans la deuxième moitié du XVIe siècle* (Paris: Droz, 1936)

Dimmick, Jeremy, 'Ovid in the Middle Ages', in Philip Hardie, ed., *The Cambridge Companion to Ovid* (Cambridge: Cambridge University Press, 2002), 264–86

Dorat, Claude-Joseph, *Julie, fille d'Auguste à Ovide, Héroïde* (The Hague, 1759)

Doré, Pascale, *Yourcenar ou le féminin insoutenable* (Droz: Geneva, 1999)

Downie, Louise, ed., *Don't Kiss Me: The Art of Claude Cahun and Marcel Moore* (London: Tate Publishing, 2006; New York: Aperture, 2006)

Doy, Gen, *Claude Cahun: A Sensual Politics of Photography* (London: I. B. Tauris, 2007)

Du Bellay, Joachim, *Les Antiquitéz de Rome et Les Regrets* (Geneva: Droz, 1960)

La Deffence et illustration de la langue françoyse, ed. Henri Chamard (1948; Paris: Société des Textes Français Modernes, 2000)

Du Bosc, Jacques, *L'Honnête Femme* (Paris: Billaine, 1623)

Dufour-Maître, Myriam, 'Les "Antipathies": académies des dames savantes et ruelles des précieuses, un discours polémique dans l'espace des Belles-Lettres', in Claudine Poulouin and Jean-Claude Arnould, eds, *Bonnes lettres/Belles lettres* (Paris: H. Champion, 2006), 271–92

Dufour-Maître, Myriam, 'Les "Belles" et les Belles-Lettres: femmes, instances du féminin et nouvelles configurations du savoir', in John D. Lyons and Cara Welch, eds, *Le Savoir au XVIIe siècle* (Tübingen: Gunter Narr, 2003), 35–64

Du Perron, and others, *Les Epîtres d'Ovide* (Paris: 1616)

Duveyrier, Charles, 'La Ville nouvelle, ou le Paris des saints-simoniens', in *Paris ou le livre des cent-et-un*, 12 vols (Paris: Ladvocat, 1832), viii, 315–44

Edwards, Catharine, *Writing Rome: A Textual Approach to the City* (Cambridge: Cambridge University Press, 1996)

Eugenides, Jeffrey, *Middlesex* (Toronto: Random House of Canada, 2002)

Eliot, T. S, *The Waste Land*, in *The Complete Poems and Plays 1909–1950* (New York: Harcourt, Brace and Co., 1952), 37–56

Elisei, Chiara, 'Sappho as a Pupil of the *praeceptor amoris* and Sappho as *magistra amoris*: Some Lessons of the *Ars amatoria* Anticipated in *Heroides* 15', in Thea S. Thorsen and Stephen Harrison, eds, *Roman Receptions of Sappho* (Oxford: Oxford University Press, 2019), 227–48

Elkin, Lauren, 'Reading Claude Cahun', *The Quarterly Conversation*, 13 (2008), http://quarterlyconversation.com/claude-cahun-disavowals>

Euripides, *The Bacchae and Other Plays*, trans. John Davie, with an introduction and notes by Richard Rutherford (London: Penguin Classics, 2005)

Fabre-Serris, Jacqueline, 'Anne Dacier (1681), Renée Vivien (1903): Or What Does It Mean for a Woman to Translate Sappho?', in Rosie Wyles and Edith Hall, eds, *Women Classical Scholars: Unsealing the Fountain from the Renaissance to Jacqueline de Romilly* (Oxford: Oxford University Press, 2016), 78–103

Fabre-Serris, Jacqueline, 'Sulpicia, Gallus et les élégiaques. Propositions de lecture de l'épigramme 3.13', *EuGeStA*, 7 (2017), 115–39

Feldherr, Andrew, 'Metamorphosis in the *Metamorphoses*', in Philip Hardie, ed., *The Cambridge Companion to Ovid* (Cambridge: Cambridge University Press, 2002), 163–79

Feldherr, Andrew, *Playing Gods: Ovid's Metamorphoses and the Politics of Fiction* (Princeton: Princeton University Press, 2010)

Felman, Shoshana, 'Women and Madness: The Critical Fallacy', *Diactrics*, 5 (1975), 2–10

Fièvre, Paul, 'Racine en querelles', *Littératures classiques*, 81/2 (2013), 199–210

BIBLIOGRAPHY   281

Filaire, Marc-Jean, ed., *Marguerite Yourcenar et la culture du masculin* (Nîmes: Lucie éditions, 2011)

Flotow, Luise von, and Hala Kamal, eds, *The Routledge Handbook of Translation, Feminism and Gender* (London: Routledge, 2020)

Fontaine, Charles, *Les Epistres d'Ovide* (Lyon: Rollet, 1552)

Fontaine, Charles, *Les XXI épitres d'Ovide* (Paris: H. de Marnef et la Veufve Guillaume Cavellat, 1580)

Françon, Marcel, 'Un motif de la poésie amoureuse au XVIᵉ siècle', *PMLA*, 56 (1941), 307–36

Fränkel, Hermann, *Ovid: A Poet between Two Worlds* (Berkeley: University of California, 1969)

Frantuono, Lee, 'Introduction', Ovid, *Metamorphoses X*, ed. Lee Frantantuono (London: Bloomsbury, 2014), 1–17

Freccero, Carla, 'Ovidian Subjectivities in Early Modern Lyric: Identification and Desire in Petrarch and Louise Labé', in Goran V. Stanivukovic, ed., *Ovid and the Renaissance Body* (Toronto: University of Toronto Press, 2001), 21–37

Freud, Sigmund, *Totem and Taboo*, trans. Abraham A. Brill (New York: Cosimo, 2009)

Fulkerson, Laurel, *The Ovidian Heroine as Author: Reading, Writing, and Community in the* Heroides (Cambridge: Cambridge University Press, 2005)

Gaensbauer, Deborah B., 'Metamorphosis and Migration in Marie NDiaye's *Trois femmes puissantes*', *Studies in Twentieth and Twenty-First Century Literature*, 38/1 (2014), Article 5

Gaillard, Jacques, 'L'Imaginaire ludique ovidien dans les *Héroïdes*', in Joël Thomas, ed., *Les Imaginaires des Latins. Actes du Colloque international de Perpignan (12-13-14 novembre 1991)* (Perpignan: Presses Universitaires de Perpignan, 1992), 101–12

Galand Willemen, Perrine, 'Les jardins de Chanteloup (Cantilupum, 1587): promenade poétique et itinéraire moral sous la plume d'une grande dame du XVIe siècle, Madeleine de Villeroy', in Lucia Bertolini, Donatella Coppini, and Clementina Marsico, eds, *Nel cantiere degli umanisti: per Mariangela Regoliosi* (Florence: Edizione Polistampa, 2014), 533–54

Garval, Michael, '*A Dream of Stone': Fame, Vision, and Monumentality in Nineteenth-Century French Literary Culture* (Newark: University of Delaware Press, 2004)

Gertz, SunHee Kim, *Echoes and Reflections: Memory and Memorials in Ovid and Marie de France* (Leiden: Brill, 2003)

Ghillebaert, Françoise, *Disguise in George Sand's Novels* (New York: Peter Lang, 2009)

Gillespie, Stuart, and Robert Cummings, 'A Bibliography of Ovidian Translations and Imitations in English', *Translation and Literature*, 13 (2004), 207–18

Gladwin, Derek, *Rewriting Our Stories: Education, Empowerment and Well-being* (Cork: Atrium, 2021)

Goff, Barbara, 'Antigone's Boat: The Colonial and the Postcolonial in *Tegonni: An African Antigone* by Femi Osofisan,' in Lorna Hardwick and Carol Gillespie, eds, *Classics in Postcolonial Worlds* (Oxford: Oxford University Press, 2007), 40–53

Goldhammer, Arthur, review of J. Kristeva, *Les Samouraïs*, in *French Politics and Society*, 8/4 (1990), 102–7

Gordon, Pamela, 'The Lover's Voice in *Heroides* 15: Or, Why Is Sappho a Man?', in Judith Hallett and Marilyn B. Skinner, eds, *Roman Sexualities* (Princeton: Princeton University Press, 1997), 274–91

Goslar, Michèle, 'Marguerite Yourcenar, une femme qui s'est voulue "hors-sexe" et dont l'écriture trahit la femme', in *Marguerite Yourcenar. La femme, les femmes, une écriture-femme? Actes du colloque international de Baeza (Jaén) (19–23 novembre 2002)* (Clermont-Ferrand: Société Internationale d'Études Yourcenariennes, 2005), 55–65

282 BIBLIOGRAPHY

Gournay, Marie de, *Versions de quelques pièces de Virgile, Tacite et Salluste* (Paris: Fleury Bourriquant, 1619)

Gournay, Marie de, *Eschantillons de Virgile* (Paris: 1620)

Gournay, Marie de, 'Epistre de Laodamia à Protesilaus', in Jean-Claude Arnould, Évelyne Berriot, Claude Blum, Anna Lia Franchetti, Marie-Claire Thomine, and Valerie Worth-Stylianou, eds, *Œuvres Complètes*, 2 vols (Paris: Champion, 2002), ii, 1455–64

Gournay, Marie de, 'Envoy de l'Epistre de Laodamie, version d'Ovide', in Jean-Claude Arnould, Évelyne Berriot, Claude Blum, Anna Lia Franchetti, Marie-Claire Thomine, and Valerie Worth-Stylianou, eds, *Œuvres Complètes*, 2 vols (Paris: Champion, 2002), ii, 1828–9

Gowers, Emily, 'Lucan's (G)natal Poem: Statius' *Silvae* 2.7, the *Culex*, and the Aesthetics of Miniaturization', *Classical Antiquity*, 40 (2021), 45–75

Graf, Fritz, 'Myth in Ovid', in Philip Hardie, ed., *The Cambridge Companion to Ovid* (Cambridge: Cambridge University Press, 2002), 108–21

Le Grand Olympe des Histoires Poétiques du prince de poésie Ovide Naso en sa Métamorphose (Lyons: de Harsy, 1532)

Greaney, Michael, 'Violence and the Sacred in the Fiction of Julia Kristeva', *Theology and Sexuality*, 14 (2008), 293–304

Green, Karen, 'Women's Writing and the Early Modern Genre Wars', *Hypatia*, 28 (2013), 499–515

Greene, Ellen, 'Sexual Politics in Ovid's *Amores* 3.4, 3.8 and 3.12', *Classical Philology*, 4 (1994), 344–50

Grudé, François, sieur de La Croix du Maine, *Premier volume de la bibliotheque du Sieur de la Croix-du Maine* (Paris: A. l'Angellier, 1584)

Guberman, Ross Mitchell, ed., *Julia Kristeva Interviews* (Columbia: Columbia University Press, 1996), 211–25

Guillou, Edouard, *Versailles, ou le palais du soleil* (Paris: Plon, 1963)

Habert, François, *Les Epîtres héroïdes, pour servir d'exemple aux Chrétiens* (Paris: M. Fezandet, 1560)

Habert, François, *Les Epîtres héroïdes, très salutaires pour servir d'exemple à toute âme fidèle* (Paris: Fezandet, 1550)

Habert, François, *Les Quinze Livres de la Métamorphose d'Ovide interprétés en rime française, selon la phrase latine* (Paris: M. Fezandat et E. Groulleau, 1557)

Habert, François, *Six Livres de la Métamorphose d'Ovide, traduits selon la phrase Latine en rime française* (Paris: Fezandat, 1549)

Habert, François, *Les Trois Premiers Livres de la Métamorphose d'Ovide, traduits en vers français; le premier et second par C. L. Marot, le tiers par B. Aneau* (Lyons: Rouile, 1556)

Hall, Edith, 'Subjects, Selves, Survivors', *Helios*, 34/2 (2007), 125–59

Hallett, Judith, 'Catullan Voices in *Heroides* 15: How Sappho Became a Man', *Dictynna*, 2 (2005), 1–15

Hallett, Judith, 'Ovid's Sappho and Roman Women Poets', *Dictynna*, 6 (2009), 1–12

Halperin, David, *One Hundred Years of Homosexuality: and Other Essays on Greek Love* (New York: Routledge, 1990)

Hardie, Philip, 'The Speech of Pythagoras in Ovid *Metamorphoses* 15: Empedoclean epos', *Classical Quarterly*, 45 (1995), 204–14

Hardie, Philip, *Ovid's Poetics of Illusion* (Cambridge: Cambridge University Press, 2002)

Hardie, Philip, 'The Word Personified: Fame and Envy in Virgil, Ovid, Spenser', *Materiali e discussioni per l'annalisi dei testi classici*, 61 (2009), 101–15

Hardie, Philip, 'Wordsworth's Translation of *Aeneid* 1–3 and the Earlier Tradition of English Translations of Virgil', in Susanna Braund and Zara Martirosova Torlone, ed., *Virgil and his Translators* (Oxford: Oxford University Press, 2018), 318–30

Hardwick, Lorna, 'Introduction', in Lorna Hardwick and Carol Gillespie, eds, *Classics in Post-Colonial Worlds* (Oxford: Oxford University Press, 2007), 1–11

Harkness, Nigel, '"Ce marbre qui me monte jusqu'aux genoux": pétrification, mimésis et le mythe de Pygmalion dans *Lélia* (1833 et 1839)', in Brigitte Diaz and Isabelle Hoog Naginski, eds, *George Sand: pratiques et imaginaires de l'écriture* (Caen: Presses Universitaires de Caen, 2006), 161–71

Harkness, Nigel, *Men of their Words: The Poetics of Masculinity in George Sand's Fiction* (Oxford: Legenda, 2007)

Harris, Steven, 'Coup d'oeil', *Oxford Art Journal*, 24/1 (2001), 91–111

Harvey, Elizabeth D., 'Ventriloquizing Sappho: Ovid, Donne, and the Erotics of the Feminine Voice', *Criticism*, 31 (1989), 115–38

Hauser, Emily, 'When Classics Gets Creative: from Research to Practice', *Transactions of the American Philological Association*, 149/2 (2019), 163–77

Haynes, Natalie, interview on 'Women's Hour', BBC Radio Four, 2 May 2019

Heavey, Katherine, 'Aphra Behn's *Oenone to Paris*: Ovidian Paraphrase by Women Writers', *Translation and Literature*, 23 (2014), 303–20

Heinze, Theodor, ed., *Der XII. Heroidenbrief: Medea an Jason. Mit einer Beilage: Die Fragmente der Tragödie Medea* (Leiden: Brill, 1997)

Herdman, Emma, 'Folie and Salmacis: Labé's Re-writing of Ovid', *Modern Language Review*, 108 (2013), 782–801

L'Héritier, Marie-Jeanne, 'Le Parnasse reconnoissant ou Le triomphe de Madame Des-Houlières. A Mademoiselle de Scuderi', *Œuvres mêlées de Mlle L'H**** (1694; Paris: Guignard, 1696), 404–24

L'Héritier, Marie-Jeanne, *L'Apothéose de Mademoiselle de Scudéry* (Paris: Moreau, 1702)

L'Héritier, Marie-Jeanne, *Les Epîtres héroïques d'Ovide traduites en vers françois* (Paris: Brunet fils, 1732)

Hesse, Carla, *The Other Enlightenment: How French Women Became Modern* (Princeton: Princeton University Press, 2001)

Hexter, R. J., 'The Poetry of Ovid's Exile', in William J. Anderson, ed., *Ovid: The Classical Heritage* (Routledge, 1995), 36–60

Hiddleston, Janet, *George Sand and Autobiography* (Oxford: Legenda, 1999)

Hinds, Stephen, 'Black-Sea Latin, Du Bellay and the Barbarian Turn', in Jennifer Ingleheart, ed., *Two Thousand Years of Solitude: Exile after Ovid* (Oxford: Oxford University Press, 2011), 59–83

Hine, Ellen M., *Constance de Salm, her Influence and her Circle in the Aftermath of the French Revolution: 'A Mind of No Common Order'* (New York: Peter Lang, 2012)

Hock, Jessie, 'Voluptuous Style: Lucretius, Rhetoric, and Reception in Montaigne's "Sur des vers de Virgile"', *Modern Philology*, 118/4 (2021), 492–514

Hoffman, Michael, and James Lasdun, eds, *After Ovid: New Metamorphoses* (London: Faber and Faber, 1994)

Hollis, A. S., 'The *Ars amatoria* and *Remedia amoris*', in J. W. Binns, ed., *Ovid* (London & Boston: Routledge & Kegan Paul, 1973), 84–115

Hornblower, Simon, Antony Spawforth, and Esther Eidinow, eds, *The Oxford Classical Dictionary* (Oxford: Oxford University Press, 2012)

Hosington, Brenda M., 'Introduction: Translation and Print Culture in Early Modern Europe', *Renaissance Studies*, 29/1 (2015), 5–18

284 BIBLIOGRAPHY

Huber-Rebenich, Gerlinde, and Sabine Lütkemeyer, 'Non Ovidian 'Immigrants' in Printed Illustration Cycles of the *Metamorphoses*, in Karl A. E. Enenkel and Jan L. de Jong, eds, *Re-inventing Ovid's* Metamorphoses: *Pictorial and Literary Transformations in Various Media, 1400–1800* (Leiden: Brill, 2020), 9–34

Hughes, Ted, *Tales from Ovid* (London: Faber and Faber, 1997)

Hult, David, 'The Roman de la rose, Christine de Pizan and the querelle des femmes', in C. Dinshaw and D. Wallace, eds, *The Cambridge Companion to Women Writers: Medieval Women* (Cambridge: Cambridge University Press, 2003), 184–94

Hurst, Isobel, *Victorian Women Writers and the Classics: The Feminine of Homer* (Oxford: Oxford University Press, 2006)

Hyginus, *C. Hygini Augusti Liberti fabularum liber* (Basel: Joannes Hervagius, 1535)

Hyginus, *Fabulae*, ed. Peter K. Marshall (Munich; Leipzig: K. G. Saur, 2002)

Ingleheart, Jennifer, ed., *Exile after Ovid: Two Thousand Years of Solitude* (Oxford: Oxford University Press, 2011)

Ingleheart, Jennifer, 'Vates Lesbia: Images of Sappho in the Poetry of Ovid', in Thea S. Thorsen and Stephen Harrison, eds, *Roman Receptions of Sappho* (Oxford: Oxford University Press, 2019), 205–26

Jacobson, Howard, *Ovid's Heroides* (Princeton, NJ: Princeton University Press, 1974)

James, Heather, 'Ovid in Renaissance English Literature', in Peter E. Knox, ed., *A Companion to Ovid* (Oxford: Wiley-Blackwell, 2009), 423–41

Jameson, Caroline, 'Ovid in the Sixteenth Century', in J. W. Binns, ed., *Ovid* (London: Routledge, 1973), 210–42

Jenkyns, Richard, 'Review of *Ovid Renewed*, ed. by Charles Martindale', *Review of English Studies*, 41/161 (1990), 152

Jolivet, Jean-Christophe, 'Pleurs héroïques, sourires mythographiques: pathos et érudition ludique dans les Epistulae Heroidum', in M. Trédé and P. Hoffmann, eds, *Le Rire des anciens* (Paris: Presses de l'École Normale Supérieure, 1998)

Jolivet, Jean-Christophe, 'La Dispute d'Ovide et des Alexandrins ou Briséis γραμματικωτάτη: trois problèmes homériques et une *quaestio ovidiana* dans la troisième *Héroïde*', in Jacqueline Fabre-Serris and Alain Deremetz, eds, *Élégie et épopée dans la poésie ovidienne* (Héroïdes *et* Amours). *En hommage à Simone Viarre* (Villeneuve d'Ascq: Université Charles-de-Gaulle Lille 3, 1999), 15–39

Jolivet, Jean-Christophe, *Allusion et fiction épistolaire dans les Héroïdes. Recherches sur l'intertextualité ovidienne* (Rome: Collection de l'École Française de Rome, 2001)

Jones, Ann Rosalind, 'Contentious Readings: Urban Humanism and Gender Difference in *La Puce de Madame Des-Roches* (1582)', *Renaissance Quarterly*, 8 (1995), 109–27

Jones, Anny Brooksbank, 'Kristeva and her Old Man', *Textual Practice*, 7 (1993), 1–12

Jordan, Shirley, *Marie Ndiaye: Inhospitable Fictions* (Oxford: Legenda, 2016)

Journal général de la littérature française, 36 (1833)

Kahn, Madeleine, *Why Are We Reading Ovid's Handbook on Rape?* (London: Routledge, 2005)

Kane, Benito Jaro, *Betray the Night: A Novel about Ovid* (Mundelein, IL: Bolchazy-Carducci Publishers, 2009)

Keith, A. M., *The Play of Fictions: Studies in Ovid's 'Metamorphoses' Book 2* (Ann Arbor, MI: University of Michigan Press, 1992)

Kennedy, Duncan F., 'The Epistolary Mode and the First of Ovid's *Heroides*', *The Classical Quarterly*, 34 (1984), 413–22

Kennedy, Duncan F., 'A sense of place: Rome, history and empire revisited', in Catharine Edwards, ed., *Roman Presences: Receptions of Rome in European Culture 1789–1945* (Cambridge: Cambridge University Press, 1999), 19–34

BIBLIOGRAPHY   285

Kennedy, Duncan F., 'Epistolarity: The Heroides', in Philip Hardie, ed., *The Cambridge Companion to Ovid* (Cambridge: Cambridge University Press, 2002), 217–32

Kennedy, Duncan F., 'Recent Receptions of Ovid', in Philip Hardie, ed., *The Cambridge Companion to Ovid* (Cambridge: Cambridge University Press, 2002), 320–35

Kenney, E. J., *Apuleius: Cupid & Psyche* (Cambridge: Cambridge University Press, 1990)

Kenny, Neil, *Born to Write: Literary Families and Social Hierarchy in Early Modern France* (Oxford: Oxford University Press, 2020)

Kline, Katy, 'In or Out of the Picture: Claude Cahun and Cindy Sherman', in Whitney Chadwick, ed., *Mirror Images: The Women, Surrealism and Self-Representation* (Cambridge: Massachusetts Institute of Technology Press, 1998), 66–81

Klosowska, Anna, ed., *Madeleine de l'Aubespine: Selected Poems and Translations* (Chicago: University of Chicago Press, 2007)

Anna Klosowska, 'Erotica and Women in Early Modern France: Madeleine de l'Aubespine's Queer Poems', *Journal of the History of Sexuality*, 17 (2008), 190–215

Anna Klosowska, 'Madeleine de l'Aubespine: Life, Works, and Auto-Mythography: An Exchange with Ronsard, ca. 1570-80', *French Forum*, 32 (2007), 19–38

Knox, Peter E., ed., *Ovid: Heroides, Select Epistles* (Cambridge: Cambridge University Press, 1995)

Kolocotroni, Vassili, 'A Little Inner Mythology: Kristeva as Novelist', *New Formations*, 21 (1993), 146–57

Krief, Huguette, *La Sapho des Lumières: Mlle de Scudéry, Fontenelle, Gacon, Voltaire, Rousseau, Pesselier, Moutonnet de Clairefort, Barthélemy, Lantier, Mme de Staël* (Saint-Étienne: Publications de l'Université de Saint-Étienne, 2006)

Kristeva, Julia, 'Le Texte clos', *Langages*, 12 (1968), 103–25

Kristeva, Julia, *Revolution in Poetic Language*, trans. Margaret Waller (New York: Columbia University Press, 1984)

Kristeva, Julia, *Les Samouraïs* (Paris: Fayard, 1990)

Kristeva, Julia, *Le Vieil Homme et les loups* (Paris: Fayard, 1991)

Kristeva, Julia, *Possessions* (Paris: Fayard, 1996)

Kristeva, Julia, 'Un père est battu à mort', *The Dead Father*, international symposium, Columbia University, 2006, http://www.kristeva.fr/pere.html

Kristeva, Julia, 'A l'Est, l'Europe en souffrance', *Libération* (19 November 2009), http://www.kristeva.fr/a-l-est.html

Kristeva, Julia, 'Comme un polar métaphysique', 2009, http://www.kristeva.fr/comme-un-polar-metaphysique.html

Kristeva, Julia, *Visions capitales: Arts et rituels de la décapitation* (Paris: Fayard, 2013)

Kristeva, Julia, *Je me voyage: Mémoires: Entretiens avec Samuel Dock* (Paris: Fayard, 2016)

Kristeva, Julia, and Vassilli Kolocotroni, 'Avant-Garde Practice', in Ross Mitchell Guberman, ed., *Julia Kristeva Interviews* (New York: Columbia University Press, 1996) 211–25. First published in *Textual Practice*, 5 (1991), 157–70

Kristeva, Julia, and Bernard Sichère, 'Roman noir et temps present', *L'infini*, 37 (1992), 75–86

Kristeva, Julia, and Margaret Waller, 'Intertextuality and Literary Interpretations', in Ross Mitchell Guberman, ed., *Julia Kristeva Interviews* (New York: Columbia University Press, 1996), 188–203

Kuizenga, Donna, 'L'Arc de triomphe des dames: Héroïsme dans *Les Femmes illustres* de Madeleine et Georges de Scudéry', in Alain Niderst, ed., *Les Trois Scudéry* (Paris: Klincksieck, 1993), 301–10

Kurmann, Alexandra, *Intertextual Weaving in the Work of Linda Lê: Imagining the Ideal Reader* (Washington, DC: Lexington Books, 2016)

286 BIBLIOGRAPHY

Labé, Louise, *Œuvres complètes*, ed. François Rigolot (Paris: Flammarion, 1986; repr. 2004)

Lacan, Jacques, *Ecrits* (Paris: Editions du Seuil, 1966)

Lachmann, K., 'De Ovidii *Epistulis*', in J. Vahlen, ed., *Kleinere Schriften zur Klassischen Philologie von Karl Lachmann* (Berlin: Reimer, 1974)

Laforgue, Pierre, 'Structure et fonction du mythe d'Orphée dans "Consuelo" de George Sand', *Revue d'histoire littéraire de la France*, 84/1 (1984), 53–66

Laporte, Dominique, 'Deux figures emblématiques de l'engagement sandien: Corambé et Gribouille (*Histoire du véritable Gribouille*, 1850)', in Simone Bernard-Griffiths and José-Luis Diaz, eds, *Lire 'Histoire de ma vie' de George Sand* (Clermont-Ferrand: Presses universitaires Blaise Pascal, 2006), 327–33

Larsen, Anne R., 'On Reading *La Puce de Madame Des-Roches*: Catherine des Roches's *Responces* (1583)', *Renaissance and Reformation*, 22 (1998), 63–75

Latimer, Tirza True, 'Looking Like a Lesbian: Portraiture and Sexual Identity in 1920s Paris', in Whitney Chadwick and Tirza True Latimer, eds, *The Modern Woman Revisited: Paris between the Wars* (New Brunswick: Rutgers University Press, 2003), 127–44

Latimer, Tirza True, *Women Together/Women Apart: Portraits of Lesbian Paris* (New Brunswick: Rutgers University Press, 2005)

Lavaud, Jacques, *Un poète de cour au temps des derniers Valois: Philippe Desportes* (Paris: Droz, 1936)

Law, Sin Yan Hedy, 'Composing *Citoyennes* through *Sapho*', *The Opera Quarterly*, 32/1 (2017), 5–28

Lê, Linda, *Les Trois Parques* (Paris: Christian Bourgois, 1997)

Lê, Linda, *Par ailleurs (exils)* (Paris: Christian Bourgois éditeur, 2014)

Lê, Linda, *The Three Fates*, trans. Mark Polizzoti (Cambridge, MA: New Directions, 2010)

Ledesma Pedraz, Manuela, and Rémy Poignault, eds, *Marguerite Yourcenar. La femme, les femmes, une écriture-femme? Actes du colloque international de Baeza (Jaén) (19–23 novembre 2002)* (Clermont-Ferrand: Société Internationale d'Études Yourcenariennes, 2005)

Leibacher, Lise, 'Speculum de l'autre femme: Les Avatars d'Iphis et Ianthe (Ovide) au XVII sièle', *Papers on Seventeenth-Century French Literature*, 30 (2003), 367–76

Le Moyne, Pierre, *Galerie des femmes fortes* (Paris: Compagnie des libraires du Palais, 1663)

Leperlier, François, *Claude Cahun, l'écart et la métamorphose* (Paris: Jean-Michel Place, 1992)

Letexier, Gérard, 'Les Exilés de la Cour d'Auguste: Mme de Villedieu entre tradition et modernité', *Littératures Classiques*, 61 (2006), 71–87

Lettres de Julie à Ovide et d'Ovide à Julie, précédées d'une notice sur la vie de ce poète et suivies d'une Epître en vers de Julie à Ovide (Paris: Delaunay, 1809)

Letzter, Jacqueline, 'Making a Spectacle of Oneself: French Revolutionary Opera by Women Author(s)', *Cambridge Opera Journal*, 11 (1999), 215–32

Leuwers, D., 'Feux et contre-feux', *Sud, Revue littéraire bimestrielle* (1990), 247–54 [special issue: *Marguerite Yourcenar, une écriture de la mémoire*]

Lewis, Charlton D., and Charles Short, *A Latin Dictionary* (Oxford: Clarendon Press, 1879)

Lewis, Lindam, *Germaine de Staël, George Sand, and the Victorian Woman Artist* (Columbia: University of Missouri Press, 2003)

Lezay-Marnésia, Claude-François-Adrien, *Plan de lecture pour une jeune dame, seconde édition augmentée d'un Supplément et de divers morceaux de Littérature et de Morale* (Lausanne: Fischer and Vincent; Paris: Louis, 1800)

BIBLIOGRAPHY 287

Lezay-Marnésia, Claude-François-Adrien, *Lettres écrites des rives de l'Ohio*, ed. Benjamin Hoffmann (Paris: Garnier, 2019)

Lindheim, Sara H., *Mail and Female: Epistolary Narrative and Desire in Ovid's* Heroides (Madison: Wisconsin University Press, 2003)

Lipking, Lawrence, *Abandoned Women and Poetic Tradition* (Chicago: University of Chicago Press, 1988)

Lippard, R. Lucy, 'Scattering Selves', in Shelley Rice, ed., *Inverted Odysseys: Claude Cahun, Maya Deren, Cindy Sherman* (Cambridge, MA: Massachusetts Institute of Technology Press, 1999), 27–42

Liveley, Genevieve, 'Surfing the Third Wave? Postfeminism and the Hermeneutics of Reception', in Charles Martindale and Richard F. Thomas, eds., *Classics and the Uses of Reception* (London: Wiley, 2006), 55–66

Loscalzo, Donato, *Saffo, la hetaira* (Pisa and Rome: Fabrizio Serra editore, 2019)

Loubère, Stéphanie, *L'Art d'Aimer au siècle des lumières* (Oxford: SVEC, 2007)

Loucif, Sabine, 'Le fantastique dans Les Trois Parques de Linda Lê', in Margaret-Anne Hutton, ed., *Redefining the Real: The Fantastic in Contemporary French and Francophone Women's Writing* (Oxford. Bern. Berlin: Peter Lang, 2009), 115–127

Loyer, Pierre Le, *Les Œuvres et mélanges poétiques de Pierre Le Loyer* (Paris: J. Poupy, 1579)

Lukacher, Maryline, *Maternal Fictions: Stendhal, Sand, Rachilde, Bataille* (Durham, NC: Duke University Press, 1994)

Lusty, Natalya, *Surrealism, Feminism and Psychoanalysis* (London: Ashgate Publishing, 2007)

Lynch, Tosca, and Rocconi, E., eds, *A Companion to Ancient Greek and Roman Music* (Chichester: Wiley-Blackwell, 2020)

Lyne, R. O. A. M, 'Love and Death: Laodamia and Protesilaus in Catullus, Propertius, and Others', *The Classical Quarterly*, 48 (1998), 200–12

McCall, Anne, 'Land Use and Property Values: The Commercial Development of Space in George Sand's *Narcisse*', *George Sand Studies*, 20 (2001), 83–101

McCallum, Sarah, '*Ego sum pastor*: Pastoral Transformations in the Tale of Mercury and Battus (Ov. *Met.* 2.676–707)', *The Classical Outlook*, 92 (2017), 29–34

Machiavelli, Niccolò, *The Prince: A Revised Translation, Backgrounds, Interpretations, Marginalia*, trans. and ed. Robert M. Adams (New York: Norton, 1992)

Mack, Peter, *A History of Renaissance Rhetoric 1380–1620* (Oxford: Oxford University Press, 2011)

Maclean, Ian, *Woman Triumphant: Feminism in French Literature, 1610–1652* (Oxford: Clarendon Press, 1977)

Manutius, Aldus, *Quae in hoc volumine continentur: Ad Marinum Lanudum epistola… Orthographia dictionum graecarum per ordinem literarum; Vita Ovidii ex ipsius operibus; Index fabularum et caeterorum… Ovidii Metamorphoseon libri quindecim* (Venice: A. Manutius, 1502)

Margollé, Maxime, 'Aspects de l'opéra-comique sous la Révolution: L'évolution du goût et du comique aux théâtres Favart et Feydeau entre *Médée* (1797) et *L'Irato* (1801)', PhD thesis, University of Poitiers, 2013

Marolles, Michel de, *Mémoires de Michel de Marolles*, 2 vols (Paris: Sommaville, 1656)

Marolles, Michel de, *Les Epistres Heroides d'Ovide* (Paris: Veuve P. Lamy, 1661)

Marolles, Michel de, *Publii Ovidii Nasonis Tristium libri V cum interpretation gallica et notis. Les Tristes d'Ovide, de la traduction de M.D.M.A.D.V [Michel de Marolles, abbé de Villeloin] avec des remarques* (Paris: L. Billaine, 1661)

288 BIBLIOGRAPHY

Marot, Clément, *Le Premier Livre de la Métamorphose d'Ovide, traduit de Latin en français* (Paris: E. Roffet, 1534)

Marot, Clément, *Le Second Livre de la Métamorphose d'Ovide*, in *Les Œuvres de Clément Marot* (Lyons: E. Dolet, 1543)

Marot, Clément, *Le Second Livre de la Metamorphose d'Ovide*, in Gérard Defaux, ed., *Œuvres poétiques de Clément Marot*, 2 vols (Paris: Bordas, 1993)

Marshall, Sharon, 'The Aeneid and the Illusory Authoress: Truth, Fiction and Feminism in Hélisenne de Crenne's Eneyde', PhD thesis, University of Exeter, 2011

Martignac, Estienne d'Algay de, *Les Œuvres d'Ovide traduction nouvelle avec des remarques, contenant les XXI Epistres d'Ovide*, 9 vols (Lyon: Mollin, 1697)

Martin, Christopher, 'Translating Ovid', in Peter E. Knox, ed., *A Companion to Ovid* (Oxford: Wiley-Blackwell, 2009), 469–84

Martindale, Charles, ed., *Ovid Renewed: Ovidian Influences on Literature and Art from the Middle Ages to the Twentieth Century* (Cambridge: Cambridge University Press, 1988)

Martindale, Charles, ed., *The Cambridge Companion to Virgil* (Cambridge: Cambridge University Press, 1997)

Martindale, Charles, and Lorna Hardwick, 'Reception', in Simon Hornblower, Antony Spawforth, and Esther Eidinow, eds, *Oxford Classical Dictionary* (4th edn; Oxford: Oxford University Press, 2015)

Martini, J. P. A., *Sapho, tragédie en trois actes et en vers, par la C[itoyen]ne Pipelet, mise en musique ... Représentée pour la 1re fois, sur le théâtre des amis de la Patrie rue de Louvois, le 22 frimaire l'an 3e de la République (14 xbre 1794 v. s.) ... gravé par le C[itoye]n Lobry* (Paris: n.p., 1795)

Massac, Raimond de, and Charles de Massac, *Métamorphoses d'Ovide mises en vers français par Raimond et Charles de Massac, père et fils* (Paris: A. l'Angelier, 1603)

[Masson de Pezay], *Lettre d'Ovide à Julie, précédée d'une lettre en prose à M. Diderot* (n.p., 1767)

Mastrangelo Bové, Carol, 'Revolution Has Italian Roots: Kristeva's Fiction and Theory', in Begnino Trigo, ed., *Kristeva's Fiction* (New York: SUNY, 2013), 45–55

Mathias, Manon, *Vision in the Novels of George Sand* (Oxford: Oxford University Press, 2016)

May, Georges, *D'Ovide à Racine* (New Haven: Yale University Press, 1947)

Méziriac, Claude Gaspar Bachet de, *Les Epistres d'Ovide* (La Haye: H. de Sauzet, 1616)

Méziriac, Claude Gaspar Bachet de, *Les Epistres d'Ovide traduites en Vers françois avec des commentaires fort curieux* (Bourg-en-Bresse: J. Tainturier, 1626)

Michel, A., 'Des Héroïdes modernes: *Feux* de Marguerite Yourcenar', in Raymond Chevallier, ed., *Colloque Présence d'Ovide* (Paris: Les Belles Lettres, 1982), 455–60

Miller, John F., 'The Memories of Ovid's Pythagoras', *Mnemosyne*, 47 (1994), 473–87

Miller, John F., and Carole Newlands, eds, *The Handbook to the Reception of Ovid* (Chichester: Wiley and Sons, 2014)

Milnor, Kristina, *Graffiti and the Literary Landscape in Roman Pompeii* (Oxford: Oxford University Press, 2014)

Mittun, Birgitte Huitfeldt, 'Crossing the Borders: An Interview with Julia Kristeva', *Hypatia*, 21 (2006), 164–77

Möller, Melanie, ed., *Gegen/Gewalt/Schreiben. De-Konstruktionen von Geschlechts- und Rollenbildern in der Ovid-Rezeption* (Berlin: De Gruyter, 2020)

Montaigne, Michel de, *Les Essais de Michel de Montaigne, édition nouvelle: enrichie d'annotations en marge, du nom des Autheurs citez, de la version du Latin d'iceux* (Paris: Sevestre, 1617)

BIBLIOGRAPHY 289

Morales, Helen, *Antigone Rising: The Subversive Power of the Ancient Myths* (London: Wildfire, 2020)

Morel, Héloïse, 'Constance-Marie de Théis', 2017,http://siefar.org/dictionnaire/fr/Constance-Marie_de_Théis

Moss, Ann, *Ovid in Renaissance France: A Survey of Latin Editions and Commentaries Printed in France before 1600* (London: Warburg Institute, 1982)

Moss, Ann, *Poetry and Fable: Studies in Mythological Narrative in Sixteenth-Century France* (Cambridge: Cambridge University Press, 1984)

Moss, Ann, *Latin Commentaries on Ovid from the Renaissance* (Signal Mountain, TN: Library of Renaissance Humanism, 1998)

Mulvey, Laura, *Visual and Other Pleasures* (London: Macmillan, 1989)

Murgia, Charles, 'Imitation and Authenticity in Ovid's *Metamorphoses* 1.477 and *Heroides* 15', *American Journal of Philology*, 106 (1984), 456–74

Myers, K. Sara, 'The *Culex*'s Metapoetic Funerary Garden', *The Classical Quarterly*, 70 (2021), 749–55

Naginski, Isabelle Hoog, *George Sand: Writing for her Life* (New Brunswick, NJ: Rutgers University Press, 1991)

Naginski, Isabelle Hoog, *George Sand Mythographe* (Clermont-Ferrand: Presses universitaires Blaise Pascal, 2007)

NDiaye, Marie, *Trois femmes puissantes* (Paris: Folio, 2009)

NDiaye, Marie, *Three Strong Women*, trans. John Fletcher (London: Maclehose Press, 2012)

Néraudau, Jean-Pierre, 'Ovide au château de Versailles, sous Louis XIV', in Raymond Chevallier, ed., *Colloque Présences d'Ovide* (Paris: Belles Lettres, 1982), 323–42

Neva, JoAnn Della, 'Mutare/Mutatus': Pernette Du Guillet's Actaeon Myth and the Silencing of the Poetic Voice', in Michel Guggenheim, ed., *Women in French Literature* (Saratoga: Alma Libri, 1988), 47–55

Newman, Karen, and Jane Tylus, 'Introduction', in Karen Newman and Jane Tylus, eds, *Early Modern Cultures of Translation* (Philadelphia: University of Pennsylvania Press, 2015), 1–24

Newman, Karen, ed. and trans., *Madeleine de Scudéry: The Story of Sappho* (Chicago: University of Chicago Press, 2003)

Norman, Larry F., *The Shock of the Ancient: Literature and History in Early Modern France* (Chicago: University of Chicago Press, 2011)

Olney, James, *Memory and Narrative: The Weave of Life-Writing* (Chicago: University of Chicago Press, 1998)

Ovid, *Ouidii Metamorphosis*, ed. Raphael Regius (Venice: Simon Bevilaqua, 1497)

Ovid, *Epistolae Heroides. Auli Sabini responsiones ad epistolas Ovidii* (Paris: Michel Le Noir, 1499/1500)

Ovid, *Epistolae heroides et Sappho et Ibis* (Lyon: Jean de Vingle for Etienne Gueynard, 1500)

Ovid, *Epistolae Heroides*, trans. Octavian de Saint-Gelais (Paris: Michel Le Noir, 1500)

Ovid, *Epistularum Heroidum Liber: interpretatione & notis illustravit D. Cripinus Helvetius; jussu Christianissimi Regis ad Vsum Serenissimi Delphini* (Paris: Posuel and Rigaud, 1689)

Ovid, *Heroides and Amores*, trans. Grant Showerman, rev. G. P. Goold (1914; Cambridge, MA: Harvard University Press, Loeb Classical Library, 1977, 1986, 1996, 2014)

Ovid, *Metamorphoses*, trans. Frank Justus Miller, rev. G. P. Goold, 2 vols (1916; London and Cambridge, MA: Harvard University Press, Loeb Classical Library, 1977 and 1984)

Ovid, *Tristia; Ex Ponto*, ed. and trans. Arthur Leslie Wheeler and G. P. Goold (1924; Cambridge, MA: Harvard University Press, Loeb Classical Library, 1988; repr. 1996)

290 BIBLIOGRAPHY

Ovid, *The Metamorphoses of Ovid*, trans. and with an introduction by Mary M. Innes (Harmondsworth, Middlesex: Penguin Books, 1955, repr. 1982)

Ovid, *Amores I*, ed. and trans. John Barsby (Oxford: Oxford University Press, 1973, repr. 1995)

Ovid, *Ars amatoria: Book I*, ed. A. S. Hollis (Oxford: Clarendon Press, 1977, repr. 1992)

Ovid, *The Erotic Poems*, trans. Peter Green (London: Penguin, 1982)

Ovid, *The Poems of Exile: Tristia and the Black Sea Letters*, trans. Peter Green (London: Penguin, 1994)

Ovid, *Les Métamorphoses*, trans. Joseph Chamonard (Paris: Flammarion, 1996)

Ovid, *Ovid's 'Metamorphoses' Books 1–5*, ed. William S. Anderson (Norman: University of Oklahoma Press, 1997)

Ovid, *Ars amatoria, Book 3*, ed. Roy Gibson (Cambridge: Cambridge University Press, 2003)

Ovid, *Metamorphoses*, ed. R. J. Tarrant (Oxford: Clarendon Press, 2004)

Ovid, *Metamorphoses*, trans. David Raeburn (London: Penguin, 2004)

Ovid, *Fasti*, trans. Anne and Peter Wiseman (Oxford, Oxford University Press, 2013)

Palmer, Arthur, *P. Ovidi Nasonis Heroides* (Oxford, Clarendon Press, 1898)

Palmer, Arthur, ed., *Ovid: Heroides*, vol. 1, with the Greek translation of Planudes, and a new introduction by Duncan Kennedy (1898; Bristol: Bristol Phoenix Press, 2005)

Pausanius, *Pausanias's Description of Greece*, trans. and with a commentary by J. G. Frazer (London: Macmillan, 1898)

Pausanius, *Description of Greece, Volume 1: Books 1–2 (Attica and Corinth)*, trans. W. H. S. Jones (Cambridge, MA: Harvard University Press, Loeb Classical Library, 1918)

Perazzolo, Paola, 'Un "animal sans pareil" sous la Révolution: la Sapho ambiguë de Constance de Salm', *Revue italienne d'études françaises*, 8 (2018) http://journals.openedition.org/rief/1773

Perrault, Charles, *Parallèle des anciens et des modernes*, 4 vols (Paris: Coignard, 1688–97)

Petrarca, Francesco, *Petrarch's Lyric Poems: The Rime sparse and Other Lyrics*, trans. and ed. Robert M. Durling (Cambridge, MA: Harvard University Press, 1976)

Pilgrim, Robert, *Que me veux-tu?: Claude Cahun's Photomontages* (Croyde, Devon: Majaro Publications, 2012)

Planté, Christine, ed., *George Sand critique 1833–1876* (Tusson: Du Lérot, 2006)

Pliny, *Letters*, trans. William Melmoth, rev. W. M. L. Hutchinson (London: Heinemann, 1915)

Plutarch, *Phocion*, in *Plutarch's Lives*, trans. Bernadotte Perrin (London: Heinemann, 1919)

Poignault, Rémy, *L'Antiquité dans l'œuvre de Marguerite Yourcenar. Littérature, mythe et histoire*, 2 vols (Bruxelles: Latomus, 1995)

Poignault, Rémy, 'Dans le miroir de Sappho. De l'impossibilité d'être femme', *Bulletin de la Société Internationale d'Études Yourcenariennes*, 11 (1993), 21–40

Puche, Océane, 'Les Epîtres héroïques de Marie-Jeanne L'Héritier: traduction et réception d'Ovide au XVIIe siècle', PhD thesis, Université de Lille, 2020

Pure, Michel de, *La Précieuse ou le Mystère de la Ruelle* (1656–1660), ed. Myriam Dufour-Maître (Paris: Champion, 2010)

Quérard, Joseph-Marie, *Les supercheries littéraires dévoilées: Galerie des auteurs apocryphes, supposés, déguisés, plagiés, et des éditeurs infidèles de la littérature française, pendant les quatre derniers siècles* (Paris, 1850), iii

Raymond, Emmanuelle, 'Caius Cornelius Gallus', in Thea S. Thorsen, ed., *The Cambridge Companion to Latin Love Elegy* (Cambridge: Cambridge University Press, 2013), 59–67

BIBLIOGRAPHY   291

Rea, Annabelle, '*Narcisse* ou la réécriture d'un mythe', in Simone Bernard-Griffiths and Marie-Cécile Levet, eds, *Fleurs et jardins dans l'œuvre de George Sand* (Clermont-Ferrand: Presses Universitaires Blaise Pascal, 2006), 231–44

Read, Kirk D., 'Poolside Transformations: Diana and Actaeon Revisited by French Renaissance Women Lyricists', in Anne R. Larsen and Colette H. Wynn, eds, *Renaissance Women Writers: French Texts/American Contexts* (Detroit: Wayne State University Press, 1994), 38–54

Read, Kirk D., 'Touching and Telling: Gendered Variations on a Gynecological Theme', in Kathleen P. Long, ed., *Gender and Scientific Discourse in Early Modern Culture* (Farnham: Ashgate, 2010), 259–77

Reeson, James, *Ovid Heroides 11, 13, & 14: A Commentary* (Leiden: Brill, 2001)

Reid, Martine, 'Post-scriptum: Naomi Schor trente ans après', in Damien Zanone, ed., *George Sand et l'idéal. Une recherche en écriture* (Paris: Honoré Champion, 2017), 449–57

Reid, Martine, *Signer Sand: l'œuvre et le nom* (Paris: Belin, 2003)

Reineke, Martha, 'Not a Country for Old Men: Scapegoats and Sacrifice in Santa Varvara', in Begnino Trigo, ed., *Kristeva's Fiction* (New York: SUNY, 2013), 57–78

Renouard, Nicolas, *Les Métamorphoses d'Ovide avec…quelques epistres d'Ovide* (Paris: Vve. Langelier, 1619)

Revue de Paris, 53 (1833)

Rice, Shelley, ed., *Inverted Odysseys: Claude Cahun, Maya Deren, Cindy Sherman* (Cambridge, MA: Massachusetts Institute of Technology Press, 1999)

Richards, Sylvie, 'A Psychoanalytic Study of the Double in the Novels of George Sand', in Armand E. Singer, Mary W. Singer, and Janice S. Spleth, eds, *West Virginia George Sand Conference Papers* (Morgantown: West Virginia University Press, 1981), 45–53

Richer, Henri, *Epistres choisies des Héroïnes d'Ovide* (Paris: E. Ganeau, 1723)

Richlin, Amy, 'Reading Ovid's Rapes', in Amy Richlin, ed., *Pornography and Representation in Greece and Rome* (New York: Oxford University Press, 1992), 158–79

Richlin, Amy, *Arguments with Silence: Writing the History of Roman Women* (Michigan: University of Michigan Press, 2014)

Ricks, Christopher, *Allusion to the Poets* (Oxford: Oxford University Press, 2002)

Rimell, Victoria, 'Epistolary Fictions: Authorial Identity in *Heroides* 15', *Proceedings of the Cambridge Philological Society*, 45 (1999), 109–35

Rimell, Victoria, *Ovid's Lovers: Desire, Difference, and the Poetic Imagination* (Cambridge: Cambridge University Press, 2006)

Ronsard, Pierre de, *Oeuvres complètes*, ed. Jean Céard, Daniel Ménager, Michel Simonin (Paris: Gallimard, 1993)

Rosati, Gianpiero, 'L'elegia al femminile: le *Heroides* di Ovidio (e altre *Heroides*)', *Materiali e discussioni per l'analisi dei testi classici*, 29 (1992), 71–94

Rosati, Gianpiero, 'Sabinus, the *Heroides* and the Poet-Nightingale: Some Observations on the Authenticity of the *Epistula Sapphus*', *The Classical Quarterly*, 46 (1996), 207–16

Rosbo, Patrick de, 'Entretiens radiophoniques avec Marguerite Yourcenar', *Mercure de France*, 1972

Ross, Sarah, and Rosalind Smith, eds, *Early Modern Women's Complaint: Gender, Form, and Politics* (Cham: Palgrave, 2020)

Roynon, Tessa, and Daniel Orrells, eds, 'Ovid and Identity in the Twenty-First Century', *International Journal of the Classical Tradition*, 26/4 (2019) [special issue]

Rüdiger, Horst, *Sapho: Ihr Ruf und Ruhm bei der Nachwelt* (Leipzig: Dieterische Verlagsbuchhandlung, 1933)

292 BIBLIOGRAPHY

Rues, François des, *Les Marguerites françaises ou fleurs de bien dire* (Rouen: Reinsart, 1611)

Rus, Bianca, 'Thought as Revolt in *The Old Man and the Wolves*', *Hypatia*, 34 (2019), 20–38

Sabot, A. F., *Ovide, poète de l'amour dans ses œuvres de jeunesse*: Amores, Heroides, Ars amatoria, Remedia amoris, De Medicamine faciei femineae (Paris: Ophrys, 1976)

Saint-Gelais, Octavian de, *Les Epistres de Ovide translatées de latin en français* (Paris: Verard, 1499)

Saint-Gelais, Octavian de, *Les Vingt et Une Epistre [sic] d'Ovide* (Paris: Chemin, 1546)

Salm, Constance de, *Poésies de Madame la Comtesse De Salm* (Paris: F. Didot, 1811)

Salm, Constance de, *Mes soixante ans, ou mes souvenirs politiques et littéraires* (Paris: Librairie de Firmin Didot Frères et Arthus Bertrand, Libraire, 1833)

Salm, Constance de, *Œuvres complètes*, 4 vols (Paris: Librairie de Firmin Didot Frères et Arthus Bertrand, Libraire, 1842

Saltonstall, Wye, *Ovid's Heroical Epistles Englished by W. S.* (London: W. Gilberston, 1636)

Sand, George, *Histoire du véritable Gribouille* (Paris: Blanchard, 1851)

Sand, George, *Correspondance*, ed. Georges Lubin, 25 vols (Paris: Garnier, 1964–91)

Sand, George, *Œuvres autobiographiques*, ed. Georges Lubin, 2 vols (Paris: Gallimard, 1971)

Sand, George, *Narcisse*, ed. Amélie Calderone (Paris: Honoré Champion, 2019)

Sarde, Michèle, *Histoire d'Eurydice pendant la remontée* (Paris: Seuil, 1991)

Sartre, Jean-Paul, *L'Être et le néant: Essai d'ontologie phénoménologique* (Paris: Gallimard, 1943)

Savigneau, Josyane, 'Quand les Samouraïs répondent aux Mandarins', *Le Monde* (March 1990)

Schor, Naomi, *George Sand and Idealism* (New York: Columbia University Press, 1993)

Sciamma, Céline, dir. *Portrait d'une jeune fille en feu* (Lilies Films/Hold-Up Films & Productions/Arte France Cinéma, 2019)

Scott, Michael, *Delphi: A History of the Center of the Ancient World* (Princeton: Princeton University Press, 2014)

Scudéry, Madeleine de, and Georges de Scudéry, *Les Femmes illustres ou Les harangues héroïques* (Paris: A. de Sommaville and A. Courbé, 1642)

Scudéry, Madeleine de, and Georges de Scudéry, 'Histoire de Sapho', *Artamène ou le Grand Cyrus* (Paris: Courbé, 1656), x, 355–608

Searle, Adrian, 'A Ghost in Kiss Curls: How Gillian Wearing and Claude Cahun Share a Mask', *Guardian*, 8 January 2008

Segal, Charles, 'Myth and Philosophy in the *Metamorphoses*: Ovid's Augustanism and the Augustan Conclusion to Book XV', *American Journal of Philology*, 90 (1969), 257–92

Segal, Charles, 'Ovid's Metamorphic Bodies: Art, Gender, and Violence in the *Metamorphoses*', *Arion*, 5 (1998), 9–41

Segal, Charles, 'Intertextuality and Immortality: Ovid, Pythagoras and Lucretius in *Metamorphoses* 15', *Materiali e discussioni per l'analisi dei testi classici*, 46 (2001), 63–101

Seidler, Sophie E., review of M. Möller, *Gegen/Gewalt/Schreiben. De-Konstruktionen von Geschlechts- und Rollenbildern in der Ovid-Rezeption*, in *Bryn Mawr Classical Review* (2021), https://bmcr.brynmawr.edu/2021/2021.06.43/

Seth, Catriona, 'L'Épître aux femmes: textes et contextes', *Cahiers Roucher-André Chénier*, 29 (2010), 41–64

Seth, Catriona, 'La Femme auteur, stratégies et paradigmes—L'exemple de Constance de Salm', in A. Del Lungo and B. Louichon, eds, *La littérature en Bas-Bleus* (Paris: Garnier, 2010), 195–214

BIBLIOGRAPHY   293

Sharrock, Alison, 'Gender and Sexuality', in Philip Hardie, ed., *The Cambridge Companion to Ovid* (Cambridge: Cambridge University Press, 2002), 95–107

Sharrock, Alison, 'Ovid and the Discourses of Love: The Amatory Works', in Philip Hardie, ed., *The Cambridge Companion to Ovid* (Cambridge: Cambridge University Press, 2002), 150–62

Sharrock, Alison, 'Gender and Transformation: Reading, Women, and Gender in Ovid's *Metamorphoses*,' in Alison Sharrock, D. Möller, and M. Malm, eds, *Metamorphic Readings: Transformation, Language, and Gender in the Interpretation of Ovid's Metamorphoses* (Oxford: Oxford University Press, 2020), 33–53

Sharrock, Alison, 'Ovid and the Ecological Crisis?' (2021), https://classicsforall.org.uk/reading-room/ad-familiares/ovid-and-ecological-crisis

Shaw, Jennifer, *Exist Otherwise: The Life and Works of Claude Cahun* (London: Reaktion Books, 2017)

Shaw, Jennifer, 'Narcissus and the Magic Mirror', in Louise Downie, ed., *Don't Kiss Me: The Art of Claude Cahun and Marcel Moore* (London: Tate Publishing, 2006), 33–45

Shaw, Jennifer, *Reading Claude Cahun's Disavowals* (Farnham: Ashgate Publishing, 2013)

Skinner, Marilyn ed., 'Rescuing Creusa: New Methodological Approaches to Women in Antiquity', *Helios*, 13 (1986) [special issue]

Smith, Ali, *Girl Meets Boy* (Edinburgh: Canongate, 2007)

Smith, Anna, *Julia Kristeva: Readings of Exile and Estrangement* (London: Macmillan, 1996)

Sophocles, *The Three Theban Plays*, trans. Robert Fagles with an introduction and notes by Bernard Knox (London: Penguin Classics, 1984)

Sorg, Roger, 'Une fille de Ronsard, la bergère Rozette', *Revue des deux mondes*, 1 January 1923

Sorg, Roger, ed., *Les Chansons de Callianthe, fille de Ronsard* (Paris: Pichon, 1926)

Spentzou, Efrossini, *Readers and Writers in Ovid's Heroides* (Oxford: Oxford University Press, 2003)

Spivak, Gayatri Chakravorty, 'Echo', *New Literary History*, 24 (1993), 17–43

Spoth, Friedrich, *Ovids Heroides als Elegien* (Munich: Beck, 1992)

Spreng, Johann, *Metamorphoses Ovidii* (Paris: Hieronymus de Marnef and Gulielmus Cavellat, 1570)

Staël, Madame de, *Corinne ou l'Italie* (Paris: Gallimard, 1985)

Steiner, Wendy, 'Bulldozer of Desires', *New York Times*, 15 November 1992

Stevens, Benjamin Eldon, 'Not the Lover's Choice, but the Poet's: Classical Receptions in Portrait of A Lady on Fire', *Frontières. Revue d'Archéologie, Histoire et Histoire de l'art*, 2 (2020), https://publications-prairial.fr/frontiere-s/index.php?id=258

Tarrant, Richard, 'The Authenticity of the Letter of Sappho to Phaon (*Heroides* XV)', *Harvard Studies in Classical Philology*, 85 (1981), 133–53

Tarte, Kendall B., 'Early Modern Literary Communities: Madeleine Des Roches's City of Women', *The Sixteenth Century Journal*, 35 (2004), 751–69

Tashijan, Dickran, 'Vous pour moi?: Marcel Duchamp and Transgender Coupling', in Whitney Chadwick, ed., *Mirror Images: The Women, Surrealism and Self-Representation* (Cambridge: Massachusetts Institute of Technology Press, 1998), 36–65

Taubin, Amy, 'Here's Looking at You': Céline Sciamma on the Path of Love and Restoring Lost Histories', *Film Comment* (November/December 2019), https://www.filmcomment.com/article/interview-celine-sciamma-portrait-of-a-lady-on-fire/

Taylor, Helena, 'Ovid, Galanterie and Politics in Madame de Villedieu's Les Exilés de la cour d'Auguste', *Early Modern French Studies*, 37/1 (2015), 49–63

294 BIBLIOGRAPHY

Taylor, Helena, *The Lives of Ovid in Seventeenth-Century French Culture* (Oxford: Oxford University Press, 2017)

Taylor, Helena, 'Marie de Gournay et le Parnasse des femmes', in M. Roussillon, S. Guyot, D. Glynn, and M.-M. Fragonard, eds, *Littéraire—pour Alain Viala*, 2 vols (Arras: Artois Presses Université, 2018), I, 227–37

Taylor, Helena, 'L'Adorateur du beau sexe': Madeleine de Scudéry et Marie-Jeanne L'Héritier, lectrices d'Ovide', in Stefania Cerrito and Marylène Possamaï-Pérez, eds, *Ovide en France du Moyen Âge à nos jours* (Paris: Classiques Garnier, 2021), 243–63

Tennyson, Alfred, Lord, *Tiresias and Other Poems* (Australia: Leopold Classic Library, 2015)

Terry, Philip, ed., *Ovid Metamorphosed* (London: Chatto and Windus, 2000)

Thompson, Thom, 'A Conversation with Cindy Sherman', in *Cindy Sherman* (Stony Brook, NY: State University of New York Art Gallery, 1983)

Thorsen, Thea S., 'Introduction: Latin Love Elegy', in Thea S. Thorsen, ed., *The Cambridge Companion to Latin Love Elegy* (Cambridge: Cambridge University Press, 2013), 1–22

Thorsen, Thea S., 'Ovid the Love Elegist', in Thea S. Thorsen, ed., *The Cambridge Companion to Latin Love Elegy* (Cambridge: Cambridge University Press, 2013), 114–32

Thorsen, Thea S., *Ovid's Early Poetry: From his Single Heroides to his Remedia amoris* (Cambridge: Cambridge University Press, 2014)

Thorsen, Thea S., 'The Second Erato and the Deeper Design of Ovid's Ars amatoria: Unravelling the Anti-Marital Union of Venus, Procris and Romulus', in Luis Rivero and others, eds, *Vivam! Estudios sobre la obra de Ovidio. Studies on Ovid's Poetry* (Huelva: University of Huelva, 2018), 141–68

Thorsen, Thea S., 'The Newest Sappho (2016) and Ovid's Heroides 15', in Thea S. Thorsen and Stephen Harrison, eds, *Roman Receptions of Sappho* (Oxford: Oxford University Press, 2019), 249–64

Thorsen, Thea S., and R. Berge, 'Receiving Receptions Received: A New Collection of *testimonia Sapphica c.*600 BC–AD 1000', in Thea S. Thorsen and Stephen Harrison, eds, *Roman Receptions of Sappho* (Oxford: Oxford University Press, 2019), 290–402

Thorsen, Thea S., and S. Harrison, eds, *Roman Receptions of Sappho* (Oxford: Oxford University Press, 2019)

Thorsen, Thea S., 'Review of D. Loscalzo, *Saffo, la hetaira* (Pisa: Fabrizio Serra editore, 2019)', *Journal of Hellenic Studies*, 141 (2021), 246–7

Thynne, Lizzie, 'Surely You Are Not Claiming to Be More Homosexual than I?: Claude Cahun and Oscar Wilde', in Joseph Bristow, ed., *Oscar Wilde and Modern Culture: The Making of a Legend* (Ohio: Ohio University Press, 2008), 180–208

Tibullus, *Elegies*, ed. and trans. C. P. Goold (Cambridge, MA: Harvard University Press, Loeb Classical Library, 1990).

Tisseron, Louis, and De Quincy, 'Notice biographique sur la vie et les écrits de Mme la princesse Constance de Salm-Dyck', *Fastes nobiliaires* (Paris: Imprimerie D'Amédée Saintin, rue Saint-Pierre-Montmartre, 1845), 3–20

Tissol, Garth, *The Face of Nature: Wit, Narrative and Cosmic Origins in Ovid's 'Metamorphoses'* (Princeton: Princeton University Press, 1997)

Traub, Valerie, 'Afterword', in Goran V. Stanivukovic, ed., *Ovid and the Renaissance Body* (Toronto: University of Toronto Press, 2001), 260–8

Traub, Valerie, Patricia Badir, and Peggy McCracken, *Ovidian Transversions: 'Iphis and Ianthe', 1300–1650* (Edinburgh: Edinburgh University Press, 2019)

Trigo, Begnino, ed., *Kristeva's Fiction* (New York: SUNY, 2013)

Tyard, Pontus de, *Erreurs amoureuses*, ed. John A. McClelland (Geneva: Droz, 1967)

Uman, Deborah, '"This Defective Edition": Gender and Translation', in *Women as Translators in Early Modern England* (Newark: University of Delaware Press, 2012), 1–16

Valois, Marguerite de, *Album de poésies*, ed. Colette Winn and François Rouget (Paris: Classiques Garnier, 2009)

Van Buren, A. W., 'A Pompeian Distich', *The American Journal of Philology*, 80/4 (1959), 380–2

Van der Poel, Ieme, 'Linda Lê et Julia Kristeva: citoyennes de la langue française', in Bruno Blanckeman, Alena Mura-Brunel, and Marc Dambre, eds, *Le Roman Français au tournant du XXIe siècle* (Paris: Presses Sorbonne Nouvelle, 2004), 241–8

Vance, Norman, 'Ovid and the Nineteenth Century', in Charles Martindale, ed., *Ovid Renewed: Ovidian Influences on Literature and Art from the Middle Ages to the Twentieth Century* (Cambridge: Cambridge University Press, 1988), 215–32

Vassallo, Helen, *Towards a Feminist Translator Studies: Intersectional Activism in Translation and Publishing* (London: Routledge, 2022)

Venuti, Lawrence, *The Translator's Invisibility* (London: Routledge, 1995)

Verdière, Raoul, 'Un amour secret d'Ovide', *L'Antiquité classique*, 40/2 (1971), 623–48

Verdière, Raoul, *Le Secret du voltigeur d'amour ou le mystère de la relégation d'Ovide* (Bruxelles: Revue des Etudes Latines, 1992)

Veyne, Paul, *L'élégie érotique romaine. L'amour, la poésie et l'Occident* (Paris: Seuil, 1983)

Viennot, Eliane, 'Revisiter la "Querelle des femmes": mais de quoi parle-t-on ?', in *Revisiter la Querelle des femmes. Discours sur l'égalité/l'inégalité des femmes et des hommes, de 1750 aux lendemains de la Révolution* (Saint-Étienne: Publications de l'Université de Saint-Étienne, 2012), 1–20

Villedieu, Madame de, *Ovide, ou Les Exilés de la cour d'Auguste* (Paris: Barbin, 1672–8)

Virgil, *Opera*, ed. R. A. B. Mynors (Oxford: Clarendon Press, 1969)

Virgil, *The Aeneid*, trans. David West (London: Penguin, 1990)

Virgil, *Eclogues, Georgics, Aeneid I–VI*, trans. H. Rushton Fairclough, rev. G. P. Goold (Cambridge, MA: Harvard University Press, Loeb Classical Library, 1999)

Vives, Jean de, *The Education of a Christian Woman*, ed. and trans. Charles Fantazzi (Chicago: Chicago University Press, 2000)

Volpilhac-Auger, Catherine, 'La collection *Ad usum Delphini*: entre érudition et pédagogie', *Les Humanités classiques*, 74 (1997), 203–14 [special issue: *Histoire de l'éducation*]

Volpilhac-Auger, Catherine, ed., *La collection Ad usum Delphini. L'Antiquité au miroir du Grand Siècle* (Grenoble: ELLUG, 2000)

Von Oehsen, Kristine, 'The Lives of Claude Cahun and Marcel Moore', in Louise Downie, ed., *Don't Kiss Me: The Art of Claude Cahun and Marcel Moore* (London: Tate Publishing, 2006; New York: Aperture, 2006), 10–23

Waller, Margaret, *The Male Malady: Fictions of Impotence in the French Romantic Novel* (New Brunswick, NJ: Rutgers University Press, 1993)

Walsh, Théobald, *George Sand* (Paris: Hivert, 1837)

Warner, Marina, *Fantastic Metamorphoses, Other Worlds: Ways of Telling the Self* (Oxford: Oxford University Press, 2002)

Watson, Patricia, 'Praecepta amoris: Ovid's didactic elegy', in Barbara Weiden Boyd, ed., *Brill's Companion to Ovid* (Leiden: Brill, 2002), 141–65

West, M. L., 'Erinna', *Zeitschrift für Papyrologie und Epigraphik*, 25 (1977), 95–119

West, Patrick, 'Theoretical Allegory / Allegorical Theory: (Post-)Colonial Spatializations in Janet Frame's The Carpathians and Julia Kristeva's The Old Man and the Wolves', *Journal of New Zealand Literature*, 26 (2008), 73–94

296 BIBLIOGRAPHY

White, Paul, 'Ovid's "Heroides" in Early Modern French Translation: Saint-Gelais, Fontaine, Du Bellay', *Translation and Literature*, 13/2 (2004), 165–80

White, Paul, *Renaissance Postscripts: Responding to Ovid's 'Heroides' in Sixteenth-Century France* (Columbus: Ohio State University Press, 2009)

Wiesmann, Marc-André, 'Verses Have Fingers: Montaigne Reads Juvenal', *Journal of Medieval and Renaissance Studies*, 23 (1993), 43–67

Wilkinson, L. P., *Ovid Recalled* (Cambridge: Cambridge University Press, 1955)

Wilson, Emma, *Céline Sciamma – Portraits* (Edinburgh: Edinburgh University Press, 2021)

Wishart, David, *Ovid* (London: Hodder and Stoughton, 1995)

Wynn, Colette H., 'Le procès du même et de l'autre. Pernette Du Guillet et le mythe ovidien de Diane et Actaeon', in Evelyne Berriot-Salvadore, ed., *Les Représentations de l'autre: du Moyen Age au XVIIe siècle* (Saint-Etienne: Publications de l'Université de Saint-Etienne, 1995), 263–71

Xavier, Subha, 'Wretched of Sea: Boat Narratives and Stories of Displacement,' in Anna Louise Milne and Russell Williams, eds, *Contemporary Fiction in French* (Cambridge: Cambridge University Press, 2021), 184–98

Yalom, Marilyn, 'Dédoublement in the Fiction of George Sand', in Natalie Datlof and others, eds, *The George Sand Papers: 1978* (New York: AMS Press, 1982), 21–31

Yandell, Cathy, 'Iconography and Iconoclasm: The Female Breast in French Renaissance Culture', *The French Review*, 83 (2010), 540–8

Yourcenar, Marguerite, *Feux* (Paris: Grasset, 1936)

Yourcenar, Marguerite, *Feux* (3rd edn; Paris: Plon, 1968)

Yourcenar, Marguerite, 'Qui n'a pas son Minotaure?', in *Théâtre II* (Paris: Gallimard, 1971), 163–231

Yourcenar, Marguerite, *Fires*, trans. Dori Katz, in collaboration with the author (Chicago: University of Chicago Press, 1981)

Yourcenar, Marguerite, *Œuvres romanesques (Alexis ou le Traité du Vain combat Le Coup de grâce; Denier du rêve; Mémoires d'Hadrien; L'œuvre au noir; Anna, soror; Un homme obscur—Une belle matinée; Feux; Nouvelles orientales; supplément: La nouvelle Eurydice)* (Paris: Gallimard, 1982)

Yourcenar, Marguerite, *La Couronne et la lyre. Poèmes traduits du grec par Marguerite Yourcenar* (Paris: Gallimard, 1984)

Yourcenar, Marguerite, *Essais et mémoires* (Paris: Gallimard, 1991)

Yourcenar, Marguerite, *Lettres à ses amis et à quelques autres*, ed. Michèle Sarde and Joseph Brami (Paris: Gallimard, 1995)

Zajko, Vanda, 'What Difference Was Made?: Feminist Models of Reception', in Lorna Hardwick and Christopher Stray, eds, *A Companion to Classical Receptions* (London: Wiley, 2008), 195–206

Zehnacker, H., and Fredouille, J.-C., *Littérature latine* (Paris: Presses Universitaires de France, 1993)

Zetzel, James, 'Rome and its Traditions', in Charles Martindale, ed., *The Cambridge Companion to Virgil* (Cambridge: Cambridge University Press, 1997), 188–203

Zimmermann, Mary, *Metamorphoses: A Play* (Chicago: Northwestern University Press, 2002)

Ziogas, Ioannis, *Law and Love in Ovid: Courting Justice in the Age of Augustus* (Oxford: Oxford University Press, 2021)

Ziolkowski, Theodore, *Ovid and the Moderns* (Ithaca: Cornell University Press, 2005)

Zuber, Roger, *Les 'Belles Infidèles' et la formation du goût classique* (Paris: Armand Colin, 1968)

Zuckerberg, Donna, *Not All Dead White Men: Classics and Misogyny in the Digital Age* (Cambridge, MA: Harvard University Press, 2018)

Zwierlein, Otto, *Die Ovid- und Vergil-Revision in tiberischer Zeit* (Berlin: De Gruyter, 1999)

Index

Introductory Note: References such as '178-79' indicate (not necessarily continuous) discussion of a topic across a range of pages. Wherever possible in the case of topics with many references, these have either been divided into sub-topics or only the most significant discussions of the topic are listed. Because the entire work is about 'Ovid' and 'reception by women', the use of these terms (and certain others which occur constantly throughout the book) as entry points has been restricted. Information will be found under the corresponding detailed topics.

For the benefit of digital users, indexed terms that span two pages (e.g., 52-53) may, on occasion, appear on only one of those pages.

abandoned women 53, 56, 144, 188-9, 208-9
abandonment 53, 100-1, 130-1, 145-7, 177-8
Académie française 11, 86-7
accuracy 74-6, 169-71
Achilles 203-7, 209-14, 218-19
  cross-dressing 205-6, 208-10, 212-14
  destiny 207, 213
Actaeon 22, 117
adulterers 70, 80-1
adultery 121, 136-9
  laws 13-14, **136-9**
Aegina 263
Aegisthus 198-9
Aeneas 140-1, 144, 198, 200-3
Aeneid 73-4, 140-1, 149-50, 202-3, 247, 271
Aeschylus 196, 199-202
aesthetics 75-6, 79, 81-7, 153-4, 166-7
affection 84, 90-1, 97-8, 101-2, 112-13, 117-18
afterlife 1
Agamemnon 198-9, 208
  murder 188-9, 196, 201-2
age 26, 124, 137, 147-8, 156-7, 221, 274
agency 11, 53, 57, 62, 184-6
  negotiation of 11
Aglaurus 10-11
  of Madeleine des Roches 32-5
  Ovid's 26-35

Agnodice 35-40, 43
Agrippina 108-10
Alba 224, 232-8
alcyon 216-17
Alcyone 216-18, 251-2
allegorical interpretations 8-11, 30
allegories 30-1, 64-5, 159-61
allusions 15, 21-2, 115-17, 142-3, 200-2, 216
  Ovidian 15, 253-4
  Virgilian 140-1, 144
ambiguity 4-5, 20, 51, 59, 61-2, 93, 184-7
  gender 20, 188-9
ambivalence 144-5, 268-9
  of Ovidian models 188-219
amor stultus 58-61
Amores 4-5, 8-9, 15, 38, 67-8, 113-16, 120, 143-4
anachronisms 188-9, 193-9
  deliberate 198-9
Ancients 11, 72, 88-90, 94-5
Andersen, Corinne 183-4
androgyny 155-6, 180-5
Andromeda 11-12
anger 34-5, 38, 178, 235, 248
Anne d'Autriche 89
Antigone 254, 256
Antigone Rising: the Subversive Power of the Ancient Myths 2, 186
anxiety 127-8, 153-4

298 INDEX

Apollo 12–13, 29, 65–6, 89, 132–3,
   175–6, 195
appropriation 58, 161
Apuleius 116–17, 151–2
Arachne 11–12
Arendt, Hannah 227–8
Argonauts 207–8
argumenta 89–94, 101–2
Ariadne 55–6, 90–1, 145–7, 189,
   197–8, 209
Ariane 92–3, 99, 101–2
Aricia 201–2
Ariosto 25–6
Ars amatoria 2, 4–5, 8–9, 15, 40–3,
   115–16, 134–7, 141, 143–4
art 50, 91–2, 94, 138–9, 152–3, 173–80,
   185–7
Artamène ou le Grand Cyrus 77–9, 123–4
   see also Scudéry, Madeleine de
artists 171–3, 183–4, 186–7
   female 86–7, 183–4, 186
Ascensius, Jodocus Badius 49
Athenian women 37, 39
Athenians 36–9, 178–9
Athens 39–40, 55, 57, 92–3, 196–8
Attica, women of 35–6, 38
Attys 198–9
Augustan Rome 148–9, 196–7
Augustus 104–12, 117, 119, 121, 137
Aulis 70
Auraix-Jonchière, Pascale 158–9, 161
authority 7, 43, 63, 79–81, 86–7, 163–4
   male 74
   patriarchal 5–6
authorship 6–8, 77–8
   female 2
autobiographies 15, 20, 121–3, 151, 154–5,
   157, 226
autofiction 5–6, 20, 220
autonomy 171, 182–3, 185
   spurious 186–7
Aveux non avenus 179–80, 185–6 *see also*
   Cahun, Claude
Avis sur la traduction de la seconde
   Philippique de Ciceron 75 *see also*
   Gournay, Marie de

Bacchantes 99–100, 234–5
Bacchus 54–5, 92–3

bad omens 116–17, 207–8
balance 26, 135–6, 162–3
   gender 135–6
Balzac, Honoré de 1, 166–7
banalisation 237
banality 16–17, 232, 238, 240
banishment 106–10, 119 *see also* exile
barbarism 273–4
barbarity 229, 231–2
Bardon, Henri 11–12
Barrin, Jean 71–2, 81–4, 89–94
Battus 27–9
beasts 269–70, 273
Behn, Aphra 12–13, 68
Belle, Marie-Alice 45–6
Bellegarde, Jean-Baptiste de 71–2, 81–2, 84
belles infidèles 67–70, 85–7
belles lettres 68–70, 79, 86–7
Benson, Fiona 2
Berchorius, Petrus 30–1
bereavement 147–8, 226–7
Berlin wall 16–17, 223, 225, 229–30, 238
Bersuire, Pierre 7–8, 30
Bertall 74, 158–9
Berthaut, Jean 74, 158–9
betrayals 26–7, 133, 235
bienséance 79, 83–5, 96
binary modes of thinking 80, 166–7, 218–19
birds 214–17, 244–7, 251–2
Bloom, Harold 153–4
blurring 143, 171–3, 177, 188–9, 211, 218,
   223, 225
boats 17–19, 133, 214, 244, 249, 268
Boccaccio 68–70
borders 232, 242–4, 269, 274
boundaries 171–3, 177, 186–9, 221, 223–4,
   236–7 *see also* borders
Bouton de rose, Le 13–14, 121, 127–8
   see also Salm, Constance de
Bovary, Emma 56–7
Bové, Carol 227–8
breasts 39–43, 206–7, 211, 213, 215
   prisoner of her 207–9, 213–14
   women's 206, 211
Bressey Lezay-Marnésia, Charlotte
   de 13–14, **104–20**
Briseis 77–8, 204–6
Brown, Hilary 72–3
Bulgaria 221, 224, 225

bulls 98–9, 250
burials 35–6, 225
Butor, Michel 149–50
buzzards 247–8

Caenis 213–14
Caenus 186
Caesar, Julius 272
Cahun, Claude 5–6, 15–16, **169–87**
  enigma 171–3
  as Ovidian Tiresias 186–7
  Penelope and the art of narration 173–7
  Sappho and the art of destruction 177–9
  self-portraiture or the act of
    inversion 179–84
  Tiresias, Narcissus, and the
    mirror 184–6
Callianthe 64–5
Callimachus 27
Calypso 175
Camille, ou Amitié et Imprudence 121–3
  see also Salm, Constance de
Canacé 98–9
cannibalism 264–6, 268–9
capitalism 159–61, 163–4
Capitol 140–50
careers 13–14, 121–7, 151–2
  literary 121, 125–6, 261
Cassandra 195, 255–6
  powers of prophecy 196
  prediction 195
catalogues 67–8, 77–8, 82–3, 101–2, 143–4,
  152–3
catastrophes 255–6, 259
categorization 5–6, 15, 157, 166–7, 171, 184–6
  gender 155–6, 186–7, 209–10, 213–14
Catullus 70–2, 189, 257–8
Cecilia/Cécile 149–50
censorship 84, 158–9
Cephalus 137
Ceres 54–5
Ceyx 217, 251–2
Chadwick, Whitney 183–4
chambre bleue 11
Chard, Chloe 149–50
charms 112–13, 147–8
chastity 30–3, 35, 38, 43
Château des désertes, Le 161 *see also*
  Sand, George

chiasmus 52, 62, 271
childhood 157–9, 182–3, 221–2,
  246–7, 264
children 95–6, 132, 143, 158–9, 162–3,
  194–5, 271–2
chora 154, 163–6
Christ child 30–1
Cicero 68, 73–5, 83
Cioran, Emil 253
circulation 9–10, 264, 267
Circus 40
Cixous, Hélène 2
clairvoyance 195–6
clandestine marriages 58
Clark, James 7–8
Clarke, Danielle 72–3
class 6–7, 153–4
classrooms 2–3, 78
Cleis 132–3, 178–9
Clericus, Ubertinus 49, 57–9, 95–6
cliffs 17–19, 131, 133, 213
  Leucadian 131–3
Clytemnestra 188–9, 194–5, 198–202, 208–9
coherence, semantic 59
Colosseum 148–9
collectivity 5–6
Comédie française 121–3
commentaries 8–10, 46, 49, 57–9, 72, 95–6
communism 221–2, 227–30
companion for women 26, 43
companionship 23–4
compassion 91–3
complete translations 49–50, 81–2
  female-authored 13, 68
complexities 5–6, 86–7, 89–90, 175–6,
  179–80, 182–4, 246
  etymological 53
  semantic 62
concealment 112–13, 119
Confidences au miroir 179–80 *see also*
  Cahun, Claude
consent 193
constancy 35, 74
Constanța 16, 221
contagion 232, 237
Corambé 15, 154–9, 162–3, 166–7 *see also*
  Sand, George
Corinna 64–6, 120, 143–4 *see also* Corinne
  ou l'Italie

300 INDEX

Corinne ou l'Italie 15, 140–50 *see also* Stael, Germaine de
Corneille, Thomas 71–2, 81–4
Cornelia 110–11
Coronis 29
correctness, moral 76, 85–6
corruption 232
Cosnay, Marie 4, 16–17, 20, 242–5, 260
couplets 52, 63, 94–5, 98–101, 138–9
  elegiac 134, 207–8
courage 36–7, 80–1, 89, 93, 212–13
courageousness 139
Couronne et la lyre, La 189 *see also* Yourcenar, Marguerite
Covid-19 pandemic *see* pandemic
creativity 151–2, 155, 166–7, 179, 186–7
  female 17–19, 177, 182–3, 186
creative-criticism 4, 16–17
Crecelius, Kathryn 155–6
Crete 90–3, 101–2
crimes 91–2, 94, 100–2, 224, 233–4, 274
criminality 91–2, 138–9, 226, 229, 232
Crispin, Daniel 89–96
Cronos 254
cross-dressing, Achilles 205–6, 208–10, 212–14
crows 28–9, 34, 267
cruelty 22, 97–8, 240, 265, 268, 271
  erotics of 10–11, 22–3, 46–7
culture 6–7, 11, 13, 44–6, 81–2, 144–5, 229–30
  ancient 11, 46, 67–8, 88, 227–8
  literary 24, 66–8, 88
  salon 5–6, 11, 67–71
Cupid 54–5, 116–17
curiosity 30–5, 116–17
  women 10–11, 22–3, 31–2
Cyane 152–3

Damophyle 123–4, 132–6
Daphne 175–6, 211
Dardanians 200–1
Darrieussecq, Marie 2, 4
de' Cipelli, Giovanni 49
de Crenne, Hélisenne 9–10
de la Pure, Michel 70–1
De mulieribus claris 68–70
Dean, Tacita 186–7

death 133–4, 161–2, 164–5, 178–9, 223–5, 255, 259–61
decorum 9–10, 23–6, 42–3, 83–5
  rhetorical 25
dedications 24, 26, 73–4, 81–3, 159
defender of women 190–1
Défense et illustration de la langue française, La 44 *see also* Du Bellay, Joachim
Deidamia 211–13
Deimier, Pierre 89–94
Delacour, Stéphanie 221–2, 224, 228–30, 232, 238–41 *see also Le Vieil homme et les loups*
Delmont, Léon 149–50
Delon, Michel 106–7
Demetriou, Tania 45–6
Demophoon 47–8, 52, 54–6, 59–63
dependence 33, 139, 173–4
Deren, Maya 173, 186–7
'dernière Olympique, La' 201–2 *see also* Yourcenar, Marguerite
des Roches, Dames (Catherine and Madeleine) 10–11, 22–6, 32–3, 35–43
Descola, Philippe 270
Deshoulières, Antoinette 88–9
Desmond, Marilynn 7–8
despair 54, 80, 108–12, 145–7, 164–5, 201–3
Desportes, Philippe 64–6
destiny 144–5, 178–9, 197, 201–4, 207, 213–14, 259
  common 268
destruction 149, 161–2, 164–5, 178–9
  art of 177–9
Deucalion 264
Diana 155
Diderot 106–7
Dido 56–7, 77–8, 144, 198, 202–5
dignity 80–1, 145–7
Dimmick, Jeremy 7–8
Dionysius 124–5
disappearance 119, 171
disaster 207–8, 255, 259, 266
discretion 33, 79, 85–6, 270
  poet's 35
disguises 35–7, 210–12, 214, 265–6
dislocation 1–2, 16–17, 20, 147–8, 252, 259–60, 262
disobedience 22–3, 26–8, 30–1

displacement 16–17, 155–6, 260
disruption 149–50, 180–2, 246
dissimulation 95–6, 101–2, 118
divine mystery 26–7, 30–1, 35
doctors, male 36–7
dogs 247–8, 264
domestication 44, 49, 67–8, 75
doors 144–5, 207–9, 212–13, 243
  double 207, 213
Dorat, Claude-Joseph 106–7, 120
drama 130–2
dreaming 110
dreams 70, 111–12, 154–5, 157, 216, 256–7
Du Bellay, Joachim 8–9, 44, 46, 50,
  63–4, 66
Du Perron, Jacques Davy 71–2, 74
Dudevant, Aurore 15
Dudevant, Solange 152–3
Dufour-Maître, Myriam 79, 86–7
Dumas, Alexandre 158–9
dust 40–1, 144

early modern reception 4–5, 22–3, 30,
  42–3, 67
early modern women 22–4, 26, 42–3, 83
Echo 152–3, 158–9, 164–6, 185, 250–1
eclecticism 151–2
ecological themes 16–17
Écouchard-Lebrun, Ponce-Denis 123–4
education 3, 6–7, 12–13, 23, 38, 43, 70–1,
  91–2
  equal 76–7
  women 10–11, 21–3, 26, 38–9
Education of a Christian Woman, The 70–1
Egnatius, Johannes Baptista 49
eighteenth century 2, 9–10, 13–14, 17–19,
  67–8, 86–7, 94–5
Electra complex 155–6
elegiac couplets 134, 207–8
elegiac epistles 51, 54–6, 59
elegiac women 143–4, 150
elegy 62, 124–5, 134–5, 143–4, 150, 204–5,
  207–8
Elkin, Lauren 171–3
eloquence 63–4, 77–80, 86–7, 142
emblems 158–9, 166–7, 182–3
emotions 108–10, 112–13, 118, 204, 262
emperor 110, 125–7, 136–9
empty time 202–4

engagement 10–11, 20, 110–11, 151–2,
  158–9, 169–71
  corrective 22–3
Ennius 129–30
Envy 22–3, 26–30, 34–5
  of Catherine des Roches 35–40
epic world 205, 207–9
Epicurus 272
epidemics 263–4
epistles 45–6, 68–72, 80, 84, 89–90, 173–4,
  177–8
  elegiac 51, 54–6, 59
epistolarity 9–10, 193–4
epistolary form 13–14, 67–8, 77–8, 106–7,
  134, 197–8
epistolary rhetoric 9–10, 67–8
Epistula Sapphus 124–5
Epistulae Ex Ponto 8–9, 106–7
epitaphs 62–3
Épître adressée à L'empereur
  Napoléon 13–14, 121, 137–8 see also
  Salm, Constance de
Épître aux femmes 13–14, 123–4, 126–7
  see also Salm, Constance de
Epîtres héroïques, Les 88–103 see also
  L'Héritier, Marie-Jeanne de
equality 85–6, 126–7, 139, 162–3, 268
Erasmus 9–10
Erichthonius 22–3, 26–7, 29–33
Erinna 79, 123–4, 132–3
erotic elegies 120
erotic focus 42–3
erotic world 204–5, 207–9
eroticism 6–7, 39, 75–6
erotics of cruelty 10–11, 22–3, 46–7
erudition 21–4, 63–4, 66, 145–7, 188–9, 228–9
escape 177–8, 193–4, 210–19, 270–1
eternity 148–9, 251, 272
etymology 53, 64–5
Euripides 201
Europa 250
Eurydice 4, 17–19, 153–4, 269–70
Eustathius of Thessalonica 200–1
Eve 169–71
evil 224, 227–8, 238
exemplarity 29, 34, 43, 47–8, 63–4, 86–7
exile 16–17, 20, 171–3, 221–2, 252–3,
  261–2 see also banishment
  poet's 4, 108–10, 116–17, 119, 224–5

302 INDEX

fables 8–9, 196–7, 266
  early modern 22–3
  political 226–7
fairy tales 68, 88, 154, 158–9, 164–5,
    167–8, 182–3
faith 35, 43, 111–12, 151–2, 221–2, 240,
    253, 264
fame 140–1, 143–4, 171–3, 212–13,
    243–5, 272
family histories 6–7, 149–50
Fasti 8–9, 15, 140–1, 144
fathers 55, 99, 163–6, 223–5, 244–7,
    252–3, 260–1
feasts 175–6, 264–5
female artists 86–7, 183–4, 186
female characters 16–17, 89–90 *see also*
    individual names
female identity 7–8
female perspective 134–6, 188–9, 194–5
female traditions 5–7, 72–3
female virtue 67–70
female voices 4–5, 20, 86–7, 164–5, 179,
    184–7, 190
feminine seduction 205–6, 211
feminine universe 204, 206, 210, 218–19
feminine world 193, 204–10, 213, 217–18
feminism 5–7, 13–14, 85–6, 139, 171–3,
    184–5
  and Classics 2–3
  ambivalent 15
  of difference 85–6
  fourth-wave 2
  French 5–6
  Ovid's 4–7, 127, 139, 190–1, 128–9
  second-wave 2
  third-wave 2
femmes fortes 67–8, 89, 101–2
Femmes illustres 68, 82–3, 89, 123–4
  see also Scudéry, Madeleine de
  rhetoric and gender in 77–81
Feux 15, 188–219 *see also* Yourcenar,
    Marguerite
fickleness 35, 56, 111–12
  women 31
fidelity 9–10, 68–71, 73–4, 77–8, 85–7
  Laodamia 70, 73–7, 85–6
films 17–19, 179–80, 196–7, 203–4
Fires 196–9, 201–6, 208–10, 212 *see also*
    Feux *see also* Yourcenar, Marguerite

Flaan, Mme de 104–6
flea 40–3 see also *La Puce des Madame
    Des-Roches*
Fleury, Laure 159
Fleury, Valentine 159
flight 65, 100–1, 214, 218, 251–2, 267–8
flood 264–6
Flora 155
flowers 162, 166, 201–2, 231, 247, 267
fluid world 193–4, 216, 218–19
fluidity 15–17, 161–3, 184–5, 209–11
  gender 2, 4–5, 183–5
  generic 135–6
Fontaine, Charles 49–50, 52–3, 56–7,
    59, 71–2, 169
forbidden knowledge 26–7, 39–40
forced marriage 110, 117–19
foreigners 242–3
fourteenth century 1, 30
France, Marie de 7–8
France *see* Introductory Note
freedom 37, 53, 110–12, 117–18, 120, 266–7
  intellectual 35–6
French Feminism 5–6
Freud, Sigmund 165–6, 226
Fulgentius 32–3
Fulkerson, Laurel 56, 63
fury 37, 100, 221, 233–4

Gaensbauer, Deborah B. 244–7
Gaillard, Jacques 202–3
galant culture 67–8, 71–2, 81–4
Galinsky, Karl 232–3
games 143–4, 190, 193–4, 201–3, 264, 271
  scholarly 199–204
  seductive 119
Garland, Emma 15
Garval, Michael 167–8
Gavarni, Paul 158–9
Gélas, Monseigneur de 74
gender 2–7, 13, 77–81, 171–3, 179–80, 184–7
  ambiguity 20, 188–9
  balance 135–6
  binaries 184–6
  categorization 155–6, 186–7, 209–10,
    213–14
  fluidity 2, 4–5, 183–4
  identity 4–6, 15, 72–3, 155–6, 167–8,
    186, 193–4, 206

male 213–14, 218–19
  non-binary 4–6, 169
  politics 4–5, 155–6
  stereotypes 59, 178, 180–2
gendered identities 15, 213–14
gendered language 44–5
gendered spaces 15
gendering 10–11, 45–6, 68–70, 86–7, 162–3
gender non-conforming writers 2, 5–7
genres 11–14, 106–7, 134–5, 204–6, 222–4
  narrative 260–1
  theatrical 134–5
Germany 106–7
ghosts 258–9
  literary 145–7
Girard, René 227–8
girls 3, 212, 264–6 *see also* individual names
  young 188–9, 198–9, 203, 215
glory 13, 88–103, 175–6
  literary 89, 102–3
  women 89–90, 102–3
gods 35, 54–5, 206–7, 269–70, 272–3
  see also individual names
Goff, Barbara 246
gold 159–61, 212
  dust 256–7
  necklaces 211
Goldhammer, Arthur 222–3
Gouget, Claude-Pierre 23
Gournay, Marie de 9–10, 68, 71–2, 77–80, 82–7
  'faithful' Laodamia 73–7
  frankness 75–6
  translation 9–10, 72–6, 82–3, 86–7
graces 38–40, 104–6, 142, 152–3, 169–71
grands opéras 121–3, 134–5
Greaney, Michael 223, 226
Greece 44, 47–8, 64
greed 28, 30–2, 161–2
Greek 3–4, 44, 64–5, 80, 163–4, 198–9, 246, 272
Green, Peter 16
Gribouille 15, 158–67 *see also* Sand, George
guests 38, 62, 162, 195
Guilleragues, Gabriel 13–14
guilt 94–100, 165–6, 258–61
gullibility 41, 272

Habert, François 8–10
Hadrian 191–3, 229
hair 38–9, 180–2, 203, 205, 211, 233–4, 267
hair dryers 205–6, 212
Halicarnassus 124–5
happiness 38, 106–11, 144–7, 256
harangues 77–8, 80–1, 89, 123–4
Hardie, Philip 70
Harkness, Nigel 155–6
Harlequin 169–71
harmony 162–3, 165–6, 246–7, 251–2
Harpies 247–8
Haynes, Natalie 68–70
health 143
  bodily 35–6, 38–9
heart 38, 110–11, 113–14, 118, 158–9, 206–7
Hebe 155
Hector 80–1, 200–1
Hecuba 70–1, 235–6
Hedélin François 71–2
Helen 70, 77–8, 201–2
Heliades 234–5
Helios 2–3
helmets 203, 205–6, 212
heresy 151–2, 155
Hermaphroditus 186, 213–14
heroes 71–2, 90–1, 93, 169–71, 193–4, 203, 218, 268
Heroides 12–16, 44–66, 67–72, 129–36, 188–91, 194–5
  corrective translation 88
Héroïnes 15, 169–71, 173–5, 180–2, 186–7
  see also Cahun, Claude
heroines 56, 89–96, 102–3, 201–2
  abandoned 51, 56–7, 63, 145–7, 209
  death 62–3
  letters of 130
  mythological 190–1, 193–4, 197–9
  Ovidian 68, 145–8, 150, 218–19
heroism 101–2, 205–6
Herse 26–32
Hetzel, Pierre-Jules 158–9
Hiddleston, Janet 155
high priests 132–3
Hipparchus 198–9
Hippolyte/Hippolytus 89–91, 93–103, 201–2
  mother 97–8

304 INDEX

Histoire de ma vie 15, 151, 154–5, 158–9
 see also Sand, George
Histoire du véritable Gribouille 15, 158–9,
 161–3 *see also* Sand, George
Hoffman, Michael 16
Homer 70, 79, 94–5, 129–30, 134,
 169–71, 173
Homeric problems 200–1
homogenization 16–17
homosexuality 144–5, 201–2
honour 145–7, 158–9, 186
Horace 151–2
hostages 268–70, 273–4
House of Fame 243–5
Howe Allen, Helen 191
Hubertinus *see* Clericus, Ubertinus
Hughes, Ted 16
Hugo, Victor 1, 14, 260
humanists 8–9, 21–2, 46, 49, 63–4
Hurst, Isobel 14
husbands 70–1, 80–1, 93, 97–9, 137–9, 207–8
Hyginus 35–6, 70–2
Hypnos 159–61
hypotexts 51, 204, 218–19

Ianthe 4–5, 11–12, 186
Icarus 65–6
ideal woman 141
idealism 166–7
identity
 female 7–8
 gender 4–6, 15, 72–3, 155–6, 167–8, 186,
  193–4, 206
 hiding 108–10
 pluralistic 15, 169–71
 trans 4–5
ideological positions 72–3
ideology, utopian 164–6
ignorance 22–3, 30–1, 35
Iliad 70, 200–3, 207–8, 271
imagery 38–9, 149, 175–6, 182–3, 243,
 256–9
 bird-of-prey 246–7
 erotic 127–8
images 142–3, 169–71, 180–7, 189, 207–8
imagination 30–2, 51, 118, 142, 148–9,
 156–7, 186
imitations 9–10, 13–14, 16, 26–7, 46, 51,
 66, 89–90

immortality 251, 273
imperfections 21–2
imprisonment 193, 204–10, 218
improbability 106–7
incarnations 94, 150, 243
incest 89–90, 93, 95–6, 98–9
inclusivity 5–6
inconstancy 26, 34–5, 43
indifference 90–1, 183, 228, 233–4, 238–40
indiscretion 22–3, 25, 30–4
infanticide 95–6
infidelity 29, 55–6, 70, 85–6, 90–1,
 101–2, 175
ingenium 118–19
ingenuity 40–1, 120
ingratitude 31–2, 90–1, 130–1
Innes, Mary 3
innocence 37–9, 41, 70–1, 84–7
 Laodamia 74, 84–5
instability 16–17, 35, 221
intentions 7, 57–9, 90–1, 94, 127–9, 131
interiority 182–3
intersections 45–6, 88, 124–5, 246, 261
intertexts 13–15, 17–20, 149–50, 152–3,
 201–3, 254–5
intertextual practices 228–9
intertextual references 116–17, 152–3,
 202–3, 222–3, 254
intertextual theory 228–9, 240
intimacy 74, 84
inversion 15, 169–71, 173, 179–80
 act of 179–84
Invidia *see* Envy
Iphis 4–5, 11–12, 186, 213–14
Iris 155
irony 70, 110, 188–9, 205, 225, 256–7
islands 17–19, 130, 209, 211–14
Italy 49, 63–4, 142, 144–5, 237
Itys 264–5, 268–9

James, Heather 9–10
jealousy 70, 118, 198–9
Jenkyns, Richard 14
Jesus 188–9
John the Evangelist 188–9, 206, 208–9
Jolivet, Jean-Christophe 200, 205
*Journal général de la littérature
 française* 157
Journal littéraire, Le 173

INDEX 305

joy 80, 113–14, 119, 162–3, 178, 255–6
Julia 13–14
  letters to Ovid 104–20
  marriage to Tiberius 108–12, 117
Juliette 152–3
Julius Caesar 272
Juno 54–5, 249
Jupiter 141, 233–4, 237, 240, 250
  eyes 196–7, 203–4
justice 94, 118, 139, 164–5

Kelly, Joan 45–6
Kennedy, Duncan 167–8
Killigrew, Anne 12–13
King Lear 253–4, 258–9
kings 61–2, 90–3, 159–61, 194–5, 200–1,
  208–9, 212–13
kisses 17–19, 39–40, 76, 84
Kline, Katy 180–2
Klosowska, Anna 47–8, 64–5
knowledge 30, 39–40, 79–81, 85–7, 159–63
  forbidden 26–7, 39–40
  male-gendered 72–3
  unlicensed 10–11, 22–3
Kolocotroni, Vassilike 232–3
Kristeva, Julia 16–17, 154, 163–6, 220–41
  see also Vieil Homme et les loups, Le
  exile mentality 221–2
  novels 222–3, 227–8
Kristev, Stoyan 220–5, 229–30
Kurmann, Alexandra 252–4

La Croix du Maine Grudé, François, sieur
  de 23, 48, 50–1
La Fontaine, Jean de 11–12, 52, 54–5,
  59–62
Labé, Louise 24
landscape 269–70
  literary 67–8
  natural 211
  pointillist 271
language(s) 50, 163–5, 221–2, 229–30,
  252–3, 261
Laocoon 144–5
Laodamia 68–72, 76–8, 80–1, 83–4, 204–5,
  207–8
  character 76–7, 84–5
  fantasies 80–1
  fidelity 70, 73–7, 84–6

grief 80–1
innocence 74, 84–5
letter 70–6, 80, 83–6, 205, 207–8
  of Marie de Gournay 73–7
  of Madeleine de Scudéry 80–1
  of Marie-Jeanne L'Héritier 83–5
  of Marguerite Yourcenar 200–1, 206–7
Laporte, Dominique 158–61
Lasdun, James 16
Latimer, Tirza True 182–3
Latin 7–9, 53, 58–9, 74–5, 98–9, 228–30,
  234–6
L'Aubespine, Madeleine de 10–11, 13,
  44–66, 75
Laura, voyage dans le cristal 167–8 *see also*
  Sand, George
law(s) 53–4, 98–9, 121, 136–9, 163–4, 259
Lê, Linda 1–2, 16–17, 246, 252–4, 256–62
Le Moyne, Pierre 89
Lear 253–4, 256–9
legacy, operatic 134–5
legends 190–1, 197, 263
legitimacy 186, 201–2
Lena 188–9, 198–9
Leperlier, François 171–3
Lesbos 123–4, 130, 132
letter writers 130, 198–9, 204–5, 217
Lettres de Julie à Ovide 13–14, 104–20
  see also Bressey Lezay-Marnésia,
  Charlotte
Lettres écrites des rives de l'Ohio 104–6
  see also Lezay-Marnésia,
  Claude-François-Adrien
Lettres Portugaises 13–14 *see also*
  Guilleragues, Gabriel
Leucadian cliffs 131–3
Leucas 131–3
Lezay-Marnésia, Claude-François-Adrien
  de 13–14, 104–6
L'Héritier, Marie-Jeanne 12–13, 68,
  81–5, 88–103
Liaisons dangereuses, Les 13–14
licentiousness 9–10, 22, 221
lightness 250–1
lightning 133, 256
Lingendes, Jean de 71–2, 75–6, 83
Lippard, Lucy 171–3
literary history 2, 4, 53, 134, 166–7,
  169–71

306 INDEX

literary self-expression 10–11, 22–4, 43
literary tradition 188–9, 193–5, 199–204
Liveley, Genevieve 2–3
Livia 108–10, 112–13, 117–18
  son 110
lockdown 263, 268
loss 16–19, 174–5, 177–9, 252–3, 260, 262–3
Louis XIV 11–12
Louvre 78, 236–7
love affairs 17, 108–10, 144–5, 188–9
  doomed 140–1, 144, 147–8
love poetry 4–5, 16, 139
love stories 17, 113–14, 149–50, 269–70
lovers 17–19, 108–15, 118, 175, 177
  unfaithful 55, 63
lovesickness 66, 131–2, 177
lubricity 94, 101–2
Lucretius 271–3
Lukacher, Maryline 155–6
Lycaon 233–4, 264–6, 268–9
  story 266, 268–9

Macarée 98–9
Macbeth 258–9
McCall, Anne 152–3
madness 99–102, 258–9
Maecenas 111–12
Maenads 234–6
magister Amoris 113–14, 119, 128–9
male doctors 36–7
male domination 4–5, 85–6
male gender 213–14, 218–19
male-gendered knowledge 72–3
Malherbe, François de 75
Malm, Mats 2–3
manual, mock 40–3
marginalization 5–6, 14, 72–3, 221–2
marital home 138
Marolles, Michel de 71–2, 81–4, 95–6
Marot, Clément 8–9, 31–2
marriage 26–8, 31–2, 75–6, 90–1, 108–12, 117, 121–4
  clandestine 58
  Julia to Tiberius 110–12, 117
marriages, forced 110, 117–19
Mars 98–9
Marsyas 267–8, 270
Martignac, Etienne de 70–2, 81–2, 84, 95–6
Martindale, Charles 4–5

Martini, Jean-Paul-Égide 121–3, 137–8
Mary Magdalene 188–9, 196–7, 206, 208–9
Massac, Raimond and Charles 8–9
Masson, Alexandre-Frédéric-
  Jacques 106–7
master of love *see* magister Amoris
maternal space 162–4
meat 264, 266, 274
Medea 9–10, 145–7, 235
Medici, Marie de 77, 89
meditations 149–50, 152–3, 226–7, 242
Medusa 2, 236–7
memories 147–50, 193–4, 251–3
Menelaus 80–1, 201–2
Mercure de France 173
Mercury 12–13, 22–3, 26–32
metamorphosis 153–4, 157, 161–2, 166–8, 211, 213–14, 218, 244–6
  playful 151–68
  vs. disguise 211–14
métamorphoses, Des 4, 242 *see also*
  Cosnay, Marie
Metamorphoses, Ovid's 3–5, 7–9, 14–23, 144, 151–4, 211, 220
  and *Le Vieil Homme et les loups* 227–40
  and George Sand 151–68
  and the Dames des Roches 21–43
metaphors 38, 44–5, 86–7, 100, 271
Metella, Cecilia 149–50
metempsychosis 13–14, 121, **127–130**, 139, 272
Meun, Jean de 7–8
Méziriac, Claude Gaspar Bachet de 89–94, 101–2
Middle Ages 7–8, 263
migrants 242–3, 249, 260–1
migration 1–2, 16–17, 116–17, 220, 242–62
  forced 260
Minerva 22–3, 26–9, 32–3, 35
Minos 90–1, 98–9
Minotaur 55, 90–1, 98–9, 101–2, 189
mirrors 4–5, 17–19, 77, 148–9, 179–86, 203
Misandra 203–4, 206–9, 211–14
miseries 108–10, 145–7, 179, 223, 265–6
misfortunes 60, 118, 195
misogyny 4–5, 7–10, 58–9, 123–4, 190–2
Missives 24 *see also* Des Roches, Dames
mock manual 40–3

INDEX 307

models 2–3, 9–10, 40, 78, 80, 86–7, 93,
    158–9
  ancient 89–90, 271
  classical 11, 44
  literary 201–3
  Ovidian 188–219
  perfect 74, 88
modernism 171–3
Moderns 11, 16, 72–3, 81–2, 88–90, 94–5
modesty 24, 34–5, 39, 79, 81–3, 86–7,
    100–1, 104
Modification, La 149–50 *see also* Butor,
    Michel
Möller, Daniel 2–3
Molossi 268–9, 273–4
money 244–5, 250
monologues 169–71, 173–6, 188–9, 197–8
Montaigne, Michel de 24–6, 61–2, 73–4
Montolieu, Mme de 104–6
moonlight 148–9, 211
Moore, Marcel 180–2, 185, 214
moral correctness 76, 85–6
moral edification 24
moral exempla 9–10, 77–8
Morales, Helen 2, 186
morality 77–8, 81–2, 102–3
moralizing 8–9, 30–2, 58–9, 83–6
morals 80–1, 104–7, 117
Morillon, Guido 9–10, 49
Moss, Ann 46, 49
mothers 104–6, 154–6, 162–4, 209–10, 242,
    244–5
Motte, Houdar de la 94–5
mourning 174–5, 179, 223, 225–6, 234–5
murder 194–5, 199–200, 224, 234, 244–5
  Agamemnon 188–9, 196, 201–2
murderers 63, 139, 159–61, 175–6, 200–1
Muses 38–9, 89, 155
music 17–19, 121–3, 137–8, 162–3
Musset, Alfred de 158–9
mutability 26, 32–3, 184–5
Myrtis 64–5
mystery 162–3, 224
  divine 26–7, 30–1, 35
mythographer 15, 151–2
mythological heroines 190–1, 193–4,
    197–9
mythology 7–8, 90–1, 116–17, 142–3, 179,
    188–9, 264–5

myths 8–9, 14–15, 17–19, 116–17, 144–5,
    151–3, 185–6, 228–9
  Narcissus 15, 166
  originary 157
  Ovidian 11–12, 15, 151–3, 230
  playful manipulation 194–9

Naginski, Isabelle 151–2, 155
naiads 131
Nantes 244
Napoleon, Emperor 13–14, 121, 137–8
Narcisse 152–3 *see also* Sand, George
narcissism 66, 183–4, 231
  female 182–3
Narcissus 11–12, 158–9, 164–6, 169–71,
    184–6
  female 185
  myths 15, 166
narration 8–9, 41, 173–7
  art of 173–7
narratives 7–8, 67–8, 199–200, 204, 243–5
narrators 41, 192, 222–3, 227–8, 231–2,
    239, 242
national literature 44, 46, 48, 66
native land 248, 252, 261
Naxos 197–8, 209
NDiaye, Marie 1–2, 16–17, 244–6,
    249–52, 261
Necker, Mme 104–6
neighbours 40, 248–50
Nelvil, Lord 140–1, 144–5
Neptune 92–3
Néraudau, Jean-Pierre 11–12
nineteenth century 14, 68–70, 106–7,
    152–3, 158–61, 166–7, 182–3
nineteenth-century France 14, 158–61, 166–7
Niobe 144–8, 218
Nodier, Charles 158–9
Nohant 152–5
Norris, Guillaume de 7–8
nothingness 239
novels 11, 104–6, 152–3, 192, 221–2, 270
nymphs 141–2, 144–5, 151, 155,
    175–6, 195

objectification 190
Octavia 110, 113–14
Ocyrhoe 27–8
odes 64–5, 123–5

308 INDEX

Odysseus 173–7, 186–7
Odyssey 186–7, 194–5
odysseys 249
Oenone 68, 77–8, 195–6
Ogier, François 83
Ombre de la Damoiselle de Gournay, L' 73–4
omens, bad 116–17, 207–8
Ondine 144–5
opera 11–14, 134–5
opéra comique 13–14, 121–3, 134–5
opposition 22–3, 26–30, 35, 80, 204–6
  figure of 22–3, 26–7, 30
  social 6–7
opulence 255
oracles 54–5, 70, 91–2, 175–6, 194–5
orgasm 127–9
Orpheus 17–19, 152–4, 222, 234, 269–71
Oswald 144–9
Othea 7–8 *see also* Pizan, Christine de
otherness 171–3, 184–5, 222
outsiders 171–3, 185, 221–2
Ovid and the Moderns 16
Ovid Renewed 4–5
Ovide moralisé 1, 7–8, 22
Ovidian models, ambivalence 188–219
Ovidius Moralizatus 7–8

pain 64, 84, 145–7, 150, 234, 239, 267–8
Pallas 155
Palmer, Arthur 197–8
pandemic 4, 16–17, 268–9, 272–3
Pandrosus 26–7
Pan's pipes 267
Par ailleurs (exils) see also to Lê, Linda
Parcae 253–5, 257–61
parentheses 65–6, 175, 270
Paris 8–9, 44, 49, 68, 121–3, 149–50, 243–4
Pasiphae 98–9
Pasquier, Estienne 23, 41
passion(s) 59, 89–96, 101–2, 239
  forbidden 101–3
pathos 17–19, 188–91, 193–4, 199–204, 218–19
patience 9–10, 80–1
patriarchy 4–5, 86–7, 139, 163–4, 175–6, 178–82, 186
Patroclus 188–9, 197, 201–4, 206–7, 212–13

peace 106–7, 202–3, 246–7
Penal Code of 1810 137–9
Penelope 70–1, 77–8, 169–71, 173–9, 194–5, 204–5
Penthesilea 197
Peray, Madame de 73–4
perceptions 169–71, 173–4, 177, 242
peroratio 202–3
Perrault, Charles 88
Perseus 11–12
personifications 35–6, 43, 151, 184–5
Petrarch 66
petrification 30, 35
Peyron, Bernardino 64–6
Pezay, marquis of 106–7
Phaedra 89–90, 95–6, 98–102, 201–3
  see also Phèdre
  suicide 199–200
Phaethon 65–6, 116–17
Phaon 12–13, 17–19, 124–5, 130–6, 177–8, 188–9
Phèdre 89–103 *see also* Phaedra
Phèdre, passion 89–94
Phèdre to Hippolyte 94–101 *see also* L'Héritier, Marie-Jeanne, de
Phemius 175–7
Philomela 4–5, 11–12
philosophers 272–4
philosophy 24, 224, 226
Phocion 35–7
photographs 179–87
photography 179–80, 186–7
Phyllis 51–2, 54–9, 62–3, 216–17
Pindar 64–6
Pipelet de Leury, Constance 121–3 *see also* Salm, Constance de
Pizan, Christine de 7–10, 15, 82–3, 149–50
Plato 151–2, 163–4, 242–3
playfulness 153–4, 166–7
Pléiade 46, 50, 64
Pliny 104–6, 229
Plotina 192
pluralistic identities 15, 169–71
Plutarch 35–6
Poème de Myrza, Le 151–2 *see also* Sand, George
poetics 11–12, 65–6, 72–4, 157
poison 22–3, 38, 196–7, 224, 235
political activists 4, 171–3

politics 16, 126–7, 136–7, 155–6, 166–7, 186–7, 192, 242–3
    gender 4–5, 155–6
    green 4
Polymester 235
Portrait d'une jeune fille en feu 17–19 *see also* Sciamma, Céline
portraits 17–19, 101, 104–6, 129–30, 134, 144–5, 179–80
    negative 93, 101–2
postal services 198–9
power 17–19, 53, 149–50, 159–63, 177–8, 259
    mystical 175–6
    transformative 153–4, 177, 234
powerlessness 173–4, 202–4
Pradher, Louis Barthélémy 127–8
Pradon, Jacques 89–90
prayers 34–5, 54–5, 127–8, 200–1
premonitions 70, 80–1, 110, 195–6
Presse, La 154
prey 41, 246–7, 265–6, 272
priests, high 132–3
prisoners 165–6, 207, 209, 213, 215
prisons 209–10, 213–14
Procne 268–9
Procris 137
pronouns 5–6, 53, 61–3, 76
prophecies 108–10, 140–1, 169–71, 186–7, 195–6, 272
propriety 6–7, 9–10, 37
prose 51, 71–2, 74, 83, 106–7, 134–5
Protesilaus 68, 70–2, 74–7, 80–1, 205, 207–8
proto-feminism 20, 190
pseudonyms 143–4, 156, 171
psyche 116–17, 165–6
public sphere 12–13, 68, 86–7, 142
Puce de Madame Des-Roches, La 42–3
Pucill, Sarah 179–80
pudor 98–101
punishment 22–3, 27–9, 59, 116–17, 137–9, 164–5
puns 144–5
Purser, Louis Claude 197–8
Pygmalion 15, 152–3, 256–7, 261
    female 86–7
Pyrrha 264
Pythagoras 128–9, 268–9, 272–4

Quarrel of the Ancients and Moderns 11, 72, 94–5
quarrels 2, 88–90
quatrains 33–4, 64–6, 94–5, 97–8, 100–1
queens 56, 77, 161–6, 186–7, 202–3, 236
querelle des femmes 2, 13, 21–2, 24–5, 88, 123–4

Rabaté, Jean-Michel 223
Rabelais, François 63–4
Racine, Jean 11–12, 89–90, 101–2, 199–202
Raeburn, David 153–4
rage 97–8, 235
Rea, Annabelle 152–3
realism 5–6, 166–7, 222–3
reception *see* Introductory Note
reconciliation 155–6, 251–2
reconfigurations 13–14, 99–100, 155
refugees 4, 242–3, 260, 274
Regrets, Les 8–9 *see also* Du Bellay, Joachim
Reid, Martine 155–6, 166–7
reification 190
Reineke, Martha 227–8, 236–7
reinvention 173–4
religion 106–7, 155, 264
Remedia amoris 7–8
Renaissance 2, 5–7, 9–10, 44–6, 51, 63–4
    commentators 51, 57–8
    France 21–43, 66
    Humanism 2, 65–6
    Ovid 8–11, 21–66
    translation 46, 72–3
repetition 228, 234–5
representation of women 2–3, 6–7, 20, 190
reputation 9–10, 89–91, 112–13, 202–3, 255
resentment 237, 248, 256
resistance 22–3, 42–3, 85–6, 100–1, 157
responses 4–6, 9–11, 15, 17, 20, 26, 106–8, 110–12
responses to Ovid 4–5, 15, 17
retributions 22–3, 137, 231
revelations 39, 108–12, 251
revolutions 125–6, 154–5, 158–9, 164–6
Revue de Paris 157
reworkings 13–15, 20, 158–9, 164–5, 173–4, 271
rewriting 7, 10–11, 20, 51, 56, 63, 194–5, 197

310 INDEX

rhetoric 9–10, 67–8, 77–81, 86–7,
  91–2, 97–8
  epistolary 9–10, 67–8
  female 78, 86–7
  persuasive 80–1
rhetorical decorum 25
rhythms 270–1
Richer, Louis 71–2, 84
Richlin, Amy 4–5, 236
ridicule 78, 200–1
rights 126–7, 138, 185, 242–3
rivers 159–62, 231, 258–9, 270
rocks 42, 131–2, 209, 269–70
role reversal 118
Roman de la rose 7–8
Romania 16, 221, 226
Rome 44, 66, 140–2, 144–5, 147–50
  contemporary 134, 137
Ronsard 1, 48, 64–6
Rosbo, Patrick de 192
Rousseau, J-J. 152–3
Rus, Bianca 227–8

sacrifice 34, 37, 42–3, 54–5, 118, 165–6
Saint-Gelais, Octavian de 9–10, 49–50,
  54–5, 59, 71–2, 75–6
Sallust 68, 73–4
Salm, Constance de 13–14, 121–39
  career 121–7
  second marriage 121–3
salonnières 15, 104–6, 149–50
salons 2, 11, 17–19, 42–3, 78, 83, 143–5
  culture 5–6, 11, 67–71
  visitors 23, 42
Saltonstall, Wye 12–13
samedis 11
Samouraïs, Les 221–3 *see also* Kristeva,
  Julia
Sand, George 15, 151–68
  autobiography 151, 154–5, 157
  Gribouille's playful
    metamorphoses **158–66**
  metamorphic muse **154–7**
  metamorphoses 166–8
Sand, Maurice 158–9
Santa Barbara 221–2, 224–5, 227–8, 231,
  233, 237–8, 240–1
Sapho, l'histoire de 79, 123–4 *see also*
  Scudéry, Madeleine de

Sapho, play/opera 13–14, **121–39** *see also*
  Salm, Constance de
*Sapho à Erinne, Vingtiesme
  harangue* 123–4 *see also* Scudéry,
  Madeleine de
Sappho 17–20, **129–36**, 142–5, 177–9,
  197–9, 209–10, 215, 218–19
  and Phaon 132–3
  and Phèdre 102–3
  and Salmacis 169–71
Sappho Phaoni 124–5
Sarde, Michèle 4
Sarton, May 191–2
scholarly games 200, 202–3
schoolboys 58–9
Schor, Naomi 166–7
Schwob, Lucy *see* Cahun, Claude
Sciamma, Céline 17–19
sciences 50, 159–63, 165–6
Scudéry, Georges de 68, 77–8
Scudéry, Madeleine de 77–82, 85–9, 101–3,
  123–4
sea 17–19, 57–8, 133, 209, 217–18, 248, 250
sea gulls 214, 216–17
secret union 95–6, 175–6
secrets 27–8, 31–5, 108–10
seducers 41–3
seduction 2, 37, 40, 100–3, 119, 204–5
  feminine 205–6, 211
  manual *see* mock manual
self 179–80, 182–5, 193, 222, 226
self-absorption 152–3, 182–3
self-control 80–1, 104–6
self-effacement 62
self-empowerment 178–9
self-expression 26, 43, 45
  literary 10–11, 22–4, 43
selfies *see* self-portraits
self-knowledge 164–6
self-portraits 129–30, 169–71, 180–4,
  186–7
self-portraiture 179–84, 186–7
self-reflection 2–3, 152–3
Senegal 16–17, 244–7, 252
sentiments 67–8, 108, 112–13, 118, 120,
  188–9, 191
separation 17, 84–5, 108–10, 229–30, 264
seventeenth century 2, 8–9, 11–13, 67–87,
  88–9, 101–2

sex workers 137
sexual violence 2, 4–5
sexuality 7–8, 169–71, 177–8, 180–2, 184–5
shame 91–2, 94, 99–102, 246
Sharrock, Alison 2–5, 143, 190, 213–14, 218
Shaw, Jennifer 183, 185–6
shawl 144–5
Sherman, Cindy 171–3, 179–80, 186–7
sibyls 144–5, 250, 256–61
Sicily 130, 132–3
silence 22–3, 27–8, 30–5, 99–100, 260
sincerity 74, 112–13, 118, 120
sixteenth century 8–11, 45–6, 48–9, 58–9, 67–8, 70–2
skills 79, 94, 159–61, 175–6, 179
Skyros 205–11, 213–14
slaves 115–16, 137, 159–61, 197
sleep 148, 157, 159–61
Smith, Ali 2–3, 186, 232–3
snakes 26–7, 38
social constructs 180–3
social conventions 54–5
social opposition 6–7
songs 135–6, 141, 164–5, 229–30, 239, 267–8, 270–1
sonnets 33, 35–6, 43, 64–6
sorrows 145–7, 261–2
soul 25, 47, 101, 129–30, 159, 258–9, 263–74
Spain 237, 244
Sparta 173–4
species 264–6, 268–9, 273–4
Spentzou, Efrossini 145–7
spinoffs 13–14
Spivak, Gayatri Chakravorty 164–6
Spreng, Johann 30–1
stability 32–3, 209–10, 213–14, 218–19
Staël, Germaine de 15, 140–3, 145–50
stags 267, 270
stars 148–9, 212–13, 215, 231, 251, 272
statues 39–40, 55, 144–7, 218
stepmothers 95–6, 143, 272
stepson 89–93, 95–6, 102–3
stereotypes, gender 59, 178, 180–2
Stesichorus 132–3, 135–6, 139, 201–2
stone 22–3, 26–9, 63, 199–200
storytelling 153–4, 173–4, 177
strength 32–3, 100, 119, 159–61, 173–4, 268–9

Styx 161–2, 196–7
subjectivity 4–5, 31, 171–4, 178–9
subplots 110–11, 116–17
subversiveness 72–3, 158–9, 169–71, 177, 182–3, 240
Suetonius 230
suicide 47–8, 56, 62–3, 193–4, 196–7, 216, 218
suitors 4–5, 174–5
Sulpicia 110, 117–18
superficiality 25
surrealism 5–6, 15, 171–3, 183–4
suspense 110, 130
sweat 218
swords 97, 239, 259–60
symbols 39, 159, 165–6, 179–80, 182–3, 206
syntax 52, 54–5, 270

taboo 264–6
Tacitus 68, 73–4, 104–6
tastes 11–13, 39, 67–73, 75, 86–7, 101–2
    literary 26, 68–70
temples 133, 162–3
tenderness 17–19, 84, 119
tension 62, 108–10, 126–7, 136–7, 139, 204, 256, 259
tercets 33–4, 64–6
Terentia 111–12
Théatre des Amis de la Patrie 121–3 *see also* Salm, Constance de
Théis, Constance-Marie de 121–3 *see also* Salm, Constance de
Theseus/Thésée 55–6, 90–3, 97–8, 101–2, 196–8
    absence 93
Thetis 194–7, 203–4, 209
Thrace 57, 59, 61–2
threats 62, 75, 149–50, 227–8, 232, 237, 273
thresholds 207–10, 212–13
thunder 133
Tiberius 104–6, 108–14, 117–18
    marriage to Julia 108–12, 117
Tibullus 207–8, 227–8, 230, 240
Tiresias 15, 169–71, 184–7, 213–14
tombs 62–3, 65, 149–50, 221–2
Tomis 16, 108–10, 221–2, 262
Tomlinson, Rowan 45–6
totalitarianism 226, 230, 232, 238

312 INDEX

traditions, female 5–7, 72–3
tragedies 134–6, 145–7, 149–50, 205,
    216, 270
trans identities 4–5
transformation 127–9, 153–4, 167–8, 211,
    213–14, 228, 232–5
transformative power 153–4, 177, 234
transition(s) 2, 99–100, 184–6, 188–9, 231
translation *see also* Introductory Note
    practice 68–70, 74, 76–7
    theory 67–8, 73–4
transmythology 186
traps 117, 191–2, 264, 269–70
Traub, Valerie 4–5, 9–10, 22, 46–7
trees 47–8, 161–2, 247, 249, 267–70
trials 97–8, 138–9
Tristes Pontiques 4 *see also* Darrieussecq,
    Marie
Tristia 8–9, 13–14, 16–17, 20, 106–7,
    111–12, 116–17, 148
triumphs 55, 89, 113–14, 117–19
Trois femmes puissantes 16–17, 244–7 *see
    also* NDiaye, Marie
Trois Parques, Les 16–17, 253–4, 261
    see also Lê, Linda
Trojan war 47–8, 197, 201–2, 205, 207–10
Troy 70, 194–5, 201–5, 207–8, 213
Truismes 2 *see also* Darrieussecq, Marie
truth 29, 166, 178–9, 201–2, 233,
    268–70, 272
twentieth century 15–16, 95–6, 179–80

Ulysses 175, 194–5
Uman, Deborah 44–5
underworld 70, 249
unhappiness 108–10, 116–17
universality 236, 238
unpredictability 16–17
utopia 161–3, 166–7
utopian ideology 164–6

Vance, Norman 14, 152–3
vanity 182–3
venality 31–2
vengeance 36
Venus 54–5, 98–9, 124, 144–5, 272
Venuti, Lawrence 45–6, 67–8, 75
vernacular 8–9, 21–2, 31–2, 44, 48–9,
    58–9, 66

verse translations 8–9, 24, 71–2, 83–4
Verteillac, Countess of 81–2, 89
Vertigo and Ghost 2 *see also* Benson, Fiona
Vespasien 224, 229, 232–7
Vesta 110–11
victims 37–8, 98–9, 101–3, 133, 223–4,
    236–7, 264–5
    direct 38
    indirect 36, 38
Vieil Homme 229–30, 232–4, 240–1
    citations of Ovid 227–8, 231
    death 224, 229–30, 233–5, 238
    funeral 236–7, 239
    identity 224–5
Vieil Homme et les loups, Le 16–17,
    220–41
    and Ovid's *Metamorphoses* 227–40
Viennot, Eliane 88
Vietnam 252–6, 261
Villedieu, Madame de 12–13
*Vingt-quatre heures d'une femme
    sensible* 121–3 *see also* Salm,
    Constance de
violence 4–7, 94, 97–9, 101–2, 165–6, 238
    lethal 227–8
    sexual 2, 4–5
Virgil 9–10, 26–7, 140–1, 144–5, 148–9,
    151–2, 271–2
virtue, female 67–70
virtuous women 37, 43
viruses 263–4, 266, 272–3
vitality 162–3
Vives, Jean de 70–1
Vivonne, Catherine de 11
voices 2–6, 175–7, 186–7, 190–1
    female 4–5, 20, 86–7, 164–5, 179,
    184–7, 190
Volpihac-Auger, Catherine 96
Volscus, Antonius 49
Von Oehsen, Kristine 169–71
Vulcan 26–7, 32–3

Walsh, Théobald 167–8
wanderings 130–1, 175, 250
war 80–1, 84–5, 101, 145–7, 192, 204–5,
    268–9
    machines 214
    Trojan 47–8, 197, 201–2, 205, 207–10
Warner, Marina 2–3, 153–5

water 158–9, 165–6, 217, 222, 249, 267–8
  oily 196–7
weakness 30–1
wealth 21–2, 159–61, 256–7
Wearing, Gillian 186–7
weaving 175–7
weddings 70, 75–6, 110, 133, 137–8
Wheatley, Phillis 12–13
White, Paul 46, 52, 57–8
Wilson, Emma 19
wind 70, 80, 208–9, 250–1
wisdom 32–3, 35–6, 43, 57, 159–63, 250
wit 23, 41–3, 46–7, 99, 112–13, 118, 120
wolves 224–6, 232, 238, 265–7, 273–4
women *see also* Introductory Note
  abandoned 53, 56, 144, 188–9, 208–9
  Athenian 37, 39
  curiosity 10–11, 22–3, 31–2
  defender of 190–1
  divine 207, 213
  early modern 22–4, 26, 42–3, 83
  education 10–11, 21–3, 26, 38–9
  and gender 4–6

glory 89–90, 102–3
historical 77–8, 173
narrow domain of 191–3, 204, 215
virtuous 37, 43
young 74–6, 78, 200, 208–10, 212, 253–4
Women's Classical Caucus 2–3
woods 130–1, 151, 211, 234–5, 249
wordplay 207–8, 211, 254, 271

Xavier, Subha 260–1

young girls 188–9, 198–9, 203, 215
Yourcenar, Marguerite 15–16, 188–219
  anachronisms and playful manipulation of classical myths 194–9
  feminine world/masculine world 204–10
  recalling literary tradition 199–204
  rigidity of gender division 210–19

Zajko, Vanda 2–3
Zeus 264–6, 269, 273–4
Ziolkowski, Theodore 16, 223, 228